To Alison + Michael

Hope you can find something of interest in this Baby boomer journey

STUMPS & RUNS & ROCK N' ROLL

" cricket - a game which the English, not being spiritual people, have invented in order to give themselves some conception of eternity"

Lord Mancroft 1979

Says it all really!

Best wishes

Tim Quelch

August 2016

p.s. while cricket anchors the story there are copious diversions — current affairs, popular culture, in particular its music, social work, caring etc. + many reflections upon race + class discrimination

STUMPS & RUNS & ROCK N' ROLL

SIXTY YEARS SPENT BEYOND A BOUNDARY

TIM QUELCH

First published by Pitch Publishing, 2015

Pitch Publishing
A2 Yeoman Gate
Yeoman Way
Durrington
BN13 3QZ
www.pitchpublishing.co.uk

A CIP catalogue record is available for this book
from the British Library.

ISBN 978 178531-051-5

Typesetting and origination by Pitch Publishing

Printed in Great Britain by TJ International

Contents

Introduction

My deceased parents gifted me a love of cricket and popular music at an early age. These twin passions have stayed with me for over 60 years, placing their distinctive marks upon the passage of time. This book is a testament to their gifts. It is essentially a Baby Boomer's account of growing up and older with cricket, in which the wildly oscillating fortunes of the English Test side are set against a changing cultural and political landscape with popular music supplying the soundtrack.

The story begins in the early 1950s, when I was still a small boy, and when Britain was recovering uncertainly from a ruinous Second World War. Here, my initial impressions of my first cricketing heroes are described, inevitably moulded by dad's accounts, and merged with the popular songs I heard on the radio, our record player and the first jukeboxes. The tale continues in a similar vein over the ensuing years, through adolescence, adulthood and later life, taking in England's various triumphs, and, until recent times, their frequent adversities, recounting the impact made by an ever-changing cast of players, and reflecting upon the times in which they played. This is a life not so much measured by coffee spoons as by cricket scores with many memories impaled upon a melody, phrase or riff. For 'popular music', for want of a better generic term, evokes fragments of my past with greater vivacity or poignancy than any other musical form, better even than albums of age-bleached photographs.

My musical taste is as eclectic as my cricketing preference is conservative – I love the drawn-out drama of the four- or five-day game more than the lusty slogging of the shorter contest. So, it encompasses everything from swing to soul, blues to metal, folk to jazz, reggae to rap, funk to punk, old rhythm 'n' blues to new rhythm 'n' blues, disco to 'techno', acoustic to electronic and various combinations of these.

For much of the 1950s, cricket united my family. Despite the unreliable summer weather of those years, cricket dominated our weekends. Dad played, mum prepared the teas and I watched. Meanwhile, I absorbed my parents' choice of music – the crooners, the classical excerpts and the show songs. And when our family reunited in the early 60s, that bond resumed with dad and mum introducing me to live County Championship and Test match cricket. By then the musical landscape was changing with the emergence of rhythm and blues bands. They also bought me a wonderful, mellow-sounding bat which was sadly wasted on my thin talent, and fed my cricketing curiosity with a generous supply of annuals, diaries and biographies, that supplemented dad's sprawling library. They loyally supported my development as a school and club cricketer, and bought me the table cricket games that lit up dark winter days – the anarchic Cricket at Lord's and the deft Discbat.

When increasing age reversed our roles, I took dad to matches in quiet, pretty villages, particularly when he fretted over mum's poor health, and when his mind began failing him following the onset of dementia. Mum also retained a sharp interest in the game even as age and infirmity made her life very troublesome. There were many occasions when visiting her in hospital that she would ask how England were doing. In health and sickness cricket remained as a key part of our lives.

The inspiration for writing this book came from Dannie Abse's poem, *Winged Back*. In *Winged Back*, Abse entwines musical, sporting and political references in evoking his 1953 past. Citing Noel Coward's observation, 'Strange the potency of a cheap dance tune,' he describes himself 'winged back' to an England shrugging off grim austerity, and celebrating a new Elizabethan age with an Ashes triumph.

I claim no cricketing authority. I once played the game for fun, or so I told myself when my competence failed to meet my modest ambitions. My credentials for writing this book are based entirely upon the vivid impressions this changing game has left with me, placed, as I have often been, beyond the boundary. My hope is that the book will resonate with all those who have shared even part of my journey, and that its sales will enable me to make a substantial donation to Cancer Research UK as it is my intention to pass on all of my royalties to this important charitable cause.

Most of the material gathered for this book derives from what I have seen and heard, supplemented by scrapbooks of newspaper cuttings, with the various books referenced on the final pages helping close gaps in my diminishing memory. Readers may not agree with my various interpretations. That is fine. It is, after all, a game of opinions as well as facts. I hope, though, that the impressions I have given of former players and past games inspire pleasant recollections.

In the appendix located at the end of this book, I have provided a statistical analysis of England's top Test performers over the last 60 years, broken down by the decade in which they played most of their Test matches. This has been done in order to provide a series of reference points in accounting for England's vacillating fortunes over this period. An analysis is also provided of England's win percentages, examined over time and compared with those of other Test-playing countries. Finally I have hazarded a selection of the players who might comprise the strongest England cricket team of my lifetime. As is the way with lists, this is merely a frivolous exercise with the intention of sparking a debate about who was best.

Finally, I would like to thank everyone who helped me to bring this book together: my late parents for inspiring my love of cricket and popular music; my wife for putting up with my long absences while writing this book; the staff at or associated with Pitch Publishing for their guidance and skill in bringing the book to production; the daily press for 60 years of cricket reports, particularly *The Daily* and *Sunday Telegraph, The Guardian* and *The Observer,* although many of these reports are retained as unattributed scrapbook entries; BBC TV and radio, Sky TV, and Channel Four for their live commentary and highlights; all books mentioned in the reference section which have bolstered my faltering memory; and last, but not least, Getty Images, who kindly granted Pitch Publishing permission to use the wonderful photographs featured in this book.

Tim Quelch
April 2015

'Great Balls Of Fire'
1952 – 1958

*England won 52 per cent of 50 Tests played between
June 1952 and August 1958*

1952
Walking My Baby Back Home

Is it really possible to recover a distant past without distortion, deception or doubt? Except where the scorching glare of trauma has left an indelible imprint, remembrance of things long past is surely tainted with misapprehension, conflation and revision, prey, perhaps, to the impact of what was later seen, read, watched, heard or felt, and edited by an ever-changing outlook.

Nevertheless, in my mind I retain a blurred clip of age-speckled film. I am lying in the long, moist grass at the edge of the village recreation field, in dappled sunlight, watching dad bat. He is wearing thick, voluminous woollen 'whites' that are actually cream coloured. I have no idea whether these images are real or imagined as I hear a succession of cracking rifle shots – 'pock', 'puck' – disturbing the languid summer hum. Engrossed, I watch dad brutally despatch one inviting delivery over the swings and into the melting road, before heaving another high over the leg side boundary where the ball clatters against the village hall slates, then smacking yet one more low past the bowler with tracer-like fury. It is an unashamedly heroic portrait drawn by a small boy in awe of his father's strength, for dad was a powerful man, at least physically, a legacy of his daily wrestling with the notoriously stiff gear levers on the gypsum mine's giant bulldozer.

It was in the summer of 1952 that my black Labrador and I began accompanying dad to his village matches, or at least that's what I'm told. Since I was barely four years old at the time, I am entirely reliant upon my deceased mum's word. If true, this was the year in which dad's hero, Len Hutton, became England's first professional captain. However, little of the great man's patience and stylistic perfection rubbed off upon dad. Much later,

I watched him bludgeon the first five balls he received to the boundary before being bowled by the sixth. It was hardly Hutton-like.

In 1952, my parents and I lived on a small, rural, council estate, huddled beneath a high Wealden ridge. The council houses were arranged in a tight circle as if defying a marauding Sioux war party. Thick woodland bordered the estate on three sides, discreetly concealing the gypsum mine where most of the local men worked. At the crest of the ridge was a sweeping view of undulating pastures and scattered woodland, stretching towards a horizon of whale-backed Downs and glimmering sea. Had Satan chosen here to make his pitch, Jesus just might have caved in.

In these early years, when still consumed by Sunday school imagery, I mistook each dazzling shaft of sunlight as the descent of the Holy Ghost, as if this remote, blustery place was divinely blessed. Not that the perishing winter gales suggested such a state of grace, when buffeting gusts of wind would breeze through our cracked walls and ill-fitting window frames with ghoulish shrieks. As for the established villagers, our reticent hosts, their frosty reception matched the elements, although the musty local grocery store was certainly rejuvenated by our custom. As the villagers' antipathy turned towards tolerance, and eventually acceptance, we, the invading 'townies', took our place in village society – helping out at its fetes, swelling its harvest festivals and participating in its sports activities. However, dad's inclusion in the village cricket team was less in recognition of his cricketing ability, as an appreciation of mum's baking skills in supplying the scrumptious scones and sponges for its summer teas. I began to understand that cricket's cliquey clubs could rarely resist a culinary antidote.

As I became older, I realised that dad's idolisation of Len Hutton was not only for cricketing reasons. Because of dad's distrust of the 'officer class', a consequence of his many wartime grudges, he had little time for first-class cricket's preferred leaders, who were typically 'amateurs' or 'gentlemen'. He trusted Hutton more because he seemed to be 'a man after his own heart', a 'professional' or a 'player'. It was not until my teens, when I began reading books from dad's large cricket library, that I understood this social division which once existed in English first-class cricket. The distinction between amateurs and professionals lasted up until 1962, although vestiges of the social divide remained for years after. I was astonished to find that even as late as the 1950s, the amateurs and professionals had separate dressing rooms, discrete travelling and accommodation arrangements, and distinct forms of address. To my untutored indignation this seemed like a caste system.

Dad told me that during wartime, pre-1939 class boundaries became diluted. It seemed as if this was an almost inevitable consequence of people, from all social backgrounds, being flung together in chaotic proximity. However, after hostilities ceased, in 1945, those pre-war class divisions were largely restored, or so I was told.

But dad was barking up the wrong tree if he thought that Hutton was a stroppy corporal prepared to take on the establishment gentry. He may have lacked MCC's preferred profile when he was offered and duly accepted the England captaincy, but, off the field at least, he conducted himself with tact and due decorum. As his book *Fifty Years in Cricket* suggests, he knew when to bend the knee. Besides, although Hutton lacked a public school or Oxbridge education, the mark of an 'amateur' or 'gentleman', he had the distinction of grammar schooling having been brought up in a solidly lower-middle-class family of master builders and teachers. He was certainly not a Jimmy Porter, or any kind of working-class warrior.

What made much more impact upon the rigidity of the British class system was an improving economy, a more egalitarian education system and the emergence of a 'rock 'n' roll culture' that resonated so strongly with restless fifties adolescents in search of a distinct generational identity. For rock 'n' roll was much more than a blues-based rhythm with an accentuated back beat. In my early years, mum and dad had little time for rock 'n' roll, but they were prepared to tolerate Johnnie Ray whose pop standard, 'Walking My Baby Back Home', was released in 1952. What links Ray to my earliest encounters with cricket was not so much this song, though, as the hysterical reaction he evoked among the sober housewives of our estate. For years after, it was inconceivable to my parents that these practical, stoical women should abandon their customary restraint in fawning ostentatiously over a lachrymose crooner, dubbed by the popular press as a 'Prince of Wails' or the 'Nabob of Sobs'. With my curiosity aroused in recent times, I sought and found one of Ray's performances on YouTube. Here I discovered a slender, pallid, apparently conservative young man with a hearing aid, arousing his female audience into frenzied squeals with his panting, writhing, sobbing performances. 'He just SENDS US,' one excitable fan gasped, as if anticipating the rock 'n' roll generation's infatuation with Elvis and the Beatles. Of course, Sinatra drew a hysterical response from his 'bobbysoxers' during the 1940s. The black gospel tradition featured similarly florid outpourings of emotion, too, as did Billy Graham's London evangelical crusade of 1954, attended incredibly by 1.7 million people. But the controversy Ray attracted spiralled once it became known that he was bisexual. This was far too much for conservative, 1950s Britons to tolerate. This was not an age in which diversity was celebrated.

1953
The Black Hills of Dakota

In this year I experienced my first summer of love. My initial obscure object of desire was bubbly, boisterous, buck-skinned Doris Day, the star of the Hollywood musical of that year, *Calamity Jane*. With her jauntily placed US Cavalry cap and her thigh-slapping androgyny – such an alluring 'pop' commodity – she exuded high-octane fun, gymnastically belting out rowdy numbers such as 'The Windy City' and 'The Deadwood Stage'. But it is her wistful version of 'The Black Hills of Dakota' which stands my test of time, perhaps possessing greater poignancy because it signifies that the heyday of the western was passing.

In our crowded, smoky cinemas, the sweeping western panoramas of Monument Valley, Montana and the Great Plains provided a perfect antidote to grey, rationed lives. But in the brighter, more prosperous years that followed the coronation of our new queen, we had less need of vicarious horizons. Not that the Coronation Day weather gave any cause for encouragement. After watching, in grainy monochrome, a heavily-bejewelled Elizabeth solemnly dedicate herself to a life of regal duty, we trudged in bedraggled procession towards the village hall, waving our miniature flags determinedly in the insistent June rain, and hungrily anticipating the feast being laid out on the trestle tables inside. For this was our celebration, too, of an end to austerity, as plates were piled high with sandwiches and bridge rolls bulging with scrambled egg, ham and cheese and tomato, not forgetting the abundance of jelly, fairy cakes and the ever-serviceable Victoria sponges. Our garish coronation mugs ensured it was a day we would never forget.

With the nation so pumped up with patriotic pride it was entirely fitting that Len Hutton's side should defeat the mighty Australians for the first time since the Bodyline series of 1932/33. At a sun-drenched Oval in August the winning runs were hit by 'pin-up' boy Denis Compton as he swivelled on Arthur Morris's wayward long-hop and smacked it joyfully to the long leg boundary. As the ball raced towards its triumphant destination, BBC TV commentator Brian Johnston shouted, 'It's the Ashes! The Ashes!' Thousands of men and women swarmed all over the turf, racing one another to embrace the not-out batsmen, 'Compo' and Bill Edrich, while women planted fat kisses on their heroes' burning cheeks. BBC radio commentator Bernard Kerr found difficulty in restraining his euphoria, 'This is staggering… In fact, it's rather moving. From the broadcasting box, you can't see any grass at all, there's just a whole carpet of humanity… It really is just a wonderful sight!'

Appearing on the pavilion balcony, Len Hutton addressed the tumultuous crowd with a pastiche of an Oxford-style diction, decidedly different from the uninhibited, native accent he adopted when interviewed after his record-breaking innings at the Oval in 1938. The Australian captain, Lindsay Hassett, seemed much more at ease as he amiably extended his heartfelt congratulations to his victorious rival. However, at the post-match party Hassett confessed that his speech had been more sporting than he felt, remarking, 'Yes, I think it was pretty good considering Lockie threw us out.'

By all accounts, this had been a very tight series in which runs were often at a premium. Early rumours of Lindwall's decline had proved premature. For England, the wily Alec Bedser was at the height of his game. His late in-swingers and fizzing leg-cutters caused mayhem, particularly at Nottingham where half of his 14 victims were clean bowled. With England continually struggling to make sufficient runs, Hutton felt compelled to use the yeoman-like Bedser in both stock and shock capacities. Only the persevering Bailey could be relied upon to be of assistance when containment became the name of the game. Indeed, had not Bailey thwarted the Aussie victory charge at Leeds by controversially bowling well wide of the leg stump, Hassett's final Ashes quest would have ended triumphantly.

Bailey's batting proved equally redoubtable, particularly at Lord's, where he held out, limpet-like, for most of the final day in support of centurion Willie Watson as England's heroic rearguard action secured an improbable draw, helped by a featherbed wicket, which drew Lindwall's and Miller's sting.

Although Bedser's sterling efforts did so much to ensure parity, it was spin that took England ultimately to victory. While the nation rejoiced exultantly, more sober voices, such as that of BBC commentator John Arlott reflected that this Ashes success said as much about the decline of an ageing Australian side as it did about a revitalised English one. Bradman's retirement in 1948 had, of course, proved pivotal. His colossal Test average of 99.94 was almost equal to the collective efforts of three top Australian batsmen in the 1953 series. Meanwhile, Hutton had proved to be as prolific as ever. His Ashes batting average of 55 runs was well ahead of anyone on either side, an extraordinary achievement given that the uncovered English wickets allowed extravagant seam movement and torrid turn. Although once again castigated, by some, for his defensiveness, Hutton proved the value of having beat the retreat at Lord's and Leeds, by grasping a decisive Ashes-winning opportunity at the Oval. Here, he turned conclusively to spin after only five overs of pace, when the Australians batted for the second time. In our village, at least, Hutton's pedigree was not in dispute. On a serenely sunny evening in August 1953, the established and the outsiders came together as one to toast Hutton's success. *Vivat* Len!

It was *vivat* Freddie too, after the Yorkshire fast bowler Trueman was restored to the England team at the Oval. Trueman had decimated the timid Indian batting in 1952, but had been overlooked for the first four Ashes Tests of 1953, on account of injury, form, and his national service commitments with the RAF. Statham had made little impact on the docile Lord's wicket in his solitary appearance. 'Fiery' Fred hoped to do better in his Ashes debut at the Oval. Within the next few years these two great fast bowlers would establish a formidable 'fire' and 'ice' partnership.

Dad told me how excited he had been at Trueman's selection for the final Ashes Test of 1953. I sensed that his knowledge of Trueman's early life in a mining community had mattered to him. Dad had been at the Oval on the opening day of the conclusive Test match which, unusually, began on a Saturday. He told me umpteen times how thrilled he was watching a tearaway

English fast bowler avenge the damage previously inflicted by the Australian pace bowlers, Lindwall and Miller.

Looking at the triumphant Pathe footage, almost 60 years later, I tried to imagine him there, sharing the buzz of expectation of a fiery riposte as Trueman marked out his run. For here was a bowler with a blacksmith's muscular physique – beefy shoulders, hefty thighs and calves – and a scowling expression beneath an unruly mop of jet-black hair. He apparently spat volleys of salty wit, too. When reproached by his Yorkshire team-mates for his feeble dismissal by a Frank Tyson 'Exocet', Trueman reputedly retorted, 'Aye, I slipped in that pile of sh*t you lot left behind.'

Like Ray Lindwall and Harold Larwood, Trueman's action was not an erratic explosion of pugilistic strength. It was finely tuned, classical, even. His curving, bounding, shirt-flapping, slightly pigeon-toed run of gathering speed was completed with a sideways twist, a thrusting aloft of his guiding left arm, a cocking of the right, and a giant stride forward, before a cart-wheeling motion catapulted a ball of singeing pace at the batsman.

Trueman was dubbed 'Mr Bumper man' by the incensed Jamaican crowd during the notorious 1953/54 series, and it was not long before he delivered the goods here. Australian opener Arthur Morris was instantly greeted with a sharp bouncer, producing a raucous cheer from the packed, partisan crowd. Morris was ill-at-ease with this unaccustomed onslaught, edging Trueman's sixth ball to Compton at slip. Alas, 'Compo' dropped it. But Trueman was not only a fire and brimstone merchant, any more than Larwood had been. He swung the ball proficiently, and sometimes prodigiously, often late in its flight. He cut the ball off the seam and was adept at varying his pace, too, quickly disconcerting Morris with a well-disguised slower ball.

But according to dad's copy of John Arlott's diary of the series, it was hard going for Trueman. The Oval wicket was apparently sluggish and the sultry conditions enervating. Although accurate and economical, Trueman did not achieve a breakthrough until a lunchtime shower spiced up the languid surface. After hatching a plan of attack with Hutton, Trueman fed Neil Harvey's partiality for the hook shot. The Australian left-hander snapped at the bait, but was deceived by the degree of lift, skying the ball with an uncontrolled shot that sent it swirling towards midwicket where the rapidly retreating Hutton pouched the chance expertly from over his shoulder. Elated at his initial success, Trueman proceeded to have both de Courcey and Hole caught at the wicket, undoing the former with a ball that climbed more than he anticipated, and tricking the latter with a teasing away-swinger that enticed a fatally expansive drive. Although the Australian tail wagged, frustratingly, Trueman dismissed Lindwall just before the close of play, to conclude the visitors' innings for 275 runs and finish with his side's best bowling figures of four wickets for 86 runs. But with the wicket taking spin in the Australian second innings, Trueman was only required to bowl two overs before Jim

Laker and Tony Lock cleaned up, with the Surrey spin twins sharing nine wickets for only 120 runs.

The Oval Ashes victory brought a year of patriotic pride to a glorious close, for a joint Commonwealth team had conquered Everest; the De Havilland Comet became the world's first commercial jetliner, and peace had been finally restored in Korea, to be celebrated by General Sir Anthony Farrar-Hockley's tale of the 'Glosters' outstanding bravery at the Battle of the Imjin River. With the nation stirred by accounts of British pluck in the face of extreme adversity, our film studios put out a series of self-reverential war dramas including *The Cockleshell Heroes*, *The Dam Busters*, *Reach for the Sky*, *The Sea Shall Not Have Them*, *The Cruel Sea* and *The Battle of the River Plate*. However this glorification of a new Elizabethan age was quickly shaken by the horrific crashes of several Comet aircraft, and the humiliation of the England football team, at Wembley, by the technically and tactically superior Hungarians.

1954
Young at Heart

In January 1954, I started my school days in an austere gothic building with oak desks and benches scarred with ancient and modern graffiti. Across one classroom wall was spread a world map with vast territories coloured red to denote British dominion. We celebrated Empire Day. We sang 'Soldiers of the Queen', 'The British Grenadiers', 'Land of Hope and Glory', 'Jerusalem', 'Hearts of Oak', 'Rule Britannia', and 'I Vow to Thee My Country'. Our daily homage was led by an ascetic, improbably aged teacher, whose imperial zealotry was of Jesuit-strength. It was her fervent belief that the British Empire had been ordained by God, as if a pith-helmeted Prime Mover had tapped around the perimeter of a colonial hill station with his silver-tipped cane.

I read much later that, by 1954, such pretensions were misplaced, as a furiously fluttering Union Jack became frayed by the blustery winds of change. Events on the MCC Caribbean tour of 1953/54 underlined this. The West Indian political climate was particularly volatile. The white colonialists were at odds with the black and mixed race liberationists, fearing that if independence was granted, their lucrative lifestyles would be threatened. It was not purely a political contest between blacks and whites, either, for the Caribbean islands were rife with parochial rivalries as well as those of class and race. The situation was complicated by the Americans, still immersed in their McCarthy-fuelled, 'Red Scare' paranoia. They were jumpy about the Caribbean independence movements lest they became hijacked by the communists, as was portended in British Guiana and later realised in Cuba.

With the series billed as an unofficial world championship and the reactionary white colonialists yearning for a symbolic white victory, it was unsurprising that ill feeling fermented throughout the tour. In this steamy political climate, thin-skinned sensitivity prevailed, as Hutton found to his cost when he inadvertently snubbed Alex Bustamante, the Jamaican Chief Minister. Bustamante was a Jamaican hero like the feted liberationist, Marcus Garvey.

The litany of controversial umpiring decisions did little to contain the heat, especially after Lock was called for throwing, but the English players' petulant challenging of the match officials' authority hardly helped. In response to one hotly disputed decision, Graveney threw the ball down in disgust. Press reports of MCC players' indiscipline, on and off the field, compounded their bad boy reputation. Trueman seemed to be a primary target, although Statham refuted almost all accusations levelled at 'Fiery' Fred. Nevertheless, the mud stuck and Trueman found himself in the Test wilderness for a couple of years after, having had his tour 'good conduct' bonus withheld. Meanwhile, Hutton was castigated for not controlling his unruly men.

Despite being under intense political and emotional pressure, Hutton scored almost 700 runs during the Test series at an average of 96.71 – a Bradman-like feat. His big hundred at Georgetown and his double century in Jamaica contributed strongly to England's recovery in overturning a two-nil deficit and squaring the series.

However, once the Caribbean touring party had returned home, MCC's selection committee met in secret to consider replacing Hutton as captain. Their preferred candidate was David Sheppard, a gifted amateur batsman, who had yet to prove himself at Test match level, at least against the strongest bowling attacks. *Daily Telegraph* cricket correspondent 'Jim' Swanton wasted little time in endorsing Sheppard's claim, believing that no one else had the qualities for the post. *The Observer*'s cricket journalist Alan Ross agreed, citing Sheppard's remarkable skill in leading Sussex to second place in the 1953 County Championship. Had MCC's intentions not been leaked to the 'popular' press, Hutton might well have been deposed. But once the cat was out of the bag, the story went viral. The controversy became a matter of excited debate in almost every cricket pavilion, workplace, club and pub in the country.

Dad was incensed when the news broke, maintaining that Hutton had been betrayed by 'cowardly men in suits who were not fit to lick his boots'. Even if there was just cause in removing Hutton, it is difficult to understand MCC's infatuation with Sheppard's candidacy. Sheppard had not played in a Test match for almost two years. He had failed badly in Australia during the 1950/51 series, when his captain, Freddie Brown, deemed him technically deficient against extreme pace. Although Sheppard had enjoyed a fine summer with Sussex in 1953, averaging an impressive 52 runs, he was still unproven in an Ashes contest. Hutton, on the other hand, had already made a stack of runs against the world's best Test sides, averaging in excess of 60 against formidable opposition, whereas Sheppard had a Test batting average of 31 –

and only 17 against Australia. Moreover, Hutton's toughness as a leader was evidenced by his courageous pursuit of victory in Georgetown in the face of a bottle-throwing riot.

More bizarrely, the MCC selectors were advocating Sheppard's candidature just as the Sussex captain was about to retire from the first-class game, having entered holy orders. In fact, Sheppard had already begun his ordination training at Ridley Hall. Admittedly, MCC had cause to question the robustness of Hutton's health, and, perhaps, his capacity to keep his players in order, at least if the derogatory Caribbean tales were to be believed. But these matters were not even broached with Hutton apparently. He was kept completely in the dark about their deliberations.

Once Hutton realised what was up, he urged Sheppard to accept the captaincy if it was offered. But Sheppard mistook Hutton's generosity of spirit as a loss of appetite. When the MCC selectors had a late change of heart, and invited Hutton to lead the winter touring party, it was clear that Hutton's keenness for the job was undiminished. Swanton was disappointed with the MCC *volte face*, though, remarking that Sheppard's exclusion was 'a loss indeed at a time when character and integrity of conduct were never more needed both on and off the field'. Hutton's new vice-captain, the 'gentleman amateur', Peter May, thought otherwise, commenting once the Ashes were retained, 'What a good job we've got Len out here because David would never have done it.'

But having plumped for Hutton, MCC resident Lord Cobham thought it advisable to counsel him and his team on their conduct, before they set sail for Australia. According to Lord Cobham it was more important that Hutton's men should not disgrace the name of English cricket than it was for them to retain the Ashes. Dad grumbled some years later, 'No wonder Hutton had a bad back given the number of times they stabbed him there.' Dad's prejudices distorted his judgement.

The summer of 1954 was a wretched affair. It rained almost continuously, as evidenced in my parents' water-stained holiday snaps. It was a sombre summer for Hutton, too, beset with physical and nervous exhaustion, a legacy of his unhappy Caribbean tour. And embarrassingly, a novice Pakistan team came, saw and drew, squaring the Test series with a sensational victory at the Oval, set up by their fast-medium bowler, Fazal Mahmood, whose proficiency with swing and seam was such that he achieved match-winning figures of 12 wickets for only 99 runs.

But my abiding memory of that summer is my startling encounter with death on a colossal scale. During that summer there were hundreds, possibly thousands, of dead or dying bodies lying outside our houses, school, and church; in the drains and ditches; in the gardens, fields and woods; and on the roads, paths and lawns. In fact, everywhere we looked there were bloodied, pustulant bodies, either rigid, or still twitching in pain.

This was death by myxomatosis, a grotesque 'genocidal' pest control, which left acre upon acre of bugged bunnies strewn across the English countryside. The brutal extermination of so many Brer and Peter Rabbits seemed like an execution of childhood. How was it possible to think of a rabbit again as a pet, a toy, a cartoon character or, ahem, food? During that awful summer, the village cricket pitch had to be regularly cleared of fluffy corpses before play could begin, subject, of course, to the sopping weather first relenting.

It was the time of my introduction to the voice of the 20th century – Frank Sinatra. I cannot remember where I first heard 'Young at Heart'. It might have been while I was wrestling with the scary hallucinations caused by a virulent fever, when my heightened heartbeat suggested that a malevolent monster was at large within me. If so, my demons were surely vanquished by Frank's gentle balm.

Strings, both lush and caressing, provide the opening to 'Young at Heart' before Frank began his tender lullaby. His voice is so assured and assuring. Like Bing Crosby and Nat King Cole, Frank sounded gently mollifying in the melodies that wafted into my bedroom late at night. Whenever our house was buffeted by an Atlantic storm, I'd lay awake anxiously absorbing the wind's shrill fury, its surging, surf-like torment in the adjacent branches and its grumblings in the grate. It was then that I listened out for Frank to calm the tempest.

With Sinatra, the singer was always so much more than his song. Each number was invested with his persona. He would intuitively apply the style – swing, jazz, pop, big band – to his chosen mood, whether carefree and exuberant or brash and boisterous or poignant and reflective. His improvisations with rhythm, and his distinctive use of intonation and rhetoric, marked him out as a unique performer, irrespective of whether his song was old or new, borrowed or blue. With each rendition he invited his listeners to share *his* world. Forget the prodigious vanity that this fantasy requires, millions of listeners believed that they had an exclusive place in his heart. In the summer of 1954 Frank came to me in the privacy of my spartan bedroom.

1955

Rock Around the Clock

The Comets' drummer cracks two bouncing rim shots and Haley is away. In ascending pitch he calls the passing hours. With a sharp, single rim shot emphasising each word, he declares his intention to rock the whole night through. The pounding piano cuts in. A back slap bass stokes the beat. The steel guitarist lets rip. A tenor sax fires short staccato bursts, leaving Haley to bring up the rear.

In 1955, the Comets' rockabilly was streaking across the firmament to crash into conservative Britain with meteoric force. In the British cinemas, crowds of teenagers were literally ripping it up as 'Rock Around the Clock' provided the rowdy soundtrack to the film *The Blackboard Jungle* which was the first cinema drama to link rock 'n' roll with juvenile delinquency.

Meanwhile, Frank Tyson had crashed into Australia with meteorological force – the typhoon kind. No one Down Under had seen this coming. A droll Len Hutton kept his powder Sahara-dry, telling the expectant Australian press, 'Noo, we 'aven't got mooch bowling. Got a chap called Tyson but you won't'ave 'eard of him because he's 'ardly ever played.' The maestro of understatement wryly reckoned that Frank would do the talking – with the ball in his hand.

Before trudging off to work in the crumpling snow, my father would wake me early so that I could hear bulletins of Frank's mighty feats via the crackling, wavering live radio commentary from the other side of the globe. With the landing oil heater providing our only protection against frozen pipes, my bleary, early memories of Frank are forever associated with the pungency of paraffin.

I first saw Tyson in action in a cockerel-crowing Pathe News clip. Expecting him to be a wild, hairy, untamed beast, I was shocked to find a balding, apparently elderly man creating so much mayhem. He didn't look particularly muscular, either. But, with the edited Pathe footage condensing the action, none of the Australian batsmen hung around long while he was strutting his stuff.

Examining those Pathe clips in recent times, the images of Tyson in action are considerably more impressive. He began his approach with a curious foot-pawing gesture as if mimicking an enraged bull. Despite his leanness he exuded wiry strength. Leaning forward into ever-lengthening strides, there is a sense of mounting elasticity, and power. His bowling action is a crescendo of force. Upon reaching the point of delivery, his head and body suddenly rose; he clawed for height before releasing the ball with ballistic fury, his left leg taking the shuddering impact of his follow-through, as he was flung far forward by the mighty effort expended.

According to dad's copy of Alan Ross's book of the series, Frank had not been an irresistible force at Brisbane. In the sweltering, sticky conditions, he was carved all around the Gabba. Depleted by sickness, injury, and a contagion of dropped catches, England lost the first Test match by an innings and 154 runs. Hutton did not lose faith in Frank, though, selecting him for the Sydney Test two weeks later. Not that the early signs were propitious after Frank was withdrawn from the attack after two wild opening overs. But in a short afternoon spell, Tyson took two vital wickets. Despite shortening his run, Tyson achieved blazing speed without losing control. Bowling on a fuller length, he continually made the ball lift and break back viciously from the off. However, Australia eked out a potential match-winning lead of 74 runs.

Fortunately for Hutton, May (104) and Cowdrey (54) rescued England's second innings from a parlous position at 55/3, taking it to a sturdier one at 171/4. But had it not been for a breezy last-wicket partnership of 46 runs between Appleyard (19 not out) and Statham (25), Australia might well have won this close contest. Crucially, Lindwall made the mistake of 'nutting' Tyson with a vicious bouncer, forcing the dazed and wobbling Englishman to be taken to hospital. Tyson returned intact but with a livid temper. Tyson took six wickets for 85 as England won by 38 runs, thereby drawing level in the series.

At Melbourne, Tyson proved even more devastating as he took seven for 27 in the Australian second innings, the hosts subsiding from 77/2 at the start of the fifth day to 111 all out before lunch, to lose by 128 runs. Tyson's searing off-cutters left those who rashly attempted to cut him with decimated stumps. Demoralised by their shattering defeats at Sydney and Melbourne, the Australians disintegrated once again at Adelaide. Despite Keith Miller's late heroics, England cantered to a five-wicket, Ashes-winning victory.

According to dad, the tour taxed Hutton's resilience to the hilt. He suffered continuously with back pain, requiring a constant supply of pain killers. Hutton worried about young Cowdrey whose father had died while the MCC party was outward bound. Before embarkation, Hutton had assured Cowdrey senior that he would look after his boy. He worried, too, about his faithful lieutenant, Alec Bedser, whom he dropped after the disastrous defeat at Brisbane. He fretted about his declining batting form. In fact, he became so immobilised by anguish that he considered pulling out of the vital Melbourne Test, after succumbing to a heavy cold. It required the combined efforts of Bill Edrich and Godfrey Evans to bundle him into a taxi and head him off to the MCG.

Hutton averaged only 24 runs in this series, with a highest score of 80 at Adelaide. Impeded by pain, his previously faultless technique faltered. Because he did not place his left foot far enough across to counter the away swing, he tended to be caught at slip or gully early in his innings. It was to his great credit, though, that he led his side so well. Even *Observer* journalist Alan Ross who, like 'Jim' Swanton, had been an implacable critic of Hutton's captaincy, conceded as much, praising Hutton's tactical acumen and astute deployment of his bowlers. Despite his Brisbane aberration – Hutton thought the Gabba wicket would assist his seamers early on, as it had in the State game – he was rarely wrong-footed, thereafter. He attacked vigorously when in the box seat, and defended doggedly when forced on to the back foot. In order to keep his prized pacemen fresh, and hold back the Australian run rate, he slowed the over rate to a funereal speed.

Hutton proved adept at mind games, too, exploiting the Australians' nervousness and flawed technique against extreme pace. Whenever one of his support bowlers – Bailey, Appleyard or Wardle – claimed a wicket, he seized the opportunity to intimidate the new batsman with one or both of his quickest bowlers – Tyson and Statham – both of whom were capable of bowling at speeds in excess of 90mph. But almost sadistically, he would typically wait until the successful support bowler was about to begin another over before suddenly clapping his hands and announcing a change of plan. He would then peer, with feign absent-mindedness, around the field for a possible replacement until his eyes finally alighted upon Tyson or Statham, as if he had no idea where his ace bowlers might be. To add to the new batsman's qualms, Hutton frequently held a prolonged, whispered conversation with his fastest bowler, Tyson, before unleashing the 'typhoon' upon his potential victim. Hutton proved equally adept at kidology, too, when at the crease. If he was batting against an Australian bowler whom he did not fear, Hutton was liberal in his praise, frequently commenting 'well bowled', hoping to discourage any change of attack.

While Hutton never resorted to sledging, at least as it is now practised, he was not averse to making a sly, derogatory remark to an incoming batsman, hoping to undermine his confidence. For example, whenever Benaud arrived at the crease, Hutton would say something like, 'Let's get you over with Richie' as if his dismissal was just a tiresome formality. He would then turn to Tyson and declare to one and all, 'Come and have a bowl, Frank, Richie's in.' After England had secured the Ashes at Adelaide, Hutton offered, without any trace of irony or sarcasm, to coach the Australian batsmen. Hutton's shyness belied a steely resolve.

Len Hutton played his final Test match in Auckland, New Zealand, in March 1955. Batting at the unaccustomed position of five, he scored 53 runs, which, fittingly, almost equalled his final Test batting average of 56.67. Hutton's reward for retaining the Ashes was an unprecedented MCC vote of confidence. He was invited to captain England in all five home Tests against South Africa. Alas, his failing health prevented this. Shortly afterwards, Hutton retired from first-class cricket. His right-hand man, Peter May, was appointed in his place, restoring the amateur succession, but otherwise it was a case of 'Meet the new boss, same as the old boss'. Under Hutton's captaincy, diligent, determined, hard-nosed professionalism had been re-invented as a virtue. May and Cowdrey – both extravagantly talented stroke-makers – learnt to adapt their style of play to their team's needs. But if May emulated his mentor's 'roundhead' style of captaincy, he did not lose his penchant for 'cavalier' batting. For three more years, at least, May's conflation of MCC's 'amateur spirit' and Hutton's professional dedication proved a winning formula for both Surrey and England.

May's first success came against Jack Cheetham's agile, athletic and resilient Springboks. But it was a very close-run thing. England controversially won the rubber 3-2 on an Oval wicket ideally suited to Lock and Laker. The Surrey spin twins shared 15 wickets for only 185 runs. Perhaps this was another patriotically prepared wicket to go with those of 1956.

To be honest, my sharpest memory of that summer was the Davy Crockett craze, in which many boys and even girls wore imitation 'raccoon skin' caps in homage to the 'King of the Wild Frontier'. Mine resembled a scraggy carpet remnant, though. However, what dad remembered better than the Walt Disney re-creation was Brian Statham's annihilation of the South Africans in the second Test at Lord's. At least that is what he told me during my teens. He insisted we watched the denouement on TV together. I doubt that because I should have been in school. But in deference to his account, I reconstructed the occasion with the help of recovered BBC video footage and contemporary reports, calling also upon later experiences of seeing Statham bowl.

The South Africans were apparently 17/2 at close of play on the Saturday, chasing only 183 runs for victory. In poor light, Statham had dismissed both openers, Jackie McGlew and Trevor Goddard, while Trueman had chipped Cheetham's left elbow so badly that the South African captain could take no further part in the match.

Monday morning was heavily overcast, too. Statham and Trueman immediately bore into the obdurate Russell Endean and nightwatchman Tayfield. While the more sturdily built Trueman bustled in off his curving run, snorting fire, the wiry and imperturbable Statham stealthily probed the South Africans' determined defence. His elasticity, from which he largely derived his speed, was remarkable. He could remove his sweater by extending a hand over his shoulder, grasping the garment at the small of his back and pulling it effortlessly over the rear of his head.

Statham had a straight, relaxed, loping approach to the wicket, leaning forward into lengthening strides, the ball cradled in both hands. Smoothly accelerating towards the crease, he skipped at the point of delivery, with a crossing of his ankles, twisting his lean torso sideways, flicking up his guiding left arm in the guise of a periscope, and, with a supple, whippy action, dispatching the ball with laser-like accuracy and penetrative pace at the batsman's off stump. Statham's five opening overs were maidens. On a pitch that was occasionally producing alarming lift, Endean and Tayfield groped and ground for an hour. Tayfield attempted to allay his insecurity by obsessively stubbing his right toe into the turf between each delivery. But Statham had him in his sights. After a further, forlorn, groping lunge, he was gone, caught at the wicket by Evans. However, with first innings centurion, Roy McLean, joining Endean with the score at 40/3, an ominous black cloud slid over Lord's, preventing play for two hours. Captain Cheetham hoped for a deluge. He was to be disappointed.

When play resumed in mid-afternoon in scarcely better light, the aggressive McLean went onto the attack, freeing his arms to cut Trueman powerfully to the boundary, thereby bringing up the South Africans' 50. However, Statham promptly produced a wicked off-cutter which bowled him for just eight. From over the wicket and close to the stumps, Statham was bowling so straight that none of the South Africans could risk leaving any of his deliveries. As Endean continued to prod and miss, Evans and the slips remained excitedly expectant. Eventually, Statham found the edge of Endean's tentative bat and

Evans gobbled up the chance. The South Africans were then 63/5 and Statham had taken all five wickets for 21 runs.

Wicketkeeper Waite and Keith added another 12 runs uneasily before Statham trapped Waite in front of his stumps (75/6). At this point Statham had bowled unchanged since Saturday evening but he had no thought of taking a breather any more than May had of asking him to. Graveney dismissed Keith off the Lancastrian, with a tumbling slip catch, at 78, but then Heine and Fuller counter-attacked heartily, if briefly, raising the score to 111, before wristy left-arm spinner Wardle dismissed both batsmen with no addition to the total. England had won by 71 runs and Statham had taken 7-39 off 29 overs with 12 maidens. This was exemplary fast bowling – relentlessly accurate, very quick, incisive and intelligent. Statham had largely played a supporting act to Tyson Down Under. But here he was the deserved hero.

1956
Heartbreak Hotel

It was the summer of 1956. The rain had been unremitting for weeks, or so I recall. As a child of the 50s I still bear the watermark of my formative years. But on this blue remembered evening, the sun dazzled, beaming on the lush, verdant recreation ground where long shadows were cast by the pines and elms at its northern perimeter. I remember being kitted out in my green and khaki Cub uniform, with my yellow scarf held neatly in place by a leather toggle. I was waiting for the village hall to open and for the other Cubs to arrive. As I did so, I became aware of a scowling teenager perched defiantly on the crossbar gate. He was wearing heavy duty jeans – coarse, prickly and sweaty. I knew that, after mistakenly borrowing a pair to play in. His grease-quiffed hair tapered at the back into a DA – a 'duck's arse'. He was affecting a sneering lip curl as he tunelessly murmured the mordant opening lines of 'Heartbreak Hotel'. The lyrics were lifted from a suicide note, but it wasn't that which gave the song so much edge. That was wholly down to the singer – Elvis Presley.

Elvis, the man, entered my life via a friend's TV. I gawped at what I saw. His legs shimmered with restless energy; he shook, twitched and rolled his hips, with what I would later understand to be combustible sexuality. His wide pants showcased every pelvic thrust. The adulatory crowd was frenzied. Young women were screaming their heads off. Meanwhile Elvis's bassist was whooping it up, riding his instrument, and hitting double licks.

Elvis Presley was a call to arms, 'a rebel without a pause' – a hiccupping, gyrating Brando or Jimmy Dean. He conflated hoarse, visceral, black rhythm 'n' blues with ecstatic, wailing gospel, and yet he was a white Dixie boy. Little Richard squared the circle, explaining, 'Elvis was an integrator. He opened the door to black music.' Elvis's view was more emotive, 'Rock and roll music, if you like it, if you feel it, you can't help but move to it… Rhythm is something you either have or don't have, but when you have it, you have it all over.'

By 1956, the Comets had begun to splutter out, exposing Bill Haley, their avuncular-looking, middle-aged vocalist, as no more than a 'Great Pretender', an improbable adolescent hero, whereas Elvis not only sounded, but looked like, the real deal. So did the gender-bending Little Richard, with his raunchy shrieks and key-bashing excitability; the leathered Gene Vincent, with his sultry Virginian whispers; and the manic, deranged, piano-pummelling Jerry Lee Lewis. This insurgent quartet blasted a giant crater in the grey conformity of the times.

It could be said that 1956 was the year of the 'Angry Young Man', when, with a growing swagger, restless adolescence barged into the narrow confines separating childhood from adult life; when the British working class flexed its muscles in response to rising prosperity; and when its children began seizing the educational opportunities granted by the Butler Education Act. It was also the year in which despotic Soviet rule crushed the Hungarian Revolution; and when Britain ceased to be a world power, following Prime Minister Eden's abject humiliation at Suez.

But England were still top of the world at Test cricket after their summer Ashes victory, although many Australians believed they had been stitched up. Neville Cardus seemed to agree, euphemistically describing the Manchester and Oval wickets as 'patriotically prepared'. The Leeds pitch seemed no less so, for, as at Manchester, it turned to dust by teatime on the second day.

In brief, the 1956 Ashes series had gone like this. After a rain-drenched, injury-scarred draw at Nottingham, the Australians had won resoundingly at Lord's by a 185-run margin. The debonair Miller defied his troublesome back – a legacy of a wartime 'pancake' landing – and bowled magnificently, taking ten wickets for 152 runs. Benaud also batted spectacularly in the second innings, smiting a match-winning 97 runs. Having arrived at the crease when the game was still in the balance, he clobbered a hostile England pace attack, comprising Statham, Trueman and Bailey, to all parts of the ground. The English batsmen could only manage a limply cautious, clamp-footed response, conceding the initiative, the momentum and, ultimately, the match.

However, parity was restored at Leeds after veteran 41-year-old opener and selector Cyril Washbrook was surprisingly restored to the ranks, not having played Test cricket for five years. He and May put together a match-winning partnership of 187 runs, rescuing England from a perilous position of 17/3 on the opening morning. Their combined efforts allowed England to reach a total of 325 which proved sufficient, for on a crumbling wicket, Laker and Lock disposed of the Australian batting, enabling England to win by an innings and 42 runs.

And so to Manchester where May once again won a pivotal toss. England batted on a bare, deceptively dead wicket, racking up 459 runs at around three runs per over – a veritable sprint by 1950s standards. Peter Richardson (104) and Rev. David Sheppard (113), on sabbatical leave from the Church, scored impressive centuries after Richardson and Cowdrey (80) had put on 174 for the first wicket. However, even by tea on the first day, a huge cloud of dust appeared when the ground staff swept the wicket. The dead Old Trafford wicket was about to become deadly. Trevor Bailey euphemistically called it a 'beach'. By the end of the England innings, Benaud was turning the ball six inches or more. In desperation, Australian captain Ian Johnson tried to rally his men, insisting that with gutsy performances from everyone, they could still save the match. Miller slowly lifted his gaze from the racing paper he was studying, before announcing, 'Bet you 6/4 we can't.'

McDonald and Burke made a steady start, though, reaching 48 without loss. Then Laker was asked to bowl at the Stretford End. McDonald was dismissed immediately, caught in the leg-trap by Lock. The left-handed Harvey followed instantly, bowled by Laker with a beauty. The ball drifted in to pitch on middle and leg, before turning sharply and clipping the off stump. Although Australia reached tea without further loss, in the 35-minute period which followed, their remaining eight wickets fell for 22 runs, to leave them 84 all out. Laker took nine wickets for 37 while an increasingly exasperated Tony Lock managed just one.

Australia made a better fist of their second innings, reaching 53/1 at the close of the second day. But during that evening session Harvey bagged a pair, after being caught by Cowdrey off Laker. Harvey had come to the crease prematurely because McDonald was forced to retire with a knee injury. Saturday was largely wet and so was Monday. In between the showers, the Australian score rose to 84 but with the additional loss of Burke. This left the Australians almost six hours to survive on the final day. In their favour, the pitch was damp and slow, offering no help to the English spinners or to Statham and Bailey. By lunch, the recovered McDonald and Ian Craig had given the Australians hope. Batting very watchfully, they had taken their side's score to 112/2.

I find it impossible to separate what I actually remember of the last rites from that seen later on film. Looking again at the BBC TV footage, on that final afternoon, Old Trafford appeared bright and blustery. The ruffling flags tugged at their masts. The square was scarred with extensive patches of sawdust, testifying to the weight of rain that had fallen over the weekend. The combination of bright sun and gusting wind dried the wicket by early afternoon, creating an ominous crust upon which the spun ball could grip. Australia had no chance. Only two runs were added to their lunchtime score when Craig, shifting fatally on to the back foot, shuffled across his stumps, prodded indeterminately at Laker's off-break and was given out leg before wicket for 38 runs. Laker then dismissed three Australians in rapid succession – Miller was bowled by a fizzing off break while Mackay and Archer were caught in the leg trap by Oakman. At 130/6, the back of the Australian batting was broken, but Benaud and McDonald dug in for 75 minutes before tea, adding

51 runs. Meanwhile Lock was fuming. He had turned the ball prodigiously to no avail. One ball had spun so sharply that it beat Benaud's bat and was fielded at second slip.

Immediately after tea, Laker resumed the attack from the Stretford End, preferring to bowl around the wicket because, with the extravagance of the turn he was achieving, there was a better chance of trapping the Aussies in front of their stumps, or of bowling them. Laker's first ball ran harmlessly off McDonald's leading pad into the leg-trap. But the second had McDonald edging the ball on to his thrusting left pad whereupon it lobbed into Oakman's safe hands.

McDonald had played eminently in scoring 89, emphasising the feebleness of his team-mates' efforts. Benaud and Lindwall scraped together a further 17 before Laker bowled both of them, Benaud for 18 and Lindwall for 8.

It was at this point that John Arlott took up the BBC commentary. With his unmistakable Hampshire drawl, he observed, 'Old Trafford redeemed itself with a last hour of flawless sunshine. Laker comes in again, hair flopping, bowls to Maddocks, it turns and Laker appeals and he's out lbw and Laker's taken all ten! The first man to congratulate him is Ian Johnson and England have won by an innings and 170.'

The final Test was a mirror image of the first, with just over two days' play lost to rain. Compton made a stunning comeback, making 97 runs without his incapacitating right kneecap. It was yet another triumph for MCC's 'golden oldie' selection policy. When the truncated game was brought to a close, the Australians were once again in a mess at 27/5.

In that dark, dank summer Jim Laker's cup had overflowed. His harvest of 46 Test wickets had cost him just 9.60 runs each. Ian Johnson's Australians came prepared to face extreme pace. Instead, they were undone by malevolent spin.

Thirty years later, Trevor Bailey added in a BBC radio interview, 'The most remarkable thing was not that Laker took 19 wickets but that Lock took only one. And the reason, of course, was temperament. The more wickets Laker took, the more Lock tried and tried and the faster and faster he bowled. Meanwhile Jim just carried on putting the ball on the spot and letting the pitch do the work... If Johnny Wardle had been at the other end there is no way that Laker would have taken 19 wickets... But an English county side on that pitch would have played better than the Australians.'

Tony Lock, in his yet unreformed, jerky, faster bowling style, exuded bristling aggression, displaying extremes of joy and irritability, his heart printed unmistakeably upon his sleeve. Whereas, the taciturn and less demonstrative Laker maintained a smooth, composed action of relaxed elasticity off a few, perfunctory steps. He seemed to be so nonchalant about his amazing feat. After he took the final wicket he swung around, grabbed his sweater from the umpire, and sauntered off the field as if completing a net session. In the dressing room he sat quietly in his chosen corner having just a sip of celebratory champagne, then after posing briefly for the obligatory press photo, he changed and drove back to London alone. Somewhere along the A6 he stopped at a pub. A crowd was gathered around a television which was showing the Old Trafford highlights. Although he was the talk of the town, no one recognised him as he stood at the bar, meditatively supping his beer.

Colin McDonald was less complimentary about Laker's performance, exclaiming, 'England cheated.' He maintained that the pitch had been doctored. MCC's chairman of the selectors, 'Gubby' Allen, denied responsibility, leaving Old Trafford groundsman Bert Flack to face the music. The appropriately-named Flack quipped, 'Thank God Nasser has taken over the Suez Canal otherwise I'd be plastered over every front page like Marilyn Monroe.'

By 1956, county cricket was struggling. County Championship attendances were falling dramatically. These were a million less than in 1947, a massive drop of 47 per cent. Cinema attendances were dropping quickly, too, 33 per cent down over the same period. Even the still popular English Football League games had seen a 2.5 million reduction in attendances. In fact, public entertainment was generally in decline after an immediate post-war boom. With prosperity levels rising, this was the age of the family saloon, and a do-it-yourself craze, affecting not only home improvements but music also, with the advent of the skiffle group. Hearth-side entertainment grew, too, following the birth of ITV in 1955. With the range of leisure and occupational interests still widening, first class cricket faced a very uncertain future. It was a challenge that MCC was slow to address.

1957

Diana

Prime Minister Harold Macmillan assured us we'd 'never had it so good'. I wasn't so sure, having been suddenly moved to a faraway town, where my kind, if eccentric and feisty, aunt began caring for me. She continually fell out with tradesmen whom she berated for taking apart her household appliances without her prior consent. It was rare for her tiny front room not to have a partially dismantled vacuum cleaner, TV or radio, while her tinier scullery often had an unserviceable fridge or washing machine. She had a habit of randomly taking in unsuspecting animals she deemed to be in need of sanctuary. I came home one day to find her bathing a hedgehog in Dettol. The poor creature smelled like a lavatory brush. Then there was the bizarre clothing she obtained from jumble sales. Once I was presented with a safari suit, big enough to accommodate my school class. Undeterred, she stuffed me with chips hoping to achieve a better fit. No wonder I left her care three years later with a stomach girth the size of the equator. By then the safari suit had 'mysteriously' disappeared.

With my new schoolmates doting on football but dismissive of cricket, it was not until dad bought me *The Big Book of Sports*, as a Christmas gift, that I rediscovered my cricketing interest. The book contained a number of photographs of MCC's 1956/57 winter tour of South Africa and of the home rubber with the West Indies.

Two shots from the South African series absorbed my attention. Both featured the miserly Springbok off-spinner Hugh Tayfield. He was the leading wicket-taker on either side with 37 wickets at an average cost of 17.18 runs. His efforts brought the South Africans back on terms after losing the first two Tests. But it was only after dad bought me Jim Laker's rather grumpy autobiography, *Over to Me*, a few years later, that the story behind those brilliantly-lit shots fell into place, although I never discovered whether the MCC tourists wore safari suits as my aunt claimed.

Jim Laker did not seem to like Tayfield. He accused Tayfield of cheating two leading English batsmen of their wickets. At Johannesburg, Tayfield insisted he had caught Compton legitimately off his own bowling. Laker disputed this, stating that the catch had been taken 'on the bounce'. However, being a man of integrity, Compton took Tayfield at his word and promptly walked off, not waiting for the umpire's decision. Troubled by the possibility that Tayfield had not caught the ball cleanly, South African captain, Clive van Rynefeld, ran after Compton, imploring him to return, but Compton ignored him. The photograph I have captures Tayfield on one knee claiming the catch. He seems exultant while Compton appears unconvinced.

Although it is a quaint practice now, up until the mid-1950s, a batsman was expected to 'walk' if convinced he was out. The Australian Neil Harvey once 'walked' on an lbw appeal, not even waiting for the umpire's decision. However, this sporting etiquette came under challenge as the decade progressed. At the Oval in 1955, May had stood his ground when Tayfield appealed vociferously for an lbw decision. This was before May had scored. The umpire reprieved May and he went on to make a series-winning score. Pugnacious South African opener Jackie McGlew was as incensed by May's refusal to walk as Tayfield had been.

Once appointed as South African captain, McGlew instructed his batsmen to remain at the crease until the umpire had made his decision. Leaving aside Compton's sporting gesture, these new rules of engagement prevailed for much of the 1956/57 series. In his book of the series, *Pitch and Toss,* the hard-hitting South African batsman Roy McLean expressed his abhorrence at this dismal decline in sportsmanship. His book was appropriately titled, given that four out of the five Tests were decided by either the state of the pitch or the luck of the toss.

The standard of much of the cricket played was dire. England's left-handed opener Peter Richardson took over eight hours to make what was then the slowest century in Test history, while three South Africans remained scoreless for an hour. But probably the most dispiriting statistic of all arose when an uninterrupted third day's play at Port Elizabeth produced just 122 runs.

Roy McLean thought the South African batsmen's preference for a 'two-eyed' stance was partly to blame. It had been adopted in Australia as a protective device against hostile, short-pitched bowling. But it also restricted scoring opportunities on the less protected off side.

In my second photograph of this series, Cowdrey is shown being caught at slip by a backward-arching Trevor Goddard. Once again Tayfield is the executioner, dismissing Cowdrey for eight runs with a delivery that had apparently gone on 'with the arm'. Goddard's reversed palms seem positioned to protect his throat as much as in anticipation of the catch. It seems as if the ball had spat on what was described as an unreliable wicket. The customarily serene Cowdrey is shown in a contorted, half-cocked position, with both feet planted outside the off stump. For all his elegance and fluency at the crease, Cowdrey seemed too easily subdued by blunting slow bowling, as practised expertly by the South African pair, Tayfield and the medium-paced all-rounder, Goddard. Cowdrey was inclined to resort to 'pad play' in protection of his wicket, believing he was immune to an lbw decision if he pushed well forward. It was a technique that served him well, though, in his matching-saving stand of 411 runs made with May at Edgbaston in 1957. The pair neutralised the West Indian mystery spinner, Sonny Ramadhin, so successfully that he rarely presented a threat thereafter.

The soporific cricket played on the South African tour prompted MCC to limit fielders on the leg side to five with only two permitted behind the wicket. Also, in order to incentivise bolder hitting, MCC introduced a new bonus points system in the County Championship and reduced boundaries to 75 yards from the wicket. But consideration of the most radical recommendation that might have reversed the decline in attendances – the creation of a limited-overs knockout competition – was deferred until its financial implications could be examined. Six more years would pass before the first one-day competition – the Gillette Cup – was introduced.

According to my *Big Book of Sports,* the summer series against the West Indians proved no less disappointing despite the mammoth May–Cowdrey stand that deprived the tourists of victory in the first Test. Thereafter, the West Indians capitulated pathetically, losing by an innings and 36 runs on a fiery surface at Lord's. Only a brave innings of 90 runs from the injured Everton Weekes, and an eye-catching one of 66 runs by the promising Garry Sobers, arrested England's charge as they won within three days. England proceeded to thrash their opponents in two of the three remaining Tests. Worrell, who scored a stunning, unbeaten 191 at Nottingham to deny England a fourth victory, was the sole member of the 'three Ws' (Worrell, Walcott and Weekes) to enhance his reputation, excelling with both bat and ball. Worrell's calm authority and his undisputed leadership qualities enabled him to unite the fractious island contingents within the team, prompting the West Indian Cricket Board of Control to offer him the captaincy on a permanent basis, thereby ending an unchallenged white succession. Worrell deferred acceptance until the 1960/61 tour of Australia, but his appointment signalled the end of colonial discrimination in West Indies cricket.

I missed my parents' passion for music. My aunt's only concession was to play *Two-Way Family Favourites* on the radio during the fat-spitting Sunday lunchtimes. Not that this was any compensation. It seemed as if the BBC was determined to suppress rock 'n' roll with battalions of bland crooners, such as Perry Como, Dean Martin and Michael Holliday, or bury it beneath the bubbly banality of Alma Cogan, Patti Page or Rosemary Clooney. I could not complain, though. My aunt cut me unprecedented slack, allowing me to head off to the town's coffee bars where thumping jukeboxes kept the faith. I was equally intrigued by the coffee bars' hissing Gaggia espresso machines which dispensed frothy coffee into glass cups. In fact, there was something deliciously salacious about these haunts. Their cane furniture, low glass-topped tables, huge rubber plants and dark recesses hinted at a garden of unearthly delights.

Feeling excluded on grounds of age, I would position myself uncertainly in their open doorways. Here, I would gawp at those inside, the truculent, brilliantine quiffed and 'draped' young men with their narrowed trousers, and their bountifully-petticoated girlfriends. Here, I could nod to the honking horns of the Upsetters or tap my feet to the panting insinuations of 'Be-Bop-a-Lula'. Sometimes, my presence proved irritating to the surly inhabitants. Then, one of the gum-chewing fraternity might emerge and cuff me around the ears, telling me to 'push off squirt'. If that happened, I would make for Woolworths' record counter where their *Embassy* covers of pop hits would be played, at industrial volume when the store was at its busiest.

It was here that I first heard 'Diana' on one sparkling Saturday morning in August 1957. I am unclear why this unremarkable love song, penned by Paul Anka, to a much older girl he hardly knew, should take such a hold of my heart. Was it the brash sax introduction that excited me? Was it his soaring expression of unrequited love, given my intoxication with those unreachable young women in the coffee bars? If so, Anka's improbable chat-up line might have struck a chord. Or was it simply because Diana was my absent mum's second name?

1958
At the Hop

The summer of 1958 was wet, weary and woeful. With the Munich disaster decimating the Busby Babes, England performed poorly in the World Cup finals in Sweden, just as they had in the 1954 and 1950 competitions. Only the plucky Welsh and Northern Ireland teams gave Britain anything to cheer, for Scotland, like England, exited ignominiously at the group stage. Brazil's dazzling skills, fluidity of movement and tactical inventiveness once again exposed the grave limitations of the anachronistic and ponderous British game. As if any further proof was needed, the England players looked like a team of ancient scoutmasters in their baggy, flappy shorts. It seemed as if the English Football Association had learnt nothing from the humiliations inflicted by the Magical Magyars in 1953 and 1954.

The summer Test series with New Zealand was a dreary, pointless, ill-matched affair. On five occasions, the Kiwis were bowled out for less than 100. Lock caused mayhem, taking 34 Test wickets with embarrassing ease, with each dismissal costing on average less than eight runs. As if the huge imbalance in strength was insufficiently challenging, the poor New Zealand batsmen had to contend with a succession of rain-affected surfaces on which they had neither the technique nor the resolution to survive for long. Only their seam attack, led by their 6ft 5in swing bowler Tony MacGibbon, posed any problems for the English team. England won the series at a canter. Yet England had only batted with conviction in two of the five Tests, and a reliable opening partner had yet to be found for Peter Richardson. Meanwhile, the Australians had emerged from their much more exacting South African tour with a 3-0 Test victory. It was not hard to guess which side was the better prepared.

As a result of this damp squib, the counties' share of the summer's Test match profits fell by a half. The 1958 Annual Report of Warwickshire County Cricket Club laid bare the malaise gripping English first-class cricket. It stated, '[This season] will go down to posterity as a depressing year... The weather was frequently wet and cold; the tempo of the game slowed to a degree... where it was difficult to define actual movement; the Laws of the game were more than ever disregarded, and throwing and dragging by bowlers became all too commonplace and most depressing of all, no apparent action to rectify the position; as a culminating result there was a very great diminution of public interest, and County match aggregate gates fell from just over a million in the season before to practically half that figure... The changes instituted 12 months ago almost entirely failed in their purpose, and that further legislative action must now be taken... to ensure that the Laws of the game are upheld, and if necessary an incentive given to ensure that the bat is applied to the ball with the basic idea of scoring runs.'

Peter May was so concerned about the state of the county game that he attempted to revive Cyril Washbrook's proposal that championship matches should be confined to the weekend in a geographically-zoned competition. He also urged that the distinction between amateurs and professionals should be dropped, with all cricketers paid by the match, as was then the case in Australia, with the freedom to take outside jobs. But an MCC Advisory Committee rejected this proposal, concluding, 'The distinctive status of the amateur cricketer is of great value to the game and should be preserved.'

On one foggy winter evening I dropped in to see my cousin. She immediately grabbed my arm and pulled me into her front room. 'Listen to THIS!!' she insisted, putting a 45 single onto the record player. After a brief hiss and crackle, I was jolted into motion by a furious chopping of the piano keys. A doo-wop harmony followed, with a succession of ascending scales. Then Danny Rapp, the lead singer, swung into gyrating action. 'At the Hop' was where it was at. Has there ever been a more exultant, exuberant call to dance? Even a bloated heifer like me couldn't resist the urge to strut and sway. We played it again and again. Even Elvis's 'Jailhouse Rock' couldn't compete. What bliss it was to lose myself in this vivacious wall of sound.

'In The Middle Of Nowhere'

1959 – 1966

England won 31 per cent of 87 Tests played between December 1958 and August 1966

1959

What I'd Say

Quite unlike the previous year, the summer of 1959 was one of torpid heat. On its many indolent afternoons I would lie in the shade of the orchard trees dully watching the droning Super Constellations and Stratocruisers heading off to an American west I would not have recognised, being infatuated with images of bronzed Apache and Sioux warriors, anarchic saloons and gruff, laconic cowboys. Having cleansed our orchard of itinerant gunslingers I found myself at a loose end. I had been as easy to miss as TV detective, Frank Cannon, and yet not one of these hoodlums could beat Tex Blubber's fumbling draw. So, I set aside my cap-firing Colt-45 and began perfecting my technique with bat and ball, using the crumbling outhouse wall, with its erratic bounce, to assist my practice. Thrusting my left knee forward as I leant into a drive, and freeing my hands to play a cut, I hoped that my newly-acquired coaching manual would help me to make the grade. With England yielding so lamely Down Under, they appeared in need of new blood.

This became clear when dad bought me the 1959 *News Chronicle Cricket Annual* which documented my first experience of England's cricketing failure. I could not comprehend the scale of their Ashes defeat. It seemed like an offence to karma. Despite the serial failures of the national football team, as a devout new Elizabethan I held the absurd belief that Britain, or at least England, was best at most things – war, sport, manufacturing. That Ashes debacle shook my faith as much as the Suez humiliation rocked the complacency of the British establishment. In the years that followed I read as much as I could about the series. It was as if I needed an exhaustive inquest before I could lay the matter to rest.

The MCC party had been exposed to the dual spectre of Australian throwing and 'dragging', although England's Loader and Lock were hardly without sin. But England did not lose the Ashes and their 'world crown' in 1958/59 on account of foul play. As with England's humiliation in Dubai and Abu Dhabi 53 years later, the questionable action of an opposing bowler was no more than a sideshow. May's side did not lose this series 4-0 because of controversial umpiring decisions, either, although there seemed to be too many of these, any more than their appalling luck with injuries was to blame. Put simply, Peter May's team lost the 1958/59 Ashes series – just as Andrew Strauss's side lost the 2012 series with Pakistan – because they did not play as well as their opponents. Only May and Cowdrey batted consistently well during this turgid series while Statham and Laker largely carried an under-performing bowling attack. Although Trueman did not lack conviction, Tyson was a spent force. His three Test wickets cost 64 runs each. Bailey, with only four wickets, performed no better, while Lock's five wickets cost an average of 75.

The greatest indictment of England's performance lay in their woeful batting. Not once did they reach a total of 300 and only exceeded 250 twice. The Australians were much better at keeping the scoreboard ticking over, frequently taking quick singles, converting ones into twos, and twos into threes, while too many of the English batsmen settled for immobile occupation of the crease.

The left-handed Peter Richardson's technical deficiencies, notably outside his off stump, were targeted ruthlessly, particularly by left-arm fast bowler Alan Davidson. Bowling around the wicket, Davidson tested Richardson with a staple diet of late out-swingers, and found him wanting. Richardson was no more at ease against Benaud. His fall from grace was represented by a dismal series average of 20 runs. Richardson was dropped for the drawn third Test at Sydney.

Graveney was one of only three English batsmen to average over 30, but his returning habit of wafting outside his off stump, at balls bowled across him, proved costly. Davidson, in particular, probed this weakness. In six out of ten innings Graveney was dismissed caught at the wicket or in the slip or gully region.

As immovable as Trevor Bailey often was, he hardly ever smote a ball in anger. His attritional defiance counted for little as he meekly conceded momentum to the fired-up Australians. Only when May and Cowdrey were batting in partnership did England threaten to seize control of a game, as happened in the second innings at Sydney. Statham's stupendous bowling at Melbourne (7-57), briefly restored parity before the bent-armed Meckiff and the irreproachable Davidson blew away the timid English batsmen, for an abject second-innings total of 87.

Lock and Trueman apart, the Australians were also vastly superior in the field, displaying astonishing athleticism, catching brilliantly and throwing from the boundary with speed and great accuracy. O'Neill, Harvey, Davidson and Benaud were outstanding in this regard.

As with any humiliating national defeat, there was much wringing of hands after England lost their world crown at Adelaide. Battered by Benaud's men, bruised by the press and afflicted by illness, May seemed to lose his appetite for the game and 1962 would be his last full first-class season.

My *News Chronicle Cricket Annual* did not have a single photograph. Instead, there were pages of figures and tables. But after studying these on my long Saturday journeys to see my mum, I began to understand what they denoted about skill and form, run rates and so on. Their indications of comparative worth, success and failure seemed agreeably definitive. I became comforted by the apparent certainties that statistics offered. Suitably encouraged, I began to work out averages for myself based on the cricket scores I found in the daily papers. Total immersion in a dimly-lit world of figures felt like a cosy burrow. Even today, I tend to bury myself in statistics at times of stress, except these exercises are now more likely to relate to health and social care data.

As for the legacy of this traumatic Ashes series, its throwing and dragging problems prompted a sterner review. However, as the leading world cricketing authority, MCC declined to grant its English umpires ultimate authority for deciding the lawfulness of a bowler's action, opting instead for an adjudicating MCC committee to which umpires should refer when concerned. It was hardly a ringing endorsement of their umpires' judgement.

The collective failure of international cricket authorities to grasp the nettle of 'throwing' enabled suspect bowlers, worldwide, to continue playing without sanction. Apart from the Australian suspects – Meckiff, Rorke, Slater and Burke – there was also a clutch of Englishmen, apart from Loader and Lock, with supposedly dubious actions. Harold Rhodes of Derbyshire, and David 'Butch' White of Hampshire were both 'called' for throwing during the summer of 1960, although umpire Paul Gibb later conceded he had been wrong to censure White. At this point Rhodes had already played for England, while White, having been cleared of any transgression, was subsequently selected for the 1961/62 MCC winter tour of India and Pakistan. As for Tony Lock, he took it upon himself to amend his ways, having been horrified by film evidence that he 'threw' his quicker deliveries.

After visiting the Caribbean in 1959/60, England's new batting star, Ted Dexter, identified three West Indians whom he considered to have suspect actions – fast bowlers Chester Watson and Charlie Griffith, and spinner Sonny Ramadhin, who later confessed his guilt to a *Daily Mail* journalist.

Jim Laker had thought that the disgraced West Indian quick bowler, Roy Gilchrist, had 'thrown' during the 1957 Test series. Although the Kiwi bowlers were apparently blameless, both the Pakistani and Indian Test sides included bowlers with apparently controversial actions. Following the 1961/62 MCC tour of the Indian subcontinent and Ceylon, England captain Ted Dexter declared that the Pakistani off-spinner, Haseeb Ahsan, and the 'tiny' Indian seamer, Ramakant Desai, 'threw'. In Ahsan's case, he had already been 'called' by a Pakistani umpire. Neil Harvey was equally convinced of the guilt of the Indian off-spinner Jasu Patel during the 1959/60 tour of India. But none of these alleged offenders were brought to book. It was as if political expediency had been allowed to triumph over regulatory valour. In such a pusillanimous climate further controversies were inevitable, as illustrated by the later Griffin, Griffith and Meckiff affairs.

On a brighter note, the long, hot summer of 1959 laid on a feast for the English batsmen. With truer tracks to trust and the sun's warmth on their backs, most of the leading English batsmen made hay. As a testament to this, in my 1959 *Big Book of Sports* there is a photograph of a relaxed Colin Cowdrey smiting a massive on-side blow off Indian leg-spinner, Gupte, on a glittering day at Lord's. *Wisden* rightly hailed the summer as a 'cricket renaissance'. It proved to be a particularly memorable one for Warwickshire and England batsman M.J.K. 'Mike' Smith, who notched over 3,000 runs. Smith's team-mate Jim Stewart had his share of fun, too, peppering a ducking and diving Blackpool crowd with 17 sixes. This remained a record for the County Championship until Andrew Symonds scattered the Abergavenny flock with 25 in 1995. No fewer than 23 English batsmen aggregated over 2,000 runs in the summer of 1959, including Surrey's newly-capped opening batsman John Edrich, who proved to be the find of the season. During the ruinous, rainy summer of 1958, only three batsmen scored as many.

Sadly, the summer's Test series against the Indians was a dismal spectacle with the tourists mauled in all five Tests by a much-changed England team. As was the case in 1952, the Indians' technical deficiencies against pace proved to be their undoing, despite the blameless surfaces on which they had mostly played. Statham and Trueman shared 41 wickets for little more than 15 runs each.

In the autumn of 1959, I failed my 11-plus examination. It was hardly surprising. I had become easily distracted and inclined to wander. If I had any spare cash I would attempt to inveigle an adult cinema-goer into escorting me into an 'A' feature, such as *The Night of the Hunter*. Otherwise, the nearby mainline station allowed me a place to hide. I was absorbed by the rocking, steam-hauled expresses that hurtled past with their fleeting scents of scorched oil, tar and peppery sulphur. On dark, winter afternoons, there was an added attraction as the reflections of the locomotives' roaring fires flickered along the grimy station walls. My mum was then 80 miles away in a sprawling Victorian hospital suffused with a smell of disinfectant and heavy polish. If I was ever in doubt about my welcome, a fellow inpatient would pinch her nose tightly whenever I passed.

I came to realise that there was little solace in solitude. It was affirmative company that I craved. Luckily I found what I was looking for in my father's cousin, a burly, genial, easy-going man who could dispel my moroseness with a quip and a relaxed smile. I envied his casual, confident command of life, his ability to ride the knocks with cheery equanimity. In time I began to share his love of black American rhythm and blues and jazz. The song I associate with this period is Ray Charles's breezy single, 'What I'd Say'. In this song, Charles conflates jazz, boogie woogie blues and gospel influences. In mimicking evangelical preachers' 'call and response' routines with his band, Charles secularised, even 'sexed up', the gospel tradition. Being oblivious, then, of such controversial ramifications, I was just grateful to be lifted out of the rut and into the groove.

1960
Cathy's Clown

Ray Charles lent tempo to the emerging US civil rights movement, as did Sam Cooke. It was not only racially segregated North America that was scarred with bloody discrimination, for in March of this year, 180 black protesters were injured and 69 killed when white policemen opened fire in Sharpeville, South Africa. This time the British public reacted. For the first time, a visiting South African cricket team was confronted with anti-apartheid demonstrations. Rev. David Sheppard also refused to captain the Duke of Norfolk's XI in their opening fixture.

BBC commentator John Arlott had been horrified at his initial confrontation with South African apartheid in 1948. It was an experience he had shared with MCC's Billy Griffith who was said by Arlott to have been shaken by the experience. As an outspoken critic, Arlott became the first person to denounce the South African regime as a 'Nazi' one on BBC radio. This was in 1950 when he took part in a panel show which was broadcasted live. Despite that, the Springbok tourists of 1951 were not challenged politically. Neither were Jack Cheetham's team in 1955, although shortly before their arrival in England, British cinemas had screened a Pathe Newsreel item, documenting the brutal dispossession of black Africans in Sophiatown, Johannesburg, by heavily-armed white South African policemen. In his 1960 book, *Over to Me,* Jim Laker also gave a grim first-hand account of a South African policeman's heartless treatment of an injured black African during MCC's tour of 1956/57. Whether or not these disturbing reports stirred consciences at Lord's or Westminster, there was no immediate action taken to curtail sporting links with a country wedded to apartheid. South Africa was, of course, an important trading partner. British businesses were based there.

Several high-ranking MCC members had strong South African connections, while May and Compton had family links there. Ethical foreign policies are easier to espouse than implement.

Nevertheless, by then, even politically conservative Hollywood was producing films which directly challenged the racial discrimination prevalent within the USA. This was illustrated by the 1958 cinematic production of the Rodgers and Hammerstein musical, *South Pacific*. John Ford's fine but complex western, *The Searchers*, and Richard Brooks's under-rated *Moby Dick* of the Great Plains, *The Last Hunt*, were also unusually challenging in their treatment of racism. There was little evidence here of the bland conservatism that shaped white, middle-class attitudes in North America and Britain for much of the 1950s.

The 1960 South African tourists were led by the dour, but indomitable Jackie McGlew. His surname was an apt reflection of his adhesive qualities. However, in this damp, dismal series, he was as easily undone as his team-mates as Trueman and Statham ran riot on the green, green grass of home. The South African mixture of aged experience and novice youth proved no match for a resurgent England side which had just won its first Caribbean rubber, having blunted the mighty blades of Sobers and Worrell, and withstood the hostility of Hall and Watson.

MCC's class of 1959/60 was very different from the team trounced in Australia. Out went Richardson, Watson, Milton, Graveney, Bailey, Evans, Mortimore, Laker, Lock, Loader and Tyson. In came Lancashire's Geoff 'Noddy' Pullar, Northants' Raman Subba Row, Surrey's Ken Barrington, Warwickshire's M.J.K. Smith, Gloucestershire's off-spinner David Allen, Yorkshire's off-spinner Raymond Illingworth and the Sussex wicketkeeper Jim Parks. Although only Allen was a Test debutant, the others had yet to establish themselves in Test cricket, particularly against opposition of the calibre of the West Indies. However, the new intake performed well on the firm, true Caribbean wickets, making light of May's absences through illness. Pullar, Barrington, Smith, Subba Row and Parks made vital contributions with the bat while Dexter excelled, setting aside his Ashes failure Down Under, and revealing himself to be a batsman of exceptional craft, dash and power.

Dexter struggled more against the South African seamers, on the moist home wickets, as did most of his colleagues, although Cowdrey (155) and Pullar (175) shared a 290-run opening partnership at the Oval to pull their side out of the mire. South African Roy McLean drove, cut and pulled with glorious fluency at Manchester (109) but, apart from belting a bold half-century in a losing cause at Edgbaston (68), he offered little resistance otherwise. By sharp contrast, the tourists' wicketkeeper John Waite patented the art of unadventurous survival, grinding out four patient half-centuries. He could not prevent a 3-0 series loss, though.

As for the South African bowling, only belligerent Neil Adcock caused the English batsmen any discomfort, once his opening partner Geoff Griffin was 'chucked out' at Lord's, having been no-balled 11 times for throwing. Griffin had been euphoric at completing a first-innings hat-trick, but concluded his Lord's debut by ignominiously bowling under-arm during an imprudently-added exhibition match. As roller coaster rides go, his was unnecessarily precipitous.

The 'Griffin Affair' reflected badly upon the South African Cricket Association. In line with a new international undertaking, the selectors had pledged not to choose any player whose action was deemed suspicious, and yet they picked Geoff Griffin knowing that he had already been 'called' for throwing by a South African umpire. MCC attempted to forestall a crisis by exhorting the South Africans to send a replacement. Poor Griffin did his best to eradicate the kink in his arm, but to no avail. Shamefully, the South African Cricket Association consigned this pleasant young man to an avoidable public execution. Upon returning to South Africa, Griffin immediately announced his retirement from first-class cricket.

Meanwhile, Tayfield was persuaded to suspend his retirement and join the tour. Having lost fitness, he was no longer the threat of old, and while he bowled with customary accuracy, his 12 Test wickets cost almost 38 runs each. Goddard was as miserly as ever, though, in taking 17 wickets at an average cost of 24.35 runs, but this did little to adjust the substantial imbalance between the sides.

In May 1960 I was selected to play in a school cricket match that took place in a posher part of town. The Everly Brothers' country-and-western-styled single, 'Cathy's Clown', was whirring around inside my head. Don Everly claimed to have renounced love. I could have done with some, though, for here I felt an imposter. I was no sportsman. I was just a fat clown. What right did I have to an attentive audience of cross-legged children? The manicured cricket pitch amid the lush, leafy surroundings made my appearance all the more preposterous, shameful even.

I looked on nervously as a blond boy from the opposing school tossed a shiny, red cricket ball from hand to hand as he marked out an absurdly long run. Before our opening batsmen had reached the crease, he charged in at full tilt and, in a blur of wheeling arms, took out the unguarded middle stump. 'Just practising,' he chirped. Whacking a tennis ball around the playground was fun, but this was a terrifying spectacle. Our ripped, stained pads and threadbare batting gloves looked hopelessly inadequate, and so were we. By the time it was my turn to slouch to the crease, most of our team were out, and we had yet to reach double figures. My class teacher, standing at square leg, reminded me to ask for a guard. But when the umpire enquired whether I would prefer middle or leg, I thought of opting for square leg, behind my teacher. At the inevitable demolition of my stumps I was confronted by the blond boy's malicious glee. 'Eight for two,' he gloated. 'Just two more to get.'

As I trudged back to our demoralised team, my wobbling weight drew the customary cat-calls. Veteran rock critic Dave Marsh reckoned that the interplay between the Everly brothers' harmonies and the grave drumbeat, suggested that Don was about to face a firing squad. I know what he means.

Not long after my dismal debut, our dog found a ragged cricket ball. I eagerly drew it from his disappointed jaws and stuffed it into my pocket, vowing to turn myself into a fast bowler. Over the next 12 months I practised with feverish compulsion, aiming at the stumps I chalked on a nearby garage door, annoying the neighbours with the incessant metallic reverberations. But nothing would deter my ambition.

During the summer of 1960, mum, dad and I reunited in the fading seaside resort of Hastings with its wash of shabby, flaking Victorian tenements, a place that was supposedly 'popular with visitors since 1066' and rightly so, for age did weary the town. However, here I re-found my feet. I began to dispense with those things which had been dragging me down. At mum's insistence, I lost weight. I stopped carrying my favourite books around in a suitcase. I gave away my toys, finally hanging up my guns for good. I exchanged my second name for my first and found that other children offered fun and companionship, rather than threats, ridicule or unwelcome intrusions into my fantasies. I discovered I could achieve things for myself. My weight and my 11-plus failure were not definitive damnations. It is sometimes difficult to grasp how bad things have become until they are better. I had come to recognise morose greyness as my lot, like the ill-fitting clothing I largely accepted in the interests of growth. I still see the 1950s in monochrome, typified by the miniature snaps my aunt took on our rain-soaked outings to Whipsnade Zoo. By contrast, the sixties seem much more colourful. So many happy family memories remain of this period, unfailingly evoked by its wonderful pop songs.

1961
Take Five

While England's football team was enjoying an unexpected renaissance, its Test side confounded both hope and expectation by failing to recover the Ashes. The first Test at Edgbaston started badly. Hopping in and out of the spring showers, England's top batsmen capitulated lamely to the insipid medium-pace of crab-like Ken Mackay. However, defeat was evaded thanks to a vigilant century from Subba Row (119), and a more disdainful one from Dexter (180), containing 31 bristling boundaries and one lordly six.

At Lord's, the mysterious ridge raised its unsightly head, forcing the bruised batsmen, on either side, to lower theirs. Australia's novice opener Bill Lawry was a noble exception, though. Defying the brunt of the fire storm meted out by Trueman and Statham, he remained tall, riding the many blows between wind and water, to reach an outstanding, brave, match-winning, maiden century (130). While Lawry hooked and drove with bullish panache, the English batting withered wretchedly against the rhythmic pace of Davidson and the muscular power of McKenzie.

At Headingley, though, Trueman's perfection of the off-cutter, at reduced pace, earned him man-of-the-match figures of 11-88 – his best return for England. It was enough to propel May's side to parity inside three days. However, the momentum achieved here was then squandered at Manchester where England failed to capitalise upon a 177-run first-innings advantage.

Many years after the event, I read Dexter's outspoken autobiography, *Ted Dexter Declares*. Here, he alleged that MCC selector Walter Robins was partly culpable. Dexter claimed that it was Robins's unwelcome intrusion at tea on the third day which wrecked England's hopes of mounting an unreachable lead. At that point May's side was handsomely-placed at 358/7, with the Australians floundering in their wake. Robins insisted that the two not-out batsmen, Barrington (78) and Trueman (0) 'got on with it', whereupon Barrington immediately lost his wicket with a reckless shot, leaving the unprotected lower order to collapse for only nine more runs, as part-time leg-spinner Bobby Simpson gleefully cleaned up. Admittedly, England had batted cautiously, but the slow Old Trafford wicket did not favour flamboyant stroke-making.

If Dexter's record of events is correct, Robins's intervention was out of order. Chairman of selectors Gubby Allen had previously proclaimed, 'As regards tactics on the field, I am certain that no definite instructions should be given. On the other hand the selectors must discuss tactics with the captain at selection committee meetings, especially when they may have some bearing on the composition of the team. Once a match has started, the chairman may offer an occasional suggestion.' Robins was not then the chairman of selectors.

The Australians batted much more productively in their second innings, removing their deficit with only two wickets down. But the match tilted decisively on the final morning when all-rounder Alan Davidson and young fast bowler 'Garth' McKenzie came together with Australia tottering again on 334/9. David Allen, England's off-spinner, had just taken three quick wickets for no runs. Davidson immediately set about Allen, blasting him for 20 runs in one over. Together, the pair bludgeoned 98 runs in a volatile last-wicket partnership that set May's side a challenging 255-run victory target with just under four hours of play remaining.

An innings of iridescent brilliance from Dexter, in which he scored 76 runs in 85 minutes, enabled England to reach 150/1 at blistering speed. But once Dexter was caught at the wicket, Benaud began to plant his leg-spinners in the roughened area, outside the right-handers' leg stump. May was immediately bowled around his legs, unaccountably essaying a sweep shot (0), and an unexpected slip suddenly became an unstoppable slide as England subsided to 171/6 in a calamity of rash shot selection. Sat intently in front of our flickering, pallid TV screen, I watched this catastrophe unfold in stunned silence. Unable to tolerate the mocking sunlight, I pulled the curtains on the funereal events. After Dexter and Subba Row had provided such a robust platform, England could have seized victory by merely batting normally. But their misplaced anxiety and Benaud's wily assortment of leg-spinners, flippers and googlies, with which he took six wickets for 70 runs, left England 54 runs short of their target, depriving them of the Ashes and the unofficial world crown.

In his autobiography, Dexter had another gripe about Robins's alleged interference. He claimed that, as MCC team manager on the 1959/60 Caribbean tour, Robins had instructed Colin Cowdrey to declare early on the final day of the fifth Test, to restore interest to a game in which Mike Smith and Jim Parks were mounting an unassailable second innings lead, knowing that a draw was sufficient for England to win the rubber. Cowdrey refused. He was not prepared to risk relinquishing a notable series victory in the interests of brighter cricket. Besides, before Smith and Parks had come together, England had been in danger of losing at 148/6. According to Dexter, Cowdrey was backed strongly by his players, with Trueman apparently threatening to eject Robins. Smith (96) and Parks (101 not out) were allowed to complete their 197-run partnership which took the game well away from the West Indians. A piqued Robins then carped to the press about the alleged slowness of England's over rates, and their excessive drinks breaks. The reality was that England scored at a faster rate (2.6 runs per over) than the West Indians (2.4), and also achieved a better over rate.

Once Walter Robins became the chairman of MCC selectors in 1962, he announced that he would not mind losing all five Tests in Australia during the coming winter tour, as long as England played in the 'right way'. In order to enforce his will, he revoked Gubby Allen's 'hands off' dictum. Henceforth, the selectors could direct tactics during a game. To reinforce the point it was agreed that each of the selectors would, in turn, assume the role of team manager during the five home Tests against Pakistan, four of which were captained by Dexter.

Three years later, MCC decided that England's successful and well-respected captain, M.J.K. 'Mike' Smith, would be answerable to an MCC manager, while on the Ashes tour of 1965/66, to ensure that the game was played in accordance with the selectors', 'not the players', wishes. Because the personable Smith worked well with his diplomatic tour manager, Billy Griffith, this arrangement worked satisfactorily. It was a very different story on the 1970/71 Ashes tour, though. But in fairness to the MCC selectors, they had justifiable concerns about the sustainability of first-class cricket, given its dwindling entertainment value, and shrinking revenue stream. Not even the startling success of the one-day game, introduced in 1963, entirely allayed their fears, as County Championship attendances continued to fall, being less than half a million by the mid-1960s, 1.7 million down on the 1947 figure.

The 1961 Ashes series concluded at the Oval with England mired in a grim, dogged rearguard action under grey, pendulous skies. Australia deservedly triumphed because they fielded better, holding on to more crucial chances, and batted with greater resilience and adventure.

However, at the end of this glum summer, I was to discover an inspirational winner. It happened as I was sprawled on the unseasonably green turf of Hastings Central Cricket Ground, watching an England XI take on a strong Commonwealth side. I became entranced by a West Indian fast bowler. His jaunty, loose-limbed stride emphasised supreme athleticism. His wide smile exuded self-belief. Again and again, he pounded in off a prodigiously long run, that began just yards from my cupped chin. His dishevelled shirt became progressively darkened with sweat. A gold chain, encircling his neck, glinted in the September sun as he accelerated to the crease. With a quivering, flailing action he completed his delivery. The ball was barely seen as it reared sharply past the batsman's tentative prod and thwacked into the upstretched gloves of the leaping wicketkeeper. Only the cackling seagulls mocked. He was so confident of his power that he had no need to flaunt it. There were no histrionics, no aggressive posturing. His jocular manner emphasised his love of a life that granted him his mighty talent. I yearned to have his relaxed conviction, his rhythmic power and his compelling presence. I wanted to become Wes Hall.

The Britain I had grown up in was changing rapidly. According to ex-US Secretary of State Dean Acheson, 'Britain had lost [*or was about to lose*] an Empire, and yet to find a role.' For all the important reforms introduced by the Macmillan government, he and his administration seemed crusty and out of touch. There was a mounting urge, at least among the older Baby Boomers, that we should be shaking off the vestiges of staid British conservatism with its 'club amateur' nepotism and embrace a sleek, shining technological future, offering greater equality of opportunity. Anthony Sampson suggested as much in his seminal work *Anatomy of Britain*. It was hardly coincidental that satire once again became chic.

A new satirical nightclub opened in London called 'The Establishment', attracting the controversial American comedian, Lenny Bruce, who traded in edgy narratives on race. *Private Eye* produced its first scrappy editions and, much as it might appear tame now, the *Beyond the Fringe* revue scoffed at 'Establishment' mores such as our self-reverential view of Britain's war effort. To mock our heroic wartime acts of selfless courage was considered almost sacrilegious, at least by those who insisted that Britain should be forever great and grateful. But while Peter Cook, Dudley Moore, Jonathan Miller and Alan Bennett were criticised, notably in the provinces, for trivialising a war from which they had been spared, this accusation could not be levelled at Joseph Heller, whose novel, *Catch-22*, first appeared here in 1961.

Heller had served as a bombardier with the US air force flying missions over Nazi-occupied Italy, in support of the allied invasion. His grotesquely funny satire savaged with nihilistic abandon the euphemisms, moral pretensions and organisational chaos of war. In a year when Britain seemed to be declining and Cold War tensions were mounting, perhaps gallows humour had more resonance.

My soundtrack to this 'shock of the new' was a jazz number. By then, rock 'n' roll had become emasculated, its rough edges hewn away by bland, 'pretty boy' performers such as Ricky Nelson, Bobby Vee and Fabian, leaving only a vapid varnish, awaiting eventual rescue by our very own 'Fab Four'. Not being an Aldermaston marcher, I plumped, not for the growing popularity of 'Trad' Jazz as performed by Acker Bilk and Kenny Ball, but for the coolness of Dave Brubeck's joltingly percussive 'Take Five', with its catchy saxophone melody and repetitive two-chord piano 'vamp' that I associate with the swish insouciance of British 'New Wave' cinema. If I had discovered a capacity for pretence, though, my tongue remained firmly in my chic.

1962

Let's Dance

MCC's 1961/62 winter tour of India, Pakistan and Ceylon was a largely dismal affair. While a worthy 1-0 victory was achieved in Pakistan, Dexter's team was deservedly beaten 2-0 by the stronger Indians who claimed a first series victory over their former imperial overlords. In dedicated homage to failure, I kept a series scrapbook made up of daily press cuttings.

Ted Dexter had attempted to inject some urgency into the generally pedestrian batting on the sluggish tracks of India and Pakistan but was ultimately forced to settle for occupation of the crease as his side came under increasing pressure. Lacking many of England's front-line performers, he was over-reliant upon the resilient 'nudge and run' accumulator Ken Barrington and opening batsman Geoff Pullar. At Calcutta and Madras, where England had to contend with batting last on crumbling surfaces, neither Dexter nor Barrington could muster sufficient runs to compensate for others' failures.

Dexter's pace attack was woefully under-powered. His fastest bowlers, David 'Butch' White, of newly-crowned county champions Hampshire, and Alan Brown of Kent, with his pronounced 'drag', made little impact on the sub-continent pitches. White was troubled by injury while Brown lacked accuracy and length. Neither Gloucestershire's David Smith, nor the Essex all-rounder Barry Knight, fared any better with their brisk medium pace. The 18 Indian Test wickets, which fell to Smith, Knight and Dexter, cost on average 50 runs each. With too many easy pickings to be had in the seamer-friendly conditions of home, English pace bowlers were ill-prepared for such challenges abroad. On the other hand, Tony Lock and David Allen bowled admirably. Between them, they completed over 1,400 overs on this arduous tour, sharing over 100 wickets at a joint average cost of 26 runs each which was slightly better than that achieved by the leading Indian spinners, Durani and Borde.

The fate of the Indian series rested upon the hosts' uncanny fortune with the toss and the greater depth of their batting. Indian wicketkeeper Farokh Engineer, batting at nine, averaged 27, almost as many as England opener Peter Richardson achieved (33.37), and yet the Kent man was fourth-placed in England's series averages. However, the English batsmen fared better against the more innocuous Pakistani bowling. At Lahore, Ted Dexter and Bob Barber clouted England to a five-wicket victory with an unbroken sixth-wicket stand of 101, made in just 85 minutes. It was a rare interlude of sparkling cricket.

This was not a happy tour. According to Gordon Ross, editor of the *Playfair Cricket Annual* for 1962, the playing schedule was intense; the heat and dust, withering; the criss-cross travelling, exhausting; the countless functions, trying; the food, often 'unpalatable'; and the accommodation, 'strange'. One unnamed player told a British journalist, 'If I could have afforded it, I would not have come.' He was not alone.

In 1960, a professional English cricketer could earn between £500 and £1,000 gross on an MCC winter tour. If the £100 Test match fee is also taken into account, he could substantially increase, if not double, his gross county salary, which was then between £800 and £1,000 inclusive of match fees and winter payments, out of which he had to pay for his equipment, travel and subsistence. To put these earnings into perspective, a county professional's salary, without Test or touring enhancements, was scarcely better than that earned by an average manual worker of this time (£750). On the other hand, an amateur England cricketer could earn as much as a professional in touring expenses alone, given their entitlement to compensation for 'broken employment time'. It was small wonder that Jim Laker thought he would be better off turning amateur for the 1958/59 Ashes tour. Also, Dexter revealed that he made a lot more from cricket as an amateur than he did from business. It is not clear, though, whether this said more about the generosity of amateurs' expenses or the calibre of Dexter's business skills.

With top English professional footballers earning up to £100 per week, following the abolition of the £20 maximum weekly wage, the disparity in earning capacity between footballers and cricketers widened considerably. But even if English cricket had then been minded to address this differential, it lacked the revenue to do so.

Dexter returned to face a reproachful Walter Robins, who had become the new chairman of MCC selectors. While Dexter had batted with authority, his captaincy smacked of the curate's egg – at times inventive and perceptive, but at others distracted, indecisive or stolid. Being dissatisfied with the tempo of the cricket played on the winter tour, Robins sought a change of helmsman. The Rev. David Sheppard was the man he had in mind. Having been granted a sabbatical from his ecclesiastical duties, Sheppard returned temporarily to first-class cricket with Sussex after an absence of two years. Robins hailed

Sheppard as a 'fine leader on and off the field' and clearly identified him as a potential captain for the coming winter Ashes series Down Under. Sheppard's fine century in the final Gentlemen v Players game at Lord's in 1962 certainly boosted his candidacy.

The situation bore a remarkable resemblance to that in 1954 when Hutton faced being replaced by Sheppard. But in the summer of 1962 the choice was not between an amateur and a professional but between three Oxbridge amateurs, for Cowdrey was also in the mix, having been chosen to replace Dexter as the England skipper at Leeds, before being ruled out because of injury. The outcome of the summer series with Pakistan gave few clues as to the selectors' final choice, for the Pakistanis took only a brief look at the grey, chilly English weather before shrivelling into meek submission. With 35-year-old Fazal Mahmood shorn of his former potency, England posted a succession of intimidating totals at a disdainful rate of 3.5 runs per over. Despite Burki's and Nasim-ul-Ghani's defiant 197-run stand at Lord's, helped by Dexter's indecision and inattentiveness, only the merciful Nottingham rain saved the outgunned Pakistanis from a series whitewash.

Eventually, the selectors reverted to Dexter because he was thought to pose a more combative challenge to the hard-nosed, tactically-astute Benaud. Cowdrey was considered too cautious, and Sheppard's brief experience of Test match captaincy dated back eight years. Besides, Sheppard had not played Test cricket since 1956. But Dexter must have thought that his re-appointment was tepid praise.

Meanwhile, Britain's beleaguered prime minister was facing credibility problems, too. In a vain attempt to boost his plummeting popularity, Macmillan sacked most of his Cabinet in July 1962, prompting Liberal Jeremy Thorpe to snipe, 'Greater love hath no man than he lay down his friends for his life.'

It was then when I first represented my secondary modern school as an opening bowler. The game was played on a clifftop blurred by low cloud and muslin shrouds of fine drizzle. But the heavily overcast conditions did not impair the startling shine on the new ball I was presented with. Not being Waqar Younis, the ragged specimen I used in practice had no chance of swinging, but this beauty hooped around like a boomerang. While our opponents struggled to lay their bats on any of my deliveries, I had less difficulty in locating their stumps. My mind went back to the humiliation I had endured two years before. As each disconsolate batsman returned to the shack-like pavilion, I mentally stapled upon their downcast faces a mask of that gloating blond boy. For several days after, my life hovered on a bloated cushion of hubris. I fantasised about playing for England on tropical islands, edged by lapping, cerulean waters of cut glass clarity, with palm fronds swishing gently in the coconut-scented sea breezes. And then a week later I was taken apart by a burly youth who proved that style was no match for substance as each of my opening deliveries whistled to the fence. I quietly slid my feet back into the comfy slippers of modest expectation.

I first heard 'Let's Dance' on 17 November less than one month after the Cuban missile crisis. It was a grey, grimy, greasy day. New South Wales were thrashing Dexter's MCC side in Sydney. I distracted myself in the morning gloom, completing my geography homework, drawing a map of the East Midlands, carefully listing the main industries of its principal towns and cities – hosiery in Leicester, bicycles and lace in Nottingham, steel in Corby and Wellingborough, and boots and shoes in Northampton. During the 1960s, our towns and cities were characterised by what they manufactured. How quaint that now seems.

As I was studiously compiling the map I listened peripherally to Brian Matthew's *Saturday Club* on the *BBC Light Programme*. It was a rare outlet for pop music on BBC radio. Amid the rockabilly standards emerged a song that insinuated itself at first hearing. The stomping drum 'intro', like a Sioux war dance, drew me instantly to my feet. Then the nasal, nerdy vocal, accompanied by an insistent, staccato organ riff, demanded that I did, just as Chris Montez stipulated, 'Let's Dance'. Being on repeat play inside my head, the song urged my rapid strides to the station. It powered the throbbing diesel as it lurched around the wet, wooded curves to Tonbridge. It drowned the anodyne fare played on the Angel Ground's PA. It orchestrated the pulsating, tingling rhythms of the football game I had travelled to watch. I need no photographic record. 'Let's Dance' illuminates this dimly-lit, drizzle-shrouded day forever.

1963
Louie Louie

1963 seemed to be a year of living pruriently. Philip Larkin's sardonic take on the Profumo Affair started with his whimsical reflection that it was then when sexual intercourse began, arriving between the *Lady Chatterley's Lover* ban and the Beatles' first album. Although embattled Prime Minister Harold Macmillan vowed, 'I was determined that no British government should be brought down by the action of two tarts', he was forced to resign a few months later due to ill health. The satirical magazine *Private Eye* had a field day mocking the Tory slogan 'Life's better under a Conservative' and spoofing Macmillan's 1957 boast with 'We Have Never Had It So Often'. With John Profumo forced to resign from his Cabinet post, the morally discredited Tories became a laughing stock. Despite Alec Douglas-Home's best efforts, electoral defeat beckoned. Contrasted with the Labour leader Harold Wilson's implied promise of a 'white heat' technological revolution, Douglas-Home's grouse moor tweeds seemed musty and by-gone.

Not that MCC's much-deliberated and reluctant decision to abolish the distinction between amateur and professional cricketers had much impact upon its familiar mode of operation. *Wisden* editor Norman Preston led a chorus of lamentation in 1963, claiming that with the loss of the amateur, cricket risked losing the 'spirit of freedom and gaiety' that its best unpaid performers contributed. But as much as his view resonated with the likes of *Daily Telegraph* cricket correspondent E.W. 'Jim' Swanton and, more oddly, with the Marxist Caribbean writer C.L.R. James, MCC's tour Down Under seemed to perpetuate the former social divisions as emphatically as before. At least that was the view of disgruntled Yorkshire professional Raymond Illingworth, who griped that MCC's tour manager, the Duke of Norfolk, and his Oxbridge lieutenants remained aloof from the foot soldiers, such as himself, separately pursuing their private and family interests, dining exclusively, and commandeering the four cars made available to the MCC party.

Although England achieved a creditable 1-1 draw in Australia, the Test series was widely condemned as a disappointing dirge. Dexter had declared, on arrival, that his side was pledged to playing a brand of attacking cricket that had won the flamboyant West Indies tourists so much popularity during the Test series of 1960/61. Naively, perhaps, he seemed unaware that his attractive stall might become a coconut shy. Despite Dexter's typically bold batting, his side averaged only 2.4 runs per six balls, a slower rate of scoring than was achieved on the dead tracks of the Indian subcontinent. Neither the sluggish Australian wickets nor Benaud's cautious tactics helped Dexter's cause, though.

Although Benaud was feted as an adventurous, enterprising leader, this is something of a myth, at least in the Test matches, in which Benaud was as risk-averse as Len Hutton. Against the cavalier West Indians, his batsmen managed no better than 2.4 an over, not daring to throw the bat until a secure total had been reached. Benaud rarely pursued victory vigorously unless the prospect of defeat seemed remote. In the Manchester Test of 1961, he had no option other than to attack, with England sailing to victory, thanks to Dexter's bold stroke-play. Fearing Dexter's destructive driving power, Benaud seemed more concerned with stifling rather than dismissing him during the 1962/63 Ashes series, consistently aiming at or outside 'Lord Ted's' leg stump, with a mid-on set deep to save the one. Lengthy periods of stalemate ensued in this poker-like contest with Dexter equally determined not to be 'bored out' through any lack of patience. Having watched Dexter compile a meticulous, obdurate, match-saving innings of 167 runs against Glamorgan in 1962 on probably the flattest surface that the Hastings Central Ground had ever produced, I realised that he was not just a gallant dasher.

What appeared to be overlooked by the brighter cricket devotees of this period was that Ashes contests were frequently won by attritional means. Among the most successful English batsmen in Ashes contests were the cautious accumulators such as Ken Barrington, Geoffrey Boycott and John Edrich who collectively averaged 53 runs, whereas a more fluent group comprising Compton, Dexter, Cowdrey, Graveney and May jointly averaged 35, an identical average to that of the swashbuckling Australian batsman Victor

Trumper. It seemed as if Don Bradman and Len Hutton were as committed to the mantra 'winning isn't everything, it is the only thing' as the cautious football tactician Sir Alf Ramsey, who first coined the expression. Surely, Alastair Cook and Michael Clarke are no different? Clamping my Dansette transistor radio to my ear, on those tingling cold mornings, I was convinced that if we could not beat the Australians, we must never, ever let them defeat us.

With both the English and Australian press corps chuffing over what Crawford White described as a 'ghastly flop of the Test series', Dexter made the imprudent quip, 'The Ashes were a bane and a nuisance and that, if abolished and each man paid £1,000 for winning, there would probably be a result.' What he meant, perhaps, was that Test cricket, and notably Ashes contests, were too constrained by their importance to ever become spectacular events. However, batsmen of the great Australian sides of the 1990s and noughties would make nonsense of this weary fatalism, as would the Ashes-winning England side of 2005, by regularly scoring at rates around four runs per over.

Thankfully, the West Indian cricket team that toured England a few months later was as refreshing as a rippling summer breeze. They played cricket that was both physically invigorating and emotionally stirring. In turn, England rose to the challenge, helping produce a Test series as enthralling as any I have seen, replete with switchback fortunes, blistering batting, scorching pace, mesmerising spin, heroic defiance, and fielding of electric intensity, watched by buoyantly-whistling, rhythmically-drumming Caribbean crowds. Here, we were introduced to a new kind of cricket watcher, one who leapt, danced, and proffered good-humoured advice, and chirpily commented on what was seen. Not content with being supine, deckchair spectators, these excited fans were as much a part of the action as the players.

A West Indian tour during the sixties offered Caribbean immigrants a chance of vicarious glory, supposing they could afford to attend. Subsequent generations have had less cause to follow suit, not only because of a decline in West Indian cricket, but because they have developed independent identities within a British way of life. Niche musical genres such as 'Jungle' are just one manifestation of this.

The West Indian victory in 1963 restored Caribbean pride, as it showcased brilliant, vibrant, black talent to a nation still consumed with racial bigotry. The Notting Hill riots were then recent history. Esteemed black Trade Unionist Bill Morris recalled, 'In 1963 we were not even at the foothills of integration.' Signs still hung in many boarding house windows stating 'no coloureds' while many British employers believed it was acceptable to cite the discomfort of their white employees as a justification for turning away black applicants.

As if in refutation of prevailing racial prejudice, the supremely lithe Sobers epitomised grace and power; Kanhai melded stridency with style; Butcher boasted brawny belligerence; Gibbs exhibited guile and potency; and Hall and Griffith possessed fearsome strength and speed. The salacious details associated with the Profumo Affair might have grabbed the headlines, but it was not sexual impropriety that was our most pernicious vice in 1963, it was implacable racial discrimination. This is why the extraordinary events witnessed during this tour seemed to stretch well beyond a boundary, suggesting, perhaps, that multiculturalism was more than a nascent hope, only for that fragile optimism to be confounded, five years later, by Enoch Powell's 'rivers of blood' rant at a time of increasing economic strife.

Frank Worrell was the man of the series. His contribution with the bat was minimal, apart from a wonderful virtuoso knock of 74 not out at Old Trafford. He averaged only 20 runs in eight Test innings. His bowling was almost irrelevant – three wickets at 35 each, and yet he stamped his authority upon his team, helping them to transcend their island rivalries. No previous West Indian leader had managed to create a united West Indian identity that the players, their families, communities and supporters could collectively embrace. Remember, the post-colonial West Indian Federation had just foundered on the rocks of inter-island division. Worrell lifted his team and the Caribbean diaspora above these debilitating rifts. And yet his charisma was not expressed in pumped-up gestures or eloquent oratory. He used words sparingly, often contenting himself with a smile or a frown, a nod or shaking of the head, deporting himself with languid calm and genial confidence. His authority was unquestioned, though. He restored stability to a historically fragmented team. Whereas the English selectors chopped and changed their team ruinously, ten members of Worrell's side played in all five Tests.

The irrepressible Fred Trueman was one of only three Ashes survivors to play throughout the series. True to form, he led the way by taking 34 West Indian wickets at 17. His 12 wickets at Edgbaston powered England to an unexpected 217-run victory, briefly restoring parity before the Windies flexed their muscles at Headingley and the Oval, to win the series comfortably by 3-1. Without Trueman, it would have been a very one-sided affair. As a measure of his pre-eminence, his bowling colleagues could muster only 41 wickets between them, at a collective average of 43.

Captain Ted Dexter relished his ordeals by fire, surpassing himself in the murky light of Lord's, by producing an innings of almost unparalleled savagery. In the space of just 80 minutes, Dexter drove, cut and hooked the ferocious new-ball pair Hall and Griffith with such imperious disdain as to imperil the safety of the crowd intruding upon the boundary ropes. Dexter raced to a personal score of 70 runs off 76 deliveries, whisking the England score up to 120/2. Sadly, Dexter's batting did not attain this sublime height again in this series. Too often dumbfounded by the sharp spin of Sobers and Gibbs, he managed a mediocre average score of 31.50. As for Ken Barrington, England's most reliable performer Down Under, his trademark resilience crumbled in the face of West Indian pace, causing him to leap into uncontrolled, back foot, defensive shots. His nervous prodding against the spinners was equally unproductive. After averaging over 72 in the recent Ashes series, his average score against Worrell's men was almost a reversal at 27.50.

The Lord's Test was a magnificent, nail-biting affair, one of the most exciting cricket contests ever staged. It was one in which Wes Hall displayed astonishing stamina and Brian Close outstanding bravery. In dingy light, Close took hit after hit on his lean body while jostling England towards their victory target. At 130/4 England's prospects looked good, but Frank Worrell, as Len Hutton had previously done, slowed the over rate to a glacial speed. England lost further wickets in trying to force the pace. Finally, with Cowdrey nursing a broken arm, tail-ender David Allen played out Wes Hall's final over to obtain a draw. England were just six runs short of victory, but with only one wicket remaining. Although England squared the series at a rainy Edgbaston, they were outclassed in the final two Tests.

England's vulnerability against high calibre West Indian pace and spin bowling forced a strengthening of the batting order. Sussex's batsman/wicketkeeper Jim Parks was recalled, and the resolute Yorkshireman Phil Sharpe made his Test debut. Sharpe averaged 53.40 during the series, placing him well ahead of his colleagues. But not once did England manage an innings total of 300 or more. England's failure to score more runs was largely due to one man, Charlie Griffith.

Griffith's series haul of 32 wickets at an average of 16 suggested that he was twice as potent as his new-ball partner Wes Hall. From a lumbering run and a laboured, wheeling action, Griffith stunned his opponents with a deadly diet of venomous 'throat balls' and sizzling yorkers. Moreover, Griffith managed to produce his lethal lift off a good length, surprising many unwary batsmen. This had been the fate of the Indian captain Nari Contractor, whose skull was cracked, almost fatally, by a Griffith thunderbolt in 1962. Contractor never played Test cricket again.

Unlike Hall whose pounding, wild-eyed sprint to the wicket presaged extreme speed, there was nothing in Griffith's trundling approach to suggest how menacing his deliveries would be. It was a common assumption then that Griffith could not generate such lightning pace legally. In fact, he had already been 'called' for throwing by West Indian umpire Lopez Jordan in the match in which Contractor almost died. Dexter was adamant that Griffith 'threw every ball'. He claimed that Frank Worrell said as much during the 1959/60 MCC tour of the Caribbean. Richie Benaud later joined the chorus of disapproval in his book, *The New Champions*, which analysed the fiery West Indies–Australia contest of 1965 which the Australians lost 2-1. Ironically, Griffith's only contribution of note in that series was the six wickets he took for 46 runs in a losing cause in the final Test in Trinidad. Benaud claimed Griffith was an 'embarrassment' to his team-mates, many of whom were certain that he threw.

Australian umpire Cecil Pepper was equally convinced of Griffith's guilt having officiated in an exhibition match between an England XI and a West Indian one in 1964. However, MCC merely noted Pepper's concerns, and thanked him for avoiding any 'unnecessary unpleasantness' by not calling Griffith. Benaud had applauded the MCC efforts in gaining international agreement to eradicate throwing in 1960, but was disappointed that Pepper's report, which stated that Griffith threw 'a great majority of his deliveries', was not passed on to the Australian and West Indian Boards of Control before the 1965 series began.

As for Griffith, he maintained his innocence, dismissing the accusation in his 1970 autobiography, whimsically entitled *Chucked Around*. Although 'called' only twice during his first-class career, once by Lopez Jordan, and once by English umpire Arthur Fagg, his protestations of innocence failed to remove the suspicion that he 'threw', particularly when striving for extra pace. Clearly, MCC had no appetite for another 'Griffin Affair'. Ironically, the most notable achievement of the MCC adjudication committee came in 1969 when Derbyshire's former England fast bowler Harold Rhodes was cleared of throwing, nine years after he had first been 'called'. Their decision was based upon slow-motion camera footage. It was the first time that new technology had been used in an officiating capacity. Ultimately, this innovation would lead to the Umpire Decision Review System or DRS of today.

The tingling *Summer Spectacular* of 1963 left both sides and their supporters hungry for more. The Imperial Cricket Conference or ICC – renamed as the International Cricket Conference in 1965 – was sympathetic to re-ordering the Test match itinerary. It had declared that nations, other than Australia, should be granted more frequent tours of England. Consequently, the West Indians were invited to return to England in 1966 once the Indians, who had been due to tour during that summer, were persuaded to accept a shared six Test match programme with their not-so-chummy neighbours, Pakistan, a year later. To sweeten the pill, MCC promised to tour India during the winter of 1963/64. Not that this hastily-arranged tour provided much entertainment. Sterility abounded as all five Tests were drawn. However the MCC tourists, led by the genial M.J.K. Smith, distinguished themselves by bravely avoiding defeat while ravaged by sickness and injury.

In 1963 cricket also saw the eventual birth of the Gillette one-day tournament after a six-year gestation. The tournament represented the first major stage in the commercialisation of English cricket which would ultimately challenge the authority of its administrators in determining the game's destiny. Ted Dexter's Sussex won the trophy in the new tournament's first and second years, and not entirely because of his or Jim Parks's batting brilliance. Dexter's Sussex side succeeded because it comprised at least five proficient medium-paced or fast-medium bowlers – Ian Thomson, Don Bates, Tony Buss and John Snow, backed by Dexter himself – who were collectively capable of bowling consistent, tight, back of a length, seam-up, to defensive fields. Nevertheless, Dexter had misgivings at his side's initial success, warning that if one-day cricket flourished, the stereotyped medium-pace bowler would prevail at the expense of the spinner, signalling the disappearance of slow bowling from the English first-class game. Ironically then, Worcestershire left-arm spinner Norman Gifford bowled marvellously in the inaugural final at Lord's, but in a flat, containing guise that any one-day medium-pacer would have been proud of.

By the summer of 1963, shrieking Beatlemania had swamped British pop culture, not that this impressed a cricketing friend of mine who insisted that this tinny Mersey beat, with its 'sappy love songs', was absurdly over-hyped. Swimming doggedly against a tsunami of popular acclaim, he preferred the reverberating twangs of US surf guitars and feral garage rock. While the teenage nation remained in thrall of the Beatles' 'Love Me Do', 'From Me to You' and 'She Loves You', he paid homage to The Trashmen's frenzied 'Surfin' Bird' and Link Wray's resonant 'Rumble'. It was he who introduced me to The Kingsmen's 'Louie, Louie', which he recently described as a 'consummate celebration of gutter glory'. It remains as one of pop's finest walks on the wild side. Like 'Let's Dance', the piece is held together by a repetitive, insinuating organ line, but it is its clattering drum beat, chopping guitar and rasping vocals that announce a rawer, rabid sound. Ridiculously, the song was once the subject of an FBI obscenity investigation. On a path from Elvis to Public Enemy, pop has regularly stirred fears of subversion. 'Louie Louie' not only presaged the Kinks' early output, it threw down a gauntlet picked up by anarchic hell-raisers such as the MC5 and The Stooges, influencing punk sensibilities of the 1970s and beyond.

1964

I Just Don't Know What to do with Myself

If the popular press reports were to be believed, the summer of 1964 was scarred by seaside violence, perpetrated by warring gangs of Mods and Rockers. The moral panic these reports aroused were largely without justification, but the bold swagger of Mod and Rocker youth cultures did represent a challenge to restrained middle-class society. The cessation of National Service played a part in their emergence as did an extended period of full employment, in supplying greater disposable income. British Baby Boomers, notably those from the working classes, benefitted enormously from the resulting freedoms denied to the youth of previous generations.

Mod and Rocker cultures were separately defined by their choices of fashion, music and wheels. With her eye-covering fringe and her long hair, Cathy McGowan of ITV's pop show *Ready Steady Go* was a prominent Mod role model. Other Mod girls had really short cuts, like the model Twiggy. Shift dresses with round collars were all the rage, usually worn with white stockings and stack-heeled shoes although tights replaced stockings once miniskirts became fashionable. Make-up was minimal and lipstick was completely out.

But Mod fashion was not just a girls' thing. Mod guys were equally fastidious. Vidal Sassoon moved in here smartly. Mod boys liked their middle partings with puffed up lacquered tops and backs, with their girlfriends supplying the lacquer. If you can remember Steve Marriott of the Small Faces, you will know the look. Many were fond of small-brimmed blue beat hats. As for the rest of the gear, it didn't come cheaply. Ivy League suits – three buttons, narrow lapels, and two vents – would cost £30 or more, megabucks in those days. To get the picture, try watching video footage of The Righteous Brothers singing 'You've Lost that Lovin' Feelin' or The Zombies performing their breathy, jazzy single, 'She's Not There'. Then there were the trousers with 17-inch bottoms and imitation crocodile or python shoes with rounded toes, although many of the cheapskates settled for desert boots. Blue suits were popular too. For those Mods who could afford wheels, this meant a Lambretta or Vespa scooter, bristling with lamps and wing mirrors. And the scooter uniform was an olive green Parka with a fur-trimmed hood.

Then there was the music. Blue beat, rock-steady artists like Prince Buster were Mod favourites until abrasively energetic bands like The Who and the Small Faces took centre-stage. The Who's centrepiece was 'My Generation' which was completed with a frantic trashing of their instruments.

As for Rocker fashion, this was strictly retro, caught up in the 1950s beat – driving rock 'n' roll, grease, leather gear and roaring bikes. The Rocker girls wore leathers too, with flat shoes, lacquered bouffants and thick make-up. They were keen on Elvis pendants, too. While Rockers remained faithful to the jive and the twist, the Mods were strictly Blue Beat, knees stiff, arms flailing all over the place.

In my hermit's cave I observed this remote world through my TV screen – the coy Lad of Shalott. Dusty Springfield's soulful rendition of Burt Bacharach's and Hal David's 'Torch' song, 'I Just Don't Know What to do with Myself', touched me from a distance. However, it was difficult reconciling Dusty's strong, self-assured stage persona with the song's meekly submissive message, underlined repeatedly by a tragic trumpet call. Little did I realise that beneath Dusty's commanding public presence remained an anxious, self-deprecating convent schoolgirl named Mary O'Brien, as susceptible to moments of vulnerability as the hapless England batsmen.

Although Bobby Simpson's Australians were dismissed by some sports journalists as the weakest side to visit these shores, they proved too good for an unsettled and ageing England team. After rain had washed away the prospect of a result in the first two Tests, the series hinged upon a startling change in fortune on the second afternoon at Headingley.

The English batsmen had previously struggled at Nottingham and Lord's against the Aussie seamers, led by the relaxed strength of 'Garth' McKenzie, and well supported by the cut and in-swing of the ungainly Neil Hawke, and the bustling out-swing of new boy Grahame Corling, who troubled Boycott outside his off stump. Despite making a confident start at Leeds, with Boycott and Dexter taking England to 129/2, this strong position was carelessly wasted, leaving the lower order to add only dribs and drabs to a below-par total of 268. Although Australia replied strongly, racing to 95/1, they stumbled, too, in the face of a tourniquet applied by Titmus and left-arm spinner Norman Gifford. Frustrated by their inability to master the two English slow bowlers, the Australians paid the penalty of impetuosity as they toppled to 178/7. Titmus took 3-27 off 29 unchanged overs. Anxious to avert further damage, Burge and Hawke settled for passive resistance. Dexter responded by taking the new ball expecting that his refreshed opening pair Trueman and Flavell would blast out the Australian tail. Alas, not so.

Presented with a litany of long hops and injudicious bouncers, Burge flayed both fast bowlers all around Headingley, in a tremendous match-winning innings of 160. Whereas Trueman had made the old ball swing menacingly, he proceeded to gorge Burge's appetite for short-pitched bowling with the harder, new one. He and Flavell bowled like drains, profligately blowing away England's Ashes chances. Although Trueman dismissed Neil Hawke with the final ball of the day when the Australian total stood at 283, Wally Grout joined Burge in a Saturday morning run-fest, raising a further 89 runs together. Barrington apart, the English batsmen performed ineptly the second time around, leaving Australia the small task of scoring 111 for victory, which they achieved with almost sadistic slowness, losing just three wickets.

Old Trafford groundsman Bert Flack seemed determined to make amends for the 1956 fiasco by producing a wicket that would last a century. Bobby Simpson won the toss and batted and batted and batted, safe in the knowledge that a draw was sufficient to retain the Ashes. Simpson occupied the crease for over 12 hours, scoring a monumental 311, declaring just before lunch on the third day with the Australians well out of sight at 656/8.

Trueman and Flavell paid for their profligacy at Leeds with their Test places. Their replacements were the stocky, bucolic-looking Somerset quick Fred Rumsey and the heavily-built Middlesex seamer John Price, with his Guardsman's posture and immense, crescent-shaped run. But there was nothing in this somnolent wicket to encourage Rumsey's slinging pace or Price's sharp bounce. So Dexter turned largely to medium-paced Tom Cartwright who bowled with metronomic accuracy for 77 overs, conceding only 118 runs. When it became England's turn to bat, Dexter (174) and Barrington (256) seemed determined to outdo the Aussies in the dirge stakes, laboriously accumulating 246 for the third wicket. In fact, only a late clatter of English wickets prevented this uninterrupted match from being concluded without two innings being completed. By the close, most spectators had departed in search of something more engaging.

The sluggish final Test at the Oval, played under suitably sombre skies, was notable for two feats only: Trueman's 300th Test wicket and Boycott's maiden Test century. If there had been any doubt about the poor state of English cricket before this series, it was now blatantly self-evident. MCC selectors could ill afford to ignore the splendid form of Tom Graveney, who had just completed his 100th first-class century, having been successfully rehabilitated at Worcestershire. But ignore him they did, choosing no fewer than 20 players for this lamentable Ashes failure.

1965
Like a Rolling Stone

With British manufacturing then in retreat, the new Labour Government faced a huge imbalance of payments. It vainly attempted to control prices and incomes as the unions pressed for an ever-increasing share of the good life, arguably more in support of their better-off members than the lowest paid, which largely comprised women and ethnic minorities.

In his recollections of Sir Winston Churchill's funeral in January 1965, Labour Housing Minister Richard Crossman referred to the faded aristocracy and weary military chiefs on show, not neglecting to mention his dreary-looking political colleagues in his glum summation. He concluded it was an end of an epoch and perhaps of a nation, too. But it was not the time to wallow in regret. The country – particularly the industrial north and midlands – remained sullied by slum, derelict and shabby pre-fabricated housing which needed to be replaced with modern, purpose-built homes. Too many people were without basic amenities, adequate shelter being the most pressing need. The BBC Wednesday Play *Cathy Come Home* would ram that point home better than any Government Inquiry. Beneath the vapid gloss of 'swinging' England there was a grim, grimy reality, a world much nearer to the abject poverty of *The Whisperers* than the atavistic preening of *Darling*, closer to the austerity of *Z Cars* than to the cosiness of *Dixon of Dock Green*.

In 1965, I bade farewell to my much-loved secondary modern school. I signed off with a last-ball winning run against our local rivals, to be chaired off for a mocking interview with a Peter West impersonator clutching a hose in place of a microphone. It was typical of the ribald, derisory sense of fun pervading our school life, where my devout Christianity became a regular target for good-natured ribbing. How often were our prayer meetings interrupted by some goon poking his head around the door and announcing, 'If you drop that cross again you'll be out of the procession' or, 'Whoever arranged this nosh up ought to be crucified.' Much as I struggled to suppress a snigger, accepting these were just harmless jibes, I was troubled more by the morality of sending an English cricket team to play in South Africa having recently read Father Trevor Huddleston's stark personal account of apartheid in *Naught for Your Comfort*.

While MCC's decision to tour South Africa, in the winter of 1964/65, met with little political opposition at home, it was one that was out of step with the world's largest sports governing bodies: the Olympic Committee and FIFA, who had suspended South African participation. MCC justified its position by claiming that matters of sport and politics should remain separate. It was, of course, a principle which had enabled India and Pakistan to play Test cricket with one another in 1952/53, when the horrific 'ethnic cleansing' that had followed partition was still a recent memory. In his 1966 book, Dexter suggested that while South African social and racial divisions might seem incompatible with a Christian society, it was hypocritical for us to demand change while we remained complicit in the oppression of others at home and abroad. However, at the point that Dexter expressed his view, Basil D'Oliveira, a mixed race Cape Town cricketer, was about to make his Test debut for England, having been denied the opportunity to represent his native country because of the colour of his skin.

It was not as if South Africa had any legitimate right to play Test cricket, having left the Imperial Cricket Conference when the country withdrew from the Commonwealth in 1961. Nevertheless, South Africa's status as a Test-playing country was tolerated by the white, MCC-dominated ICC, at least for a few more years, despite the rightful protests of India, Pakistan and the West Indies, who had been denied the opportunity to play the Springboks at home or abroad because of the Pretoria government's apartheid policies.

With Dexter having chosen to stand for Parliament in the general election of 1964, MCC selectors reverted to another amateur, M.J.K. 'Mike' Smith, to captain England in South Africa. As MCC's captain in India during the previous winter, Smith did well to hold his beleaguered squad together. He was no less effective in South Africa, instilling confidence and achieving unity with his positive manner, while commanding respect with his fearless fielding at short leg.

England's top batsmen seemed to recover their form and confidence in the South African heat. Barrington averaged just over 100 in seven Test innings, and rejuvenated opener, Bob Barber, batted boldly and blithely to average over 70. Meanwhile Barber's more cautious partner, Geoff Boycott, averaged almost 50 in his eight innings.

Having recovered from his electoral humiliation at the hands of Jim Callaghan, Dexter enjoyed a successful tour which he crowned with a magnificent century (172) in the second Test at Johannesburg. Here, he shared a 191-run partnership with Barrington (121) that threatened to win the game. Had it not been for Colin Bland's resilient innings of 144 not out on the final day, Allen and Titmus might well have bowled England to a successive innings victory.

Because of the benign batting conditions, Smith's vulnerability against high pace was rarely tested. His vital century in the third Test at Cape Town

(121) helped his side avert the follow-on and save the game. But while Smith's batsmen proved to be robust and reliable, only his off-spinning duo Allen and Titmus caused any consternation for an equally strong South African batting order. Allen and Titmus shared 567 overs during this series, taking 35 wickets between them, which comprised almost half of England's haul. But after the second Test, Smith used them largely in a run-saving capacity as he sought to protect a narrow series lead.

Deprived of Trueman and Statham, Smith's pace attack posed little threat after an injury-prone John Price and the admirable Sussex workhorse Ian Thomson made surprising early inroads on a deteriorating first Test wicket at Durban. Here, the South Africans were replying wearily to England's hefty first innings score of 485/5 declared, in which Barrington (148) and wicketkeeper Parks (108) had shared an unbroken 206-run fifth-wicket partnership.

Fred Trueman had spluttered with indignation at his exclusion from the touring party claiming that his replacements were 'good, honest county bowlers' only. His opinion might have smacked of sour grapes, but that did not invalidate its truth. Nevertheless, the gutsy, beefy Thomson earned his unexpected call-up, coming shortly before his retirement. Thomson had routinely taken over 100 county wickets each season for Sussex, delivering in excess of 1,000 overs in a typical summer's work. While his in-dippers and leg-cutters were often challenging on the wet or dusty county pitches, these were rarely penetrative on the Union's flat tracks, although he produced a peach of a delivery, at Durban, to dismiss Eddie Barlow for two, spearing the new ball into the South African's pads before finding sufficient bite to clip the off stump. Thomson took only nine wickets in the series, at a cringing cost of 63 runs each, but his unrelenting accuracy, maintained over 248 Test overs, meant that he conceded little more than an average two runs per over. He provided essential support to Allen and Titmus in restraining the South African stroke-makers, reducing the time available in which the Springboks could gain a winning advantage.

However, in the ensuing short series played in England a few months later, South Africa proved to be a much tougher proposition with both bat and ball, helped considerably by the resurgence of the Pollock brothers, and the brilliance of the South African fielding, in which Colin Bland excelled. Such was Bland's celebrity status as a fielder that, during a break in play at Canterbury, he enthralled the crowd with an electrifying demonstration of his prowess. Former Springbok captain Jack Cheetham had led the way in this regard, during the early fifties. He revolutionised the calibre of South African fielding, insisting upon an arduous succession of day-long fielding drills during the 1952/53 tour of Australia. Through dogged batting, tight bowling and, above all, alert, agile, predatory fielding, Cheetham guided his side of supposed no-hopers to a 2-2 draw against the world's then strongest Test side.

England's home defeat by the Springboks in 1965 was their fourth series loss on their own soil since 1960. The thrashing of New Zealand at the start of this cold, wet summer seemed almost irrelevant. This one-sided series was notable only for John Edrich's belligerent triple century at Leeds, containing a world record number of boundaries. The truth, though, was that on wickets offering batsmen and bowlers equal opportunities of success, the present English Test side was inferior, not only to Australia and the West Indies but probably to South Africa as well.

Edrich's spectacular knock paled by comparison with Graeme Pollock's superlative display on a tricky, wet wicket at Nottingham in the second Test. Pollock's innings featured astonishing stroke-play, turning the series decisively in South Africa's favour. Pollock possessed prodigious talent. Although naturally right-handed, he chose to bat left-handed at an early age, emulating the technique of his Scottish father. He found that by placing his dominant right hand at the top of the bat handle he always led with his stronger hand, helping him keep the bat straight. Although his superb balance and uncanny judgement of line, length and bounce meant that he could cut and pull with assurance, his trademark shots were his drives. He was a forceful yet elegant driver, with his right hand enabling him to keep the ball down when striking the ball on the up. Pollock preferred a heavier bat, in line with modern practice. During the 1960s it was unusual for a Test batsman to use a bat as weighty as 3lb. But the extra weight gave Pollock's driving uncommon power as many hand-wringing cover fieldsmen testified, although the precise placement of Pollock's shots meant that the fielders were often bisected. Pollock did not accept that left-handers were at a disadvantage in having to cope with scuffed areas outside their off stumps. He thought that being left-handed gave him more room to play his shots, and, until he developed his leg-side play, he countered a containing leg stump line of attack by making room to drive into the off side.

On the first morning at Trent Bridge, Pollock arrived at the crease with his side in trouble at 16/2. England's medium-pacer Tom Cartwright was causing carnage on the green wicket with his devilish cut and swerve. As wickets continued to fall, Pollock began by soberly repelling Cartwright. He realised that putting up the shutters would not remedy his side's precarious position. Consequently, he began to express himself against England's wayward opening pair, Larter and Snow. Although Smith tried to unnerve Pollock by calling upon his winter nemesis, Titmus, the young South African was not to be restrained. Smith strengthened the off-side field but to no avail as a flurry of drives scorched to the ropes. Pollock was not prepared to throw all caution to the wind, though. He spent 95 minutes in reaching 50 despite producing seven boundaries. But with his confidence increasing, his next 50 runs took just 33 minutes, with nine fours. Although Cartwright and Titmus continued to bowl well, even some of their best deliveries were whipped to the boundary by Pollock as if this was a festival bun fight. I watched every ball on the BBC, grudgingly conceding my admiration for I sensed I was witnessing one of the greatest Test innings I would ever see.

The Nottingham Test also featured the renaissance of Graeme Pollock's older brother, Peter, who twice blew a gaping hole in England's top order. He finished with match-winning figures of 10-87 off 47.5 overs. Peter Pollock, father of Shaun, was a tall, brawny, genuinely quick bowler of immense strength and stamina. His approach to the wicket comprised a long, rocking, high-stepping run which concluded with a heavy stamp and a muscular, wheeling action with which he produced deliveries of fearsome pace and bounce, as John Edrich found to his cost in the opening Test at Lord's. Here, a sharply rising ball from Pollock felled the resolute Surrey opener, forcing his dazed retirement, as England stuttered and stumbled in chasing a 191-run winning target, ultimately settling for an uncomfortable draw at 145/7.

During the Springboks' tour of Australia and New Zealand in 1963/64, Pollock harassed all opposing batsmen with his hostility, taking 25 Australian Test wickets at an average cost of 28. However, in the winter series against England he was much less menacing, with his 12 wickets costing, on average, 37. And until Edrich's calamity he had made little impact at Lord's. But at Nottingham, in conditions more conducive to seam bowling, Pollock recovered his 'mojo', adding a yard or so of pace. Only Cowdrey (105) in the first innings, and Parfitt (86) in the second, handled him effectively as South Africa won by 94 runs. With a heavy downpour wiping out an exciting finale at the Oval, South Africa gained their revenge for their narrow winter defeat.

While the South African Test series was an absorbing contest, the same could not be said of the County Championship which continued to haemorrhage fans and funds at an unsustainable rate. Having spent most of the summer of 1965 nursing a broken leg, a disillusioned Ted Dexter announced his retirement from the first-class game early in the following season so he could focus upon his business interests. As a parting shot, he complained about the contrived third-day finishes in the County Championship which, he argued, made a mockery of the game.

Certainly, the county game was in big trouble. By 1966, attendances had fallen by over three-quarters from the immediate post-war figure. MCC's Clark Committee boldly attempted to address the malaise by recommending a reduction in the number of three-day games to 16 per side in order to make room for a new one-day competition to complement the popular Gillette Trophy. It was hoped that an increased quota of one-day games would generate greater public interest and higher revenue. As carefully considered as these Clark Committee proposals were, they were rejected by the cautious counties, most of whom were concerned not to upset their members, whose numbers were dwindling. It was said that many members objected to any reduction in the number of county games because there would be less cricket to watch for their money. Instead, an experimental 65-over limit was introduced in the first innings of selected championship games during the following season. It was hoped that the first innings cap might encourage more attacking play at the start of a game, allowing more positive results to be achieved without the contrivances that Dexter had criticised. Once again the law of unintended consequences applied, though. As with the first innings bonus points scheme, the innovation merely encouraged the adoption of greater containment tactics by sides in the field while the 65-over first innings limit starved many middle-order batsmen of opportunities to build an innings, particularly when there were voracious openers around, like Geoffrey Boycott, who gobbled up the reduced allocation.

Of immediate concern to MCC selectors was the impending Ashes tour. After Statham and Trueman had ended their Test careers in 1965, there appeared to be a dearth of ready replacements. Too many English seamers had figures flattered by poor English wickets giving them little incentive to raise their game. Despite taking 137 first-class wickets in the summer of 1965 at an average cost of 12.52 runs, Brian Statham made light of his achievement, attributing this largely to 'the atrocious wickets up and down the country'.

The selectors eventually plumped for a quartet of pace bowlers, comprising Warwickshire's David Brown, Glamorgan's Jeff Jones (father of Simon), Lancashire's Ken Higgs and Northamptonshire's David Larter. Brown and Higgs had made impressive debuts during the summer Test series whereas Jones had made only one, inauspicious, Test appearance, on the wretched tour of India in 1963/64.

The 6ft 7in Larter was the most experienced member of the quartet. But he had been in and out of the Test side for four years. His ten caps were spread over five series after making an impressive debut at the Oval in August 1962, when he took nine wickets as England thrashed a fragile Pakistan side. His bumper Oval haul recommended his selection for MCC's winter tour of Australia and New Zealand, but he was too injury-prone and unreliable in line and length to be considered for the Ashes Test side. His slender frame proved vulnerable on the harder surfaces Down Under. Although capable of troubling good batsmen with his sharp pace and bounce on sympathetic pitches, his Test record abroad was generally unconvincing. His single telling return abroad was achieved against the demoralised Kiwis on a deteriorating wicket at Auckland at the end of the 1962/63 tour. Nevertheless, at Nottingham in 1965, he overcame his first innings waywardness to take five South African wickets in the second.

David Brown had earned his selection with his indefatigable enthusiasm and insatiable appetite for hard work. With his bustling approach and high, hurried action he swung the ball agreeably at a brisk pace although he, too, tended to be troubled by niggling injuries, as happened after his promising debut against the South Africans at Lord's. As for Ken Higgs, he took eight

South African wickets on debut at the Oval. His short, economical approach to the wicket belied thrust and nip. In fact, Higgs's great accuracy and command of cut and swerve probably made him the leader of the pack. But after a draining first Ashes Test in which he failed to disturb the Australian big guns Bill Lawry (166) and 19-year-old debutant Doug Walters (155) until the damage had been done, he, too, succumbed to injury, leaving the left-arm paceman Jeff Jones to replace him in the four remaining Tests. With Larter also out of action for most of the tour, because of bruised feet and various muscle strains, and Brown troubled by less persistent ailments, the Essex all-rounder Barry Knight was summoned from England as reinforcement.

I had previously watched Jones bowl on a duvet surface at Hastings in 1962 after his side had run up a colossal score thanks to centuries from Alan Jones (121) and Tony Lewis (151), establishing a club record second-wicket partnership of 238 runs. Whereas the Glamorgan centurions had mastered the Sussex attack in carpet slippers, Jones managed to extract astonishing life from the dead track. He began each delivery with a curious devotional gesture. Cradling the ball in both hands he brought it to his lips, his raised elbows spread as if making an ostentatious show of prayer, before scampering off to the wicket, leaning slightly to his right, and releasing the ball with a whippy, low, slinging action. Poor Richard Langridge had spent all day in the Sussex slips waiting vainly for a chance, gloomily ruminating on the wicket's lack of pace and bounce. But then he had to contend with a sharp lifter from Jones which he could only fend to Gilbert Parkhouse at first slip, departing disconsolately for 0. With Jones hitting his straps this had become a different ball game.

Jones claimed 15 Aussie Test victims during the 1965/66 Ashes contest, six of which were acquired during the Simpson–Lawry run-fest at Adelaide. But, as expected, the English pace attack struggled to wrong-foot the strong Australian batting order, particularly after Bobby Simpson had recovered from an illness that had ruled him out of the third Test at Sydney, where England had won helped by a wearing wicket. This was the only Test in which England spinners Allen and Titmus disturbed the strong Australian batting order, sharing ten wickets. Their combined series wicket haul was just 18 with each dismissal costing on average 51 runs. Titmus was disappointingly defensive, offering little to entice a mistake, and while Allen was more attacking, he, too, was instructed by the cautious Smith to restrain the run rate. In such a wary mindset, it was no surprise that Barber's leg-spin was rarely risked for more than a handful of overs at a time.

Brown achieved his first five-wicket Test haul at Sydney, complementing the efforts of Allen and Titmus, in bowling England to an unexpected innings victory, set up by a thumping century from Bob Barber (185) and an unyielding one from John Edrich (103). However, the insult was returned emphatically in the next Test at Adelaide. Here, most of England's batsmen, apart from

Barrington, underperformed badly, possibly because of a critical reduction in the intensity of their preparations during the intervening period, which was described by English cricket journalist E.M. Wellings as 'two weeks of holiday cricket'. Barrington (115), Edrich (85), Cowdrey (79) and Parks (89) ensured that normal service was resumed in the final Test at Melbourne but Cowper's triple century (307) and Lawry's third ton of the series (108) enabled the Australians to avert defeat with ease, thereby retaining the Ashes.

It was a disappointing conclusion. While MCC tour manager Billy Griffith had urged the adoption of adventurous cricket, there were only rare glimpses of this as the series drew to an uninspiring close; Barber's glorious bash at Sydney and Barrington's bludgeoned hundred in the final Test being notable exceptions. Not that the Australians were any less risk-averse under Simpson than they had been under Benaud.

Evening Standard correspondent John Thicknesse thought that Smith became distracted when he was joined by his wife and young children at Christmas. Colin Cowdrey's wife had arrived simultaneously. According to Jeff Jones, the preferential treatment given to Smith and Cowdrey caused some resentment within the ranks, notably with Ken Higgs who had left his wife and two young boys behind in England.

By the end of the tour, Smith's captaincy appeared to be flagging, mainly on account of his wretched form with the bat. The Australians encouraged Smith to play, as he preferred, on the leg side, or the 'man's side' as he called it. In fact, they packed the off-side field to encourage his inclination, knowing that on their quicker wickets, Smith was often fractionally late when trying to whip a ball on or just outside his off stump to midwicket. Smith managed to score only 107 runs in the Ashes series at an average of 18, inferior to that of tail-ender David Allen, although Smith did fare better in the subsequent drawn series in New Zealand, averaging 42.

Bob Dylan's rancorous and confrontational hit single 'Like a Rolling Stone' dominated the cool summer of 1965. Renouncing the acoustic folk guitar in favour of an electrified sound, with Al Kooper contributing a swirling, hurdy-gurdy organ backing, Dylan was propelled out of New York café society, where he had honed his nasal, acerbic craft, and into the glare of the stadium spotlights as an electric rock god. I bought the single in celebration of my unexpected GCE O Level success. It was to set me on a path to a faraway university and a life so much better than I then thought possible.

A 6ft 5in Surrey colt fast bowler, of almost identical age, had experienced a similar epiphany. He was to express his reverence by adding 'Dylan' to his name. Sixteen years later he would demolish the Australian batting order to win one of the most extraordinary Test matches of all time. For Bob Willis, Dylan has been a constant source of inspiration. I wondered subsequently whether it was 'Like a Rolling Stone' that had spurred him on during his devastating spell at Headingley in the glorious summer of 1981.

1966

Tomorrow Never Knows

In a year of World Cup glory for Sir Alf Ramsey's England football team, there was a further cause for English celebration as a result of Bob Barber's blistering innings at Sydney. Here, he hooked, pulled, cut and drove with carefree ferocity, scoring 185 unforgettable runs in just under five hours. After Dexter's regrettable departure from Test cricket, ruthless mastery seemed to be the prerogative of our opponents. In one incandescent innings Barber obliterated that presupposition. He had an uncanny ability to hit the ball on the rise off his front foot, almost irrespective of where the ball pitched. So confident was he of his ability to improvise that he was prepared to play premeditated shots. How the Australian spinners, Philpott, Sincock and Cowper, suffered during that long, hot afternoon session. Because he adopted an unusually high grip on the bat handle, he commanded maximum leverage when swinging through the line. Like Graeme Pollock, he achieved control in driving forcefully by placing his stronger hand – his right – at the top of the bat. But it was his ferocious hooking of the short-pitched bowling of the Australian opening pair, McKenzie and Hawke, which shook me out of my bleariness on that icy, winter morning.

Although Barber seemed at ease on the true, firm wickets of South Africa and Australia, his vision from his left eye was blurred. He had compensated for this by learning to bat left-handed at an early age. He was right-handed in all other respects. This adjustment brought his stronger eye into line. Sadly, for Barber and England, his Sydney knock was almost his swansong. He would play in only five more Tests.

Upon resuming county cricket, he wryly observed that he had left his best form Down Under. England's less reliable wickets were to blame. But it was business commitments which presented a bigger obstacle. He played in only two Tests against the West Indians during that summer. Barber smote a bright, confident half-century at Leeds but it failed to prevent the West Indians from taking an unassailable 3-0 series lead. Barber's comrade-at-arms, in his all-too-brief expression of defiance, was beefy, big-hitting Colin Milburn (46), a suitable heir apparent, it seemed. It had been Milburn's exhilarating unbeaten century (126) at Lord's which had saved the game for England and momentarily interrupted the West Indians' bulldozing dominance. Tragically, Milburn's Test career would be regrettably short, too, after he lost the sight of one eye in a catastrophic car crash.

The West Indians' triumphant tour of England in 1966 was not without its setbacks, though. I was to witness the first of these at Hove on a sparkling, humid Saturday on 11 June. England had just capitulated wretchedly inside three days at Manchester. In almost a replica of their one-sided victory there in 1963, Hunte (135) and Sobers (161) piled on the runs, leaving Gibbs to run through the hesitant England batting order. On a newly prepared surface that progressively favoured spin, Gibbs took ten wickets for 106 runs and the West Indians won by an innings.

This abject defeat signalled the end of Mike Smith's period in charge. As MCC's captain at Lord's in May, Smith had made an aggressive century against the tourists, but had been liberally indulged by West Indian left-arm spinner Rawle Branker, who fed Smith's penchant for the sweep. However, at Old Trafford, Smith found no easy pickings as he struggled to cope with the pace of Griffith and Hall and with Gibbs's sharp turn. According to his successor, Cowdrey, the selectors were alarmed that the bespectacled Smith might incur a fearful injury since he seemed to be late in picking up the length, direction and height of fast, short-pitched deliveries. But it was Gibbs who sealed his fate, dismissing him twice for single-figure scores.

Since the second Test was only five days away, the astonishing events I witnessed at Hove on 11 June had no bearing upon the selection of the England team for Lord's. Geoff Boycott was preferred to Eric Russell and Tom Graveney was belatedly recalled to replace Smith in the middle order. Basil D'Oliveira made his debut in place of off-spinner David Allen while Essex all-rounder Barry Knight was chosen instead of the Warwickshire paceman David Brown. England's tail had proved too long at Manchester, but this revamped side batted down to Titmus at nine. The crucial omission, however, was Sussex fast bowler John Snow.

Sussex appeared to pose little threat to Sobers's unbeaten touring side. They had completed the 1965 County Championship season second from bottom and had managed only two victories in their opening ten county fixtures of 1966. Dexter had recently turned his back on county cricket, leaving Sussex largely reliant upon Jim Parks and the Indian captain, the Nawab of Pataudi junior, for runs, although both players performed well below their capabilities during the season. Sussex seemed to have a lot of bits and pieces players like Ken Suttle who would head their 1966 County Championship averages with a score of 29.36. While Tony Buss and Don Bates gave admirable seam support to Snow, Sussex were largely dependent upon Alan Oakman's part-time off-breaks in the spin department. Translated into modern football terms this fixture seemed like Brighton, or even Crawley, taking on Germany.

Sussex's captain was 'Pataudi'. Although he was known as Mansur Ali Khan in India, where royal titles were no longer recognised, he retained the name Pataudi while in England. Here, he won the toss and put the West Indians into bat. Pataudi was understandably reluctant to expose his fragile batting line-up to Griffith, Cohen and Sobers in such helpful conditions. Statham, Higgs and Shuttleworth had needed only 43 overs to bundle Sussex out for 69 two weeks before, and that was with Dexter in their side. Although many in the 10,000 crowd had been attracted by the prospect of the West Indians throwing the bat, the unevenness of the competition seemed to sharpen their support for the underdogs. Instead of basking in the appreciation of polite admirers, the

West Indians found themselves facing an intensely partisan crowd that was clearly up for a scrap as if this was a feisty football derby.

Snow began the proceedings, bowling up the slope from the sea end, and immediately made the ball fly off a length, forcing wicketkeeper Parks into a series of leaping takes. Parks and his slip cordon promptly retreated a yard or so. The West Indian opening pair, 'Joey' Carew and Easton McMorris, looked ill at ease at Snow's daunting pace and seam movement, but there was little respite at the other end, either, where Tony Buss, with his pumping approach, was achieving extravagant swing. Carew and McMorris were made to look like novices as they groped unconvincingly outside their off stumps, with each false shot greeted by a hail of 'oohs' and 'ahhs' from the crowd. Frustrated at his attempts in laying bat on ball, McMorris flashed rashly at a wider, climbing delivery from Snow, slicing a catch to Pataudi at backward point (14/1). An explosive roar greeted his dismissal. This was not an occasion for gracious applause.

Urged on as if he was a prize fighter, Snow let rip at the incoming batsman Seymour Nurse. The moody and introspective Snow was no Freddie Trueman. But if his aggression was less volatile than Trueman's, it steamed with smouldering menace.

Snow had been bitterly disappointed at his exclusion from the Ashes squad of 1965/66, but had spent the winter productively, perfecting his approach on the true wickets of South Africa. Dexter had noticed that when bowling over the wicket, Snow made an involuntary step to his left at the point of delivery, leaving him too open-chested and confined to bowling in-dippers. In South Africa Snow practised straightening his approach, bowling closer to the stumps, and bringing his torso around into a more sideways aspect, enabling him to achieve greater accuracy and swing although he moved the ball more by cut than curve.

Snow's considerable bounce owed much to his 6ft height, his wiry elasticity and shoulder power. Upon reaching the crease from a relaxed, loping run, Snow swayed slightly to his right, bringing him as close to the stumps as possible, flinging his guiding left arm across his chest, as if mimicking a cross-bow, before drawing his right across his waist, cocking his right shoulder with a hunched gesture, and propelling the ball with a whipped rotation. As he matured, Snow learnt to vary his pace, and conserve energy better, relying more upon lateral movement but here he was on trial against fearsome opponents. Having ambitions of an England recall he proceeded to let rip.

While the damp surface encouraged Snow's darting seam movement, the steamy atmosphere assisted his colleague's threatening swing. Somehow, West Indian opener 'Joey' Carew survived Snow's early onslaught, riding his luck with a succession of edges that sent the ball scurrying to the third man and fine leg boundaries. Meanwhile, Carew's new partner, the strapping Seymour Nurse, began to play him and the probing medium-pacer Tony Buss with growing assurance. But just as Nurse appeared to be mounting a solid recovery, Sussex's first-change seamer, Don Bates, castled him with a late swinging delivery – Nurse was out for 24 runs and the West Indies were 45/2.

Pataudi then brought Suttle into the attack with his busy, restrictive left-arm spin, so Snow could have a well-earned breather. Suttle did more than contain, though, trapping Basil Butcher (12) in front of his stumps when the tourists' score had reached 60. Butcher's departure brought the great Garry Sobers to the crease. Surely, he would throw off the shackles and dominate the proceedings? Sobers would complete the summer's five-match Test series with a Bradman-like average of 103 runs. But here, he stayed for less than five minutes before edging a wide delivery from Bates to Parks, and departing for no score. The roar that went up must have been heard over a mile away at the Goldstone Ground where Don Bates had once served the Albion with distinction. The West Indies tottered into lunch, four down for 70 runs.

Immediately after the break, Pataudi recalled Snow, arousing a cacophony of well-lubricated hectoring and hollering. Snow did as he was rowdily urged to do and blew away the remaining West Indian batting, uprooting Lashley's and Gibbs's stumps in spectacular, cart-wheeling fashion. The West Indians were dismissed for 123 in less than four hours Carew was the only man to make a substantial score, albeit with a large slice of fortune. Snow put the record straight, though, by trapping him lbw for 56. Snow had achieved what was then his best first-class bowling return of 7-29 in 16.5 overs.

Although the incensed West Indian fast bowlers, Griffith and Cohen, reduced Sussex quickly to 40/6, Pataudi (32) and 20-year-old Peter Graves (64) led a stirring recovery which enabled Sussex to close the day on 122/7. Sussex had done extraordinarily well to stand their ground against such strong opponents. The whole team richly deserved their standing ovation.

Monday morning was heavily overcast and gloomy. Most of those who had been there on Saturday had returned to work or school, leaving the ground more than half empty, and without the partisan spirit that had fortified Pataudi's men so well. Peter Graves continued to bat with brave resilience and skill, though, supported stoutly by a lower order comprising Alan Oakman, once of England (31), Tony Buss (21), John Snow (5) and Don Bates (10 not out). Graves's 64 runs was his then highest first-class score. Eventually, Sussex gained an unexpected 62-run first innings lead. It was equally astonishing that Sobers failed to take a wicket in conditions ideally suited to his faster style of bowling.

If the West Indians' paltry first innings score was a careless aberration, their second innings total of 67 was a grave humiliation. The tourists were dismissed in two and a quarter hours, and 36.3 overs. Buss and Snow were almost unplayable, sharing eight wickets equally, and conceding just 18 runs each, while Bates cleaned up the tail. Sobers avoided the indignity of a pair but made only eight before being clean bowled by the estimable Buss. Snow bagged 11 West Indian wickets in the match for 47 runs. Surely, he had to be re-selected for the Test team after this?

Sussex needed just six runs to win. Griffith was apoplectic with rage. During Sussex's first innings he had held himself in check, choosing not to strive for that lethal extra yard of pace which had courted so much unwelcome attention. He was mindful that he had been called once for 'throwing' just prior to the first Test at Old Trafford and had no wish to arouse further controversy with the second Test so close. But when Sobers placed nine men behind the bat, and a tenth at short leg, Griffith knew exactly what was expected of him. It was the fastest, most deadly over I have ever seen. Griffith's first ball flew off the wicket, just short of a length, and 'chinned' Suttle as he imprudently tried to hook. Suttle staggered from the crease as if smashed by a juggernaut. The alarmed Sussex support staff quickly summoned an ambulance which despatched Suttle to hospital. Mercifully, the X-ray confirmed that he had suffered only severe bruising. Suttle later quipped that Griffith must have slowed up, reckoning that when he was hit by him in 1963, it had been *before* he made his stroke.

With Suttle having retired hurt, Pataudi promoted his first innings hero Graves to take Sussex over the line, but Griffith's first ball hissed past his ear before he could blink. There was a call of 'no ball'. However, this was for overstepping, not throwing. Graves's second ball was his last. A spearing yorker crunched his right boot leaving him hobbling in acute pain. As Graves looked up he was almost relieved to see the raised finger of umpire John Langridge. Parks was the next man in, and immediately faced a brute of a delivery that grazed his ear. The fourth was shorter and flew over his head as he ducked. The fifth was another lightning yorker which Parks dug out just in time while the sixth flashed past his forehead barely seen. Parks swivelled around to see the ball still rising as it reached Hendricks, 20 yards back, the West Indian wicketkeeper leaping frantically to stop it flashing to the boundary. Parks and Griffith exchanged glares. It was only then that Sobers relented. He had made his point and allowed Lenham and Parks to calmly score the five runs they needed for victory from his part-time bowlers, Solomon and Lashley. It was Solomon's and Lashley's reward for being the only West Indian batsmen to reach double figures in their side's pitiful second innings.

As if rocked by this embarrassing defeat, the West Indians stumbled at Lord's where they were reduced to 95/5 in their second innings, only nine in front of England. Cowdrey's side had been rejuvenated by major innings by Boycott (60), Graveney (96) and Parks (91). But with Cowdrey reluctant to attack the new batsmen, Sobers (163) and his inexperienced cousin David Holford (105), they first stopped the rot and then turned the game around with a record unbroken stand of 274 runs. The day was only saved by a scintillating century from Colin Milburn (126 not out), and a brave innings by Graveney (30), nursing a badly bruised finger.

But England's stay of execution was brief, despite having the better of the opening exchanges at Trent Bridge. Helped by Snow's recall, and substantial contributions from Graveney (109), Cowdrey (96) and D'Oliveira (76), England led by 90 runs at the end of their first innings. However, Butcher then made an unbeaten double century (209) while Kanhai (63), Nurse (53) and Sobers (94) took the tourists to 482/5 declared, placing them out of sight. With only Boycott (71) and D'Oliveira (54) managing respectable second innings scores, in the face of Griffith's ferocity and Gibbs's guile, England were defeated by 139 runs.

The loss of their stalwart middle-order batsman Ken Barrington, due to nervous exhaustion, was keenly felt. Much responsibility had fallen upon Barrington's broad shoulders in shoring up the English batting order, but as brave and determined as he clearly was, he was often troubled by the hostility of the West Indian pace bowling.

The Leeds Test was an unmitigated disaster for Cowdrey's men. Sobers (174) and Nurse (137) blasted the West Indies to a total of 500/9 declared, while England failed to mount a total of substance in either innings, losing by an innings and 55 runs at 3pm on the fourth day. D'Oliveira (88), Barber (55) and Milburn (42) did themselves justice with the bat, as did tail-ender Higgs (49), but no one else seemed capable of defying Hall, Sobers or Gibbs for long.

Realising that England needed a more forceful leader, the selectors turned to Brian Close who had been leading Yorkshire to the County Championship. Whereas Cowdrey was a gentle, courteous, urbane and circumspect leader, Brian Close was abrasive, blunt, brave and combative. The commissioned officer had been passed over in favour of the NCO. It was the first time since Len Hutton's time in charge that a non-Oxbridge player had been chosen to captain England. Close immediately set the tone with his intimidating presence at silly mid-off or short leg, also rattling the West Indians with his shrewd bowling changes. Unlike Smith and Cowdrey, Close had no compunction about employing Barber's leg-spin early in the game, reaping the reward for his boldness as the under-used Barber took five wickets for 127 runs.

Close was one of five changes made by the selectors. In came John Edrich, Dennis Amiss, Raymond Illingworth and wicketkeeper John Murray, and out went Milburn, Cowdrey, Parks, Titmus and Underwood. Having dismissed the West Indians for 268, England were struggling at 166/7 in reply before an elegant Tom Graveney (165) and an equally fluent John Murray (112) added 217 for the eighth wicket. To cap it all, an astounding last-wicket partnership of 128 runs between Snow (59 not out) and Higgs (63) took England to the dizzy heights of 527 all out. Snow and Higgs registered their maiden first-class fifties.

Like so many other football fans, I had my ear pressed to a transistor radio on that third day of blazing heat, while ostensibly watching my home football team's opening fixture. Snow celebrated his mighty feat by having

West Indian openers Hunte and McMorris caught at the wicket with only 12 scored. England won by an innings and 34 runs just after lunch on the fourth day, Close having masterminded Sobers's instant dismissal by instructing Snow to 'bounce' the great man. Close positioned himself square in the leg trap in readiness for the miscued hook which duly followed. Unlike Cowdrey, Close led aggressively from the front. England's emphatic innings victory at the Oval was an agreeable patriotic conclusion to a summer of World Cup glory, although English cricket had much work ahead if it was to emulate the success of the national football team.

But Ramsey's 'wingless wonders' were not the only English combo sitting on top of the world in 1966, for the Beatles and the Rolling Stones had also become world leaders, having stolen and re-peddled the black American blues. By 1966, though, the Beatles had turned their attention to 'feeding our heads'. Inspired by Dr Timothy Leary's mantra, 'turn on, tune in and drop out', the Beatles recorded their first 'trippy' song, 'Tomorrow Never Knows'. Less than three years before, the mop-haired Fab Four were still churning out soppy love songs such as 'I Want to Hold Your Hand', but by 1966 they had become beaded, bearded hippies intrigued by notions of cosmic love and metaphysical meanderings. In 'Tomorrow Never Knows' a spectral-sounding John Lennon emerges from a droning swirl of instrumental distortion, agonised seagull-like cries and a pounding Indian drumbeat, to insist it was time to leave reality behind and drift listlessly downstream. The narcotic age of pop had arrived.

'Tomorrow Never Knows' set the pace for a swathe of psychedelic compositions from both sides of the Atlantic, as exemplified by Jefferson Airplane's 'White Rabbit', The Jimi Hendrix Experience's 'Purple Haze', The Velvet Underground's 'Heroin', Procol Harum's 'Whiter Shade of Pale', Pink Floyd's 'See Emily Play' and, of course, the Beatles' later composition, 'A Day in the Life'. It was left to the iconoclastic Kinks to deconstruct the venal vapidity of mid-1960s pop culture, mocking Carnaby Street narcissism in 'Dedicated Follower of Fashion', scorning parvenu decadence in 'Sunny Afternoon', and itemising debilitating poverty in 'Dead End Street'. Even Hogarth might have been impressed. Meanwhile, in his sardonic 1966 film, *Blowup,* Italian film director Michelangelo Antonioni scoffed at the vacuity of 'Swinging London' values.

'Breakin' Down The Walls Of Heartache'

1967 – 1972

*England won 39 per cent of 44 Tests played
between June 1967 and August 1972*

1967

Respect

I did not get the 'Summer of Love'. To be fair, I didn't try too hard. San Franciscan radiance seemed an anathema to sour, de-flowered Hastings. Besides, I had winter in my blood. My compass pointed resolutely northwards. Lancaster was on my radar and independence was on my mind. In the meantime I settled for the womb-like warmth of the local chess club, heavy with the scent of polish, tea, toasted teacakes and cigars. Here, an ancient gas fire popped and flared all day, every day, whatever the weather. It was an ideal bolt-hole for the socially lame. Little was said, just a brief exchange of courtesies, followed by hours of silent, furrowed concentration to the accompaniment of so many ticking clocks. An elderly woman clad in heavy woollens shuffled mutely in and out of the oak-panelled room with trays of refreshment. It was a place untouched and unnoticed by the passing years. Here, the liturgy of chess was respectfully recited – the Queen's Indian, the Ruy Lopez, the Sicilian – in its musty imperial or consular glory.

But if I was an equivocal subscriber to the present and a bashful advocate of the past, I was not alone, not by a long chalk. Take the Beatles, for instance. As much as they pushed the margins with 'Tomorrow Never Knows' and 'A Day in the Life' they seemed, as George Melly observed, 'at their happiest when celebrating the past'. George Harrison's dismissive take on the trippy, hippie

STUMPS & RUNS & ROCK 'N' ROLL

San Francisco scene was 'a load of horrible, spotty drop-out kids on drugs'. Their *Sgt. Pepper's Lonely Hearts Club Band* album, released in 1967, evoked a fading image of greasy cobbled streets, travelling circuses, and raucous music halls. The Kinks championed the past with equal enthusiasm with their 1968 album, *The Kinks Are the Village Green Preservation Society*. It was almost as if, like novice swimmers, we needed to remain at a safe depth as we tentatively entered uncharted waters. With the nation in love with the televised *The Forsyte Saga*, and Victorian fashions revived by Biba and Laura Ashley, this ambivalence about releasing the past and embracing an uncertain future was more pervasive than sixties caricatures suggest.

In the Kinks' 1967 single, 'Autumn Almanac', Ray Davies sang of traditional working-class routines such as Saturday football, the Sunday roast and Blackpool holidays. How this sentiment resonated with British photographer, Tony Ray-Jones. In the posthumous exhibition, *Only in England,* his visits to fading English resorts in the summer of 1967 are depicted in stark monochrome. Here, we find images that are alternately surreal, tender, melancholic and hilarious. Above all, they remind us that these were primarily conservative times.

Having spent my adolescence in a decaying seaside resort I was familiar with the silent majority who resolutely refused to swing. I recall their arrivals on summer Saturdays, hardy holidaymakers from another age, transported in their Zephyrs, Wolseleys and Anglias. I would find them huddling together on the tar-struck shingle in their utility plastic raincoats, or sheltering behind flapping windbreaks, gazing dubiously at the foam-flecked sea and the leaden sky, while sipping their stewed Thermos tea. They seemed to regard holidays as a solemn duty, an unquestioned annual routine. There appeared to be little expectation of fun or flamboyance beyond what might be found at a beauty pageant, a dog show, a penny arcade, a children's parade or on a choppy trip around the bay.

The ill-matched home Test series against India and Pakistan proved to be as disappointing as the glum summer weather. Barrington recovered his appetite for hefty scores, making three centuries against Pakistan and three 'big' fifties against India. Graveney enjoyed a profitable summer too with a 'daddy' hundred (151) against India at Lord's and further substantial scores of 81 and 77 against Pakistan.

Neither India nor Pakistan batted well enough to put England under any sustained pressure. Nevertheless, Pakistan captain Hanif Mohammad displayed admirable resolution at Lord's, batting for over nine hours in making 187 not out, which enabled his side to grasp a well-earned draw. Here, Pakistani all-rounder Asif Iqbal gave notice of his batting prowess by contributing 76 runs to what was then a Pakistani record eighth-wicket partnership of 130. Asif surpassed that feat at the Oval where he and his team went down with all guns blazing. His second innings century (146) included two sixes and 21 fours in a dazzling display of twinkling footwork, whipped and wristy shots. His driving was both elegant and commanding while his cutting and pulling were ruthless. Helped by leg-spinner Intikhab Alam (51), Asif's runs enabled Pakistan to avoid a crushing innings defeat which seemed certain after they had crumpled to 65/8. However, England still won easily by eight wickets, to take the series 2-0.

As for India, captain Pataudi shook off his poor county form with Sussex in 1966, when he had averaged only 20.91, to produce a mighty century (148) in his second innings at Leeds. It was a remarkable achievement for a man who lost the sight of his right eye in a car accident in 1961. Wadekar, Engineer and Hanumant Singh also contributed at least one innings of note, but their efforts were in vain as England won all three Tests by substantial margins.

The summer season was mired by controversy, the most serious of which concerned Brian Close, who had won six and drawn one of his seven matches as England's captain. And yet he was relieved of the position before the winter tour of the Caribbean began. His alleged crime was time-wasting in a vital top-of-the-table clash with Warwickshire. It was hardly a mortal sin. In 1953, aided and abetted by Hutton, Trevor Bailey stemmed the Australian victory gallop at Leeds by bowling well wide of the leg stump. Even Freddie Brown, who was then chairman of the selectors, admitted, 'I do not pretend to like the method by which England saved the match, but there was nothing new about it.' Close was also accused of hitting a spectator who had taken issue with his tactics. However, Warwickshire skipper M.J.K. Smith denied this happened. The selectors were not appeased, though. They decided that Close had to go, returning once more to the less adventurous Colin Cowdrey. Ironically, Cowdrey then proceeded to employ blatant time-wasting tactics in the decisive fourth Test at Port-of-Spain. Here, he slowed the England over rate to only 11 per hour, five less than Close managed in the final stages of the Warwickshire game. On the basis of the available evidence, Close's sacking seemed to be rough justice.

MCC made a further controversial decision during that summer in dropping Geoff Boycott for 'selfish batting' in the Leeds Test. Boycott had spent a whole day making an unbeaten century against India. He eventually progressed to 246 not out with his second 100 runs scored at a considerably faster rate than his first. This did not save him, though. Boycott protested he had been out of form, but the selectors refused to accept this as mitigation. In fairness to the selectors, they were concerned by the sparseness of the first-day crowd at Leeds. Only 5,000 spectators turned up. With Boycott eking out 25 painful runs in the two hours of play before lunch, they had just cause for concern that such slow progress would result in even smaller crowds.

Because the myopic counties vetoed almost all of the Clark Committee proposals for improving the game's attractiveness, MCC was left with few realistic options, other than to reduce the qualification period for overseas players. While players of the calibre of Sobers or Kanhai raised the level of interest in the county game it was difficult to see how their clubs could continue to afford such expensive imports without the game's finances receiving a considerable shot in the arm. The overseas players' county salaries then ranged between £1,500 and £2,500 per year, although Sobers was probably paid more. In contrast, a good home grown player received between £800 and £1,200 depending upon bonuses. This was less than the national average salary which was then £1,380.

Two years later, a new one-day competition was introduced on a Sunday afternoon. It replaced the successful Rothmans international cavaliers' games. The new competition was expected to provide the necessary financial boost, without falling foul of the 'Lord's Day' observance restrictions, and without drastically reducing the number of County Championship fixtures – a sticking point for most counties in thrall of their members. Another tobacco sponsor, John Player, was found for the competition, while the BBC agreed to pay for weekly TV coverage. So, despite the county players' complaints about playing too much cricket, MCC's solution was to add a further day's play to their existing six-day itinerary. This was not good news for England's prospects. Like the summer of love, I didn't get it.

Detroit did not appear to get the summer of love, either. It was the home city of my favourite artist of that time, Aretha Franklin. In the summer of 1967, Detroit was in flames. The motor industry, which had sustained its huge growth, had collapsed or moved on, leaving an urban wasteland of abandoned, burnt-out dwellings, offices and shops. The massive Motown record business was about to ship out to California, too. Crime abounded and the city prickled with racial tension.

In Otis Redding's original version of 'Respect', he insisted that a man is entitled to receive the respect of 'his woman' when he gets home. In Aretha Franklin's strident re-interpretation, she altered Redding's tempo and phrasing, re-presenting the song as a manifesto for the oppressed – for women striving for equality and for black Americans struggling against poverty and institutional racism. In her rendition, Franklin gave stabbing emphasis to each letter of the song's title, R-E-S-P-E-C-T. This was punchy, funky, political soul, as challenging as James Brown's stomping, 'Say It Loud (I'm Black and I'm Proud)' or Marvin Gaye's lament, 'What's Going On'. The US civil rights movement was gaining pace. A year later, US sprinters, Tommie Smith and John Carlos gave the Black Panther salute from the Olympic podium.

The West Indian touring sides of 1963 and 1966 commanded considerable respect and popularity, but as the 1960s drew to a close racial divisions were intensifying in Britain, exacerbated by the economic hardship that accompanied devaluation in 1967. Although intended satirically, the racist rants of TV's Alf Garnett probably did more to confirm than challenge discrimination. Meanwhile Enoch Powell was about to make his inflammatory 'rivers of blood' speech. All he could envisage was a hostile future of racial disharmony and bloody discord of North American proportions.

1968
All Along the Watchtower

1968 was a year of even greater unrest. Martin Luther King was gunned down in Memphis, triggering race riots across the United States. Soviet tanks ground Dubcek's liberal reforms into the Prague dust. The Palestinian, Sirhan Sirhan, assassinated Bobby Kennedy. Paris seethed with revolt and South African Prime Minister Vorster angrily cancelled the 1968/69 MCC tour of South Africa upon hearing of Basil D'Oliveira's selection. There were also two anti-Vietnam War demonstrations outside the US Embassy in Grosvenor Square, the first of which turned ugly, although the violent scenes here were almost trivial compared with what happened at Kent State University, Ohio, two years later.

But there was more joy for the England cricket team. They returned from the Caribbean having unexpectedly beaten the unofficial 'world champions' on their own soil. Admittedly, their solitary Test win at Port-of-Spain was made possible by Sobers's remarkably generous declaration. That said, England had mostly held the upper hand in the previous three Tests, although they were required to fight hard to avoid defeat at Kingston after a riot had interrupted their winning momentum, allowing Sobers to turn the tables astonishingly.

Had Barrington not been so insistent, Cowdrey might not have pursued victory in Trinidad. For Cowdrey fretted about the state of the wicket which he thought might be pitch perfect for the West Indian spinners, Rodriguez and Gibbs. Butcher had already given notice of the pitch's perils in taking five wickets with his part-time leg-breaks in England's first innings. On the other hand, Cowdrey was comforted that Griffith was unfit to bowl. Once convinced of the feasibility of victory, Cowdrey (71) and Boycott (80 not out) batted boldly and delightfully, sprinting to a winning score of 215 at a rate of four runs per over.

But the battle was not yet won for there was a further scare in the final Test at Bridgetown. Here, Cowdrey and young wicketkeeper Alan Knott rescued their side from disaster although they were ultimately indebted to Jeff Jones's sturdy defiance of Gibbs in the final over. The Caribbean tour was a particularly successful one for Sussex quick John Snow, who broke Freddie Trueman's record Caribbean haul by taking 27 wickets in only four Tests. Snow's steepling bounce and bruising hostility worried most of the West Indian batsmen.

After England's sunny success in the Caribbean, the subsequent home Ashes series was a damp squib. England performed disastrously in the opening Test in Manchester, not helped by some strange selections. Only three specialist bowlers were chosen – Snow, Higgs and Pocock – while a ring-rusty Bob Barber was preferred to Underwood on a wicket that seemed tailor-made for the Kent man. It was as if the selectors were more concerned with avoiding defeat than in pursuing victory. England were in trouble once Lawry had won the toss, and decided to bat on a wicket that was at its best during the first two days. Lawry (81), Walters (81), Sheahan (88) and Ian Chappell (73) capitalised upon their fortune in posting a first innings total of 357. In reply, the England batsmen played stodgily and ineffectually, crawling to a total of 165 in 104.3 overs. Bob Cowper's part-time off-spin was treated as if they were facing Jim Laker, gifting the Australian flattering figures of 4-48 runs off 26 overs.

England's second-innings effort was scarcely better with only D'Oliveira (87 not out) batting with distinction. Not that his efforts were considered good enough to command his retention at Lord's – a strange decision that would attract suspicion in light of the later 'D'Oliveira Affair'. Australia won at Old Trafford by 159 runs. To compound Cowdrey's frustration, heavy rain at Lord's reduced the playing time by more than a half, depriving England of a deserved victory, after they had dismissed Australia for 78 to seize a 273-run first innings lead. At Edgbaston, England were once again in control having taken a 187-run first innings lead, but with rain washing out day one and preventing much play on the final day, Cowdrey was unable to force home his advantage.

For the vital fourth Test at Leeds, Cowdrey was short of top-order batsmen. He was ruled out, having pulled a muscle when making his 21st Test hundred at Edgbaston. Both Boycott and Milburn were injured, too. So, a desperate Cowdrey rang Dexter to ask whether he might be interested in playing again for England. Dexter missed the cut and thrust of international competition, but wondered whether he could recover his touch in time, given his two-year absence from first-class cricket. Moreover, the knee that Charlie Griffith had damaged at Lord's in 1963 was still causing him pain. He was unsure whether it would stand up to a five-day examination. But in Milburn's absence, Cowdrey needed a forceful batsman of Dexter's calibre if England were to score quickly enough to allow them an opportunity of victory. Dexter decided the opportunity was too good to miss, and made himself available for Sussex's next County Championship game against Kent in Hastings. Cowdrey assured Dexter that if he performed well he would be recalled.

I had spent a considerable time at Hastings Central Cricket Ground during my teenage years, watching club and county cricket and practising in its nets. My remaining time in Hastings was short so I decided to make a farewell visit, not having any expectation that I might see Dexter play one of his finest innings.

It wasn't as if Dexter seemed prepared for the challenge. Jim Parks recalled that Dexter entered the dressing room at Hastings clutching a tattered cricket bag that contained mouldy kit and an untreated bat. He had not touched his cricket stuff in the two years he had been away from the game.

Sussex were then captained by Mike Griffith, son of MCC's Billy Griffith. It is unclear whether he was unduly influenced by Dexter's need of batting practice when he chose to bat upon winning the toss. It looked a bold decision for the wicket was green and still wet. It threatened to favour not only the Kent pacemen but also Underwood who cut the ball as ruthlessly as he spun it. After only an hour of play, Griffith must have rued his choice. Four of his top order had been dismissed for only 27 runs. Crucially, however, Dexter had survived.

Kent opened with David Sayer, a stocky, genuinely quick bowler, who managed to generate considerable speed from a relatively short run. Like Ken Higgs, Sayer habitually waved his guiding arm at the point of delivery, as if he was bidding the batsman adieu. Sayer was known to his team-mates as 'Slayer', and quickly justified his nickname by ripping out Mike Buss's stumps with only one run on the board.

Sayer's opening partner was the giant Northumbrian medium-fast bowler Norman Graham, whose trudging approach and laboured action belied his mastery of seam, swing and bounce. Graham had been in the selectors' mind, early in the season when they picked him to play in an MCC team of England hopefuls. Much to Graham's disappointment he would be the only member of that side not to be selected for Test cricket. On this humid morning, however, he proved too good for hardened battler Ken Suttle. Having located the outside edge of the left-hander's bat, Knott took the resulting catch (6/2). Derek Semmence also struggled to add to his solitary run before being caught at backward point by Denness off Graham (17/3). His dismissal brought Dexter to the wicket, bearing the disdainful expression he reserved for his toughest challenges.

Dexter was greeted by Tony Greig, a 6ft 6in, young South African-born all-rounder. Greig was abrasive and brash. He relished playing booming front-foot drives on the rise, in thrashing the ball through the covers. Cannily, Kent captain Alan Dixon turned immediately to Underwood believing that Greig and Dexter, who were confident and belligerent players of pace, might find sharply spun deliveries more difficult to play. Greig duly obliged, presenting Underwood with a simple catch off his own bowling having miscued an expansive on-drive (27/4).

With Sussex's last accomplished batsman, Jim Parks, joining him, Dexter knew he had to keep his head down, repel the Kent bowling, and re-find his touch before progressing to his 'lordly' repertoire. Whenever possible, Dexter pressed well forward in playing Underwood, employing a deftly relaxed grip on the bat handle to evade the clutches of the encircling close fielders.

In 1963, I had watched Parks (136) and Dexter (107) destroy the Kent bowling at Hastings with a flurry of graceful yet admonishing shots, but with Underwood turning the ball spitefully here, both batsmen confined their scoring shots to nudges and deflections. Underwood was an unlikely assassin.

Flat and splay-footed, he waddled to the wicket with the menace of a reclusive accountant bewildered by his sudden exposure to the dazzling daylight. Appearances were deceptive, though. He had a smooth, gliding, repeatable action with which he delivered heavily-spun or cut balls at probing pace and with nagging accuracy. On wet or crumbling wickets he was lethal, hence his sobriquet 'Deadly'. Underwood's fielding was also sounder than his laboured movement suggested, being a reliable catcher away from the wicket. While his batting seemed rudimentary, he was a brave battler as he had demonstrated after Griffith felled him with a vicious bouncer during the 1966 Test series. Having worked hard at his batting, he became a proficient nightwatchman, eventually recording a first-class century in 1985, coincidentally at Hastings. In fact, the Central Cricket Ground became a very happy hunting ground for him. It was here that he achieved his best innings figures of nine wickets for 28 runs in 1964. He also returned his best match figures in England here, too, when he took 14-82 in 1967. In 1973, he achieved a startling second innings return here of 8-9, giving him match figures of 13-52. After his drubbing by Dexter and Parks in 1963, Underwood certainly made Sussex pay heavily for the indignity he once suffered as a novice.

In measured fashion Dexter and Parks took the Sussex score past 60 just before lunch. Although this was a sounder position than an hour before, Sussex were not yet out of the woods. After lunch the clouds dispersed allowing the verdant ground to become bathed in warm afternoon sunshine. Although, the wicket began to lose its bite, Underwood and brisk off-spinner Dixon periodically troubled the Sussex pair. Underwood undid Parks with a ball that turned and lifted, resulting in a catch by future England opener, Bob Woolmer (85/5).

There were few frills about Mike Griffith's batting. He accumulated most of his runs with an assortment of swipes and swats. But playing within his limitations he provided excellent support to Dexter who had decided it was time to seize control. Tiring of the shackles that Dixon and Underwood had imposed, Dexter began driving both bowlers with increasing assuredness, piercing the field with shots that skimmed to the boundary. The clouds briefly returned in mid-afternoon, producing a sharp shower that forced the players off just as Dexter had progressed to 99. An early tea was taken but the short interruption did not trouble Dexter, as he calmly proceeded to his century at the resumption of play. It was then that he moved into overdrive, smiting the ball with utmost ferocity. While Dexter showed scant respect for line and length, he never relapsed into unruly slogging. Before lunch, Underwood had conceded less than two runs per over, but by the final session even he was unable to restrain Dexter's brutality. One of his deliveries was hoisted over long on and on to the Town Hall roof, a monstrous blow. This was the cue for Dixon to bring back Sayer and Graham. But their extra pace only ensured that Dexter's shots flashed to the boundary with even greater speed.

Training my binoculars upon Dexter's face, it bore a supercilious sneer. He was no longer content with dominating his opponents, he was intent upon humiliating them.

Alan Dixon was a sound county pro. He batted usefully and bowled seam up and off-breaks with a jolting action at a hurried pace. After helping Underwood apply tight restraint during the pre-lunch session, he took increasing flak from Dexter. But amid the mayhem, Sayer bowled Mike Griffith for 69. It was one of Griffith's finest innings for Sussex, helping Dexter put on 162 for the sixth wicket. Thanks to his doughty assistance, his team was more securely placed at 246/6.

Sussex all-rounder Graham Cooper continued the restorative work, adding 41 before he also fell to the persevering Sayer. By this time Dexter was a man in a hurry. Wrongly believing that close of play was nigh, he launched a blistering 'aerial' attack, reaching his double century with 23 runs taken from one over from Dixon, including two sixes and a brace of fours. By the time Dexter had holed out at extra cover, off a relieved and very weary Underwood, Sussex had 313 on the board, almost two-thirds of which had been made by Dexter (203). Underwood's 44 overs had cost him 144 runs while Dixon's 18 overs had cost 77.

Dexter had proved his point and was duly selected for the Leeds and Oval Tests. Alas, he was unable to repeat his Hastings form in either match. However, he was able to celebrate the end of his glittering Test career, in which he averaged 47.89 runs, with victory at the Oval. A frenzied drying operation, involving both ground staff and spectators, enabled England to overcome their sternest opponent, the wet summer weather, and draw the rubber. But the grim conclusion was that for the fifth time in succession, the Ashes had eluded England's grasp.

England's heroes at the Oval were centurions John Edrich (164) and Basil D'Oliveira (158), and 'deadly' Derek Underwood who recovered from his pasting at Hastings by taking seven wickets for 50 runs in the Australians' second innings. It was commonly assumed that Basil D'Oliveira's showpiece hundred would confirm his selection for the planned winter tour of South Africa. Unfortunately this was not the case, at least not at first.

The late 1960s was a difficult time for MCC. Because of the worsening financial climate, it was compelled to reorganise the running of first-class and recreational cricket so that the cash-strapped game might receive Sports Council funding, offered by the Wilson government, but ultimately provided by Ted Heath's administration. Being a private club, MCC was unable to retain its role as cricket's governing body and avail itself of public funding. Consequently, an independent Test and County Cricket Board (TCCB) was set up to administer the professional game while a National Cricket Association (NCA) replaced the MCC Cricket Association in looking after recreational cricket. That said, MCC continued to exert power by filling most of the influential positions within these new bodies, while continuing to have a powerful voice within the International Cricket Conference.

As unsettling as these changes were for an organisation bound by convention, its embroilment in the D'Oliveira affair created a greater stir. In March 1968, South African Prime Minister Vorster told Lord Cobham, a former MCC president, that if the mixed race D'Oliveira was selected as a member of the MCC party, the winter tour was off. Although the South African response was predictable, it was initially concealed from the full MCC committee. Meanwhile the senior MCC officials who had been made aware of Vorster's position, strove, in collaboration with their South African counterparts, to find a way of circumventing the impasse. Their clandestine efforts are described in Guy Fraser-Sampson's excellent book *Cricket at the Crossroads*.

Once the MCC selectors announced that D'Oliveira had not been chosen for the South African tour, there was a furious public and media outcry. John Arlott was predictably outspoken in opposition. It seemed as if D'Oliveira had been sacrificed so that the tour could progress. As Richie Benaud pointed out, D'Oliveira had a higher Test batting average than anyone else in the party, other than Ken Barrington. He was also in fourth position in the national bowling averages in 1968.

The Rev. David Sheppard, backed by future England captain Mike Brearley, called for a special MCC meeting to cancel the tour. Although their motion was headed off by a full MCC committee, led by Sir Alec Douglas-Home, had the committee members known what Lord Cobham already knew, Sheppard's motion might well have been carried.

Once Ken Barrington's heart condition and Tom Cartwright's injury brought about their withdrawal from the touring party, the selectors had no option other than to invite D'Oliveira. This came too late, though, to prevent MCC's integrity being called into question, not only by the British public and media, but also by the South African government who, in angrily cancelling the tour, accused MCC of political chicanery. The one person caught up in this sorry affair to survive it with his dignity intact was Basil D'Oliveira.

I arrived at Lancaster University in a damp, overcast autumn of 1968 to find a 'Klondike town' minus the gold. It was a building site with mud spattered everywhere. Discreetly isolated in rural splendour, our stay became one of experimental living. Joss sticks abounded if only to subdue the rancid smell of our clothing. Vitamins were at a premium. They had a better diet on the *Bounty*. Christmas was duly celebrated with scurvy. Those arriving with short back and sides, horn-rimmed glasses and sports jackets went home with flowing locks, John Lennon specs and beaded buckskin. Student relationships with the nearby city seemed less like 'town and gown' than 'town and clown'. *Withnail and I* had come to Lancaster.

But it was here that I met Liz, who was to become my wife. Jimi Hendrix's version of the Dylan song 'All Along the Watchtower' defines our early days together. I recall first listening to it on BBC's *Pick of the Pops* one autumn afternoon, while enjoying her tower room view of a grazed winter sky, the fading sunset mirrored by the gleaming sandbanks of Morecambe Bay, set before a faint wash of Lakeland fells.

Dylan adores Hendrix's cover: the strummed acoustic intro; the four-part solo; the bottle sliding improvisations; the 'wah wah' interlude and the apocalyptic climax that mimics the howling wind of Dylan's dystopian imagery. Just play me Hendrix's 'All Along the Watchtower' and I am whisked back to the couple Liz and I once were, almost half a century ago. I sometimes wonder whether our much younger selves would have liked the people we have become. I hope so.

1969

She Moves Through the Fair

On 20 July 1969, the 'Eagle' landed on the moon. A triumphant Neil Armstrong celebrated this amazing feat with the immortal words, 'One small step for man, one giant leap for mankind.' Not that many parts of the developing world were listening. For independence had not guaranteed a new dawn or a giant step forward. Too many former colonies had succumbed to coups, dictatorships, civil unrest and wars, and in some places, widespread starvation, as in Biafra. The inherent fallacy was in granting independence according to former colonial boundaries rather than in recognition of the preceding political, cultural and tribal territories.

In 1969 North American youthful idealism receded. If Woodstock's three days of 'peace and music' represented its zenith, a brief interlude in which young hearts ran, or slithered, free, then the Altamont festival signalled its nadir, particularly when coupled with the Manson nightmare and the televised horror of Vietnam. Fittingly, *Easy Rider*, one of the films of the year, charted the death of an American hippie dream. Ironically, Fonda and Hopper's freedom ride was financed by a hard drugs deal, presumably underwritten by less free narcotic addicts. As Jack Kerouac found, uncomplicated freedoms, on the road or elsewhere, are hard to come by.

In Britain there was a different backlash against 'hippie values'. Entering from the right were the thuggish skinhead gangs. They appeared to be living in the past. Their right-wing hatred resurrected the 1930s as much as their braces did. In fact, their tribal, racist and homophobic hatreds seemed to be a defining identity, more than their bovver boots or their taste for reggae or Tamla Motown.

An ill-advised England tour of Pakistan was hastily arranged to fill the gap left by the cancelled South African tour. Pakistan was immersed in serious political strife which preceded the bloody separation of its eastern

Bengali territory. It was rumoured that the impetuous Pakistani opener and law student Aftab Gul was only chosen to play at Lahore and Karachi in order to placate the protest movement of which he was a leading member. He became the first player to appear in a first-class match while on bail for political charges. It was rumoured that he had a surface-to-air missile under his bed, but that was probably apocryphal. Play was frequently interrupted by protesters. At Dhaka, the tourists were alarmed by a background noise of gunfire, and horrified to find gagged and bound bodies floating in a nearby river. Neither the local police nor the Pakistan army seemed capable of providing much protection, and actually allowed the students to remain in charge during the Dhaka Test.

All three Tests were drawn, with Cowdrey (100), Graveney (105) and Milburn (139) scoring their final Test tons, and Knott (96 not out) narrowly missing his first. It was remarkable that any play was possible in such disturbing circumstances.

This was the year in which Liz and I were introduced to Fairport Convention's rendition of the Celtic folk song, 'She Moves Through the Fair'. Sandy Denny's powerful, lilting voice, supported by her band's ethereal guitars, and solemn beat, emphasises the song's spectral poignancy, concerning two young, star-crossed lovers, parted by death.

It was not serious illness which threatened to separate Liz and me, though, it was my mistaken idea that I should become a 'man of God'. It took an ordination selection conference in the summer of 1969 to rid me of the fug. Ignoring my censorious room-mate, I probably spent more time in the retreat's TV room, watching England beat the West Indians, than I did in religious devotion. Other than that I spent much time helping the nuns in the kitchen. In return, they fed me their delicious leftovers. I did not so much walk away from this secluded haven of peace, as roll out having stuffed an awful lot of pie into my flagging piety.

The summer of 1969 was a good one for newly-appointed England captain Raymond Illingworth. He replaced Colin Cowdrey who had ruptured his Achilles tendon. Illingworth proved to be a revelation not only with bat and ball, but with his remarkable tactical shrewdness. After defeating the West Indians with surprising ease at Old Trafford, Illingworth (113) and debutant John Hampshire (107) rescued England from a disastrous start in the second Test at Lord's, with Illingworth and Snow adding 83 for the last wicket. This was Illingworth's maiden Test century. He also helped keep the West Indians at bay late on the final afternoon, after England had stumbled from 263/3 to 292/7, when in pursuit of 332 for victory. Illingworth seemed to have had a happy habit of reserving his best and longest innings for times of strife. In fact, captaincy did wonders for his batting form, with his average Test score almost doubling at 33. Unlike Laker, he was never a prodigious finger spinner, but, by virtue of subtle changes in flight and pace, he was capable of deceiving the world's best batsmen, particularly those who failed to spot his well-disguised, drifting 'arm ball'.

Thanks to stout lower-order defiance, Illingworth was able to set the West Indians a challenging victory target of 303 at Leeds. Fredericks was dismissed for six by Snow, but then Camacho, Davis and Butcher batted with growing aggression, to place the West Indians in command at 177/2. It was at this point that I turned on the retreat's TV. As if by divine command, Underwood had Camacho (71) caught by Hampshire at short leg. Butcher (91) departed soon after with the total at 219, to a disputed catch at the wicket, again off Underwood.

With Sobers's arrival, Illingworth baffled me by taking off the successful Underwood, replacing him with medium-paced Knight. Knowing Sobers's aggressive instincts at the start of his innings, Illingworth instructed Knight to tempt Sobers with a wide, out-swinging half-volley. Sobers threw the bat as Illingworth had predicted but over-compensated for Knight's out-swing. The ball clipped the inside edge of his flashing blade and clattered into his stumps. Sobers had gone for a duck and it was 224/5. Perhaps England might have won at Lord's in 1966 had Illingworth been in charge instead of a hesitant Cowdrey.

After Sobers departed, it was expected that Underwood would be recalled, but no. Instead, Illingworth brought himself on to bowl, believing that the left-handed Clive Lloyd was more vulnerable to a ball leaving the bat. Sure enough, Lloyd, the last remaining West Indian batsman of stature, nicked one such delivery to Knott, to leave the tourists reeling at 228/6. Underwood was then brought back, and immediately dismissed the injured Kent all-rounder John Shepherd for no score. Having decided to reprimand his fastest bowler, Snow, for not bowling flat out as instructed, Illingworth put his faith in Knight and Brown to finish the job. England won the match by 30 runs and the series 2-0.

After blowing away the New Zealanders in the summer's subsequent Test series, Illingworth made an emphatic claim for the English captaincy on an extended basis. England would need a steely, tactically sharp leader Down Under, if they had any chance of recovering the Ashes. However, it seemed as if the TCCB selectors were less sure, feeling less comfortable, perhaps, with Illingworth's combative professionalism than with Cowdrey's cultured civility.

1970
54-46 Was My Number

In March 1970, US President Richard Nixon stepped up B-52 bombing raids on the Ho Chi Minh Trail in a forlorn attempt to stop the North Vietnamese Army moving supplies through Laos and Cambodia to the Viet Cong in the South. For me, the Vietnam War had moved closer to home. Al had made that difference. He was an American student on a year's exchange. It was merely a 12-month reprieve for his draft number was almost up. As the year passed, Al's wretched anguish mounted. He talked quickly and slept badly. I often kept him company while he indulged the former and coped with the latter. Our cheap cigarettes and cheaper coffee helped see us through.

Al was fond of expletive-laden diatribes. Here, he spat out his ire with contorted distaste. Obviously, I cannot recall exactly what he said, but it went something like this, 'Tell me this? How come we are mixed up in a legitimate struggle for national unification? It's got f*** all to do with communist expansion. The g***s [he wasn't averse to using military slang] just want their country back. Jesus f***ing Christ don't you think it's time! The f***ing French colonialists grabbed it from them over a hundred years ago. Jesus, they even got the defeated Japs to guard it for them after the war ended! No wonder the Vietnamese are so p***ed off... All we're doing over there is wasting lives – theirs and ours. And for what, may I ask? We're trying to prop up a corrupt, puppet government that no one wants except those Saigon leeches on the make. It's incapable of defending itself. And after the f***ing fiasco of the Tet Offensive, we know we can't protect them, either, no matter how many thousands of bombs we drop on the jungle trails.'

It was as if Al was rehearsing his desperate pitch for an imaginary draft board, hoping that honed logic and furious invective might save him from his appalling fate, although we never found out what that was.

The Vietnam War politicised rock music. Country Joe and The Fish released their anti-war song, 'I-Feel-Like-I'm-Fixin'-to-Die Rag'. In 'Fortunate Son', John Fogerty of Creedence Clearwater Revival railed furiously against an inequitable draft system that had originally protected the privileged sons at the expense of the poorer boys. Then Crosby, Stills, Nash and Young rushed out 'Ohio' following the fatal shooting of four Kent State University demonstrators by the National Guard. Meanwhile in politically turbulent, post-colonial Jamaica, Fred 'Toots' Hibbert and his close-harmony reggae group The Maytals released '54-46 Was My Number', a protest song about Toots's alleged false imprisonment on trumped-up drug charges. Other black reggae and ska artists would pick up his torch of dissent including Bob Marley and the Wailers, Burning Spear and Steel Pulse, influencing a swathe of British punk, new wave and 2 Tone bands.

If the late 1960s were caricatured by fanciful notions of peace, love and music, these glib hopes soon withered in the face of bitter discord, not only in Vietnam, but also in Bangladesh, the Middle East, Iran, Latin America, Africa, Thailand, Kampuchea and Afghanistan, while extreme forms of terrorism abounded at home, with the IRA, and abroad, with the Red Brigade, PLO and the Baader-Meinhof Red Army Faction.

In the summer of 1970, English cricket became embroiled in a bitter political feud, too. This concerned the planned South African cricket tour of this country. During the winter of 1969/70, the Springbok rugby union team's tour of Britain and Ireland had been heavily disrupted by violent demonstrations and civil disobedience. The prospects for the South African cricket tour did not look good. Nevertheless, in December 1969 the TCCB confirmed that the tour would go ahead, hoping that any anti-apartheid demonstrations would be conducted peacefully. Yet by the end of January 1970 it was reported that 12 county grounds had been vandalised in protest. With South Africa refusing entry to black US tennis champion Arthur Ashe and a mixed-race International Cavaliers side, the heat of opposition began to climb. Kenya reacted to the TCCB confirmation of the South African tour by cancelling a visit by an MCC team. Eight African countries stated that they would not participate in the summer Commonwealth Games if the tour went ahead. John Arlott also announced that he was unwilling to commentate on the series. MCC attempted damage limitation by reducing the size of the South Africans' itinerary, realising it would be impossible to protect all venues against angry demonstrators. The British anti-apartheid and 'Stop the 70 Tour' movements were well organised, fiercely determined and well-supported. The England Test players were so concerned about their personal safety that life insurance policies, valued at £15,000 per player, were taken out.

The TCCB and MCC initially attempted to 'tough it out'. Resorting to a familiar mantra, they demanded that matters of sport and politics should remain separate. Nevertheless, security was tightened at Lord's with the square protected by barbed wire, floodlighting and 24-hour dog patrols. The 'Stop the 70 Tour' campaign, led by Peter Hain, was not to be deterred, though. Hain, who had been brought up in South Africa, co-ordinated a highly persuasive, carefully-planned campaign to thwart the ambitions of the English cricket authorities. Eventually, the threat of an African boycott of the Edinburgh Commonwealth Games prompted Labour minister Jim Callaghan to order the TCCB to withdraw its invitation. The International Cricket Conference (ICC) then voted to suspend South Africa from international cricket because of its apartheid policy. This ban would last until 1992.

South Africa's Minister of Sport, Frank Waring, was furious, claiming hypocritically, 'It amounts to bowing down to irresponsible elements that manifest a total disregard for sport and the rights of others.' Whereas Peter Hain commented, 'We had been determined to stop [the tour] and had lots of ingenious protests planned. We'd discovered that a disused branch line of the London Underground had an air vent that led directly up to the concourse inside Lord's.'

Deftly avoiding the political implications, England captain Raymond Illingworth said, 'We were bitterly disappointed that South Africa weren't coming. We had a very good side with [fast bowlers] Alan Ward and John Snow – so I reckon we had them in the bowling department. Of course they batted right the way down and had just whopped the Australians. So it would have been a marvellous series.'

Ironically, almost half of the all-white South African side were included in a multi-racial Rest of the World team that faced England in a five-match series during that summer. Graeme Pollock commented, 'We could have made a bigger noise about apartheid at the time... In hindsight, perhaps we should have done more. You have to remember that in South Africa at the time if you criticised things your life became very difficult. In the end our conscience demanded that we had to show our hand.'

The series was an outstanding success and although the Rest of the World team won the series by 4-1, the contest was much closer than this scoreline suggests. More importantly, it provided Illingworth's England side with the toughest possible examination of technique, tactics and tenacity. Although later stripped of its Test status, the series was an ideal preparation for the tough Ashes challenge ahead.

For much of the summer, Illingworth was uncertain whether he would be chosen to lead England Down Under. But his record eventually spoke for itself, silencing his detractors. Cowdrey was hugely disappointed, and deliberated for an unseemly three weeks before accepting the role as Illingworth's deputy. Illingworth told Sam Pilger and Rob Wightman, authors of *Match of My Life – The Ashes*, 'If a bloke takes that long to decide, he's not in the right frame of mind.' Illingworth was right. Cowdrey had a poor tour, underperforming with the bat and in the field. As vice-captain it was his job to organise net practice but he often arrived late.

1971
Changes

The Gay and Women's Liberation movements of the early 1970s did much to challenge the supposition that men and women are distinguished by innate differences. And here Glam Rock lent a hand. Gary Kemp, who became a member of the 1980s New Romantic band Spandau Ballet recalled, 'Gender-bending was suddenly far more rebellious than drugs and violence.' It became chic for male rock stars to daub themselves with garish cosmetics, and strut around in florid, feminine designs. The camp, androgynous, glamorous look was in – thanks to pace-setters such as Marc Bolan and David Bowie.

In Bowie's song 'Changes' he describes the generational tensions underlying this time of social upheaval. The song bore testament to his chameleon personality, too, as he repeatedly reinvented his image with striking innovations of style and song.

Meanwhile, Raymond Illingworth was reinventing the England Test side as an Ashes-winning team. Illingworth was a bold, brave, authoritative leader. He made his position clear at the outset, asserting his right of say on the final composition of the squad he had been asked to lead. Although it had become customary for an England captain to have a casting vote in selection decisions, it was not an automatic right as Mike Denness revealed after he succeeded Illingworth. In fact, Denness claimed that he did not have any say in the selection of the two overseas touring parties he led.

Illingworth won his first battle, insisting that D'Oliveira should be in his squad. The Test and County Cricket Board (TCCB) selectors had considered picking Tony Greig instead. Illingworth rightly recognised D'Oliveira's worth as a patient, resilient batsman, and as a useful change bowler who could 'bottle up' one end. Had Illingworth been in charge during the summer of 1968, the D'Oliveira Affair might not have happened.

Illingworth also claimed the right to decide his team's tactics, and manner of practice. He assumed responsibility for all decisions made on the field of play, while expecting that his tour manager, David Clark, would consult him on all matters concerning the health and well-being of his players, including day-to-day living and travelling arrangements, and any change in the tour itinerary. He maintained, too, that tour bonuses should be subject to his prior recommendation. Illingworth's confident grasp of what he considered to be his brief would soon bring him into conflict with Clark.

Clark had a different background to that of Illingworth. He had received a public school education at Rugby. He was formerly an officer with the First Airborne Division of the Second Parachute Regiment which had fought so valiantly at Arnhem in 1944. He had also been a thoughtful, far-sighted chairman of an MCC committee, charged with the responsibility of recommending necessary changes to the ailing English first-class game.

Although generally genial, Clark was a stubborn, authoritarian man, displeased by any challenge to his authority. It seemed as if he had been chosen as tour manager on the presumption that his trusted Kent skipper, Colin Cowdrey, would regain the England captaincy. For both Clark and Cowdrey had been amateur captains of Kent, and, in their respective roles as club chairman and club captain, they had enjoyed a harmonious working relationship. In his previous assignment as an MCC manager, on the blighted 1963/64 tour of India, Clark had worked well with captain Mike Smith. Perhaps Clark was more at ease with those of a similar social status.

Illingworth had been brought up on the opposite side of the tracks, socially, educationally and financially. He was a gritty, shrewd and independently-minded. If Clark had expected Illingworth to be deferential he was to be disappointed. Unlike the diplomatically-minded Hutton, Illingworth was unwilling to 'bend the knee'. For him, respect was to be earned, not presumed according to social status.

Illingworth was happy with his triumvirate of resolute openers, Boycott, Edrich and Luckhurst, all of whom were expected to play in the Test matches. Cowdrey was pencilled in to bat at four while Keith Fletcher deservedly took the 'promising young batsman' place, instead of Dennis Amiss. This followed Fletcher's impressive batting performances against the Rest of the World XI, notably at Leeds. John Hampshire, England's saviour at Lord's in 1969, took the final batting slot, with two top-notch wicketkeepers, Alan Knott and Bob Taylor, almost picking themselves.

Like Hutton, Illingworth knew he needed his fastest men in Australia. Snow and Ward were earmarked to be his spearhead, while Lever, whose speed had sharpened appreciably during the summer, was designated in a support role, possibly alongside his lanky county colleague, Ken Shuttleworth. Alas, the tall, slender Ward was undone by the Australian hard surfaces, just as David Larter had been on previous tours. Ward suffered shin splints and returned home before the first Test began. His surprising replacement was the apprentice Surrey fast bowler Bob Willis, whose speed, bounce and general hostility had impressed his county colleague, John Edrich. Accepting Edrich's strong recommendation, Illingworth requested that the TCCB selectors arrange for Willis to be flown out instead of the more experienced David Brown. Willis would soon prove his worth.

Illingworth did not expect he would bowl much in the Test series because, with the exception of Tayfield, Titmus and Laker, few off-spinners had found any joy on the Australian tracks. His priority was to have bowlers capable of making the ball leave the right-handers' bat. But while recognising Underwood's devastating ability on a wet or crumbling wicket, Illingworth was less certain of his value on a flat track. Consequently, he persuaded the TCCB selectors to choose the Yorkshire left-arm spinner, Don Wilson, as a back-up.

Despite suffering an embarrassing defeat against Victoria on a poor surface, Illingworth's men recovered strongly at Brisbane to finish well on top. England's cause was not helped when umpire Lou Rowan decided controversially that Australia's double centurion Stackpole (207) had made his ground when this seemed not to be so. Stackpole had not reached 20 at that point. Undeterred, Luckhurst batted splendidly, scoring 79 runs before being run out by Knott who atoned for his error by scoring 73 himself. Edrich (79) and D'Oliveira (57) also batted durably, and with Snow contributing 34 valuable runs, England managed to reach a total of 464, 32 ahead of Australia for whom Walters (115) had batted well. Had it not been for Lawry's obstinate batting (84) in their second innings, Australia might well have lost, having been bundled out for only 214. Snow had returned match figures of eight wickets for 162 runs while Shuttleworth's 5-128 in the second innings was a fitting reflection of his threat on a placid surface. Also Illingworth and Underwood had dismissed five top-order Australian batsmen, primarily by playing upon their patience.

At Perth, England once again batted solidly with Boycott (70) and Luckhurst (131) posting 170 for the first wicket. Although Australian fast bowlers Thomson and McKenzie pulled their side back into the game, dismissing England for 397, the hosts were soon in trouble at 107/5 with Snow and Lever making an early breakthrough. But then Redpath (171) and debutant Greg Chappell (108) rescued them with a 219-run sixth-wicket partnership. The composed and stylish Chappell was particularly harsh on the English pace bowlers as 74 runs were added in only ten overs. Australia finally achieved a 43-run first-innings lead with wicketkeeper Rodney Marsh chipping in with a valuable 44 runs. England were briefly in peril of losing at 152/5, before Edrich (115 not out), D'Oliveira (31), Illingworth (29) and Knott (30 not out) dragged them out of the mire, allowing Illingworth to declare at 287/6. Lawry was typically risk-averse, refusing to chase a 245-run winning target in just under two and a half hours, so this engaging, switchback game petered out into a disappointing draw.

The Perth Test match featured further controversy involving Australian umpire Lou Rowan who refused Illingworth's rightful request of the roller. Rowan also wrongly warned Snow about bowling bouncers when the ball was pitched only marginally short of a length. Snow's indignation was hardly assuaged when tour manager Clark added his disapproval, criticising England's supposed short-pitched bowling and slow scoring. Snow had already experienced David Clark's wrath, having been told curtly to 'bowl properly' during net practice. Snow had reduced his pace on account of tiredness. He had bowled the equivalent of 72 six-ball overs at Brisbane, and was disinclined to push himself too hard with a punishing workload ahead. But Clark would have none of this. An angry confrontation ensued, resulting in the truculent Snow storming off. While having some sympathy for Snow's point of view, Illingworth regarded his discourteous behaviour as inexcusable, warning him that he would be sent home if there was any repetition. Snow heeded the warning.

Illingworth was in a difficult place. Most of the team, including the reprimanded Snow, stood full-square behind him; the only exception being Cowdrey who remained loyal to David Clark. The division in the camp was exacerbated when Clark told the press that he would prefer to see results in the remaining four Tests, even if Australia won. With the exception of Cowdrey, the England players were outraged by Clark's remarks having striven hard to deny Australia a winning opportunity in the first two matches. They were miffed, too, that Clark had chosen to convey his criticisms to the press rather than to them.

To complicate matters, Clark agreed that a further Test match should be inserted into his team's already crowded schedule, after the Melbourne Test was washed out without a ball being bowled. Illingworth was furious that Clark had not consulted with him first. Illingworth pointed out to Clark that the revised itinerary committed his men to playing 28 days of cricket, including four Tests within the space of six weeks. Once Illingworth realised that the decision was irreversible, he sought extra remuneration for his players in recognition of their increased workload. The Australians had already been promised this, but Clark was initially reluctant to pursue the matter with the TCCB until the players joined Illingworth in demanding that something was done. Although they eventually received extra payment it was allegedly less than the normal Test fee of £150.

At Sydney, the series turned decisively in England's favour thanks to Geoff Boycott's supreme batting and Snow's devastating bowling. England started well again with an unusually fluent Boycott and a composed Luckhurst posting another century opening partnership. Despite Edrich adding a fifty, England's middle order stumbled when facing Australian 'mystery spinner' Gleeson and off-spinner Mallett, both of whom found disconcerting turn. Nevertheless, the England tail wagged, with Snow (37), Lever (36) and debutant Willis (15 not out) converting a disappointing score of 267/7 into a more robust total of 332 all out.

When the Australians began their innings, their captain Bill Lawry was surprisingly accompanied by Ian Chappell. Talk about blunt and biff. Snow and new boy Willis opened the bowling with all guns blazing. For Ian Chappell, Illingworth positioned Underwood at fly slip 25 or 30 yards from the fence. He reasoned that Chappell was inclined to play an uncontrolled open-blade slash if presented with a short delivery outside his off stump. Snow supplied the bait, Chappell snapped and Underwood pocketed a swirling catch. Australia were 14/1.

Before seeing Willis bowl on the nightly TV highlights, I had imagined him to have the sleek athleticism of Statham, Sobers or Snow and the classical action of Hall, Trueman or McKenzie. Instead, what I saw was a frisky young man, with an unruly mop of curly hair, bounding in off a curved, knees-up run which had the finesse of a galloping shire horse. As he ran in he seemed to be whipping his backside with the ball as if it was a riding crop. Upon reaching the wicket he leapt rather ungracefully, before releasing the ball with a whirling, open-chested action. But my, was he quick! As Willis admitted in his autobiography *Lasting the Pace*, his action was not a pretty sight, but he sent down almost 50,000 deliveries with it during his career. Surrey coach Arthur McIntyre had tried persuading Willis to modify his action, when the Guildford lad was still an apprentice, citing Alec Bedser as an exempla. Fortunately, wiser counsel prevailed from Surrey senior Mike Edwards. Edwards urged Willis to concentrate upon bowling as fast as he could. Willis's height also meant that he was capable of achieving steepling bounce. But in order to conserve energy in the enervating Australian heat, Illingworth wisely kept his spells short, often turning to Lever or D'Oliveira after four overs or so.

I had first watched Lever in action almost ten years before, when he was a member of the Lancashire team beaten by Sussex at Hastings. Then he seemed to be of no quicker than fast-medium, not as fast as his county colleague Colin Hilton. But having seen him bowl at the Oval against the Rest of the World XI, it was evident that he had added a yard or two of pace. Helped by a run of greater speed and a rhythmic, rolling action, he utilised this extra momentum without reducing his ability to swing the ball late in its flight. At Sydney, Lever appeared almost as quick through the air as Snow, without achieving the Sussex man's alarming lift. Nevertheless, he still managed to get one ball to kick viciously outside Lawry's off stump, which found the shoulder of the bat, and flew to Edrich in the gully. The curmudgeonly Lawry departed for just nine (38/2).

Redpath (64) and Walters (55) then mounted a recovery, although both were dropped in the slips before making double figures. Illingworth eventually had Walters caught by Luckhurst at short leg (137/3), while one of D'Oliveira's deceptively innocuous out-swingers found the edge of Redpath's bat as he played a defensive back-foot shot. Fletcher nonchalantly pouched the chance at first slip (160/4). There was more to D'Oliveira's bowling than met the eye. Thereafter, the Australian innings fell apart, undone by Underwood's pace and turn. Greg Chappell miscued an on-drive, presenting Underwood with a simple return catch. Marsh then launched an ugly slog across the line that sent the ball soaring towards D'Oliveira on the midwicket boundary. Mallett was bowled neck and crop by a delivery that Underwood speared into him. Stackpole spanked a flighted delivery from Underwood to Boycott at extra cover and Gleeson nicked another D'Oliveira outswinger to Fletcher. The Australian innings was suddenly in tatters at 219/9. With nothing to lose both McKenzie and Connolly swung lustily, 'Dolly' unaccountably shelling two 'dollies' at deep mid-off. But Lever summarily ended the frivolities by clean bowling Connolly, leaving Australia 236 all out, 96 runs in arrears.

It was the cue for Geoffrey Boycott to play one of his finest innings for England. Boycott was so adept at taking runs from balls which were just short of a length and moving into him, deliveries which less talented batsmen might meet with a dead bat. Having moved into line, Boycott made a belated adjustment of his feet in playing the stroke, allowing him the room to punch or push the ball away in an arc between cover and third man. By virtue of his sprightly footwork and exquisite timing, Boycott could exert as much force with this shot as others did with a square cut.

At Sydney, Boycott savaged the Australian attack, driving the dangerous Ashley Mallett on either side of the wicket with sublime timing and placement. Boycott had worked out that the best way to play the mystery spinner Gleeson was to treat him primarily as an off-spinner. D'Oliveira twigged this, too, but Boycott mischievously urged D'Oliveira not to spill the beans to their team-mates. Boycott's confident mastery of Mallett and Gleeson was emphasised with a succession of flowing drives and crashing pulls. Although he ran out Edrich, leaving England stuttering at 48/3, he completed a supreme unbeaten century (142) supported by invaluable half-centuries from D'Oliveira and Illingworth. The upshot was that Australia were left with over nine hours to score 416 runs to win or, more realistically, to save the game.

It was then that John Snow became England's other hero at Sydney. As Illingworth observed, Snow was often bored by humdrum county cricket, but if a baggy green cap was put before him, he immediately fired into life. On a track which had begun to disintegrate, Snow proved vicious. Ian Chappell disappeared almost as soon as he arrived, fending a brutal rising ball to D'Oliveira at second slip (1/1). Redpath fared little better. His thick edge ballooned to Edrich at gully (11/2). Walters then imprudently slashed at an out-swinger from Lever only to nick a regulation catch to Knott (14/3). Although the obdurate Lawry applied himself in time-honoured fashion, he found himself rapidly running out of partners, particularly when Greg Chappell had his leg stump knocked back as he moved across his stumps to play a leg-glance off Snow (21/4). With Illingworth having set a 'Carmody' cordon behind Stackpole, the Australian tried to lift the siege by hitting out. For a short while he prospered, exploiting the wide gaps left in the outfield, but a snorter from Snow abruptly cancelled his fun, with Lever, at third slip, taking an astounding, left-handed catch at full length (66/5).

Not to be outdone, Willis immediately emulated Lever's feat in dismissing the left-handed Marsh with a catch of superb athleticism (66/6). Willis was then rewarded with his first Test wicket, dismissing Mallett with a fast rearing delivery that the off-spinner attempted to hook, but could only glove to Knott down the leg side (86/7). Poor McKenzie was so bewildered by this firestorm that he ducked into a rising, but by no means short, delivery from Snow, bringing about his immediate retirement. It was time for the limpet-like Lawry to go on to the offensive, and in a flurry of hooks, pulls and cuts he attained a redoubtable half-century, only to find himself stranded on 60 not out once Snow clean bowled an angrily slashing Gleeson, and had Connolly caught at the wicket, both for ducks. The Australians were all out for 116, losing by 299 runs. Snow had achieved second-innings figures of 7-40, the best of his Test career.

The fifth (re-played) Test at Melbourne was remarkable for the ferocity of the heat. Batting first, Australia made 493. Having been dropped twice by Cowdrey early in his innings, Ian Chappell reached an invaluable century (111), which probably saved his place, if not his Test career. He was well supported by Marsh who added 92 belligerent runs. In reply Luckhurst compiled a courageous century (109) after breaking a little finger early in his innings, while D'Oliveira's ton (117) helped restrict Australia's first innings lead to 101. Although Lawry declared once Australia were 270 runs ahead, Boycott and Edrich silenced the boorish crowd with an obdurate, unbroken opening partnership of 161 runs.

Snow was under fire again, this time from umpire O'Connell, who warned him about his excessive use of the bouncer, despite bowling fewer than the ungainly Australian fast bowler 'Froggy' Thomson. Having been recalled in place of Fletcher, Cowdrey had a poor match, scoring only 13 runs and downing four chances at first slip.

The result of the sixth Test at Adelaide was equally disappointing. Batting first, England made 470, with major contributions from Edrich (130), Boycott (58), Fletcher (80), Hampshire (55) and D'Oliveira (47).

Although Lever, Snow and Willis dismissed the Australians for 235, they were exhausted by their fine efforts in the scorching sun. Illingworth chose, therefore, not to enforce the follow-on. Boycott scored another unbeaten century (119), enabling Illingworth to set Lawry's side a winning target of 469 in 500 minutes, but the Adelaide heat-wave sapped the wicket and the English bowling of any demons, allowing the Australians to save the game with ease. It was not enough to save Lawry's Test career, though. He was replaced as captain by Ian Chappell, and as opening batsman by fellow Victorian Ken Eastwood. England were glad to see the back of Lawry. While his ten-year Test career was drawing to a close, Dennis Lillee's was just beginning. The fearsome Western Australian fast bowler made his Test debut at Adelaide.

With his dark, unruly hair and bushy moustache, Lillee oozed bandit machismo. Turning at the end of an angled run, the ball cradled in both hands, he would lean into a lengthy, rocking sprint to the wicket. As he approached the crease he made a fending-off gesture, as if pushing aside an unwelcome intruder, before leaping mightily, like a triple jumper, twisting sideways, and delivering a swinging ball at blistering speed. His hurried high action was merely a blur while his immense momentum thrust him far down the wicket where he would glare malevolently at the opposing batsman. Although still raw and inclined to spray the ball about, he was easily Australia's most potent pace bowler at Adelaide, celebrating his Test debut with a five-wicket first innings haul.

Geoff Boycott, who had averaged 93 in this Ashes series, was cruelly ruled out of the seventh and final Test at Sydney, on account of a broken left forearm. He had sustained the injury when facing McKenzie in an intervening one-day game. The tourists' injury problems were mounting, not helped by the crammed itinerary they were obliged to fulfil. To make matters worse they lost what threatened to be a crucial toss. With the SCG wicket still wet at the start of play, new Australian captain Ian Chappell gleefully put England in to bat. Luckhurst was dismissed for a duck and England struggled not only against Australia's apprentice pace bowlers, Lillee and Dell, but also against their inexperienced leg-spinners, Jenner and O'Keefe. Illingworth top-scored with 42 in an inadequate England first-innings total of 184 runs, accumulated at a painful rate of 1.8 runs per six-ball over. England roared back, though, with Snow, Lever and Willis taking four wickets for 69.

Nevertheless, with Greg Chappell (65), Redpath (59) and Walters (42) resisting well, Australia passed England's score with seven wickets down. Greg Chappell's 57-run eighth-wicket partnership with Terry Jenner (30) threatened to snatch the Ashes from England's grasp. With Jenner proving to be a thorn in England's side, Snow bowled him a shorter delivery to dissuade him from remaining on his front foot where he seemed more comfortable. Unfortunately, Jenner ducked into the path of a ball which jagged back into him, hitting the left side of his head, and causing him to retire hurt. Umpire Rowan reacted immediately, by giving Snow an official warning. Illingworth objected, maintaining that the ball had not been unduly short.

A fracas then ensued involving Rowan, Snow and Illingworth, which triggered an outbreak of crowd disorder on the Sydney hill, resulting in beer cans and bottles raining on to the outfield near where Snow had resumed fielding. A drunken spectator then grabbed Snow by the shirt, although the fast bowler was quickly released by more sober spectators. But the angry scenes continued, eventually spurring Illingworth into leading his players off the field, whereupon Rowan confronted him, threatening to award the match to Australia if he and his players did not return. Illingworth insisted that the outfield should be cleared of clutter, and order restored, before they would resume playing. At this point David Clark intervened, angrily ordering Illingworth and his players to return to the field immediately. Perhaps Clark was unaware that Colin Cowdrey had twice done as Illingworth had done, in response to riots on the Caribbean tours of 1959/60 and 1967/68. Eventually, play was resumed, and Australia closed the day on 235/7, 51 in front.

On the following day, Australia extended their lead to 80 runs before being dismissed. England desperately needed a good start and managed to achieve one with Luckhurst (59) and Edrich (57) putting on 94 for the first wicket. Thereafter, the going became a lot tougher. But with almost everyone making some contribution, England managed to scrape together 302 runs, giving them a lead of 222. Snow immediately hit back by yorking debutant Eastwood for a duck. However, in trying to catch Stackpole's swirling hook off Lever, Snow jammed his right hand between the pickets, dislocating a finger. England had lost their main strike bowler. Undeterred, Lever produced a perfect out-swinger which took the edge of Ian Chappell's bat, leaving Knott to grasp the catch (22/2). With Snow out of action, Illingworth brought himself on. He knew he had to curtail Stackpole's stroke-play which threatened to take the game away from England. Illingworth did not just blunt, though, he bit hard, or at least his off-break did, and Redpath's tickle off his pads was neatly snaffled by Hampshire at backward short-leg (71/3).

Knowing that Walters was a nervous starter, inclined to slash impetuously at any short, rising delivery outside his off stump, Illingworth set a trap, deploying D'Oliveira at deep gully. Willis bowled a ball for Walters to go after, and the Australian batsman duly obliged. D'Oliveira hardly needed to move to pocket the miscued shot (82/4). Stackpole was then joined by the last specialist batsman, Greg Chappell. Becoming restless at the shackles Illingworth was applying, Stackpole essayed an extravagant sweep at a ball that he wrongly judged to be an off-break. Instead, it went on with the arm and he was bowled (96/5). Stackpole's innings of 67 runs was the highest score in the match. The day could have ended even better for England, as seven runs later, the ever-reliable Knott missed an easy stumping chance off Illingworth. At close of play Australia were 123/5, exactly 100 runs away from victory.

I stayed up late on the final night to listen to the climactic live commentary. I knew Chappell and Marsh could easily knock off the required runs, so when Chappell skipped down the wicket only to miss Illingworth's out-floater, I hollered with joy as Knott stumped him (131/6). Marsh followed soon after, bowled by Underwood having gone for an injudicious slog over mid-on (142/7). Surely England would win now? Thankfully, O'Keefe did not linger, flicking a shot off his pads to substitute fielder, Ken Shuttleworth, at square leg (154/8). Having had a belated share of the spoils, D'Oliveira seized an extra slice by having Lillee caught, first ball, by Hampshire at second slip (154/9). Lillee was unhappy with the decision, looking ruefully at umpire Rowan while touching his right pad, but he eventually slunk away.

Sadly for D'Oliveira he was denied the rare distinction of winning an Ashes series with a hat-trick. It was left to Underwood to clean up with a quicker ball, bowled from around the wicket and very wide of the crease. Jenner stabbed at it uncertainly and Fletcher exultantly took the bat-pad chance. Illingworth was chaired chaotically off the field by his ecstatic team-mates. With the exception of Cowdrey, they had backed him wholeheartedly throughout the tour. Greg Chappell reckoned that Illingworth's side of 1970/71 was the toughest England team he had played against, citing the mental intimidation created by Illingworth's aggressive field placements, and the physical intimidation meted out by his fast bowlers. As Illingworth said, Test cricket is not for the faint-hearted.

I presumed that the nation would be united in euphoric celebration of a famous Ashes victory, but I was wrong. The *Daily Telegraph*'s cricket correspondent 'Jim' Swanton wrote, 'The Ashes [had] been re-taken at a heavy and wholly unnecessary cost in terms of sportsmanship.' It seemed as if Illingworth was damned for his manner of victory as Hutton had been before him. Not that the Australians had any complaints. They were only too happy to share a drink or two with their English opponents at the end of each day's play. Perhaps Swanton failed to appreciate the new rules of engagement which were about to become a lot harsher.

A weary England side then moved on to New Zealand, winning one Test and drawing another, before returning home to face the Pakistani and Indian tourists. I had expected the Ashes victory to herald a new 'Golden Age' of English Test cricket, in which the Test-playing nations of the world would bow in homage to England's newly-acquired prowess. The Pakistanis and Indians had other ideas, though. At Edgbaston, Pakistani batsmen Zaheer Abbas (274), Mushtaq Mohammad (100) and Asif Iqbal (104 not out) trounced the England bowling in reaching an overpowering total of 608/7 declared. Having been required to follow on, England averted defeat only because of the obduracy of Knott (116), Luckhurst (108 not out) and D'Oliveira (73), and the mercifully poor weather on the final day.

Although persistent rain at Lord's washed away any chance of a result there, at Leeds, Pakistan wasted an excellent chance of winning their first series in England, after collapsing from a dominant position at 160/4, with Sadiq Mohammad (91) and Asif Iqbal (33) apparently in command, to 205 all out, losing by just 25 runs. The Indians also came close to victory at Lord's where they were chasing 183 runs to win a Test match in England for the first time. However, rain after tea on the final day left them 38 runs short of their target with two wickets remaining.

Although rain probably rescued India at Old Trafford, when hazardously placed at 65/3 in pursuing 420 runs for victory, they deservedly won by four wickets at the Oval. Here, the brisk googlies of Chandrasekhar broke the back of the English second innings on the fourth afternoon. Chandrasekhar, with second innings figures of six wickets for 38 runs, was largely responsible for England's catastrophic total of 101. Liz and I listened to the radio coverage of England's collapse while waiting at Shrewsbury in our broken down car, staring sullenly at the gliding Severn. Snow was back in the naughty corner, too, having been reprimanded for roughly pushing Sunil Gavaskar aside at Lord's. This was hardly the stuff of world champions.

1972
I Can See Clearly Now

It was a bleak mid-winter. As Conservative Prime Minister Edward Heath slugged out a losing battle with the miners, we had to contend with daily power cuts. Frustrated by primitive conditions at the coalfaces, and comparatively poor levels of pay and holiday allowances, the National Union of Miners (NUM) was ready to do battle. In January 1972, a new and decisive tactic of industrial action was introduced – the 'flying picket'. The dispute at Saltley power station, Birmingham, was its crowning glory. But if this was Arthur Scargill's 'Battle of the Bull Run', what transpired at Orgreave, 12 years later, was Mrs Thatcher's Gettysburg. Meanwhile, the Northern Irish 'troubles' were multiplying in the advent of the Bloody Sunday massacre, so was terrorism abroad, despite the capture of leading members of the Baader-Meinhof gang. A Palestinian militant group, named Black September, murdered a German police officer and all 11 Israeli athletes taken hostage at the Munich Olympic compound, after the Israeli authorities refused to release 234 jailed Palestinians.

With electricity supplies subject to strict rotas, thousands of factories were forced into three-day weeks. Millions were laid off. During the regular four-hour blackouts, Liz and I emulated John and Yoko and took to our bed. It was not so much a love-in as an eat-in, though, as we hesitantly consumed the enigmatic leftovers Liz brought home from her canteen work.

Although Raymond Illingworth, then aged 40, led England to a successful retention of the Ashes during the summer of 1972, the resurgent Aussies appeared to be the stronger side by the end of the series. However, England struck the first blow in winning the opening Test at Old Trafford, after John Snow and Geoff Arnold, under heavy skies, had dismissed the Australians for 142 in their first innings. Not even Rod Marsh's late blast of 91 runs could save his team from an 89-run defeat.

It was at this point that I began work in a Midlands children's home. The wrecked lives and surging hormones of its adolescent residents often found expression in explosive rages and heedless destructiveness. However, a laconic, brooding, black Jamaican boy stood apart from the scrum. His interests, in so far as he revealed anything about himself, did not extend much beyond reggae and cricket. No one penetrated his morose aloofness. But we would spend half an hour or so together silently watching the Ashes Test matches on TV or listening to his reggae singles, of which Johnny Nash's 'I Can See Clearly' was his favourite. Did he really see his situation as clearly as his few words and jaded maturity suggested? I would never know.

At Lord's the tables were turned, largely due to Bob Massie's booming swing bowling. On his Test debut, Massie achieved the incredible match figures of 16-137. Although the side-burned Massie was no quicker than medium-fast, none of the English batsmen could play him with any comfort, particularly when he bowled around the wicket. Boycott was quickly clean bowled by a huge indipper with only 11 runs on the board. Then Lillee, at top speed, blasted out Luckhurst and Edrich to leave the English batting order in shreds at 28/3.

M.J.K. Smith (34) and D'Oliveira (32) managed a partial recovery although both fell to Massie before England had raised their first 100 runs. Greig (54) and Knott (43) then batted resolutely, almost doubling their side's total, but they, too, succumbed to Massie, leaving Illingworth (30) and Snow (37) to complete a barely adequate salvage operation, with a 60-run eighth-wicket partnership. The England first innings closed on 272 with Massie taking eight wickets for 84. With Greg Chappell reaching a consummate century (131), and his brother Ian, alongside Rod Marsh, chipping in with bright fifties, the Australian first innings closed 36 ahead of England. This slight lead was quickly converted into an overwhelming advantage as, in murky light, Massie dismissed seven English batsmen while Lillee, at frightening speed, despatched two, leaving England nine down and only 52 in front by close of play on the third day. Gifford and Price had a brief bash on the Monday morning, taking the England score to 116, before Australia jogged home with eight wickets to spare.

The Trent Bridge wicket had a reputation for being helpful to seam bowling in the early stages of a game. So, after winning the toss, Illingworth asked the Australians to bat first. Despite making a shaky start, the Australians found few gremlins in the wicket thereafter. Snow bowled well, taking 5-92 in 31 overs, but found a composed Stackpole (114) difficult to budge as Australia reached 315. When England batted, Lillee and Massie once again ripped through their hesitant ranks once Boycott and Luckhurst had completed a half-century stand for the first wicket. England managed only 189 runs in reply.

In order to nullify Massie's menace, the England batsmen took guard in front of the popping crease. Their idea was to force Massie into bowling a shorter length, hoping this might reduce his degree of swing. The tactic made little difference initially, not helped by poor shot selection. It was much more effective in England's second innings, though, when the sun-bleached wicket became flatter still, and the dry atmospheric conditions were less conducive to swing. After taking four wickets in England's first innings, Massie managed just one in 36 overs the second time around. It was if the intense Nottingham sun had burnt his wings. Few cricketers have risen so high, as quickly, and yet fallen so low, as fast as Massie did. Aghast at his diminishing magic, Massie strove for extra pace, only to compound his problem. With illness also curtailing his form, he was left to ruminate upon a six-match Test career, notable only for an extraordinary debut.

When the Australians batted again, Ross Edwards smote a big, unbeaten hundred (170), allowing Chappell to declare at 324/4. This left England's batsmen with a theoretical victory target of 451. In reality, survival was the name of the game. Luckhurst led the way, compiling 96 very patient runs, but the rescue mission was completed by D'Oliveira (50) and Greig (36) with an unbroken fifth-wicket partnership of 89, taking England to 290/4 before Chappell conceded the draw. The Australians left Nottingham confident that the Ashes were theirs for the taking, but at Leeds they would receive a nasty surprise.

As in 1956, the Australians thought that the Leeds wicket had been 'patriotically prepared'. It was unquestionably suited to Underwood's medium-paced spin. The Headingley ground staff denied the accusation, of course. They claimed that the grass on the prepared strip had suddenly disappeared as a result of a fungal disease called fusarium, an inadvertent by-product of recent heavy rain. The Australians remained unconvinced by their explanation, though.

Whatever the cause, the Test wicket was clearly sub-standard. Its unbound surface disintegrated early on the first day, allowing extravagant turn. Underwood took match figures of 10-82 as Australia were bundled out twice, for 146 and 136. This left England with only 20 runs to find for victory, and retention of the Ashes. But as was the case in 1956, the pitch was not unplayable as Illingworth (57) and Snow (48) proved during their craggy, eighth-wicket partnership of 104. Together they took England's first innings total to 263, 117 runs in front. Without their resilience, England might not have prevailed, despite Underwood's deadliness. Australia's failure to support Ashley Mallett with a specialist spinner was a crucial oversight, too.

Nevertheless, Australia deservedly squared the series at the Oval, winning by five wickets. England had little chance of preventing an Australian victory with D'Oliveira, Snow and Illingworth disabled at various points during Australia's successful run chase. Twin centuries Ian and Greg Chappell had led the way with a formidable first-innings stand of 201, although Dennis Lillee's superb match figures of 10-181 ensured that England could not set an unreachable winning target. Hell fire and brimstone would await the 'Poms' when battle resumed two years hence.

Illingworth had reason for satisfaction, though. He had retained the Ashes despite not knowing whether he would retain the captaincy for the whole series. Len Hutton had endured similar uncertainty in 1953. However, Illingworth, like his team, was ageing. The need for change was imperative and yet there was a shortage of convincing successors, particularly in the middle order. Among the newcomers only Tony Greig, with his spirited batting and useful medium-paced bowling, seemed to have a bright Test future. As evidence of England's limited batting options, veteran M.J.K. 'Mike' Smith was recalled for the first three Tests, despite his vulnerability against short-pitched bowling. Lillee ruthlessly exploited this weakness, dismissing Smith in four of his six innings. On the Ashes tour of 1970/71, Bob Willis's fiery bowling suggested he would become a fixture in future England sides, but sadly he returned home in a debilitated state, taking some time to recover form. His contractual dispute with his native county, Surrey, did not help either. After moving to Warwickshire, his Test career had to be put on hold while he served a period of qualification for his new county.

'Life In The Fast Lane'
1973 – 1976

England won 21 per cent of 42 Tests played between December 1972 and August 1976

1973

Angie

This was the year of Watergate and a major international oil crisis. With the Arabs sore about a successive defeat by Israel, in the Yom Kippur War, Britain was also made to pay for American Zionist sympathies. There may have been oil in the North Sea but the task of extracting it was fraught with difficulty, requiring hugely expensive technology to be imported, worsening the UK's already troubling trade deficit. Oil yields would remain insignificant until the end of the decade. As a result, we were caught up in a scramble for petrol and shackled with a 50mph speed limit. For several months, petrol rationing seemed inevitable. To add to our winter woes, the coal miners, the railwaymen and the power workers prepared to inflict yet more power cuts and three-day weeks. Without sufficient investment in the long-neglected British manufacturing sector, the Conservative Chancellor of the Exchequer's 'dash for growth' did little to raise British economic prospects, merely raising demand for a glut of foreign goods that pushed up inflation further. Even before Britain felt the full weight of the Arabs' wrath, Tory Chancellor Tony Barber had to scale back public spending severely and raise interest rates.

I then began work as a qualified, if unprepared, social worker. I was soon assigned the responsibility of dealing with out-of-office-hours emergencies on my own. I rescued abandoned infants, returned confused older people to their homes, drove runaway young offenders back to their residential schools, and admitted mentally ill adults to psychiatric hospitals. Without Liz's help, I would not have managed. She once had to cradle a baby in the back of the car while I drove, and later exchanged places as I attempted to restrain an agitated, mentally ill man. Among my memories of this time, one stands out starkly. I was inside a bleak flat, immersed in a brutalised, can-sprayed, concrete warren. I recall being perched tentatively on the arm of a ragged armchair. The hour was small and the heat, absent. I was huddled in a black great-coat, my eyes pricking with fatigue. My distressed client was stomping around the room, gesticulating wildly, oblivious to the cold and the lateness of the hour, his fractured state firing a manic energy. He told me, 'By the marks on my hands and the marks on my feet, I am the man that all should fear.' He said that there were fragments of human bone in his larder. Uneasily, I accepted his invitation to see for myself. As I awaited the overdue ambulance, I heard rustling litter being blown this way and that on the windy walkway outside. Former Velvet Underground bassist John Cale announced, 'Fear is a man's best friend.' I was less sure.

The song I associate with this memory is the Rolling Stones' 'Angie'. It was written by Keith Richards, not in homage to Angie Bowie, as some have claimed, or as a dedication to his daughter Angela as he once suggested, but as an ambivalent farewell to heroin, despite 'angie' also being slang for cocaine. By the early 1970s the perils of addiction were more widely acknowledged in rock music. Lou Reed seemed to imply this in his song 'Perfect Day', and rightly so, as a colleague tragically blew her life away on 'hards' in another part of that same concrete warren.

The winter tours of India and Pakistan were not a success. The England team, led by Oxford double blue Tony Lewis, won the first Test against India but lost the next two, and subsequently the series. It was England's second successive defeat by Ajit Wadekar's men. A weakened side, lacking Boycott, Luckhurst, Edrich, Illingworth and Snow, proved to be no match for the Indian spinners, led by the bewildering Chandrasekhar whose fizzing googlies, top-spinners and occasional leg-breaks accounted for 35 dismissals. In Pakistan, England's cause was helped by Dennis Amiss who finally came good at the top of the order, reaching a maiden Test hundred (112) at Lahore, and making further big scores at Hyderabad (158) and Karachi (99). All three Tests were drawn although the Pakistanis had the better of the first two Tests while a dust storm, and yet more crowd disorder, truncated the third. Illingworth spent the winter at home, earning more as a fireworks salesman than he had done as England's captain. Nevertheless, Tony Lewis led his side well in the Indian subcontinent. He batted well, too, making a debut ton at Kanpur (125), and half-centuries at Delhi (70 not out), in a victorious run chase, and also at Lahore (74) and Karachi (88).

There was some doubt whether Tony Lewis or Illingworth would lead England against the Kiwis. However, once Lewis had been ruled out on grounds of form and fitness, Illingworth resumed the captaincy, but made only one contribution of note with either bat or ball. This was at Headingley where he made 65 runs in the first innings, helping to take the game away from the tourists. Nevertheless, it seemed as if the selectors had other candidates in mind, one being the Kent skipper Mike Denness. He had batted satisfactorily, if unremarkably on the winter tours, averaging 32.13 in India and 34.6 in Pakistan, but did not play in any of the summer Tests.

Under Illingworth's leadership, England beat New Zealand 2-0 in the three-match series. And yet at Trent Bridge, New Zealand failed by only 39 to chase down an improbable winning target of 479, while Fletcher's timely weighty hundred (178) at Lord's propped up a last-day rearguard action. New Zealand captain Bev Congdon was the star of both shows, scoring 176 at Trent Bridge and 175 at Lord's with Vic Pollard supporting him sturdily with centuries at both grounds. Only at Leeds did the Kiwis capitulate as Snow, Arnold and Old despatched them for 142 in their second knock enabling England to win by an innings and one run. However, the resurgent West Indians quickly exposed the fragility of Illingworth's side in the second of the summer series.

England were thrashed by an innings and 226 runs at the Oval, an abject defeat which marked the end of Illingworth's Test career. This was the West Indians' biggest margin of victory over England. Lloyd, Fredericks, Kanhai and Sobers were outstanding with the bat. Even pace bowlers Bernard Julien and Keith Boyce, at eight and nine in the order, played major innings. England were overwhelmed by their opponents with bat and ball, Boyce proving to be decidedly slippery with the latter, taking 19 wickets in all, and 11 in his side's 158-run victory at Lord's.

Illingworth retired from Test cricket at the age of 41. During his time in charge of the England team, he inspired and cajoled his players into producing exceptional performances. His steely leadership, astute tactics, stubborn batting and artful bowling helped England recover a standard of tough competitiveness that had been largely absent since the days of Len Hutton and Peter May. But if England had finished with Illingworth, he had not finished with cricket. As proof of his stature as one of the best English captains, he led a previously unfancied Leicestershire side to four one-day titles and their first County Championship triumph in 1975.

1974

Lady Marmalade

At the 1974 General Election, the Conservative Prime Minister Edward Heath asked the nation who should be running the country – the government or the unions. The nation replied by restoring Harold Wilson to power, although it was hardly a conclusive Labour victory. Despite his prickly and huffy manner, Heath was at heart a consensus politician. He was ultimately undone by the deadly duo of union might and economic blight. With inflation rising by around 14 per cent a year, the press were jumpy about union agitators, restrictive practices and excessive wage claims. The 20 per cent hike in the cost of living during 1974 did little to assuage concerns, as did a 26.5 per cent leap in the average national wage.

There was better news from the Caribbean, though. Tony Greig's startling experimentation with medium-paced off-spin transformed England's fortunes in the final Test at Port-of-Spain. Here, Greig took eight wickets for 86 runs in the West Indians' first innings to reduce them from a position of strength at 224/2 to 305 all out, while his second-innings figures of 5-70 helped England achieve an amazing 26-run victory, and a 1-1 drawn series.

In truth, though, this was a 'smash and grab' raid. The West Indians should have been out of sight before the concluding Test. During the series, England were indebted to Boycott's and Amiss's magnificent efforts at the top of the order, and to some telling knocks from Knott and Greig, who added two centuries to his haul of 24 wickets.

Amiss completed the series with an average score of almost 83. In the first Test at Port-of-Spain, he made 174, albeit in a losing cause. He then made a match-saving 262 not out at Kingston in the second, and 118 at Georgetown in a drenched fourth. Boycott's most important contributions were made in the final Test match, also in Trinidad, where he scored 99 and 112, giving Greig the scope to rescue England with the ball. Apart from Greig, an England attack comprising either Willis, Arnold or Old, or spinners Underwood, Pocock or Birkenshaw, carried little threat. Underwood was particularly disappointing in that he offered little variety in flight, pace or direction, preferring to spear the ball into the batsmen's pads from around the wicket. His five Test wickets cost almost 63 runs each.

Snow's absence made little sense, particularly given his outstanding success on the 1967/68 Caribbean tour. Snow thought that chairman of the selectors, Alec Bedser, had excluded him. England's new captain, Mike Denness thought otherwise, later telling *Daily Telegraph* journalist Hugh Turbervill that it was MCC's 'Gubby' Allen who had vetoed Snow's selection, adding that he had no say in the matter. The Gavaskar incident still rankled, apparently. It is hard to imagine Ray Illingworth accepting this, at least while he was England's captain. Later, as England's manager, he took a different line. George Mann, a much admired amateur captain of Middlesex and England, once said, 'If a player is picked for England, it does not mean that he is naturally easy, or even a nice person. What it does mean is that he is a bloody good cricketer. As a manager or captain, you have to cope with misdemeanours and try to help players to avoid them.' It seems as if his wise counsel was overlooked here.

Amiable Mike Denness had an undistinguished Caribbean tour, averaging less than 26 in his nine Test innings. He was not made in Illingworth's image. Like Colin Cowdrey, his former Kent skipper, he was more deferentially inclined, at least to those in authority. And yet, despite his inexperience at Test level, he seemed reluctant to consult with his senior professionals. This aggravated Geoffrey Boycott who resented the appointment of a relative 'rookie' as England's captain when he believed he had a better claim. It was a contentious issue that would resurface during the summer of 1974.

During that summer, Pakistan provided sturdy opposition whereas India did not, capitulating pitifully to Arnold, Old and new paceman Mike Hendrick, while indulging the England batsmen's insatiable appetite for easy runs. Debutant English opener David Lloyd made an imperturbable, unbeaten double century (214) against the Indians at Edgbaston, while Edrich, Denness and Amiss also filled their boots, each achieving average series scores in excess of 90.

Regrettably, Geoff Boycott withdrew from Test cricket after his soft dismissals by the apparently innocuous Indian opening bowlers, Abid Ali and Solkar. What we hoped would be only a temporary sabbatical turned out to be a three-year exile. Boycott explained his reasons for this in Pilger's and Wightman's book *Match of My Life: The Ashes*. Boycott said that he refused to serve under Denness because he did not respect him as a captain. He was also concerned that he might lose the captaincy of Yorkshire if he did not arrest the slide in their fortunes. In 1973, Yorkshire completed the County Championship fourth from bottom, having won only three times. Their County Championship form in 1974 had not been much better (11th), while their one-day form was awful. Despite heading the Yorkshire first-class batting averages, Boycott was criticised by Yorkshire committee members for not doing more to deliver success. Not feeling able to cut himself in two, as he put it, he opted to leave Test cricket and focus on sorting out his county side. Not having a surfeit of world class batsmen, England could ill afford to lose him, particularly Down Under.

India's 3-0 series defeat by England was so bad that their shattered captain Wadekar immediately announced his retirement from first-class cricket. Several members of his party travelled home under cover or by circuitous routes in order to avoid a public mauling by the angry Indian supporters.

Had England played a five-match series against Pakistan instead, the TCCB selectors might have had a better yardstick in choosing their side to tour Australia and New Zealand, not that they were spoilt for choice. For only on a featherbed surface at the Oval did England bat with any comfort against the exacting seam attack of Sarfraz Nawaz and Asif Masood, and the accurate, probing wrist-spin of Intikhab Alam and Mushtaq Mohammad. Rain played havoc with the other two Tests. All three matches were drawn. However, Pakistan humbled England in both Prudential Cup one-day games. Majid Khan made a scintillating century at Trent Bridge (109) as Pakistan galloped to victory by scoring almost six runs per over.

This dashing run rate was almost unheard of in English one-day cricket. The 1974 Gillette Trophy was won by Kent, having scored only 122 runs in 46.5 overs. As for their losing opponents, Lancashire, featuring the free-hitting Clive Lloyd, they could only muster 118 from their full allocation of

60 overs. It was hardly a blast. The Benson and Hedges Cup Final between Leicestershire and Surrey was little better. In the 1973 winter annual of *The Cricketer*, esteemed coach and former Yorkshire and England fast bowler Bill Bowes said how he deplored the defensiveness miring the one-day game. But his proposed remedy involved a convoluted tinkering with the rules rather than encouraging bolder styles of play.

My year closed with a change of job. The catalyst was another dismal court appearance involving one of many young offenders on my caseload. The boy had been convicted for a minor theft and was ordered to pay a fine by weekly instalments. He thought he could haggle over the size and regularity of these payments. This was too much for a grouchy police officer who hissed in his ear, 'What do you think this is son, a f***ing Christmas club?' The boy's indignation was then magnified when the magistrates demanded that he paid compensation for damaging a police patrol car when arrested. His disgruntled response was to send the police a postal order which read: 'pay the f***ing fuzz, Fifteen f***ing pounds, fifty f***ing pence'. Amazingly, the Post Office paid up.

Adolescent offenders absorbed most of my time, arranging jobs, education, and accommodation, and even fixing a Football League club trial for one. However, I also had legally protective duties for younger children. I had to grasp quickly where the line should be drawn on child safety, and deal with the bitterly contested court cases that ensued. Setting aside my habitual self-deprecation, I learnt how to deal with mocking lawyers who tried to take the player before the ball. My training gave little or no preparation for this. It was simply a battle of wits. The knack was to stick with the most compelling evidence. I am sure I failed to spot some child abuse. It was such a steep learning curve. I hope no child suffered because of my inexperience. I knew, though, that if I was to succeed in this difficult profession, I needed more experience and skill in working with troubled families. This would not happen while I was pursuing young offenders around the police stations, courts and corrective institutions of the north-west. Not that my boss understood this, as he played the grizzled, frontier sheriff to my supposed greenhorn. I had a sense then of how it might feel to face a macho Aussie slip cordon. My farewell was crowned with an impromptu performance of Labelle's sassy, soul-funk classic 'Lady Marmalade' by three female colleagues. Their customary maternal, empathic manner was abruptly shed, as they transformed themselves into a pack of prowling predators. As send-offs go, this one was about as scary as they come.

1975

Gloria: In Excelsis Deo

The England team flew to Australia without two of their best performers – Boycott, who refused to play under Denness, and Snow, who was perversely passed over. No one envisaged the ordeal by fire awaiting them, though. Thus far, Thomson had barely featured in international cricket. He had made just one inauspicious, hobbling Test appearance against Pakistan in December 1972. Unaware that he had broken a bone in his foot, the lame and ultimately wicketless Thomson was thrashed around the MCG by Sadiq Mohammad (137) and Majid Khan (158).

The only Thomson then known to the English Test and County Cricket Board (TCCB) was the underwhelming quick, 'Froggie' Thomson, who had been seen off by Boycott et al during the 1970/71 series. As for Lillee, he had sustained serious back injuries in early 1973, the first symptoms of which had been felt during the 1972 Ashes tour. But Lillee had failed to heed the warning. On a tour of the West Indies six months later, the pain became so bad that it forced his early withdrawal. Lillee was found to have stress fractures in his lower vertebrae. His career hung in the balance. Although surgery was successful, and the intense physiotherapy helped a lot, it was still uncertain whether Lillee would ever recover his former menace. But he proved to be a very determined patient.

Even without Boycott, Denness considered he had sufficient batting power at his disposal. He had a resilient opening pair with John Edrich and Brian Luckhurst. In reserve he had David Lloyd who had made a spectacular start to Test cricket. Meanwhile, Dennis Amiss had added to his burgeoning reputation as a prolific run-maker. In the middle order Denness had Keith Fletcher's experience, Tony Greig's bludgeoning power and Alan Knott's impish improvisations. He also believed that he might have a pace attack of greater menace, in Geoff Arnold, Chris Old, Mike Hendrick, Bob Willis and Peter Lever. Battle-hardened Aussie captain Ian Chappell knew better, though, as did his brother Greg. Lillee seemed to be recovering quicker and better than anyone had anticipated, and in Jeff Thomson they thought they might have Australia's fastest ever bowler. They were not about to let on about their weapons of mass destruction, though.

Queensland captain Greg Chappell kept Thomson well under wraps. When England arrived in Queensland for the state game, just prior to the first Test, Chappell told Thomson to 'just f*** around'. Thomson duly pulled his punches, leaving England with little warning of the hail of thunderbolts that would be coming their way a few days later.

What was so disconcerting about Thomson was that he achieved his extreme speed from a casual, shuffling approach. His power seemed to derive from his immense shoulder strength and the elasticity of his upper body. In reaching the crease he suddenly swung his body around into a sideways position, his left leg extended high in the delivery stride, in the style of a kick-boxer. His guiding left arm was thrust aloft, while his right bowling arm was flung well behind him, where its slinging release was loaded with a pronounced arching of the back, similar to a javelin thrower. Like Charlie Griffith, Thomson exacted frightening lift from deliveries pitched just short of a length, while his toe-crushing yorkers were equally devastating. But unlike Griffith, Thomson achieved this with an action that was beyond reproach. Needing to guard his healing back, Lillee was not yet at full pace, but he was no slouch, being quicker than anyone in the England pace pack, with the possible exception of Willis. And in reserve there was the admirable seam bowling of Max Walker, who like 'Froggy' Thomson and the South African Mike Proctor, bowled off his 'wrong' right foot.

At Brisbane, when replying to Australia's first innings score of 309, only two England batsmen defied their ordeal by fire for long. These two were the valiant and durable John Edrich (48), and boldly destructive Tony Greig (112). Greig seemed to be the only member of Denness's side capable of taking the fight to Lillee and Thomson. Time and again, he used his great height to smash their kicking deliveries through and over cover while also flipping their bouncers over the slip cordon, sending the ball scuttling to the third man boundary. Greig refused to be cowed, goading Lillee and Thomson by imperiously sweeping his right arm back and forth whenever one of his crashing shots found the boundary. The faster they bowled at him, the harder Greig hit out. Greig won these mind games, hands down. Lillee and Thomson were so incensed by his provocation that, instead of probing the technical deficiencies in his cavalier style, they settled for redundant head-hunting, not helped by a febrile Australian crowd lusting for revenge.

At the close of the England innings, Ian Chappell berated Lillee and Thomson for allowing themselves to be suckered into mindless retaliation, which enabled England to recover strongly from their wobbly position at 168/7. Almost 100 runs were added by England's last three wickets, leaving Denness's side only 44 short of the Australian first-innings score. Lillee and Thomson heeded their captain's instruction in the fourth innings, though, when England were chasing a tough victory target of 332. When Greig returned to the crease, with England in a heap of trouble at 94/4, Thomson pitched on a fuller length. Greig had only made two runs when Thomson speared a sizzling yorker beneath his extravagant backlift and took out the middle stump. Thomson captured six wickets for 46 as England lost by 166 runs.

Edrich and Amiss were then ruled out of the following Test at Perth having sustained respective fractures of the hand and thumb, collateral damage of the Brisbane firestorm. With England in urgent need of reinforcement, Cowdrey loyally answered the call despite having not played in a Test match for over three years. He was quickly drafted into the side for the second Test at Perth, impressing with his courageous determination to move into line against the Australians' heavy artillery. But as sound as his technique still was, he no longer had the speed of reaction to counter-attack, particularly on Perth's fiery track. Nevertheless, in the second innings, when England faced a deficit of 273, Cowdrey creditably scored 41 as an emergency opener in a 62-run first wicket partnership. He could do little, though, to help avert another crushing

England defeat. Meanwhile, the casualty list was growing. Lloyd was the latest victim, having been hit in the groin by a venomous delivery from Thomson that splintered his protective box. Lloyd joked that the blow had caused his voice to rise by a few octaves.

The Perth Test was distinguished by a destructive century by Australian Doug Walters. He had endured a wretched tour of England in 1972 when his vulnerability outside the off stump was ruthlessly exposed by Arnold and Snow. But here he had taken his revenge, walloping 103 runs, and completing his hundred with a massive pulled six off Willis, from the last ball of the day, to win a handsome bet.

At Melbourne, England recovered lost pride by holding Australia to a tight draw. Defying pain from his damaged knees, Willis bowled magnificently in the first innings, taking 5-61. He was largely responsible for hauling his side back into the game after England had been dismissed for 242 with only Cowdrey (35), Edrich (49) and Knott (52) displaying much staying power. Willis's task was made even more daunting when Hendrick broke down with a pulled hamstring after bowling only a couple of overs.

When England batted again, one run ahead of their hosts, Amiss (90) and Lloyd (44) added 115 runs for the first wicket. But once off-spinner Mallett had made the initial breakthrough, Lillee and Thomson ran through the rest of the English batting order although Greig (60) resisted doughtily. Greig then led a fightback with the ball, worthily assisted by veteran off-spinner Fred Titmus. Together they achieved disconcerting turn as Australia circumspectly pursued a 246-run winning target. Eventually the Aussies ran out of time, but it was a close call. When stumps were drawn Australia were merely eight runs short of their target with two wickets to spare.

Any hope England had of thwarting Australia's recovery of the Ashes disappeared at Sydney, where the hosts won by 171 runs on the final afternoon with just 4.3 overs remaining. Denness had controversially dropped himself following a miserable run of form. His deputy, Edrich, did better, batting well before having his ribs broken by a sharp, rising delivery from Lillee. Forced to retire at 70/2, when his dogged defence had given England an outside chance of saving the game and possibly the series, Edrich was unable to return until the fall of the sixth wicket, by which time hope had almost vanished.

It was Thomson's turn to retire hurt at Adelaide after he tore fibres in his right shoulder while playing tennis during the rest day. Although unable to bowl again in the series, his 33-wicket haul was the third highest achieved by an Australian in an Ashes rubber. Ian Chappell was not unduly troubled by Thomson's loss, though, as Australia won easily by 163 runs. For England, their only saving graces were Knott's unbeaten century (106) and Underwood's best match figures of the series, 11-215.

The result of the sixth and final Test at Melbourne underlined how reliant the Australians had been upon the combined threat of Lillee and Thomson.

With Thomson already ruled out, and Lillee reduced to bowling just six overs before hobbling off with a foot injury, England were able to bat in much greater comfort. And how they exploited this with Denness (188), Fletcher (146), Greig (89) and Edrich (70) making hay. England's first-innings score of 529 was sufficient for them to win by an innings and one run. After a wicketless display at Brisbane, Lever ensured that his final Ashes appearance was more glorious, capturing a match-winning haul of 9-103.

England then moved on to New Zealand. Denness scored another big Test hundred (181) in Auckland, while Fletcher made a double century (216), enabling England to thrash their hosts by an innings and 83 runs. However, the game was overshadowed by a horrific head injury suffered by Kiwi pace bowler Ewan Chatfield, having been struck on the temple by a lifting ball from Peter Lever. Chatfield sustained a hairline fracture of the skull, a blow which caused his heart to temporarily stop beating. Had England's physiotherapist Bernard Thomas not been so vigilant, Chatfield might have lost his life. Peter Lever was distraught at Chatfield's plight. Fortunately Chatfield made a full recovery and continued to play Test cricket. But for Lever it was a distressing conclusion to his Test career.

Time was about to be called on Denness's Test career, too. This came after England's heavy defeat by Australia at Edgbaston on Bastille Day in 1975. This was the first of four Test matches which followed the inaugural Prudential World Cup competition, won by the West Indies in a gripping final with Australia at Lord's. At Edgbaston, just about everything went wrong for Denness. He won the toss and invited Australia to bat in conditions apparently conducive to seam bowling. However, Rick McCosker and Alan Turner, his new opening partner, put on 80 for the first wicket as Australia proceeded to make 359 by mid-afternoon on the second day. The skies then darkened and a thunderstorm broke over the ground. When it passed, England found they had to bat for three hours on a juicy wicket in gloomy light, with Lillee and Max Walker in devastating form. England limped to 101 all out. They did not do much better when asked to follow on. Denness had a dismal match with the bat, too, mustering 11 runs from two attempts. It was unsurprising that the combative Tony Greig was appointed in his place for the next Test at Lord's. Although mercurial, brash and sometimes volatile, Greig proved to be the charismatic and inspirational leader that England needed.

Realising the English middle order was vulnerable, Greig took soundings from Illingworth and Close about how he might strengthen here. They both suggested he had a look at the Northamptonshire batsman David Steele. Appearances were deceptive. The prematurely greying Steele seemed like a mild-mannered civil servant, but beneath his calm, businesslike demeanour was a cricketer of considerable skill and tenacity. Helped by the docility of the wickets prepared for the remainder of this series, Steele immediately lived up to his name, thrusting his left leg well forward in blunting the Australian pace menace, while rocking on to the back foot whenever possible to cut, hook or clip the ball away behind square.

Greig (96), helped by Steele (50) and Knott (69), transformed England's fortunes at Lord's, helping his team post a respectable first innings score of 315. This came after Lillee had reduced England to 49/4. Having re-emerged from the cold, Snow promptly reminded us of what we had missed by taking four wickets as Australia subsided to 133/8. However, Ross Edwards (99) and Lillee (73 not out) then led a bullish recovery, enabling Australia to reach 268. Although Edrich produced an unruffled, dominant hundred (175), his last in Test cricket, Australia saved the game with comfort on the last day.

The somnolent cricket played in the latter stages of the game was too much for merchant seaman, Michael Angelow. He became the ground's first 'streaker'. BBC TV commentator John Arlott described the incident thus, 'We have got a freaker down the wicket now. Not very shapely and it is masculine. He is being embraced by a blond policeman and this may well be his last public appearance – but what a splendid one!' The two remaining Tests also ended in draws, helped by sluggish surfaces and David Steele's adhesive batting. Nevertheless, England recovered some lost pride and confidence, despite losing the series 1-0.

Steele's summer achievements won him the BBC Sports Personality of the Year award. Dubbed as 'a bank clerk marching to war', his copious fund of Test runs earned him a huge consignment of meat from his local butcher who promised to supply him with a chop for each Test run he scored and a steak for each fifty. For the first time in the history of British farming, livestock tuned in to *Test Match Special*.

While driving to Headingley for the fourth day's play, Patti Smith's 'Gloria: In Excelsis Deo' came on the radio. Patti Smith was one part a scowling punk poet, and four parts a proto 'Riot Grrrl'. With 'Gloria: In Excelsis Deo' she reinvented Van Morrison's paean to raw heterosexuality as a fantasised lesbian lust-fest, introduced with a growling sneer at Christ's atonement and climaxing with Morrison's glorious chorus. It provided the perfect, high octane start to a day of palpitating action.

Tony Greig seemed similarly wired as he thumped each of Jeff Thomson's first three deliveries to the cover boundary. Steele (92) played fluently while the nimble Knott (31) extemporised cheekily, using his reversed top-hand grip to flip the shorter balls over the slips or leg-side catchers. Collectively, they lifted the England total to 291, setting Australia 445 runs to win. Sadly, this compelling contest fizzled out after the pitch was vandalised on the fourth night by the 'Free George Davis' campaigners. It was alleged that Davis had been wrongfully convicted for armed robbery. However, with heavy rain setting in at Tuesday lunchtime it was unlikely that the game would have been completed. This Test match also featured the remarkable debut of young Middlesex left-arm spinner Phil Edmonds, who took 5-28 in the Australian first innings. However, he was the fortunate beneficiary of three shockingly soft dismissals. There were no such easy pickings for him in the second innings or in the final Test at the Oval. It was here that Rick McCosker (127) and Ian Chappell (192) secured the Australians' 1-0 series lead by taking their team to an unbeatable first innings total of 532/9 declared. Thanks to major contributions from Woolmer (149), Edrich (96), Roope (77), Steele (66) and Knott (64), England evaded defeat easily.

1976
Dancing Queen

It took me a long time to appreciate arid places. Being my parents' son, limited horizons were taken for granted. For years, my idea of a holiday jaunt was a grey, choppy trip off the 'Costa Geriatrica' fortified by a zipped-up windcheater. This seemed so much better than cowering in the quavering heat of those dusty, sun-bleached Mediterranean resorts. But my blinkered calculations were confounded by the British summers of the mid-1970s. If the summer of 1975 was unseemly hot, that of 1976 was hotter still. Temperatures topped 30°C on 21 days. A Surrey local paper declared 'Woking Del Sol' while a national tabloid urged us to 'share a bath with a friend and save water'. Rivers dried up, ponds disappeared, trees wilted and crops failed just like 'grovelling' Tony Greig and his humiliated England cricketers. Large crevices appeared in the baked clay beds of the receding reservoirs. Ladybower Reservoir in the Peak District was compelled to reveal the village it had once drowned. It seemed like an exhumation.

So did the selection of the 45-year-old Brian Close. On a frayed, corrugated wicket at Old Trafford, he bravely defied the ferocity of the West Indian pace trio Holding, Roberts and Daniel, taking countless hits on his body, which left him with a mass of dark contusions, angry welts and seam tattoos. Downing a restorative Scotch with alacrity, Close dismissed the suggestion that he should have a precautionary X-ray, quipping that his body might be battered, but it had stripped the new ball of its shine. His unflinching opening stand with the equally hardy John Edrich remains as one of the most courageous acts I have seen on a cricket field.

It was to no avail. Once their second innings partnership was broken at 54 runs, no one else had the cussedness or durability to stay for long. In a clatter of falling wickets, England staggered to a 425-run defeat. The TCCB rewarded Close and Edrich for their outstanding bravery by never asking them to play for their country again. Steele's Test career was ended abruptly, and surely prematurely, after scoring more runs than any other England batsman at Manchester. He had also made a debut Test ton at Trent Bridge (106), and a half-century at Lord's (64), in helping keep the West Indians at bay. Steele, Close and Edrich remained reproachfully at the head of England's batting averages for the entire series.

While their defiance was admired, the brutality of the West Indian pace attack was not. Not that this concerned their captain Clive Lloyd. He had been equally unmoved by Bedi's protests at the decimation of the Indian batsmen at Sabina Park during the previous winter. Here, the Indian captain had controversially declared his side's second innings closed at 306/6, thereby forfeiting the match. With two batsmen unfit to return, Bedi made this decision out of concern for the safety of his tail-enders.

Only at Headingley did England possess a pace attack with sufficient bite and retaliatory fire to trouble their opponents. It was the only time in this series when England's fastest bowlers, Snow, Ward and Willis, were fit enough to play together. Unbowed by the punishment meted out by Fredericks, Greenidge, Richards and Rowe, this trio proved to be as penetrative as the West Indian pace quartet. Between them, they took 18 wickets in this match, helping England's centurions Greig (116) and Knott (116) to set up a winning opportunity on the last day. However, Wayne Daniel's fiery burst on the final morning left England 56 runs short.

The West Indian openers Roy Fredericks and Gordon Greenidge cut, hooked and drove with spectacular savagery throughout the series, but England's greatest punishment was inflicted by Viv Richards's flashing blade. Richards seemed to be a man on a mission, determined not only to win the series but to demoralise his English opponents also. Away from the heat of battle, Richards was a warm and engaging personality, but once on the field of play his swagger and flinty expression said it all. While he had a tendency to play around his front pad, sometimes hitting across the line, while he retained his uncommon sharpness of vision this was rarely an exploitable weakness. Convinced of his invincibility, Richards hit the ball all around the wicket with contemptuous power, and not just off poor bowling. He positioned himself so quickly, instantly identifying length and line. No field or bowling ruse seemed capable of halting him once he had stamped his authority at the crease. Richards averaged almost 120 runs per innings in the five-match series, helped by a brace of double centuries, the second of which came at the Oval (291) which set up a 231-run victory and a 3-0 series win.

Before the series began, Greig declared to a sceptical journalist that England had a good prospect of winning. Frustrated at the reporter's negativity, Greig talked up his team's chances, with typical bumptiousness, pointing out that while the West Indians were on top they were extraordinary cricketers, but when they were not, 'they grovel'. He added that his team intended to make them grovel. 'Grovel' was a particularly offensive term to those whose forebears had endured abhorrent slavery. Greig's South African background only inflamed the West Indian recriminations. They were determined to make England pay, and Greig in particular. Regrettably, he had allowed his irrepressible competitive zeal to overcome his better judgement, as he freely admitted afterwards. Greig was not a racist, though, and when he prostrated himself penitentially before the West Indian supporters at the Oval, they generously acknowledged his humility.

With the series resulting in record takings of £950,000, Greig's *faux pas* had proved to be good business, particularly with so many of a Caribbean heritage eager to see Greig being made to eat his words. The National Front might have attracted a fifth of the votes cast at a Leicester by-election, but in a continuous cacophony of clanging cans and beating drums the West Indian cricketers had re-asserted the pride and prowess of black African-Caribbean people.

In the late summer of 1976, the British singles charts were dominated by the Swedish pop phenomenon that was ABBA. Their song 'Dancing Queen', sung in glorious alto harmony by the twin female leads, swooned across the radio airwaves. 'Dancing Queen' presaged the heyday of disco, to be celebrated a year later with the cinematic blockbuster *Saturday Night Fever* and Donna Summer's dancefloor classic, 'I Feel Love'. If punk fed on drabness, decay and disillusionment, disco offered a swish, colourful and sparkling alternative.

On the final morning of the Test at the Oval I was asked to drive a troubled 15-year-old boy to a residential child psychiatric unit. His social worker had rung in sick so I substituted. But when I arrived at the boy's home he seemed unaware of why I had come, or at least that was what he told me. He was a cricket fan. I found him in his bedroom, sat in front of a small portable television waiting for the TV Test coverage to begin. He showed me an exercise book in which he had been scoring each day's play. He had recorded every ball, for here were the full details of Amiss's and Richards's double tons. I was concerned by his vagueness, though, so I spoke with his adoptive parents. They confirmed that they had been expecting me, but were initially evasive about what their son thought about his admission. I asked whether they would help in clarifying the situation with him but they refused. The father maintained that his son knew what was happening and why, and thought it better if they did not go over it again with him. He spoke resentfully of his son's destructive rages while his wife remained silent. I sensed that he felt cheated by the adoption process. Neither parent was young. They seemed frightened of their boy's growing strength. As uncomfortable as I felt about how their boy's departure was being handled, I decided I must trust my colleagues' decisions.

I returned to the boy and asked whether there was anything he wished to ask me. He was watching the Test match by this time. Without taking his eyes off the screen, he gave a noncommittal answer, then started elaborating upon the poor state of English cricket. So I asked him whether he would like me to help him pack. I wasn't sure whether this might spark an angry reaction. To my surprise, he stood up, reached for a suitcase and silently filled it with his belongings. He then turned off the TV and filed his scoring book and pens away in a drawer. As he left the house he did not bid his parents farewell and they did not acknowledge his departure. I put my head around the door of their lounge, just in case they had not realised we were leaving. The father looked at me momentarily and mumbled something inaudible. The mother just stared at the floor. I left them a card with the unit's contact details and said the boy's social worker would be in touch shortly. Once in the car, I asked the boy whether he would like the radio commentary on. He declined but continued to talk about cricket until our arrival at the unit. He ignored my attempts at discussing what he might expect there.

Whenever I reflect upon that day, I see a parched Oval, its herringbone drainage system skeletally exposed in the glaring sunlight. I see Holding's lithe acceleration, his graceful leap, his sleek, high action and his effusion of bumpers and blistering yorkers. I see a freeze frame of Greig in stooped dejection, his leg stump is pinged out, and the middle one is leaning awry. On this supposedly flat track, Holding had decimated the England batting, twice flattening Greig's stumps.

But I also see an image of that unhappy boy with dishevelled blond hair. I hope that in the short time we spent together, talking mainly about cricket, he found a comforting diversion. And yet I remain displeased with the part I played in his cold parting from his home. The unit required the full commitment of their young patients and their families if their therapeutic work was to be successful. In this boy's case, that commitment seemed absent. All I could detect was stubbed-out hope. The unit was not intended to be a halfway house for care, yet that is what it became, for the boy never returned home. His admission still feels like an abdication of responsibility in which all of us were complicit. I still wonder what became of him.

'Anarchy In The UK'
1977 – 1979

*England won 55 per cent of 33 Tests played between
December 1976 and September 1979*

1977
Pretty Vacant

With the economy spluttering and the pound falling sharply, Labour Chancellor of the Exchequer, Denis Healey, looked to the International Monetary Fund for financial help. The price was punitive – swingeing cuts in public spending of six per cent and eight per cent over the next two years. As it turned out the crisis was not as bad as was first feared. The Treasury's figures were shown to be untrustworthy with the estimated public-sector borrowing requirement overstated. But if the patient was not terminally ill, it was still ailing. At least the crisis gave Prime Minister Callaghan the leverage to turn off the subsidy tap for unproductive commercial ventures, such as at British Leyland. In February 1977, the British Leyland bosses laid down the gauntlet to 'Red Robbo' and his striking car workers. They announced, 'End the strike or face plant closures.' It was about time

The tawdry, decrepit, seedy image of Britain in the late 1970s spawned a 'bleak chic'. Apart from punk rock and fashions, there were nihilistic films such as *Radio On*, *O Lucky Man!* and *Jubilee*. There were novels, too, describing emotionally impoverished lives as in *The Ice Age*, *High Rise*, *Dead Babies* and *The Cement Garden*. And yet this year was meant to be one of patriotic celebration – Queen Elizabeth's Silver Jubilee. Virginia Wade did her patriotic best by winning the women's singles at Wimbledon, while the England cricket team, fresh from their impressive triumph on India's low, slow turners, recovered the Ashes from the visiting Australians.

This was England's first home Ashes victory since 1956 and how I enjoyed the occasion. Because it was then still possible to turn up on spec for a Test match, Liz and I watched the decisive phases in play at Manchester, Trent Bridge and Leeds. At Manchester, the game-changer was Derek Underwood, but at Trent Bridge it was Geoffrey Boycott. Here, he renounced his self-imposed Test exile and batted and batted and batted. Aghast at his running-out of local hero Derek Randall, he atoned for his error by making a first-innings century (107) and by taking England to a seven-wicket victory with an unbeaten 80.

With mum once again restored to better mental health, she and dad joined us as we reclined on Scarborough's sunny castle cliff taking in the sparkling sea, the hurdy-gurdy fairground sound and the gliding gulls, while listening to *Test Match Special* commentary from Trent Bridge. Here, Boycott and his opening partner Brearley (81) were driving England to the brink of victory and a 2-0 series lead.

Liz and I, and a huge contingent of Barnsley colliers, then watched Boycott progress patiently to his 100th first-class century at Leeds (191). Sat on the rowdy Headingley western terraces, Liz and I found ourselves surrounded by a massive wall of Watney Party Seven beer cans, constructed, rather precariously, by Boycott's cheerily inebriated 'kinfolk'. We thought heaven help us if Geoffrey fails in his mission. This group of ardent supporters were likely to kick the lot over in frustration, leaving us buried under tons of metal. Thankfully, Geoffrey did not choke, punching Greg Chappell's half-volley through mid-on to take him to his coveted goal and towards an Ashes-winning total. As well as England played, the Australians seemed distracted by the rift brought about by Kerry Packer's World Series Cricket.

Kerry Packer was the audacious chairman of Australian TV Channel 9. He was furious that the Australian Cricket Board refused to do business with him. He wanted the exclusive TV rights to cover Australian Test matches, and bid considerably more for this than his rival, the Australian Broadcasting Corporation. But the Australian Cricket Board would not accept his bid. So, he decided to set up a rival international cricket competition, World Series Cricket (WSC), which Channel 9 would cover. By offering lucrative financial incentives he managed to contract 51 current or former international players for WSC. Eighteen of these were current Australian Test players, including the Chappell brothers, Redpath, Walters, Marsh, Walker and Lillee. The England contingent comprised Greig, Knott, Woolmer, Underwood, Snow and, eventually, Amiss. Meanwhile, others were recruited from Pakistan, South Africa and the West Indies, including Viv Richards and Andy Roberts.

The International Cricket Council (ICC) took a dim view of this. Although the Australian and English 'defectors' were allowed to participate in the 1977 Ashes series, the battle lines were being drawn. However, the Test and County Cricket Board (TCCB) decided to relieve Greig of the England captaincy which was understandable since he had breached their trust by acting as Packer's clandestine recruiting officer while retaining this position.

The Times's cricket correspondent John Woodcock reacted by disparaging Greig's credentials, claiming that he was 'only English by adoption' which was not 'the same thing as being English through and through'. The mud-slinging had begun in earnest.

Greig attempted to defend himself by stating that he had acted in the best interests of his Test colleagues whom he considered to be under-remunerated. It was a moot point, though, whether self-interest was the greater part of his self-ascribed valour. But English Test cricketers were under-remunerated, just as the English Football League players had been before Jimmy Hill's successful campaign for the abolition of the maximum wage in 1961. But whereas Hill had encouraged those whom he represented to break their contracts with their employing clubs, Greig did no such thing with regard to his English recruits.

An England player could serve WSC in the winter months without infringing his contractual obligations to his employing county. Of course, what galled the TCCB was that WSC was depriving them of their leading players during England's winter tours. But since there was no contract of employment between the TCCB and its Test players, it had no jurisdiction over what they chose to do during the winter.

As far as the various national cricket boards were concerned, WSC represented an affront to their authority. They had become accustomed to calling the shots on all aspects of the game, particularly what players earned from Test cricket. Besides, WSC represented a considerable financial threat should Test match revenues dwindle because of Packer 'defections'. The cricket authorities' best hope seemed to be that WSC would fall flat on its face, with the 'Packer circus' seen by the watching public as a poor alternative to Test and one-day international (ODI) cricket. Initially, it seemed as if this hope might be realised, but after the dismal, one-sided Ashes series of 1978/79, the Australian public found WSC's razzamatazz more appealing, and turned to the Packer games in their thousands. Certainly, there was little prospect that the TCCB or any other national cricket board could entice their Test players away from WSC by offering better earnings.

As Bob Willis explained in his autobiography *Lasting the Pace*, the financial benefits of joining the Packer 'circus' were considerable. Willis was offered around £15,000 per year by WSC over a five-year period, before win bonuses and advertising deals were taken into account. When this offer was put to him, he was then receiving £210 for each home Test match appearance and around £3,000 for a winter tour. This was on top of a senior county player's salary of around £3,500 per year although overseas stars were paid up to three times this figure. Consequently, the £15,000 annual salary offered by WSC to Willis was almost double the figure he earned by playing county and Test cricket, without taking into account bonuses or commercial endorsements.

Although Cornhill Insurance's £1m Test match sponsorship enabled the TCCB to raise its Test match appearance fee to £1,000 per home Test, and its winter tour payment to £5,000, this still did not provide an English Test cricketer with a comparable level of pay to that being offered by WSC. While an English player continued to draw a county salary, he was around £4,000 a year better off playing with WSC, even if he was no longer selected by England to play Test cricket.

Given the greater financial benefit offered by a WSC contract, the TCCB sought to deter English players from joining the Packer initiative by imposing a Test *and* county cricket ban upon all those deciding to sign up. It was thought that this measure would substantially reduce the cash incentive of joining WSC, while provoking a fear among its signatories that they would be forced out of the game, as a consequence of being denied access to English first-class cricket.

However, the TCCB threat was deemed to be illegal. High Court judge Mr Justice Slade ruled that it was an attempt to break a legitimate contract between two third parties – that is between WSC and its English cricketers who had a contractual relationship with their counties and *not* with the TCCB. Mr Justice Slade also ruled that the TCCB ban was tantamount to a wrongful restraint of trade, a matter which had already been subject to legal scrutiny in a sports context. For, in a landmark High Court judgement in 1963, Newcastle United were judged to have acted unlawfully by preventing their player, George Eastham, from playing for another club of his choosing when his contract with Newcastle had expired. Newcastle had attempted to hold Eastham to ransom by retaining his Football League registration, which was in effect his licence to play English professional football. Their message to Eastham was play for us or not at all in England. The TCCB was equally culpable by attempting to impose a ban which would deny the WSC 'defectors' the opportunity to play English first-class cricket. It had also wrongfully sought to deny English cricketers the opportunity of increasing their earnings by playing for WSC during the winter months, when this did not interfere with their contractual obligations to their employing counties. As a result of its misguided legal action, the TCCB faced public humiliation and £250,000 losses in legal costs. Its members were hardly pleased to discover that their Australian counterparts, whom they sought to support by this proposed ban, had decided to come to terms with Packer.

Robin Marlar, a former Cambridge blue and Sussex captain, was incensed that a media tycoon should dare to challenge the will of the cricketing authorities. In May 1977, he and Jim Laker were invited to participate in an open debate with Packer on *The Frost Programme*. While the laconic Laker remained restrained, Marlar angrily berated the Channel 9 mogul for 'not knowing how to behave'. But Packer proved too deft for the irascible Marlar, easily outwitting him with a confident, amusing and clearly articulated account of his actions and aims.

Eventually, peace broke out with compromise and conciliation replacing confrontation. But while English WSC players, such as Knott, Woolmer and Underwood, were restored successfully to their Test and county cricket folds, not all of the WSC 'defectors' were happily re-accommodated. Sussex reluctantly dispensed with Greig's services on account of the ill will his WSC recruitment role had aroused among the county 'loyalists'. Nottinghamshire and Lancashire went as far as petitioning the TCCB to have Sussex expelled from the County Championship when they attempted to re-appoint Greig as their captain in 1978. And while Asif Iqbal remained as a player with Kent, his county club thought it diplomatic to relieve him of the captaincy, lest this arouse the angry reactions that had been directed at Sussex. As for Dennis Amiss, he found himself ostracised by his Warwickshire team-mates. Much to the chagrin of many of their members, Warwickshire County Cricket Club felt they should not renew Amiss's contract when it came to an end.

Packer closed his 'circus' in 1979, having obtained from the chastened Australian Board of Control exactly what he wanted in the first place. Thereafter, all of the Australian WSC players became eligible for Test selection once more – albeit at a higher rate of pay. The cash-strapped West Indian and Pakistani Boards followed suit, despite incurring indigestible costs. They, too, faced 'loyalist' resentment. Ultimately, the legacy of the Packer 'revolution' was to bring about important changes in how the players, the watching public and commercial interests were considered by those who ran the game.

With the higher WSC pay deals raising its players sense of their financial worth, henceforth, professional cricketers would exercise greater clout in negotiating their pay, and in determining who they would play for and where, as the 1980s 'rebel tours' of South Africa illustrated. As had happened in English football after the abolition of the maximum wage, the administrators were no longer able to dictate the players' conditions of service as they had before. Closer consideration had to be given to players' safety requirements, too. While the ICC and the national boards of control seemed to do little to protect their players from the hazards of intimidating fast bowling, WSC responded quickly to the injury of its Australian player David Hookes by introducing the mandatory usage of protective helmets.

WSC also demonstrated greater flexibility in accommodating the interests of the watching public, by arranging games at unfamiliar and remote venues and by meeting a public appetite for floodlit limited-over games that fitted in better with the spectators' work and family commitments. As proof of that, over 44,000 turned up at Sydney Cricket Ground in 1978 to watch a floodlit WSC game. Without WSC it is unlikely that this innovation would have been adopted not only in Australia, but also in South Africa, the Indian sub-continent and the West Indies. Although there was greater scepticism about floodlit cricket in England, at least up until the 2000s, this was because of concerns about the cost of implementation in a country renowned for its unpredictable weather.

Besides making its entertainment more accessible and conveniently-timed for the spectators, WSC enhanced the attractiveness of what was on show, not only by staging intensely contested games involving the world's best players, but by its shrewd marketing, as revealed by its eye-arresting advertising, its catchy jingles, and its range of merchandise. The razzamatazz that surrounds current limited-over games owes much to the vibrancy of WSC innovations. As much as this may seem irritating to traditionalists, like me, even I have to concede this is a widely welcomed element of a modern entertainment package.

And surely the lesson to be drawn from the bitter feud that raged between Packer and the Australian board over TV rights, is that commercial organisations needed to be encouraged and welcomed as potential partners and friends of cricket, rather than haughtily spurned or treated with suspicion, if the game is to sustain itself as an attractive, financially-viable, public spectacle. In short, the WSC initiative suggested that the game needed to be run in ways that incentivise and benefit the innovators at least as much as the traditionalists if professional cricket is to survive in a rapidly changing, commercially-competitive world.

The impact of the Packer revolution upon the English cricket establishment was much like the impact of punk culture upon conservative Britain. With both Packer and punk stirring febrile moral panics, the resulting ascriptions of folk devilry assumed Salem-like proportions. Whereas Robin Marlar confronted the allegedly villainous Kerry Packer with righteous indignation, ITV *Today* presenter Bill Grundy confronted the supposedly notorious Sex Pistols with scoffing disdain. And both came a cropper. Looking to make fools of the band, Grundy unwisely goaded them into making puerile, foul-mouthed comments live on prime-time television. While Grundy's TV career fell apart as a result, the band's notoriety ratings shot up stratospherically. Frontman John Lydon (aka Johnny Rotten) knew which buttons to press in pumping up the outrage. Hamming up Sir Laurence Olivier's risible *Richard the Third* characterisation, Lydon sneered in 'Pretty Vacant' that the band was permanently 'out to lunch'. Steve Jones's caustic riff, nicked improbably from the ABBA hit 'SOS', underscored their sardonic point. It was all too much for London's river police who halted the Pistols' boat concert as it reached Westminster, deeming their iconoclastic performance to be disrespectful to Her Majesty during her Jubilee. Had they mistaken the Pistols' song 'Anarchy in the UK' for the real thing? Punk, both edgy and confrontational, probably gave rock music its last rebel yell for thereafter that distinction would belong mainly to hip-hop.

1978

Sex and Drugs and Rock 'n' Roll

The 1977/78 tour of Pakistan was a dismal affair, not helped by the resentment aroused by the Pakistan board's decision to fly back its three

WSC cricketers – Imran Khan, Zaheer Abbas and Mushtaq Mohammad – with Packer's approval, to take part in the third Test. It was an action opposed by the 'loyalists' on both sides. Following negotiations conducted with the TCCB, the Pakistan board withdrew their invitation to the WSC players and the game went ahead. This was much to Geoffrey Boycott's relief as he had been chosen to captain the side in the absence of the injured Ashes-winning skipper Mike Brearley. While Boycott was delighted to achieve his cherished ambition, the game, like the series, ended in a bore draw. Sarfraz's first ball of the rubber bounced twice before reaching wicketkeeper Bari, and thereafter, there was little improvement in the pace of the wickets or in the speed of the play, with England labouring to stay in the game in all three Tests. According to Bob Willis, the hospitality was not up to much either. He described their accommodation as cold, the rooms cramped and spartan, lacking any hot water for bathing, while the food was limited in choice and flavour.

But the England players' delight at moving on to New Zealand evaporated quickly after being hammered on a shocking wicket at Wellington. Here, Richard Hadlee took 6-26 in England's second innings, as Boycott's men collapsed to 64 all out, losing by 72 runs. It was England's first defeat by New Zealand in 48 Test matches, and their lowest score since being annihilated by Bradman's 'Invincibles' at the Oval in 1948.

Tall and rangy, with a military officer's bearing, Richard Hadlee proved to be a formidable foe. From a relaxed, rhythmic approach, he delivered the ball with an economical, high action which made the most of his wiry strength. With a classical side-on stance and bowling close to the stumps, he was as accurate as Brian Statham. And like Statham he presumed that if the batsman missed, he would hit. Hadlee rarely gave any easy pickings. He was capable of bowling with the utmost hostility, but cleverly varied his pace, commanding impressive control of cut and curve. And like Ian Botham, he was a belligerent, game-changing batsman.

After the Wellington fiasco, Ian Botham stepped up to become the star of the show at Christchurch. Here, he recorded his maiden Test ton (103) and had match figures of 8-111, helping England to a 174-run victory. The final Test at Auckland was played on the one true surface of the tour. Kiwi Geoff Howarth scored a century in each innings while Middlesex batsman Clive Radley ground out a weighty first Test ton (158), which was then the fourth slowest on record. The match was drawn as was the series.

The summer of 1978 belonged largely to Botham and Gower. A lightweight Pakistan side, deprived of the injured Sarfraz for much of the first Test and all of the second, proved no match for Botham, who averaged 70.66 with the bat and 16.07 with the ball. Botham scored successive centuries against the Pakistanis and took 37 wickets in the six summer Tests at an average cost of 14.8 runs per wicket. A still slender Botham had become 'the man with the golden arm' capable of dismissing the best Test batsmen not only with late or booming swing but also with apparently lame long-hops.

Meanwhile Gower burst on to the Test match scene with the unruffled composure of a veteran. His first Test century, made at the Oval against the New Zealanders (111), was blithely elegant, full of delicate dabs, effortless drives and assured cuts and pulls. While Botham's batting possessed punitive power, Gower's exuded finesse of touch and flawless timing. Unlike Botham, Gower never seemed to be in a hurry. At the crease he was sometimes described as 'languid' or 'nonchalant' but there was no doubting his speed of thought and movement in the field where he caught brilliantly and returned with speed, power and accuracy, benefitting from an ambidextrous ability. His first six Test matches left him with a batting average of 54.75, almost Hutton-like.

If Ian Botham and David Gower bestrode England's summer of 1978, Ian Dury bestrode mine, for it was then when I first saw him in concert with his funky, jazzy blues band, the Blockheads. They had emerged from the Pub Rock scene that had spawned luminaries such as Dr Feelgood and Graham Parker and the Rumour. Here, the raw, rootsy essentials of rock 'n' roll were raucously revived, a cooling blast of oxygen after the stale stultification of pompous 'progressive' rock. Dury was a throwback, a reprobate Cockney uncle, an inveterate tease, a wise-cracker with a penchant for coarse humour. Above all, he was a sparky wordsmith, pithy, whimsical, and poetic in thrall of the British music hall tradition. In 'Sex and Drugs and Rock 'n' Roll', Dury delivers a rebuke those who settle for grey, confining, conformity, the song's provocative title and refrain being playfully ironic. But if grey clothing is a pity, as Dury suggests, there was a time when I, like John Major's *Spitting Image*, fully embraced such breeze block-like anonymity.

1979

Transmission

The 1970s began with 'glam' rock but, notwithstanding the spinning, high kicking exuberance of Northern Soul, the decade ended with the 'glum' kind. Bands such as The Fall, Bauhaus, Public Image Ltd., Gang of Four and Killing Joke produced jagged, jarring, desolate sounds. In one of Britain's coldest winters, doom-laden rock music provided a fitting soundtrack as the rubbish piled up, operations were cancelled and the dead remained unburied. Industrial dereliction abounded. 'Labour isn't working' announced the Saatchi brothers. It was hard to disagree.

Arguably the most nihilistic and most compelling of the 'glum' bands was Manchester's Joy Division. In their ominous rendition of 'Transmission', baritone vocalist Ian Curtis urged us repeatedly to dance to the music as if our lives depended upon it. The rising desperation in his voice was complemented by his hypnotically glazed stare and robotically pumping arms, as if mocking his epilepsy. Listening to the song now, the hurried, chugging bass, scraping guitar and echoing drum beats grow in intensity as Curtis's twitching agitation mounts. If this was an invitation to a last waltz before the apocalyptic darkness closes in, it was no pretence for Ian Curtis took his life a few months after the song's release.

At the start of the 1978/79 Ashes series Down Under, the Australian cricket board members were despondent. WSC had not fallen flat on its face. On the contrary, after a sluggish first season in 1977/78, WSC had grasped the imagination of the Australian public. The WSC stadia were filling as the spectators warmed to its PR razzamatazz, singing along heartily to the booming jingle, 'Come On Aussie, Come On'. By sharp contrast, the official Ashes contest produced a dirge of a series. 'Jim' Swanton described the cricket as 'deplorably slow and most of the batting woefully poor'. Nevertheless, England's record margin of victory (5-1) made Mike Brearley the most successful English captain Down Under. Without discrediting Brearley's astute captaincy, his feat was achieved against an Australian second XI.

At Brisbane, new Australian skipper Graham Yallop won the toss, and despite the steamy conditions, chose to bat. Eighty-five minutes later, his side were staring at a heavy defeat, having lost six wickets for only 26 runs. Australia were eventually dismissed for 116. Although Australia's debutant fast bowler Rodney Hogg arrested England's charge, Derek Randall (75) managed to steer his side to a 170-run first-innings lead. Yallop (102) and Kim Hughes (129) then staunchly added 170 runs in reply but it was not sufficient to prevent Randall (74 not out) and Gower (48 not out) leading Brearley's side to a seven-wicket victory.

South Australian pace bowler Rodney Hogg seemed to be the only Australian capable of consistently troubling the England batsmen. He made a sensational debut in Test cricket having played in only two seasons of first-class cricket. While strong, accurate and very fast, he leant over so far in his approach to the wicket that his legs struggled to keep pace, leaving him at risk of toppling over. Because of a mild asthmatic condition he bowled mostly in three- or four-over spells. Not that this impaired his effectiveness as he smashed an Australian record, previously held by Arthur Mailey, by taking 41 wickets in the six-match series, including five 'five-fors'. He was adept at exploiting the many indifferent wickets that tainted this series. Randall remarked that Hogg hit the bat as hard as Lillee, while film evidence suggested that he might have been as quick as Willis. The genuinely fast Victorian opening bowler Alan Hurst supported Hogg well without posing so much of a threat.

The second Test at Perth was almost decided on the first day as a wretchedly out-of-form Boycott (77) and a fluent Gower (102) put together 158 runs for the fourth wicket. England's total of 309 proved too much for Australia who struggled to reach 190 in their first innings, with only Peter Toohey (81 not out) offering much resistance. Willis took 5-44. Hogg then took his second 'five-for' as England set Australia 328 runs to win. Thanks mainly to John Lever (4-28) and Geoff Miller (3-21) they failed by 167 runs.

However, having benefitted with first use of a deteriorating surface at Melbourne, Australia turned the tables in the third Test, winning by 103 runs. Graeme Wood (100) had set them on their way while Hogg's second ten-wicket match haul destroyed England's batting.

Buoyant at this unexpected change of fortune, the Australians began well at Sydney. This time it was Hurst's steepling bounce that undid England, as he took 5-28, helped by some scintillating catching. England were bundled out for 152 with only Botham (59) collaring the Aussie bowlers. Most of the Australian top order then made runs against a depleted England attack, with first Willis and then Hendrick forced to withdraw because of sickness. As determinedly as Botham and Emburey bowled, Darling (91), Border (60 not out), Hughes (48) and Yallop (44) mounted a potentially match-winning lead of 142 runs.

England started their second innings badly with Hogg dismissing Boycott lbw for a duck, having deceived him with a well-disguised, slower break-back. It seemed as if Boycott's grief at his mother's death, and his distress at being stripped of the Yorkshire captaincy, sat heavily upon his shoulders. He appeared unusually leaden-footed at the crease, finding difficulty in playing attacking shots.

Despite surviving a close lbw call himself, when on three, Randall then mounted a cautious revival with Brearley (53), their partnership compiling 111 runs in three and a half hours. As successive partners came and went, Randall remained resolute, eschewing risk in favour of patient accumulation. In the Centenary Test at Melbourne in 1977, Randall had played with greater freedom, driving, cutting and pulling 21 fine fours, bewildering and infuriating Lillee with his shambling, quirky and restless mannerisms. But here in Sydney, he remained fiercely focused. In the gagging heat, in which he continually had to wipe his brow and clear his vision, Randall knew that a single error of judgement might prove fatal to his team's chances.

Although the wicket was offering little encouragement to the pace bowlers, Hogg kept chipping away at the England batsmen, ending up with 4-67 off 28 eight-ball overs. But the greater peril was posed by Jim Higgs, who was then probably the best Australian leg-spinner since Benaud. Higgs had a strong flipper which had proved too good for Gooch, Taylor and Emburey in the first innings. Realising this, Randall played Higgs watchfully, trying to keep his aching feet moving, shifting back and forth in the crease, adjusting to the wrist-spinner's variations in flight and length, playing the more threatening deliveries with supple, soft hands, while remaining alert to any scoring opportunity that the odd loose ball might allow. There were few gifts to capitalise upon, though. Higgs bowled the equivalent of 80 six-ball overs during England's second innings, taking 5-145. Randall's furrowed mastery of Higgs, maintained over almost two days of play, was a remarkable feat of concentration and determination.

After Brearley had departed, Gooch dutifully stayed with Randall until close of play on the third day when England had reached 133/2, Randall on 65, and Gooch on six. The pair continued their restorative work on day four as the England total crept to 169 before Gooch was dismissed by Higgs for 22. Renouncing his characteristic flair, Gower helped add a further 68 before he wafted at a Hogg delivery and was caught at the wicket for 34. Not to be outdone in the tenacity stakes, Botham applied himself, too, tarrying for 97 minutes over just six singles as 30 more runs were banked. England were still only 125 runs ahead.

By then, Randall was clearly struggling, slumping upon his bat handle in between overs, his unusually clouded countenance etched with fatigue, as he wearily lifted his sodden cap, smoothing away the perspiration from his matted black hair. His jaunty cap-doffing in the Centenary Test seemed an eternity away. Nevertheless, he pressed on. Twice, he berated himself for losses in concentration after offering chances that were spurned. Frustratingly, though, he was a mere 11 minutes away from seeing out the fourth day when Hogg trapped him in front of his stumps. Randall slouched regretfully from the wicket having batted nine and a half hours for his outstanding 150. This was undoubtedly his best and most important innings for England.

At his departure, England were 292/6, exactly 150 runs in credit. Brearley knew he needed more runs, though, and fortunately for him, Miller (17), Taylor (21 not out) and Emburey (14) obliged in helping set Australia 205 runs to win, but surely this was only a modest target on such a placid surface? The Australians started well, putting on 38 runs for the first wicket, but there was a curious lack of conviction about their subsequent efforts as if they knew their chance had gone. Wood (27) was run out and Darling (13) and Yallop (1) fell quickly to a recovered Hendrick. Apart from an admirable innings from Allan Border who made an unbeaten 45, the remaining Australians capitulated meekly to Emburey's and Miller's off spin. Australia were dismissed for 111 runs. England had retained the Ashes.

While Brearley batted poorly, prompting one Australian heckler to shout 'Breely, you make Denness look like Bradman!' he led his side astutely. He was an inclusive leader, inviting his players' contributions to his game plans. At Adelaide, it was collectively decided that Emburey should maintain a restrictive off-stump line of attack when bowling at the left-handed Wood, with an agile fielder (Randall) positioned on the sweep, around 20 yards from the boundary, at deep square leg. An increasingly restless Wood obliged, hitting against the spin and providing Randall with a comfortable catch. Wood's dismissal resulted in another Australian batting collapse and, ultimately, a 205-run defeat.

The summer of 1979 was one of disappointment. England lost their first Prudential World Cup Final against the reigning ODI champions, the West Indies, having failed to contain the explosive batting of Viv Richards and Collis King. Although England began their four-match home series against India with a thumping innings victory, set up by an unbeaten double century by Gower (200) and a mighty hundred by Boycott (155), Sunil Gavaskar's superb innings of 221 at the Oval almost took his side to a series-saving win. At 429/8 the Indians were only nine runs short of their target when stumps were drawn. The other Tests at Lord's and Leeds were spoilt by bad weather although Botham (137) rescued England from a poor start at Headingley.

With the Packer players returning to international duty, Australia beat England 3-0 in a hastily-arranged three-way series, Down Under, which also involved the West Indians. It was a confusing format, perhaps contributing to a loss of intensity and focus. On his own admission, Brearley was not at his best, seeming less attentive to his players' needs than during the 1978/79 tour. Boycott also cited a lack of discipline and haphazard net practice as contributory factors in England's poor performances. Brearley admitted he was in need of a rest. Nevertheless, the winter tour ended triumphantly, with a grand ten-wicket victory over India in the Golden Jubilee Test in Bombay. It featured a stunning return to form by Ian Botham who took 13 wickets for 106 runs in the match, on top of a match-winning century. After England had sunk to 58/5 in reply to the Indian first-innings score of 242, Botham (114) and wicketkeeper Bob Taylor (43) added 171 for the sixth wicket, ultimately giving their side a 54-run lead. Botham then reduced the Indian second innings to rubble by dismissing seven of their batsmen for 48.

It has been said that the length of a fashionable skirt or the height of a new building are measures of national optimism. In Britain, the miniskirt was the product of the hopeful 1960s as were high-rise dwellings. As we entered the 1970s, hemlines fell and we became increasingly disenchanted with our tower blocks, particularly after the Ronan Point disaster. Although technological innovations continued to multiply in the afterglow of the Moon landing, ranging from the cheap electronic calculator to the first test tube baby, accelerating inflation, fuelled by the rising cost of oil, created a widening rift between the British political left and right. Meanwhile, the gulf in standard between the West Indian cricket team, indisputably the world's strongest Test side, and their English counterparts continued to grow.

'Oscillate Wildly'
1980 – 1986

England won 24 per cent of 81 Tests played between December 1979 and January 1987

1980

Food for Thought

Surprised to find that we were expecting our only child in the autumn, Liz and I moved to Bristol where our closest friends lived. By this time Margaret Thatcher had seized power from the hapless Labour administration. There was little surprise about her rise to power. In times of despair, nothing seems to roll so fast through the vacuum as a bandwagon. Her bandwagon was fuelled by mounting exasperation with union activists, and fear and loathing of Britain's desolate towns and cities. In decaying Britain, punk had articulated disaffection, but this became edged aside, first by disco, and then by the flamboyant New Romantics with their pretty boy synthesizer bands. With the growth of MTV, vision began to trump sound as a more engaging pop vehicle. 'Video Killed the Radio Star'.

As national unemployment figures were about to pass the two million mark, their highest level since 1935, there were the first signs of serious unrest near our new home. A riot in the St Paul's area of Bristol seemed to be the catalyst for inner city disturbances occurring elsewhere. Chronic unemployment, poor housing and racism provided the tinder while a breakdown in family discipline and over-zealous policing probably supplied the sparks.

As Liz's waters broke, I was listening to UB40's debut single, 'Food for Thought'. The song begins with a harrowing portrait of a famine-scarred landscape. Set to a punchy reggae beat and supplemented with blaring brass assaults, the song is a scathing indictment of Catholic missionaries and western politicians, the impotent or disreputable saviours of the starving millions. As I joyfully cradled Lydia, our new-born child, I reflected guiltily upon our privileged status.

That summer, Ian Botham became England's captain after Mike Brearley turned to psychotherapy. Botham could not have had a tougher baptism, leading England in back-to-back series against the West Indians, who had been reinforced by their returning WSC stars. Botham started well at Trent Bridge. Had it not been for some spilt chances in the tense final stages, his side might have won rather than losing by two wickets. Rain then washed out chances of a result at Lord's, Leeds and Manchester. However, England gained a 105-run first-innings lead at the Oval. With West Indian captain Clive Lloyd indisposed with a pulled leg muscle, Botham's side seemed on course for an equalising victory. But after torrential rain had ruled out any play on the fourth day, England's second innings collapse threatened to give the game away.

That heavily overcast final afternoon remains etched in my memory and not because of England's parlous situation. I was investigating an anonymous report concerning the alleged physical abuse of a pre-school child. I barely registered the tumbling wickets as I drove to my destination. But I was aware that England's last man, Bob Willis, was on his way to the crease as I stopped the car engine. England were only 197 runs in front with at least four hours left for play – hardly a daunting target for Greenidge, Haynes, Richards or Kallicharran.

I would not know the final outcome until much later. For the little boy's abuse was severe and his home circumstances complex. His back was covered with angry welts. It was difficult to obtain a clear account of what had happened. The boy's single mother had a profound hearing and speech impairment. This important detail had not been disclosed in the referral. Until a signer could be found, who was acceptable to the mother, we had to communicate by written messages. Her brief explanations and anxious questions were scribbled furiously, her eyes flashing and bottom lip trembling. And yet our stilted means of communication helped in dispelling some of her emotional heat, allowing her to describe how troublesome life had become. She told me that her son was very boisterous and disobedient. Their communication difficulties did not help. She received no assistance from the boy's absent father and was seriously short of money. Her extended family were not close at hand. Although she had local friends she did not wish them to know about my visit. She admitted losing her temper with her son but denied hitting him, claiming that the severe abrasions were caused when he accidentally fell down the stairs. After she allowed me to look at his back, it did not seem to be a plausible explanation, but I let her tell, or at least write down, her account without interruption.

Once I was able to arrange for an acceptable signer to join us, I asked whether she would permit me to arrange a medical examination for her boy. She was understandably hesitant but agreed once I said it could take place at her GP practice in her presence. I hoped I might avoid invoking statutory powers at this stage. By this time, she was a lot calmer, helped by the signer's support.

The examination confirmed what I had suspected and what she subsequently admitted. I explained to her that I needed to obtain a short-term protective order for her boy while we worked out with her a viable way forward which ensured her son's future safety. Given the severity of the boy's beating, I told her that a police investigation needed to be undertaken. While she was distressed at learning this, I said that only when this was completed could a rehabilitation plan be considered, involving her, and, with her agreement, her wider family. After a precautionary overnight stay in hospital, the boy was placed temporarily with foster parents, while a fuller assessment of his home circumstances and future risk was carried out.

It was very late when I returned home. Our little daughter was contentedly asleep in her cot, her arms stretched upwards as if surrendering to her slumbers. I thought of that sad, young mother whom I had returned to her empty home after she had helped settle her boy down for the night in hospital. With her permission I notified the maternal grandparents of what was happening. A social worker specialising in hearing and speech impairment was allocated the case on the following day. She helped the mother arrange for a legal representative and a signer to be present during the police interview. Working also with the maternal grandparents a restorative process began. As for our daughter, she needed only four more years before deciding that our parenting was not up to scratch, suddenly announcing, 'The trouble with you is that you do not know how to bring up a child.'

On the following morning, I discovered that surly Peter Willey had completed a defiant, unbeaten maiden Test century (100), assisted admirably and unexpectedly by Bob Willis (24 not out). Incredibly, this last-wicket pair survived for almost three hours, adding 117 runs against arguably the world's most formidable pace quartet. It seemed to be a very agreeable conclusion to a tough day.

The reverse Centenary Test against Australia proved to be a damp squib, though, as ten hours were lost to rain. Commentator John Arlott was rightly given a standing ovation as he tuned out after a 35-year career.

1981

Ghost Town

Coventry's multi-racial reggae/ska band The Specials released their 2 Tone single, 'Ghost Town', in the spring of 1981. This hit the top 20 in June just as riots hit the streets of Peckham. There had already been serious outbreaks of violence in nearby Brixton. Copycat inner-city disturbances in Toxteth and Birmingham would follow, coinciding with the rise of the song to the top of the UK singles chart. Its opening is pure Grand Guignol: a macabre whistling wind; ascending, ominous organ chords; and a quavering clarinet phrase, punctuated with blasts of brass. Over a spare reggae beat a grave Jamaican voice tells us how bad it is – no jobs, widespread anger, and too much fighting in the clubs. While describing the deprivation and decay then disfiguring many British towns and cities, 'Ghost Town' refers specifically to the band's home city of Coventry. Having risen pluckily from the ashes of Luftwaffe destruction, the city had been brought low by harsh economics. Like Detroit, the bottom had fallen out of its car industry.

Mrs Thatcher remained resolute. She insisted, 'The lady is not for turning... We have paid ourselves 22 per cent more for producing four per cent less.' With high interest rates and an overvalued pound savaging British manufacturing industries, she was adamant that commercial salvation lie in the growth of financial services and tourism and not in our ailing heavy industries. For the first time since the Industrial Revolution we were importing more manufactured goods than we were making.

Looking at England's disastrous Caribbean visit in 1981, our supposed skills in tourism did not seem that hot. For this tour nearly collapsed when Guyana insisted that England's fast-medium bowler, Robin Jackman, should be deported on account of his South African associations. The England party refused to accept this, and promptly left Guyana with Jackman, bringing about the immediate cancellation of the second Test, and a potential scrapping of the entire series.

Like many English cricketers, Jackman had played in South Africa during the winter months, coaching black and white players. Despite the Test match ban imposed upon South Africa in 1970, a series of private international cricket tours had taken place there during the 1970s. These tours were outside the jurisdiction of the TCCB. Millionaire Coventry City FC chairman Derrick Robins was responsible for three of these. Black West Indian Test cricketer John Shepherd was allowed by the Pretoria government to join the second tour, although he had to suffer the indignity of having 'honorary white' stamped on his passport. His admission was no more than a cynical South African ploy to subvert an international ban that was weakening its sporting prowess.

Whether these tours helped incentivise multi-racial cricket in South Africa is open to question. Colin Cowdrey made a well-intentioned but vain effort in 1971 to take a mixed race team to South Africa to play both white and black national sides. This initiative was the first and last of its kind while the international ban remained. By 1976, Commonwealth opinion had hardened on the matter of apartheid after a protest by black children in Soweto at discriminative education had been brutally suppressed. Twenty-five African countries had also boycotted the 1976 Montreal Olympics in protest against the All Blacks tour of South Africa. Consequently at the 1977 meeting of Commonwealth leaders at Gleneagles, each Prime Minister pledged to eradicate racism by discouraging *any* sporting contact and competition with South Africa while its apartheid policy remained in force.

Bob Willis insisted that his former Surrey team-mate Jackman was not a racist. But after the Gleneagles Agreement this was not the point. Nevertheless, many white English cricketers continued to believe this injunction did not apply to them, seeing no reason why it should curtail their customary winter employment in South Africa. Geoff Boycott went further, suggesting that the Gleneagles Agreement represented a wrongful restraint of trade. He was certainly not alone in identifying the hypocrisy of the Commonwealth ban while Great Britain remained one of South Africa's leading trading partners. It was undeniable that South African gold and other precious minerals were coveted by British businesses. Besides, the rewards of playing in South Africa were considerable as the Pretoria government sought to split the Commonwealth consensus, hoping to enhance its political status and re-incentivise South African sport.

The TCCB should have foreseen the possibility that Jackman might be denied admission by one or more of the Caribbean countries, particularly given Guyana's sensitivity on this subject. In 1970, the then Guyanan Prime Minister, Forbes Burnham, had taken Garry Sobers to task over his participation in a double wicket competition in Southern Rhodesia (now Zimbabwe), having naively expressed his high regard of its premier, Ian Smith. Sobers was told by Burnham that he was not welcome in Guyana unless he apologised for his actions. With the ensuing political crisis threatening to break apart the West Indian team, Sobers reluctantly did as he was told. So, not even the selection of Roland Butcher, as England's first black, West Indian-born player, did anything to assuage Guyanan concerns. For it was not so much Britain's record on racial equality which was in contention, as its commitment to supporting a Commonwealth resolution to eradicate South African apartheid.

After careful deliberation upon the Gleneagles Agreement, the other West Indian governments decided not to emulate Guyana's decision in excluding Jackman. It seemed as if expedience had prevailed, influenced, no doubt, by the adverse financial consequences of cancellation.

Little did any of these West Indian administrations realise that their own players were about to breach the Gleneagles Agreement. For two 'rebel' West Indian teams proceeded to tour South Africa in 1982/83 and 1983/84, comprising capped players such as the Guyanan pair Alvin Kallicharran and Colin Croft, Jamaican Lawrence Rowe, Trinidadian Bernard Julien, and Bajans Sylvester Clarke, Albert Padmore and Collis King. While the West Indian tourists appeared to boost the liberalising credentials of P.W. Botha's South African government, the black South African majority continued to be brutally suppressed and excluded from a new 'multi-racial' parliament, provoking further angry protests. The West Indian 'rebels' found they were not welcomed in the black South African townships where they had been previously worshipped. Instead, they were accused of betrayal having collaborated with the apartheid regime.

Although the remainder of the 1981 Caribbean tour went ahead as planned, it was almost inevitable that similar difficulties would re-emerge when England toured the Indian subcontinent a year later. Sure enough, Indian premier Indira Gandhi took exception to Geoff Boycott's inclusion in the England touring party on account of his South African links, but more of that later.

The 1981 tour was a very unhappy affair and not just because of the vexed politics. The sudden death of Ken Barrington, the much-loved England assistant manager, was particularly distressing to all members of the touring party and many others besides. Predictably, England were thoroughly outplayed, having made only one score in excess of 300 during the four-match series. England were heavily defeated in the opening Tests in Trinidad and Barbados while also having the worst of the two draws in Antigua and Jamaica. Their few bright spots were Gooch's centuries at Bridgetown (116) and Kingston (153), and Boycott's and Willey's unbeaten tons at St John's, while Gower's superlative unbeaten century at Kingston (154) saved the final Test after England had slumped to 32/3 in their second innings. Gooch headed the English Test averages with an impressive 57.50, followed by Gower with 53.71, while Boycott and Willey also averaging over 40.

Although Botham was England's most penetrative bowler with 15 Test wickets, these came at a higher than usual cost of almost 33 runs apiece. As for Botham's batting, he averaged only 10.42 in seven series innings. While the burden of leadership seemed to impede his all-round talents, the high quality of the opposition and the upsetting circumstances of the tour gave the TCCB good reason to suspend judgement on his captaincy. But this was merely a stay of execution.

After losing a low-scoring, opening Ashes Test in which a rash of missed chances proved crucial, Botham was relieved of the captaincy following an undistinguished draw at Lord's. Botham had managed just 34 runs in four Test innings which included a pair at Lord's. His bowling appeared to have lost its verve, too. Meanwhile 'Dennis the Menace' was back, taking eight wickets for 80 in the Australians' victory at Trent Bridge.

Although Lillee had lost his lightning pace, he could still deliver a mean bouncer while still troubling the world's best batsmen with lateral movement and canny changes of pace. At Nottingham he bowled almost 30 overs – not bad for someone recovering from pneumonia! Terry Alderman was new to Test cricket and English conditions but nobody would have known. He made the ball dart and swing alarmingly, and despite appearing no more than medium-fast in pace, his deliveries hit the bat with greater force than expected. With the dangerous yet unpredictable Rodney Hogg and the genuinely quick Geoff Lawson in support, Australia appeared to have a daunting seam quartet, although Hogg would play in only two Tests because of fitness problems.

For the pivotal third Test at Headingley, Brearley was recalled as captain while Botham was given the freedom of the ranks, content to serve again under a leader whom he respected greatly. On the eve of the game, Brearley discussed with his team how the Australian batsmen might play.

Opener John Dyson was adept at leaving the new ball. Brearley stressed that it was important to make him play, possibly employing slower in-swingers for variety. It was suggested that a silly mid-off and short square leg should be employed as Dyson tended to lunge at quicker deliveries.

Because Dyson's opening partner Graeme Wood was inclined to move far over to the off side, Brearley proposed employing a leg-slip who might be able to pick up one of Wood's finer flicks off his pads.

Captain Kim Hughes was considered to be a fine batsman but risked being dismissed lbw. Brearley was right, Hughes was lbw on seven occasions in this series. The game plan agreed was for the quicker bowlers to push Hughes on to his back foot, before slipping in a fuller delivery. Brearley cautioned against bouncing him as this fed his adrenalin drive.

Graham Yallop was known to be a jittery starter, inclined to subdue his nerves with brazen stroke-play, hence his nickname 'Banzai' which the England team coined during the 1978/79 series. It was agreed that Yallop should be blitzed by high pace at the start of his innings.

Allan Border was inclined to go a long way back early in his innings, so the quicker bowlers were encouraged to pitch a little fuller to him.

Wicketkeeper Rodney Marsh was known to be a strong, straight driver with an ability to heave mightily to leg and slash savagely in an arc between cover and third man. His Achilles heel was the ball which moved into him.

Despite England's careful planning, Australia seemed to have the third Test in their pocket by the close of the second day, when they declared at 401/9. Dyson played impeccably (102), demonstrating greater aptitude for off-side shots than had been recognised, while Hughes (89) and Yallop (58) added steadfast half-centuries. England's pace quartet of Willis, Dilley, Old and Botham did not bowl with conviction or vigour on the first day when only three wickets fell. Once again, missed chances had cost England dearly. Although there was considerable improvement on day two, with Botham taking six wickets for 95 runs, the horse had surely bolted. Hughes was cock-a-hoop. He thought that his side's total of 400 runs was 'worth 1,000 on this pitch'.

Hughes seemed spot on as Lillee, Alderman and Lawson cut a swathe through the English batting on an 'up and down' surface that produced unplayable 'grubbers' and rearing 'chin music'. Botham's bellicose half-century provided England with their only blows in anger as his side were dismissed feebly for just 174. A jubilant Kim Hughes enforced the follow-on, whereupon Lillee immediately dismissed Gooch for a duck.

When play resumed on the Monday morning – the experimental abolition of the Sunday rest day did not apply here – Boycott (46) and Willey (33) offered some resistance while the other batsmen melted away. When Botham arrived at the crease, England were 105/5 and in imminent danger of a crushing innings defeat. Botham began circumspectly hoping to help Boycott take the game into the final day. But at 133, Boycott departed, lbw to Alderman, and only two more runs were added before Taylor was dismissed, caught at short leg. On *Test Match Special* Trevor Bailey gravely announced, 'The writing is on the wall.'

Dilley had been struggling with his bowling. Next to Willis, he was the fastest England had. But his self-belief was fragile. Brearley had attempted to protect him from well-meaning experts, who had attempted to remodel his action. Brearley was worried that he might lose the plot completely. Dilley's first innings performance with the ball had been undistinguished. He knew his place was in jeopardy. Having nothing to lose he arrived at the crease in a pugnacious mood. The bookies had England at 500/1 to win.

Dilley boldly told a dubious Botham that he was ready for some 'humpty' and immediately set about Alderman, lashing him twice to the vacant point boundary off the back foot. As if grieving for the departed Boycott, Botham remained uncharacteristically subdued, compiling only 39 runs in the hour and a half of play before tea. He later joked that he had been playing for a 'not out'. Meanwhile Dilley planted his front foot in line with his middle stump and swung and swiped at any ball he could reach. A tiring Alderman ensured that he was well supplied.

While tea did little to rejuvenate the Australian pace trio, Botham resumed batting in a much more aggressive frame of mind. Alderman had removed Boycott, Gower, Gatting and Taylor with exemplary swing and seam bowling. His slip catches, off Lillee's bowling, had also accounted for Gooch and Brearley. Now he was the man to pay. Botham immediately drove an out-swinger over mid-off with hissing force, before cutting a shorter ball past gully, and then slogging a good length delivery on off stump over wide mid-on to take him to his fifty. Botham's half-century had come off 57 balls in 110 minutes.

Not content with that, he then skipped down the wicket to smash a respectable delivery from Alderman straight for six, scattering those seated in the rugby end stand. The century partnership was raised in 70 minutes. Dilley then celebrated his maiden Test fifty with a crashing cover drive off Lillee. It was Dilley's last shot in spite as soon after he played on to an exhausted Alderman who had belatedly chosen to bowl round the wicket. The change of direction gave Botham and Dilley less room to play their shots. Dilley had demonstrated astonishing élan in making 58, but at 252/8, England were still only 25 ahead.

Dilley was replaced by Chris Old, a talented and sometimes big-hitting batsman, but with a habit of backing away from the fastest bowling. He was duly despatched from the dressing room with strict instructions to stay in line. Old did as he was bid, although Willey took the precaution of propping a bat handle against the TV screen whenever Old was in shot to keep him in line. His ploy worked. Old creditably added 29 in a stand of 67 with Botham during which the latter raced to his hundred with two mighty back-foot blows off Lawson.

Botham had reached three figures in only 87 balls. From the dressing room balcony, Brearley commanded him to stay put. Botham did more than that, though, thrashing the undisciplined Lawson to all parts of the ground, highlighted by a massive pull shot that sent the ball bouncing high over the mid-wicket boundary rope before the deeply-set Australian fielders could twitch. Lillee fared no better as a series of wild slashes from Botham sent the ball scudding to the third man boundary. Botham seemed impregnable. No matter how outrageous his shots were – hoicks, edges, miscues – everything came off. The ball either flashed to the boundary or fell just out of reach of the converging Australians.

Old departed with 319 runs on the board, 92 in front. Lawson had at last managed to pitch a delivery on the right spot after bowling a dreadful concoction of beamers and disorderly bouncers. Kim Hughes had lost control hours before. He had persevered with pace because his faster bowlers had brought England to its knees. Shell-shocked by the blistering assault that followed Dilley's arrival, he failed to realise a change of plan was needed. Willis was certain that had left-arm spinner Ray Bright been introduced earlier, Botham's bludgeoned shots would not have carried as far, probably resulting in him holing out for 50 or 60 fewer runs. When Bright was belatedly brought on he almost bowled Botham with his first delivery. But if Hughes thought that salvation was imminent, with the last pair at wicket, he was mistaken as Botham shielded Willis so well that 31 more runs were added before the close when England were 351/9 – 124 runs ahead. Willis had faced just five balls. The disconsolate Australians were in no mood for sharing an end of play drink with their opponents. Slumped in morose silence, the Australians sensed that the momentum had passed to England, as had Brearley.

On the final day, I left the office at lunchtime to buy a sandwich. The baker's shop TV was tuned in to the Test match coverage. The score was not encouraging. The Australians were proceeding in apparent comfort at 56/1. I stopped to watch a stone-faced Willis as he bounded to the wicket, and with a flurry of arms, deliver a brute of a ball to Trevor Chappell, the youngest and least talented of the Chappell brothers. The degree of bounce was so sharp that Chappell could only fend off the ball from his face with the bat handle, whereupon it hit his right shoulder, and lobbed into Taylor's waiting gloves.

Taylor did a skip of delight but Willis was unmoved. He seemed lost in a faraway zone untouched by those around him. Paradoxically, his intensity of approach seemed heightened. I could not remember seeing him bowl with such strength, rhythm and ferocity. The Headingley pitch was clearly unreliable, but the right spots needed to be found to exploit this. Willis proceeded to home in on these with unerring accuracy making the ball leap into the batsmen's faces from just short of a length. He had braved many setbacks in his career on account of dodgy knees, muscular strains and debilitating sickness. But here he seemed driven by an irresistible force.

I lingered in the shop. So did several others. In fact a small crowd had gathered in front of the TV by the time Willis galloped in to bowl at the new batsman, Hughes. Once again the ball lifted alarmingly. Hughes stretched upwards but could not counter the bounce, edging the ball to the left of Botham at third slip, who picked up an astonishing diving catch – 58/3.

The febrile roar from our growing throng shook the small bakery. Willis must have heard us for he threw his arms up in a brief gesture of jubilation before turning abruptly on his heels and trudging back to his mark, ignoring the excited celebrations of his team-mates. His morose mask was re-applied.

Yallop was the next man in – at the best of times a poor starter. Willis gave Yallop the works, knowing that a 40-minute pit stop was imminent. 'Fast and straight' demanded Brearley and that's exactly what the edgy Yallop received. Willis delivered yet another vicious ball that steepled into Yallop's ribcage. Caught unprepared, left-handed Yallop could only brush the rising ball away with an awkward jab, whereupon it fell into the safe clutches of the stooping Gatting at short square leg – 58/4. The bakery had never known such times as a rush of newcomers surged into the shop in response to our explosive cheer, wedging themselves into the few remaining spaces. Talk about bread of heaven.

After lunch I had social work visits booked but the first family I visited was absorbed by the TV Test coverage. While driving there, Border was dismissed, having edged an in-swinger from Old into his leg stump – 65/5. But I arrived on cue to see Dyson swivel too quickly on a bouncer from Willis only to glove a catch to Taylor down the leg side – 68/6. This family and I had not often seen eye-to-eye, but here we all cheered uninhibitedly, celebrating a rare moment of unity.

Marsh was next to go, hooking Willis to Graham Dilley who took a composed catch inches in front of the long leg boundary – 74/7. And when Lawson meekly nicked another climbing Willis delivery to Taylor – 75/8 – it was as if we had been lifetime friends.

Alas, our unexpected reconciliation did not survive a bruising recovery led by Lillee and Marsh, as they blasted 35 runs off only four overs. Like Alan Knott, Lillee employed the ramp shot adeptly, cleverly evading Brearley's attempts at picking him off. Accepting that this was not the occasion for discussing their son's difficulties, I moved on to my next visit.

Before I arrived, Lillee spooned a half-volley from Willis to Gatting, diving forward at mid-on – 110/9. Lillee had mistakenly renounced his successful slash and burn approach in favour of tentative orthodoxy. Willis pressed his stooping head into Gatting's commodious chest as a gesture of humble gratitude.

Willis had been disconcerted by Lillee's late assault, but now he was back in the groove. It took just one fast yorker directed at Bright's middle stump to confirm England's incredible victory by 18 runs. After briefly thrusting his arms aloft Willis charged off the field, evading all who attempted to congratulate him, his eyes distant, and his brow furrowed. It was as if he was oblivious of the magnitude of what had been achieved.

After the incredible events at Headingley, lightning struck again at Edgbaston. England batted ineptly in their first innings, raising only 189, Alderman having bowled superbly on a dead track taking 5-42. Despite some very aggressive bowling from Willis, and miserly restraint from Emburey, who took 4-43 off 26.5 overs, Australia established a more-than-useful 69-run first innings lead.

Australian left-arm spinner Bright then strangled the English batsmen in their second innings, taking 5-68 off 34 overs. Only a bold rearguard action by Old (23) and Emburey (37), supported by a stubborn Taylor (8), enabled England to reach a still inadequate total of 219 – 150 in front. Surely this was not enough to avert defeat on such a benign wicket? However, Old found some swing in the closing overs, trapping Wood lbw for two. Meanwhile Willis managed to achieve unexpected lift, forcing Dyson and Border to cling on desperately. At the close of play on the third day, Australia were 9/1, 142 runs short of a 2-1 series lead.

As at Nottingham, there was no rest day. So on a bright, hot Sunday morning, Edgbaston was packed and expectant. A defiant roar greeted the emergence of the players. Brearley's men were clearly up for a scrap, notably Willis who was as fired up as at Headingley. He steamed in from the City End, firing venomous rising deliveries into the chests of Dyson and Border who retreated uneasily on to the back foot. With Brearley posting two men on the boundary, backward of square, the Australian batsmen were hesitant about hooking. So having softened them up with a volley of fast, rearing balls, Dyson was unprepared for the one that kept low and trapped him lbw for only 13 – 19/2.

Hughes arrived at the wicket with a grim-faced determination, intent upon taking the fight to the English bowlers. He quickly espied a lifting delivery to hit, smacking the ball fiercely but high in the direction of the long leg boundary. Emburey was waiting, though, and nonchalantly plucked the ball out of the air as if this was a perfunctory fielding drill. The Edgbaston crowd had looked on in hushed hope only to burst into explosive joy at Emburey's catch.

Hughes was gone for only five and Australia were 29/3. The jumpy Yallop was then put through the wringer by Willis. One ball grazed his off stump. Another was flicked over the slip cordon, and most frustratingly of all, one found the edge of his bat, only for Brearley to shell the chance at slip. Riding their luck, Yallop and Border, began an unconvincing recovery. And yet they survived until lunch when Australia was 62/3. Only 50 runs had been scored in the morning's 30 overs.

After the break, Border and Yallop played with greater conviction and fluency. The English attack, so menacing in the morning session, appeared tamed by the burning sun. Australia approached 100 with seven wickets in reserve. The ball was worn and softer, and the pitch unsympathetic. I glumly watched as Emburey sauntered in to bowl at Yallop. Trusting his luck, Yallop launched his favourite on-drive, but was deceived by the flight and turn, edging the ball into his pad, whereupon it plopped into Botham's eager hands at silly mid-off. Yallop was out for 30 and Australia were 87/4. A relaxed-looking Martin Kent replaced Yallop but he was immediately tucked up by Emburey who denied him any width to play his flowing off-side shots. Meanwhile, a grizzled Border was struggling, not so much with the bowling as with his stomach that had been giving him as many runs as his broad bat. Hughes asked Brearley if he would allow Border a toilet break when necessary. Brearley refused, indicating that Border should retire hurt if indisposed. But Emburey then ended Border's uncomfortable vigil with a ball that unexpectedly sat up, hitting the Australian's glove before being pouched by Gatting at short leg. The Australians were 105/5 with Marsh the last accomplished batsman left.

Brearley's plan was for Botham to bottle up one end while Emburey tucked into the remaining batting. However, Botham was not convinced that he should have been chosen. There was no swing, little seam movement, and with Willis played out, no bounce either. But Botham was never one for half measures. Seizing the ball he charged in like an avenging juggernaut.

Brearley had been disturbed by Botham's declining potency as a swing bowler, despite performing better on day two at Headingley. Brearley had dubbed Botham the 'Sidestep Queen', having noted Botham taking a step to his right at the point of delivery when bowling over the wicket. Because he was carrying greater weight, Botham used the sideways step to bring his trunk around more as he released the ball, which helped his out-swing. It interrupted his momentum, though, meaning his swing was gentler and easier to combat.

Here, Botham had no qualms about his loss of swing, putting his faith in brute force and speed. In the space of 28 balls he blasted out the five remaining Australian batsmen, clean bowling Marsh, Kent and Alderman while trapping Bright in front of his stumps, and having Lillee caught at the wicket. He was indomitable, taking five wickets for just one run. It was a devastating spell of enraged fast bowling. Having scattered Alderman's stumps, Botham grabbed one and powered towards the pavilion, chest pumped up in pride and exultation. As a result of this astounding 29-run victory, England led Australia in a series that they should have already lost.

Australian captain Kim Hughes suffered badly in defeat. Under his command Australia had squandered excellent winning opportunities in both the third and fourth Tests. He knew that he was no more than a caretaker captain after Greg Chappell had chosen to remain at home. He must have wondered, too, why the battle-hardened Marsh, a combative and inspirational wicketkeeper, had been passed over. His position as captain must have felt precarious. To make matters worse, he was now short of pace bowlers following injuries to Hogg and Lawson. He was forced into calling upon inexperienced left-arm quick Mike Whitney, who was playing for Gloucestershire. Whitney had played in only six first-class games, so was hardly a ready-made replacement.

Meanwhile, Brearley fretted about the strength of his batting. Dilley led the batting averages at 37.50, fractionally ahead of Botham's Headingley-boosted score. The England top order kept keeling over. During this series, England's first five wickets had raised on average only 136 runs. Although Boycott had batted skilfully and adhesively on difficult wickets, particularly at Nottingham and Headingley, he had not contributed his customary weight of runs, averaging 26. Woolmer had failed to make any impact in his four innings and Brearley had struggled in his four knocks despite achieving the top individual score on either side (48) at Edgbaston.

After his outstanding success on the truer Caribbean surfaces, Gooch was humbled in his eight Ashes innings, averaging 15.5. Boycott was concerned by Gooch's tendency to play around his front pad which left him vulnerable when the ball moved into him. Gatting seemed similarly inclined, and he averaged little better at 27.5. Gower had compiled an impressive second innings score of 89 at Lord's, but had been dismissed caught at the wicket or in the slips in six out of eight innings, suggesting that he was still prone to playing loose shots outside his off stump. He averaged 28.25. Some critics thought Willey's exaggerated two-eyed stance made it difficult for him to play controlled off-side shots although he cut and drove square with uncommon power.

At Manchester, Brearley chose Chris Tavare of Kent instead of Willey to add resilience to the shaky top order, while Knott was recalled instead of Taylor to strengthen the lower-order batting. Lancashire fast-medium bowler Paul Allott made his debut in place of the injured Old.

England won the toss and batted. Once again their top-order batsmen disappointed. Without Tavare's dour occupation of the crease (69), and a brisk last-wicket partnership of 56 between Allott (52 not out) and Willis (11), England would not have reached 200. Their first-innings total of 231 seemed well below par until the Australians self-destructed in 30 overs of reckless hitting. Kent (52) made Australia's single score of note as they were hustled out for a paltry 130.

But with the Ashes almost in their grasp, England stumbled to 104/5 on the Saturday morning having become becalmed with excessive caution. Once again their saviour was Ian Botham, who produced a peerless century (118). If his Headingley ton was largely a carefree slog, his Old Trafford one was a consummate combination of style and power. Tavare (78) dropped anchor, allowing Botham the freedom to blast England towards an unreachable total of 404 – 505 ahead of the Australians – with rear-gunners Knott (59) and Emburey (57) strafing their defenceless opponents. Perhaps feeling that they had nothing left to lose, Yallop (114) and Border (123 not out) led a brave pursuit of victory, although Australia ultimately fell 104 runs short. Nevertheless, buoyed by their second innings showing at Manchester, the Australians took control of the sixth and final Test at the Oval, helped by another unbeaten ton from Border (106) and a hundred, on debut, by Dirk Wellham (103). However, Boycott's century (137), and Gatting's brace of fifties kept England in the game, while Knott's innings of 70 not out shut out the Aussies on the final afternoon.

England's glorious Ashes victory that summer provided a welcome diversion from Britain's financial hardships and woeful unrest. It even trumped the royal wedding of Prince Charles and Diana Spencer. Over 30 years on, that summer still retains a legendary flavour. The euphoria was short-lived though. A dismal winter Test series in India followed, beset by political controversy and funereal over rates, dumping us back in mundane mediocrity.

1982
The Model

Mrs Thatcher's popularity had fallen to 25 per cent, the lowest satisfaction rating achieved by any British Prime Minister. And yet she seemed unchallengeable. Labour was still not working, riven with internecine squabbling and a doctrinaire left-wing agenda few would buy. As for the new party at the centre, the SDP, it appealed only to footloose privileged types with pricking consciences. Despite the estimable efforts of Shirley Williams, the new party's image seemed imbued with suave wealth.

It was no surprise that the 1980s should have spawned a rapid growth in self-help and action groups. Frustrated by the perceived inadequacies of the democratic process, the allure of direct action was grasped by environmentalists, animal rights activists, nuclear disarmament protesters and a variety of anti-discriminatory campaigners. Given the prevalence of sexism, racism and homophobia within British workplaces and the media during the 1970s, it was small wonder that equal rights campaigners should voice their views with increasing stridency.

As for the economic malaise afflicting the 1980s lower classes, this was dramatised on TV in a variety of ways. We had the chirpy duckers and divers in *Only Fools and Horses*, and the cheery strength of kith and kin in *Bread*. We had the solidarity of mates forced to work abroad in *Auf Wiedersehen, Pet*, but we also had the abject despair of the *Boys from the Blackstuff*.

Then came the Argentinean invasion of the Falkland Islands. 'We're a Third World country, no good for anything,' wrote a despairing maverick MP, Alan Clark. This was no time for hand-wringing, though, as Mrs Thatcher ordered a direct military response. Some sneered but many more cheered. It wasn't just the 'Ere we go' pub jingoists who became excited. Reminded painfully of past dictators, a bellicose Michael Foot lent the government his passionate support. But was this the growl of a cornered underdog, eager for a restorative military triumph? Was this the lost British Empire striking back? And was this not a fortuitous distraction from our social and economic woes? Mrs Thatcher thought it was no time for indecision. Like a latter day Palmerston, she promptly sent her task force cruising while *The Sun* played upon the basest of terrace, tribal instincts, by printing T-shirts bearing slogans, 'Stick it up your Junta' and 'Buenos Aires is full of fairies'. After *The Sun*'s controversial 'Gotcha' headline, *Private Eye* was moved to lampoon its crassness with a spoof invitation to 'Kill an Argie and win a Metro'. Of course, Mrs Thatcher took a mighty risk. Had the task force failed, her political prospects would have sunk faster than the *General Belgrano*. But thanks to acts of outstanding bravery and flawed enemy fuse timings, the task force prevailed – just. No wonder Mrs Thatcher was exultant. 'Rejoice' she exclaimed once victory was assured. Many Britons thought she had put the 'Great' back into Britain.

There was certainly nothing great about England's winter tour of India and Sri Lanka, though. With just weeks left before the touring party was due to travel, the Indian government announced that neither Geoff Cook nor Geoff Boycott would be admitted on account of their South African connections. The TCCB stood firm, though, refusing to replace them, despite previously warning its leading players that their participation in 'rebel' tours of South Africa risked Test disqualification. Indian Prime Minister Indira Gandhi eventually relented a week before the tour was due to start, but only after Boycott drew attention to a passage in his book which purported to offer proof of his opposition to apartheid.

With Brearley concentrating upon a career in psychotherapy, Keith Fletcher was asked to captain the side, only to be cast aside abruptly on his return. The task proved to be a poisoned chalice. England's lamentable second innings collapse at Bombay (now Mumbai) resulted in a 138-run defeat, clouded also by disputed umpiring decisions. Thereafter, a combination of low, slow wickets and dilatory over rates (around 12 per hour) ensured that the remaining five Tests were drearily drawn. Fletcher's frustration spilled over when he flicked off a bail in disputing his dismissal at Bangalore. That moment of pique cost him the captaincy. England's sole winter Test victory came in Colombo, but not before a novice Sri Lankan side had given Fletcher's side a considerable scare. Thanks to Chris Tavare's and David Gower's runs and Derek Underwood's and John Emburey's wickets, England eventually prevailed.

Geoff Boycott seemed a reluctant tourist in India. Willis thought he was uncomfortable with both the country and the food. However, Boycott had his eye on the world record for the highest number of Test runs individually scored. This, he duly achieved when he reached an aggregate total of 8,114.

STUMPS & RUNS & ROCK 'N' ROLL

Despite making a century (105) in Delhi, his last in Test cricket, Boycott seemed out-of-sorts. He attributed this to sickness which caused him to return home early.

After the Indian tour was completed, Boycott joined a 'rebel' tour of South Africa, sponsored by South African Breweries. The 'rebel' party was captained by Graham Gooch. It was contracted to play three unofficial 'Test matches' and three one-day internationals. The squad also included Dennis Amiss, John Emburey, Mike Hendrick, Geoff Humpage, Alan Knott, Wayne Larkins, John Lever, Chris Old, Arnold Sidebottom, Les Taylor, Derek Underwood, Peter Willey and Bob Woolmer. The news of the tour broke when the party arrived in Johannesburg in March 1982. The players expected some public criticism and perhaps a slap on the wrist by the International Cricket Conference (ICC). However they underestimated the opprobrium they would receive for defying the Gleneagles Agreement. Both India and Pakistan were vociferous opponents of apartheid. Consequently, all members of the 'rebel' party received bans from international cricket lasting three years. These suspensions ended the Test careers of over half of them, including that of Geoffrey Boycott. With the 'rebels' subjected to widespread Commonwealth disapproval, they were labelled as 'the Dirty Dozen' in the British Houses of Parliament. The TCCB could ill afford to be compassionate. India and Pakistan, the most vocal opponents of the 'rebel' tours, were due to visit England in the summer of 1982. The TCCB was rightly concerned at the political and financial consequences if they refused to play.

The subtext to the summer Tests against India and Pakistan was an unofficial competition to determine the world's best all-rounder. Richard Hadlee had already staked his claim, but in 1982 the focus shifted on to three other nominees: Botham, Kapil Dev and Imran Khan. All three wielded the bat with audacious, pugilistic power while commanding cunning curve with the ball, Imran being the quickest of the trio, as he had demonstrated when opening the bowling for Sussex, in harness with South African, Garth Le Roux. The first three Tests pitted Botham against Kapil Dev. However, Randall's match-winning century at Lord's (126) trumped their initial duel. Botham began the contest by taking five wickets in the Indian first innings, but Kapil Dev bettered this after aggregating 130 runs and grabbing eight wickets in the match. This was Bob Willis's first Test as England's captain. It was an auspicious start as his nine wickets in the game, including 6-101 in the Indian second innings, helped secure a seven-wicket win.

At Old Trafford, Botham turned the tables, making a fine, restorative ton (128). Kapil Dev managed 65 in reply, although he reached his half-century in only 33 balls. Neither player impressed with the ball in a rain-affected draw.

Botham then established his superiority at the Oval with a dazzling double hundred (208) made off 220 balls in 268 minutes, helping England to a total of 594 all out, with newly-qualified South African Allan Lamb making a maiden

Test century (107) and Randall 95. Kapil Dev's response was to slam 97 runs off 93 balls. Once again, neither player made much impact with the ball in a high-scoring draw.

The ensuing contest was between Botham and Imran Khan. Imran had the better of the opening Test at Edgbaston. He took seven wickets for 52 in England's first innings of 272, and a further two in their second innings of 291. However, a gritty ton from experimental opener Randall (105), and a last-wicket partnership of 79 between Taylor and Willis, set up a 113-run England victory. For his part, Botham took six wickets in the match, including four in the second innings which hastened England's win. Imran batted longer, though, hammering 65 in a late show of defiance after Pakistan had slumped to 98/7. Botham managed just two runs in the game.

Following Mohsin Khan's stupendous double century (200) and Mudassar Nazar's astonishing figures of 6-32, Pakistan won by ten wickets at Lord's. As for the all-rounder sideshow, neither player contributed much to this final result.

Nevertheless, in a low-scoring series decider at Headingley, Botham's match figures of 9-144 played a crucial part in securing England's seven-wicket victory, although Graeme Fowler's outstanding second-innings score of 86, on debut, was equally significant. As for Imran, his match figures of 8-115 kept Pakistan in contention, taking his series aggregate to 21 wickets, a new Pakistani record in a rubber with England. Imran batted better, aggregating 113 runs for once out, whereas Botham compiled 61 runs in his two completed innings. Arguably, though, the series hinged less upon the all-rounders' performances than upon the extraordinary number of extras Pakistan conceded – 221 runs. This was a higher aggregate than any of the England batsmen achieved in the series.

The most unsavoury features of the summer Test series were the Indian and Pakistani gripes over umpiring decisions. The Pakistanis were particularly critical of David Constant, but also objected to decisions made by David Evans and Ken Palmer during their defeat at Edgbaston. The Indians were equally distrustful of Constant. They remained resentful about the decisions he made at a crucial stage in the nail-biting finale to the Oval Test of 1979. They claimed that Viswanath had not been caught cleanly by Brearley, although given out by Constant, and that Venkataraghavan had made his ground when adjudged run out by him. The Indians' conflict with Constant reignited in 1982 when they played Yorkshire at Bradford. Here, they queried two of his decisions. They also disagreed with his assessment of the playability of the Headingley pitch for a Prudential one-day international which they lost heavily.

To Constant's disgust, the TCCB replaced him with Barry Meyer for the Test series against India. It seemed a 'tit-for-tat' response since Keith Fletcher and his manager, Subba Row, had successfully objected to Indian umpire Mohammad Ghouse standing in the Bombay (Mumbai) Test during the previous winter tour.

Pakistan then upped the stakes by complaining about Constant's decisions in the deciding third Test at Leeds. Pakistan captain Imran Khan told reporters after Pakistan's narrow defeat, 'I don't want to give an excuse for us losing the series but Constant made what, for us, were some costly mistakes in this match.' The first and third Test matches in this series were fractious affairs, marred by dissension and a barrage of raucous appeals which subjected the umpires to intolerable pressure. The case for neutral umpires made a tentative step forward. However, it was at Imran Khan's instigation that two neutral umpires stood in Pakistan's home series against the West Indies in 1986, and again in their 1989/90 series against India. He said he was sick of the carping about umpiring decisions which had dogged previous Tests in Pakistan. However, the ICC prevaricated. Although they agreed in 1992 that one of the Test match umpires would be neutral, until 1994, this remained on an experimental basis. It was not until 2002, twenty years after the dismal disputes of 1982, that the ICC agreed that all Test matches would be officiated by a pair of neutral umpires.

While England had won both summer series, the robustness of the English bowling attack was causing concern. With Hendrick, Old, Emburey and Underwood ruled out because of their South African involvement, the selectors were hard-pressed to find adequate support for Willis and Botham for the coming Ashes tour. Pringle had yet to justify the hype that he was Botham mk 2. Allot had not 'cut the mustard', while Hemmings had neither Emburey's control nor bite. It wasn't as if the batting was that sound either, except on the flattest of tracks, although Tavare had done well as an experimental opener, and Lamb had undoubted Test quality despite his failures against Pakistan. Not that the Australians were in great shape, having been thrashed 3-0 by their hosts Pakistan in an autumn mini-series.

Kraftwerk's 'The Model' was, for me, the outstanding pop song of 1982. Its appeal lies in its catchy melody and pulsating, electronic rhythms, while its whimsical, robotic vocals and spare, but knowing, lyrics remain captivatingly cool. The song satirises the vacuity of a celebrity culture in which fame too often rests upon someone's sleekly manufactured image and cosmetic lifestyle rather than upon the worth of what they do, say or produce.

1983
Beat It

Speaking of celebrities, they did not come much bigger than American pop star Michael Jackson. Despite his freak show lifestyle, earning him the sobriquet 'Wacko Jacko', his brilliance as a performer, producer, choreographer and composer is undeniable. His 1982 album *Thriller*, on which 'Beat It' features, is the highest-selling album ever with 65 million worldwide sales. In 'Beat It',

Jackson rails against gang violence and alpha-male macho posturing. Jackson's detestation of violence stemmed from the abuse he allegedly suffered as a child. The funky guitar riff is provided by heavy-rock guitarist Eddie Van Halen. This represented a new departure for Jackson. He explained, 'I wanted to write a song, the type of song that I would buy if I were to buy a rock song.' I have no argument with that.

By 1983, macho posturing was no longer a male prerogative in British politics. Denis Healey might have dismissed her as a 'bargain basement Boadicea', but Mrs Thatcher proved to be as tough, if not tougher, than any of her male political colleagues or opponents. Her reward for a decisive response to the Falkland Islands crisis was a landslide victory at the polls in June. Labour was almost wiped out as an electoral force in the south of England with the Liberal/Social Democratic Alliance runners-up in two-thirds of these southern constituencies. No matter how much Conservative values were condemned by their detractors, such as the makers of the Emmy award-winning film, *The Ploughman's Lunch*, in 1983 Mrs Thatcher's stock could not have been higher.

But as England cricket fans know only too well, a slip has a wretched habit of becoming a slide, and when the luck runs out, a trickle can quickly become a torrent. During her second term in office, Mrs Thatcher lost her disgraced aide Cecil Parkinson; her Brighton hotel was bombed by the IRA; she was humiliated by the *Spycatcher* revelations and discredited by the Westland affair; and then challenged not only by the obstreperous Greater London Council, but by her own MPs in disputes over pay, pension, tax concessions and welfare reforms. This was a year of living dangerously. Trigger fingers were very itchy as a South Korean 747 found to its cost having strayed into Soviet airspace. *Star Wars* was high on the US agenda but Glasnost was not yet in sight.

Meanwhile back on the cricket field, an England touring party led by conscientious Bob Willis failed to retain the Ashes. On balance, Willis's men acquitted themselves as well as might have been expected given the unavailability of some of England's best and most experienced players. In the absence of Boycott and Gooch, the opening positions were never satisfactorily filled, although Tavare played with commendable adhesiveness at Perth (89) in the first Test, where important contributions by Randall (78 and 115), Gower (72), and Lamb (46 and 56) helped earn a creditable draw.

Despite losing Lillee and Alderman to injury – Alderman dislocated his shoulder at Perth following an oafish pitch invasion – Australia proved far too good at Brisbane, winning by seven wickets. Geoff Lawson proved to be a much more dangerous opponent than in 1981, achieving match figures of 11-134. Thomson shared the second-innings booty in taking 5-73.

Willis admitted that the Brisbane result hinged on his side's failure to subdue the adopted Australian debutant Kepler Wessels (162), who, like Lamb, was South African-born. Willis lamented his tactical blunder in feeding the opening batsman's off-side bias, mistakenly believing the looseness of Wessels's stroke-play would bring about his demise. Willis subsequently discovered it was more profitable to tuck up Wessels by targeting his leg stump. As proof of the effectiveness of this plan, after Brisbane, Wessels averaged only 29.67 in his remaining six innings.

Against his better judgement, Willis was persuaded by his senior batsmen to put the Australians in at Adelaide. On a flawless surface, Greg Chappell scored his second century of the series (115). Assisted well by Hughes (88) the pair steered Australia to a commanding first innings total of 438. While Gower (60 and 114), Lamb (82) and Botham (35 and 58) resisted valiantly, the rest of the English batting was shattered by Lawson who returned match figures of nine wickets for 122. Thomson, Hogg and off-spinner Bruce Yardley mopped up the rest. Having followed on, England could only set Australia a puny winning target which was achieved with the loss of only two wickets. Two successive defeats left Willis fearing a 4-0 thrashing but then England rallied superbly at Melbourne.

Having been invited to bat first at the MCG, England slumped to 56/3 with Hogg and Thomson disposing of Geoff Cook, Graeme Fowler and David Gower. Relieved to be excused the vexed opening position, Tavare was at his dogged best (89). He and Lamb (83) dug in, putting together a fourth-wicket partnership of 161. Renouncing his former dourness, Tavare unexpectedly set about the off-spin of Yardley, thrashing him repeatedly to the boundary. But having established a strong platform, Yardley ran through the lower order, taking 4-89.

The England attack, led by Willis, responded well, though, restricting Australia to a first-innings total of 287 – a lead of just three runs. But once again the England top order failed against Thomson and Hogg, although Fowler (65) hung around without appearing in command. At 160/6 England were careering towards defeat before lower-order resistance led by Botham (46), Pringle (42) and Taylor (37) enabled England to reach 294 runs, 291 in front.

Willis and Botham had largely carried the English attack, thus far, being responsible for almost 60 per cent of Australian dismissals. They were desperate for support. Willis had regretted the omission of Middlesex left-arm spinner Phil Edmonds from his touring party. While Edmonds was sometimes difficult to manage, he was a fine bowler, capable of dismissing the best batsmen. Of the remaining bowlers at his disposal, Miller was the most experienced, accurate and persevering, but unlikely to run through the Australian top order. The same could be said of Eddie Hemmings. That left the Essex medium-paced all-rounder Derek Pringle and the tearaway, raw, young Middlesex fast bowler Norman Cowans.

Pringle had been steady but hardly penetrative. As for Cowans, he had occasionally troubled Chappell, dismissing him cheaply at Brisbane. But as quick as he was, his erratic length and line had been punished ruthlessly.

In fairness, his selection had been a long-shot. The Jamaican-born 21-year-old had only 43 first-class wickets when he stepped on to the plane. He was delighted with the hard, bouncy Australian wickets, but could sustain his pace and accuracy for short spells only.

I had watched him dismiss Dyson and Chappell, during the Australian first innings, on the TV highlights. His approach was fast, strong and upright, completed with a mighty leap, an exaggerated swivel to bring his left shoulder around, and a wheeling, slinging action with which he delivered the ball at speeds of around 90mph. His proximity to the stumps helped his accuracy, at least while he maintained rhythm and stamina. And when it came together, his wicket-to-wicket trajectory posed problems. His dismissal of Dyson lbw was achieved without much seam movement or swing, just naked pace. Dyson didn't seem to fancy facing him much.

When on his game, Cowans was the quickest bowler England had. Willis was still very brisk, of course, capable of producing disconcerting bounce, but had borne a heavy burden in England's cause. He looked wan, his face lined with worry, his tread laboured and weary. By contrast, Cowans was sprightly, and lithely athletic. This young man appeared to be the real deal.

On the night of 29 December I took the transistor radio into the spare bedroom. With the game so fascinatingly poised, and having the latitude of a week's holiday, I decided to listen to entire night-time coverage. As I tuned in I heard that Norman Cowans had been given the new ball instead of Botham. With the first innings TV footage still in mind, I had a vivid mental impression of him as he raced to the wicket. There were no immediate fireworks, though, as Dyson drove Willis to the cover boundary while Wessels spanked a wider delivery from Cowans to the fence. The Australian opening pair seemed composed and in good nick.

And then suddenly the early calm was splintered. In line with the agreed game plan, Cowans speared a faster delivery at Wessels's leg stump. The South African left-hander seemed slow to react. Before he could blunt the danger, the ball either flicked his pad or inside edge before clattering into the middle stump. Cowans extended both palms to his converging team-mates inviting 'low fives' congratulations. Wessels had been dismissed for 14 and Australia were 37/1. Two runs later Chappell was facing Cowans. The lad was said to be giving it his all, sweating copiously, his saturated shirt clinging to his back. In he stormed and released another lightning delivery, pitching just outside the off stump. Chappell attempted to force it away with an airy drive, his feet rooted to the spot, only to find substitute fielder Ian Gould at cover who jubilantly threw the ball aloft. Chappell was gone for two and Australia were 39/2. Cowans had dismissed Chappell twice in the match for just two runs.

However, at 71/2, Hughes and Dyson seemed to be regaining control. It was at this point that Botham enticed Dyson into driving at a slower leg-cutter, only for the ball to find the outside edge and fly to the left of second slip where Tavare, at full stretch, managed to grasp the ball with both hands. Dyson departed for 31 while Botham honoured the MCG jeer leaders with a one-fingered salute. With Border unsettled by a desolate run of form, Hookes was promoted ahead of him.

The partnership between Hookes and Hughes flourished, placing Australia in charge by mid-afternoon at 171/3. Whereas Willis had been unusually expensive, Miller had restrained the Australian run rate by bowling wide on the crease from around the wicket. He did not seem very threatening, though. But once the left-handed Hookes began to collar him, slashing a succession of back-foot drives and cuts to the point and cover boundary, Miller reverted to over the wicket. Almost out of the blue, Hughes essayed a slog sweep at a Miller off-break which pitched on middle and leg. Deceived by the flight and pace of the ball, Hughes badly mistimed his shot. The ball clipped the back of his bat in its follow through, whereupon it fell behind the stumps, initially wrong-footing Taylor. But with amazing reflexes, the England wicketkeeper recovered, diving and scooping up the ball with his right glove just before it hit the ground. Hughes was out for 48 and Australia were still 121 runs from victory, but with six wickets remaining.

With Border's arrival, Cowans was restored to the attack. He was immediately on the money. A short, rising delivery persuaded Hookes to live up to his name, but like Chappell he misjudged the pace of the ball, sending the ball soaring towards mid-on. Willis belied his exhausted demeanour by getting quickly into position to take the catch. While Hookes trudged off to the pavilion, out for 68, Willis led an excited pied piper parade at the other end of the ground. The Australians were beginning to falter. For 'falter' please read 'collapse' as Marsh went back to a short delivery from Cowans which, to his horror, shot along the ground and trapped him lbw for 13. Australia were 190/6. Suddenly, the pitch had begun to produce unreliable bounce. Sensing his opportunity, Cowans produced an identical delivery for Yardley that smacked into the base of his middle and off stumps. Yardley was out for a duck and Australia were now collapsing at 190/7. Pringle then came to the party with his tippy-toes run to the wicket. Lawson had a dart, hooking the ball in the direction of Cowans at long leg. The young fast bowler could do no wrong, calmly pocketing the gift. Lawson had departed for seven and Australia were 202/8. The Australians were capitulating, having tossed their wickets away so carelessly. Hogg was no exception, out lbw, having shuffled across his crease to another fizzing delivery from Cowans.

It was here that Willis blundered. Believing that last man Thomson was the one to target, he invited Border to take easy singles in order to expose his more limited batting partner. Thomson proved remarkably stubborn, though, while Border's easy acquisition of runs played him back into form. With the England bowlers tiring the Australian last-wicket pair added 37 runs in the final overs without displaying many signs of alarm, although Border once played too early at a straight delivery from Willis, almost popping up a gentle return catch. At the close of play Australia were 255/9, 37 runs from victory. Suddenly a heroic triumph seemed possible. At least many Australians thought so as 18,000 turned up for a final day's play that might have lasted for only one ball.

The introduction of the new ball did not achieve the expected breakthrough. The pitch was still sluggish, and no matter what changes Willis made to the attack or the field, Thomson and Border continued to progress serenely. The target continued to narrow. The 20s were safely negotiated and so were the teens, just, since Botham found the outside edge of Thomson's bat only for Tavare to shell the chance wide to his right at second slip. Despite the extra hardness of the new ball, Taylor and the slips moved up a pace or two to ensure that any snick would carry.

With Australia just one boundary from victory, Willis arranged his fielders in a tight circle around the edge of the square. Although Border was on strike, Willis managed to prevent him from scoring, forcing the Australian to dig out a yorker and block a good length ball on his middle and off stump. So it was left to Botham to bowl at Thomson. He needed a magic ball but did not deliver one. It was a long-hop, pitched outside Thomson's off stump, begging to be driven. Thomson moved into position to hit the loose ball hard, but in the pressure of the moment, fatally checked his shot, deciding to push it away for a single instead. The ball swung, found the edge, and travelled quickly, at chest height to Tavare at second slip. Whether his advanced position left him with insufficient time to react, or whether he, too, was bitten with the nerves, Tavare fluffed the chance.

For a split second Thomson espied a reprieve, only for Miller to dash behind Tavare and grasp the ball before it fell to earth. Miller hurled the ball high into the air with relief and elation. Meanwhile, on the third man boundary, Pringle flicked a double V-sign at his Australian critics. The MCG became hushed in disappointment. England had won by three runs, almost the narrowest margin of victory ever achieved in a Test match. An ecstatic Ian Botham declared, 'Don't ever let anyone tell you Test cricket is dead – one-day matches are marvellous fun but in terms of satisfaction – for player and for spectator – comparing them with Tests is like comparing take-away chicken with a banquet.' Amen to that.

Jeff Thomson reacted to his intense disappointment by angrily barging into the England dressing room, berating them for their 'stupid fields' and tactics, threatening dire reprisals in the final Test at Sydney. He had no cause for concern, though. Another poor first innings effort by the England batsmen – Gower (70) and Randall (70) excepted – meant that Willis's men were behind in the game at the halfway stage, and when Hughes (137), Border (83) and Wessels (53) took Australia to a second innings total of 382, the Ashes slipped from England's grasp. Nevertheless, England's night-watchman, Eddie Hemmings, lifted English spirits with a stirring innings of 95, ensuring that the game, unlike the Ashes, was not lost.

Undoubtedly, the better side won. Although some pundits carped that Willis was tactically deficient, he put so much effort into this campaign, constantly rallying his troops in the face of adversity and exhausting himself in carrying an under-strength attack. He should be proud that his side gave a superior Australian team a tough fight.

The highlight of the ensuing summer was India's unexpected victory over the vaunted West Indians in the Prudential World Cup final. Indian Prime Minister Indira Gandhi was so impressed that she took Farokh Engineer's advice to heart and awarded Indians a national day's holiday in celebration.

Having been beaten easily by India in the World Cup semi-finals, England progressed to a comfortable 3-1 Test series victory over visiting New Zealand. Lamb came to the fore with a series average of 65.33 after completing unbeaten centuries at the Oval (102) and Trent Bridge (137) while Gower recorded an average of 57.71 with an unbeaten hundred in a losing cause at Headingley (102) and by scoring 108 in a winning one at Lord's.

Hampshire's South African-born opener Chris Smith made an unspectacular debut against the Kiwis. The TCCB was beginning to have qualms about South African players qualifying for the England Test side on the basis of parental nationality, for they agreed to consider a longer qualification period than the current four years. Their problem was, of course, the shortage of Test-class British players. Although Leicestershire's left-arm spinner Nick Cook made a highly impressive Test debut against New Zealand, taking 17 wickets in the series at only 16.17 runs each, the new-ball attack was too dependent upon Willis's ageing legs. Neither Cowans nor Botham had a remarkable series with the ball. In the all-rounder stakes, Kiwi Richard Hadlee performed better than Botham. Hadlee averaged 50.16 with the bat whereas Botham managed 35.25, despite making a ton at Trent Bridge (103). But it was with the ball that Hadlee triumphed most emphatically, taking 21 wickets at 26.61 compared with Botham's ten wickets at 34.

1984
Smalltown Boy

By the mid-1980s the divisions between the north and south of England were widening substantially. Around 75 per cent of new jobs created between 1983 and 1987 were located in the south-east. Meanwhile, youth unemployment had reached horrifying proportions in the formerly industrial north. In areas of Liverpool, up to 90 per cent of young people were without work. In 1984, Tory MP Matthew Parris attempted to live for a week in Newcastle on a basic Social Security income. He failed. In a *World in Action* TV documentary, he stated, 'Perhaps the sharpest lesson I drew... was that unemployment is not only a problem of the pocket but of the spirit; and once the spirit is broken, neither money nor training can easily help.'

It was small wonder that coalmining folk chose to defend their livelihoods and communities so tenaciously when the NCB threatened pit closures. Mrs Thatcher strode into the conflict, framing it in familiar Falkland terms. Arthur Scargill was a dictator to be crushed like Argentina's General Galtieri, although Orgreave became her Gettysburg rather than her Goose Green.

The 'casuals' seemed to be to the eighties what the punks and skinheads were to the seventies, and what the mods and rockers were to the sixties. Like their 1960s predecessors they seemed more obsessed with style than notoriety. And like the yuppies they donned the latest designer gear, with the more affluent, London-based football fans flaunting their sartorial wares in front of their less-privileged northern opponents. It was their obnoxious contempt which inspired Harry Enfield's 'Loadsamoney' TV character. While the pits and manufacturing sector were going down the tube, the leisure and style industry was flourishing, helped by the 'casuals' patronage.

As was the case in 'Swinging London', style outstripped substance. The huge success of the controversial Liverpool band Frankie Goes to Hollywood spawned a market for 'Frankie' T-shirts with printed messages such as 'Frankie says Relax' or 'Frankie says arm the unemployed'. Once the band's over-hyped period of fame had quickly spluttered out, those who marketed the style cashed in on the backlash, producing T-shirts telling Frankie basically 'where to go'. The asinine moral panic that the 'Frankies' aroused seemed no more than commercial artifice. In 1984, another band with a gay frontman, Bronski Beat, released their song 'Smalltown Boy', one of the year's best singles. Above a sad, swishing synth-pop melody with an incongruously bouncing beat, falsetto Jimmy Somerville poignantly describes the family rejection, bullying and loneliness that gay men suffer on account of their sexual orientation. There was no banal commercial artifice here.

This was the year when Bob Geldof, leader of Irish rock band The Boomtown Rats, inspired a swathe of fellow rock and pop stars to mount a Christmas famine relief appeal. Please ignore the sniping, sneering cynicism that their efforts attracted from some quarters, this was an immense achievement, which was more than could be said of the languishing England cricket team which lost rubbers, for the first time, in New Zealand and Pakistan on their cheerless twin winter tours.

Botham (138) and Randall (164) rescued England from a bad start in the first Test at Wellington with a sixth-wicket partnership of 232, but big innings from Jeremy Coney (174 not out) and Martin Crowe (100) ensured that England's first-innings lead of 244 was not converted into victory. At Christchurch, New Zealand batted first on a deteriorating wicket. Richard Hadlee whacked a rapid 99, taking advantage of some imprudently short-pitched bowling. Hadlee then took 8-44 as England were blasted out twice on a cracked, rain-affected surface for 82 and 93, to lose by an innings and 132 runs. The final Test at Auckland ended in a high-scoring draw in which Randall made another century (104), but so did the Kiwi trio John Wright (130), Jeff Crowe (128) and Ian Smith (113 not out). And so ended what one paper described as the 'sex, drugs and rock 'n' roll tour', during which the tourists' alleged misbehaviour had greater coverage than the cricket.

In Pakistan, England lost the opening Test at Karachi with twirling leg-spinner Abdul Qadir taking eight wickets for 133 and Sarfraz Nawaz 6-69. Only Gower showed much resolve with the bat, scoring a brace of half-centuries, while Nick Cook's 11-83 ensured that Pakistan struggled in making the required 65 runs for victory. Pakistan won by three wickets.

Gower took over the captaincy at Faisalabad after illness had forced Willis to return home. He celebrated the honour by scoring 152 as England replied to Pakistan's first-innings total of 449/8 declared with 546/8 declared. Gatting (75) and Chris Smith (66) had added 127 for the first wicket, in yet another of England's ever-rotating opening pairings. This was the 11th different combination attempted since the Nottingham Test of 1981. With Marks (83), Randall (65) and Fowler (57) lending essential support, the game ended in stalemate.

The final Test at Lahore was drawn also, despite an exciting finish. England began poorly, being dismissed for only 241 runs with Qadir (5-84) and Sarfraz (4-49) inflicting the main damage. England were indebted to Marks (74) and Fowler (58) once again in getting them past 200. This pair shared a 120-run sixth-wicket partnership. At 181/8 Pakistan were in trouble, too, but a 171-run ninth-wicket stand between Zaheer (82 not out) and Sarfraz (90) took them to a 102-run lead. Qadir was equally mesmerising when England batted again, taking 5-110, but Gower's brilliant, unbeaten century (172) enabled him to set Pakistan a 243-run winning target. Openers Mohsin Khan (104) and Shoaib Mohammed (80) shot out of the blocks, blasting 173 before the first wicket fell with Cook and Marks copping most of their punishment. However, Cowans came belatedly to England's rescue, taking five wickets in 22 balls, prompting Pakistan to settle for a draw after stumbling to 199/6, thereby taking the series 1-0. Cowans's second-innings return of 5-42 was his best since his 6-77 at Melbourne.

I had listened to the radio commentary from Lahore in a freezing apartment in Eastbourne. Lydia, our three-year-old daughter, was staying alone with my parents for the first time in nearby Hastings. The weather was as grey as much of the cricket in this series, although that explosive final session at Lahore was a welcome exception. It was so cold that Liz spent much of the time reading under the bed covers while I ran for miles and miles over the Sussex Downs, in a state of glazed oblivion, when my body operated as if on auto pilot, and the vanishing point remained ever distant – an ideal state for following England's cricket team.

The summer series against the West Indies was the first of successive 'Blackwashes' as England were thrashed in all five Tests. If this had been a boxing match it would have been stopped well before the fifth round. At Edgbaston, West Indies won a typically tight contest by an innings and 180 runs. Gomes (143) and Richards (117) made centuries, the former diligently, the latter destructively, as the West Indies totalled 606 in reply to England's pathetic first-innings score of 191 with only Botham (64) putting up a fight. Poor Andy Lloyd celebrated his Test debut in hospital having been hit on the temple by a rising ball from Malcolm Marshall.

England made a much better fist of the second Test at Lord's, at least until the final day. Debutant Chris Broad (55) and his opening partner Graeme Fowler (106) put on 101 for the first wicket only for the remaining nine England wickets to fall for just 185 more. The chief destroyer was Malcolm Marshall (6-85) with his skidding pace and lethal short-pitched deliveries. However, Botham led an inspiring fightback, taking 8-103 as the West Indians were dismissed for 245. Lamb (110) and Botham (81) then helped England to 300/9 before Gower declared, setting West Indies 344 to win in 78 overs.

On that final day I was in the High Court opposing an application made by the mother of a ten-year-old boy to have him restored to her full-time care. He had been a Ward of Court since the age of three, with my employing council having had caring responsibility for him since the original order was made. During the intervening years, the boy had remained happily with local long-term foster parents. I respected the mother's efforts in re-establishing her life after a chaotic past of drug and alcohol addiction, nomadic wandering, and erratic contact with her son. However, in the six years she had taken to sort out her life with a more stable partner, her son had put down roots with his foster family. Although fond of his mother, he seemed to regard his life as being with the family who had looked after him for much of his childhood. My heart sank, though, when the mother assured the court that it was her and her partner's intention to get some 'bondage going' with her son, prompting some quickly suppressed smirks among the court officials. I felt sorry for her. Having finally kicked her damaging addictions, and established a settled life, I no longer had any reason to doubt that she was a capable, caring parent. I freely acknowledged this in court. I was more concerned that her botched jargon might discredit her, exposing her, perhaps, to unfair ridicule.

Not that it seemed to have any impact upon the judge's decision. In declining the mother's application, the judge referred to the strength of the boy's attachment to his foster family. While the foster family recognised the mother as the boy's parent, actively supporting his continuing relationship with her – his father's whereabouts were unknown – they intended to look after him until the court deemed otherwise or he made a decision to leave, when of age to do so. In the meantime, he would continue to have regular contact with his mother and her partner, including overnight stays, and they would remain welcomed visitors at the foster family's home. The mother was crushed by the court's decision. The restoration of her self-esteem seemed to rest upon her son returning to her care. She had difficulty in understanding that her son wanted to remain with his foster family, wrongly believing that her application had failed because the court and the council's children's services had lingering doubts about her fitness as a parent. This was neither the time nor place to discuss this crucial issue so we agreed to meet on the following day.

Driving away from court I re-examined the veracity of the case I had put forward. I did not hide behind the court's judgement. After all, my recommendation carried considerable weight in this process. Nor did I indemnify myself by citing the boy's expressed wishes. His loyalty to his foster family and his understandable uncertainty about returning to his mother's full-time care had obviously played a significant part in what he said. By opposing the mother's application, I thought I had been protecting a vulnerable boy who had found love and stability in his foster home after a very disruptive and distressing start to his life. And yet, upon subsequent reflection, I began to feel increasingly uncomfortable with an outcome I had sought and secured. I was not to know, of course, that four years later this boy would request the court's leave to be reunited permanently with his mother and her partner. Long before that happened, though, I belatedly grasped the principle that it is *always* to be presumed that children should live, and are generally better off, with their natural families, unless there are *compelling* reasons to the contrary. In this court hearing that burden of proof was reversed with a presumption made that the boy was better off remaining with his foster family, leaving the mother to demonstrate compelling reasons why this should not be so, which she could not do without impugning her boy's foster care. Knowing how much her son loved his foster family and how much they had done for him, she was unwilling to go so far.

Turning on the Test match radio commentary, I learnt that David Gower had suffered a disappointing day, too. Gordon Greenidge had reached a double century, while his partner 'Larry' Gomes was in sight of his hundred. Only one wicket had fallen. The West Indian victory target was just a few runs away. With the exception of the persevering Willis, the England attack had been murdered by Greenidge, who had despatched 29 rasping boundaries and a couple of towering sixes. It was a massacre. The West Indies would overrun England in the remaining three Tests, too.

Willis made his 90th and final Test appearance at Leeds, the ground of his greatest triumph. While his first innings dismissal of Holding took his total Test haul to 325 wickets, his bowling received scant respect from the West Indian batsmen who contemptuously took 163 runs off his 26 overs. It was an ignominious end to a marvellous Test career. His retirement left an enormous chasm in the England attack. It was hoped that Cowans might become his successor, but with his performances remaining frustratingly erratic, this seemed increasingly unlikely.

England's summer of submission was completed when Sri Lanka had the better of a high-scoring draw at Lord's. Against his better judgement, Gower was persuaded by Peter May, the chairman of selectors, to put the visitors in to bat. Wettimuny (190), Mendis (111), Ranatunga (84) and Silva (102 not out) underlined the folly of this decision as they rattled up 491 runs. Lamb's fourth ton of the summer (107) restored a smidgen of home pride but the grim reality was, that since the glorious summer of 1981, England had been defeated by all of their opponents except Sri Lanka who had outplayed England in this one-off Test.

The blight of dangerously short-pitched fast bowling was back on the agenda. Former England captain Tony Lewis wrote in the *Sunday Telegraph*, 'The memory of last summer in England was of helmeted, arm-padded, rib-padded anonymous procession of batsmen doing their best not to get their skulls cracked or being caught off the bat handle.' While intimidating pace bowling continued to serve the interests of its perpetrators, self-regulation remained a vain hope, and while the ICC refrained from issuing firmer directions, it was unrealistic and unfair to expect umpires to exercise greater control.

1985
Running Up That Hill

As in 1977, England recovered from a brutal West Indian pasting by unexpectedly defeating India on an ensuing winter tour. It was a remarkably courageous achievement. For the England team had arrived in India on the day that Indian Premier Indira Gandhi was assassinated. The country was gripped by violent disorder. As if this was not sufficient cause for alarm, British Deputy High Commissioner Percy Norris was murdered in Mumbai just prior to the first Test starting there. Understandably, the England players were worried that they might become a terrorist target. The shambolic security arrangements, which allowed strangers to reach their dressing room unchallenged, gave them little assurance of their safety.

It is amazing that the British Foreign Office did not direct the TCCB to cancel the tour. But as was the case during the politically volatile tour of Pakistan in 1969, this did not happen. It was little wonder that England lost the first Test by eight wickets, although the situation was no better for their opponents. Mike Gatting demonstrated his nerves of steel by making an admirable maiden Test ton. But once the Test was completed, England tour manager, Tony Brown, was urged to take the team home not only by vociferous press men but also by some of his players. Brown desisted, but arranged a brief period of respite for his players in Sri Lanka, only for the party to encounter a bomb explosion at Colombo bus station on arrival.

Thereafter, the tour progressed without further incident. Much credit should be given to captain David Gower for holding the squad together, and for bringing about England's eventual success. His relaxed, inclusive and enabling style of captaincy was exactly what was required. It was an approach that was panned during the disastrous 1985/86 Caribbean tour, but proved perfectly judged here. As worried as they must have been for their safety, players such as Graeme Fowler, Mike Gatting, Tim Robinson, Phil Edmonds and Neil Foster produced superb match- and series-winning performances. For Gower's class of 1984/85 recovered astonishingly to take the series 2-1, after winning by eight wickets at New Delhi, and by nine wickets at Madras (Chennai), where both Fowler and Gatting made double centuries, and Essex paceman Foster took 11 wickets for 163 on a dispiritingly slow surface.

With Gooch and Emburey once again available for Test selection, having served their three-year bans, and Botham having recovered from a back injury, which had excluded him from the Indian tour, England were able to call upon a much stronger squad for the home Ashes series of 1985. As for the Aussies, they had been rocked by the news that seven of their touring party had signed for a 'rebel tour' of South Africa in 1985/86. Among them was former captain Kim Hughes who had tearfully resigned as Australian Test skipper after two thumping defeats by the touring West Indians in 1984. This time Kerry Packer was on the side of the Australian Board of Control as the 'defectors' were threatened with ten-year bans. The Board's bullish stand induced Graeme Wood, Murray Bennett, Wayne Phillips and Dirk Wellham to change their minds and remain loyal to them.

The summer of 1985 was wet, cool and sometimes wild. Liz, Lydia and I donned heavy woollens for our blustery stay in north Cornwall. We had hoped we might enjoy a short, balmy holiday in the south-west before a change of work took us all to London. Not so. Red warning flags flapped furiously all week. The vast, gleaming Cornish sands were largely deserted apart from clutches of hardy surfers who, under storm-tossed clouds, braved the relentless assault of lurching, cream-crested rollers. The sudden, searing slashes of sunlight startlingly exposed their zigzagging descents. Denied the opportunity to swim, we were drawn towards the hissing, translucent waves that toppled before us, each of which broke upon the beach with a shuddering boom, spewing spume in pursuit of our giggling retreat. Undeterred, we repeatedly returned to our positions once the seething ocean had sucked back its spent surges and glinting hostages.

During that squally week I ran for hours over the steep, surrounding hills that afforded magnificent views of the foam-capped ocean, driven onwards and upwards by Kate Bush's imploring single, 'Running Up That Hill'. Actually, the song has nothing to do with jogging. For it is about how angry disputes between men and women might be reconciled if they swapped roles and presuppositions. So much for the hard-wired gender stereotyping of *Men are from Mars, Women are from Venus*.

In contrast with the wild summer weather the Ashes series became becalmed after the Australians had squared the series at Lord's. The sluggish pace of play was not helped by the torpid surfaces at Trent Bridge and Old Trafford. England had begun the series brightly at Headingley. Inspired by his winter success, Tim Robinson struck a punchy hundred (175). Botham added a ruthless half-century (60), while returning 'rebel' exile John Emburey took 5-82, leaving England with only 123 runs to find for victory. This was achieved with five wickets to spare.

At Lord's, Allan Border's typically pugnacious first innings knock (196), wonderfully supported by Greg Ritchie (94), gave the visitors a winning advantage which they did not squander. Leg-spinner Bob Holland took 5-68 in England's second innings, which mustered only 261 runs, despite Botham's stubborn resistance (85). Bustling young Australian fast bowler Craig McDermott had a fine match, being responsible for eight dismissals at a cost of 154 runs. Australia won by four wickets.

Trent Bridge produced a high-scoring draw in which the questions posed by Gower's radiant innings of 166 were answered emphatically by more workmanlike ones by Graeme Wood (172) and Greg Ritchie (146). Ritchie scored another worthy ton at Old Trafford (146 not out), helping Australia secure a draw after England had seized a 225-run first-innings lead, thanks to Mike Gatting's domineering innings of 160. Here, McDermott became the youngest Australian to take eight wickets in a Test innings.

The start of the crucial fifth Test at Edgbaston coincided with the final days of our Cornish holiday. Believing the steamy conditions might be conducive to swing bowling, Gower put the Australians in to bat. Unfortunately, another sluggish wicket offered little encouragement to his revamped seam attack, comprising Botham, Leicestershire's muscular former coalminer Les Taylor, and Kent's brisk swinger Richard Ellison. With debutant Taylor and Ellison bowling too short, and rain once again intruding, Australia were comfortably placed at 181/2 at the close of the first day. Although Ellison bowled splendidly in between the showers on the second day, quickly reducing the Australians to 208/6, a lower-order recovery led by Lawson (53) meant that, with two days gone and the weather still unsettled, Border's side looked immune from defeat at 335/8.

On the Saturday we began our long drive to Hastings. Unbroken summer sunshine had returned not only to Cornwall but also to Birmingham. In the first over, Lawson was run out by Gower without adding to his overnight score while Ellison dismissed Holland for a duck. The chase was on. While our daughter slept or listened to her audio books, the *Test Match Special* commentary entertained Liz and I for much of our seven-hour journey. Determined to make up for lost time Robinson (148) and Gower (215) set about the Australian attack with unfamiliar savagery. Their second-wicket partnership of 331 was achieved in only 343 minutes, and studded with thudding boundaries from Robinson and refined ones from Gower. Not that Gower's princely grace lacked anything in power with almost half of his runs coming from boundaries. At the close of a memorable day's play, England were 20 in front at 355/1. Failing to contain his irrepressible enthusiasm, radio commentator Brian Johnston announced, 'I'm sorry for any Australian listeners. There can't be much joy listening but here is an English crowd revelling in sunshine, which we haven't had much of, who have been given a treat today and I'm sorry if we sounded a bit too pleased.' When it came to gloating inoffensively, Johnston had few equals.

On the Monday, Liz and I drove to London to begin our house-hunting while the fun continued on *Test Match Special*. Robinson and Gower departed only for Gatting (100 not out) and Lamb (46) to continue the carnage. Not to be outdone, Botham smashed a straight, towering six – his 75th of the season – off the first ball he received from the decidedly quick Craig McDermott, as England rocketed to 595/5 declared.

This left Australia an awkward hour to survive at the end of the fourth day. Botham in his faster style made the initial breakthrough, dismissing Hilditch for ten. But it was Ellison, bowling full and straight with sharp, late away-swing, who broke the back of the Australian batting. Cleverly varying his pace, Ellison induced Wessels into playing an injudicious drive at a slower ball that drifted across him. Wessels edged to wicketkeeper Downton and Australia were 32/2. Hapless nightwatchman Bob Holland was immediately lbw to a much faster delivery that evaded his stumbling shot, leaving captain Border to successfully prevent a hat-trick. But his partner Graeme Wood did not stay long, launching a rash drive off another hooping delivery. The resulting thick edge caused the ball to fly high, if not mightily, to Robinson at cover. Australia were now 35/4. But while Border remained, Australia still had a chance of saving the game. Stubbly, in the guise of Desperate Dan, and squinting with the steeliness of Clint Eastwood, the hickory-hard Border was at his dogged best when the chips were down. He was always the prize scalp, but even he could not keep Ellison out as a late in-swinger took his off bail (36/5).

The bad news for England was that wet weather was forecast for the final day. Border giggled with delight as the dense drizzle duly arrived, threatening to rule out any play. Unfortunately for him the elements relented by mid-afternoon, allowing a resumption of play shortly after. However, Gower remained frustrated as Aussie wicketkeeper Phillips played with growing authority, adding 77 runs for the sixth wicket with an imperturbable Greg Ritchie. It took a freak dismissal to wreck their recovery plan. Phillips, surrounded by close catchers, slashed hard at a shorter delivery from Edmonds. Lamb at silly point immediately leapt out of the way, but while in mid-air

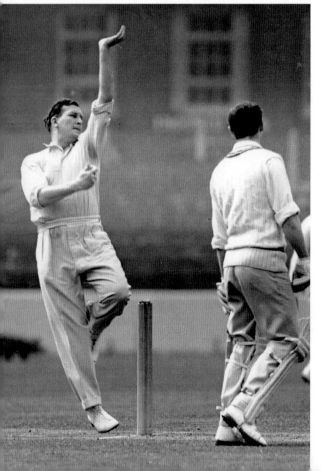

19th August 1953: The England cricket team captained by Len Hutton, prior to the Ashes victory over Australia at the Oval. Back row (left to right) Trevor Bailey, Peter May, Tom Graveney, Jim Laker, Tony Lock, Johnny Wardle (12th man), Fred Trueman. Front row (left to right) Bill Edrich, Alec Bedser, Sir Len Hutton (captain), Denis Compton and Godfrey Evans (wicket-keeper).

Surrey off-spinner, Jim Laker who bowled England to Ashes victory in 1953, and again in 1956 when he took 46 wickets during the series at an average cost of 9.60 runs each, including world record match figures of 19 wickets for 90 runs at Old Trafford.

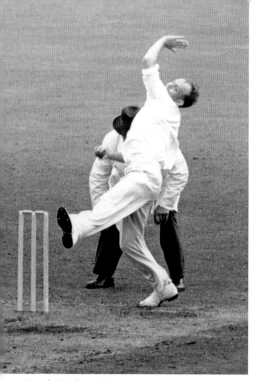

Frank 'Typhoon' Tyson in action against South Africa in 1955. His ferocious pace in Australia during the 1954/55 Ashes series was a major factor in England's Ashes victory.

Ted Dexter, England's captain 1961-64, in typically belligerent style.

England batsman Ken Barrington cuts a ball from Australia pace man, Graham McKenzie, during the drawn final Test in Sydney in February 1963.

A victorious England team carry their captain Ray Illingworth off the field after clinching the Ashes by a 62 run win in the seventh Test match in Sydney.

West Indian fast bowler, Wes Hall, in action in England during the spectacular Test series of 1963.

John Snow of Sussex and England clean bowls West Indian fast bowler, Michael Holding, in the fourth Test match at Headingley in July 1976. Snow was England's leading pace bowler during the late sixties and early seventies, playing a major part in England's victory in the Caribbean in 1967/68 and in the recovery of the Ashes in 1970/71.

August 1968: Umpire Charlie Elliot raises his finger to signify John Inverarity's dismissal and England's victory in the final Ashes Test at the Oval. Derek Underwood took seven wickets in the Australian second innings, seizing a series-saving win with only five minutes to spare.

'Life in the fast lane'. Geoff Boycott evades a Michael Holding bouncer during the third Test against the West Indies at Old Trafford in July 1980. Boycott made 86 invaluable runs in the second innings helping England achieve a creditable draw.

Sir Ian Botham at Edgbaston July 1981. His second innings bowling figures of five wickets for 11 runs enabled England to win by just 29 runs. Botham's bowling and unforgettable centuries at Headingley and Old Trafford propelled England to a magnificent 3-1 Ashes victory. Botham made 5,200 Test runs for England at an average of 33.54 and took 383 wickets at an average cost of 28.40 runs each.

24th July 1981: Willis's sixth victim, Geoff Lawson is out for one run, caught by wicket-keeper, Bob Taylor, who is dancing in jubilation with Mike Gatting. Australia are 75 for 8 on the final day of the third Test match at Headingley. Willis took eight wickets for 43 in the Australian second innings and England won by 18 runs after following on.

Colin Cowdrey ducks under a bouncer from Dennis Lillee, while David Lloyd is backing-up during the second Ashes Test in Perth, December 1974.

Jeff Thomson is bowling
to David Gower, with
Rod Marsh keeping
wicket, during the second
Ashes Test at Brisbane in
November 1982.

Viv Richards in typical
punishing form on the
West Indian tour of
England 1984.

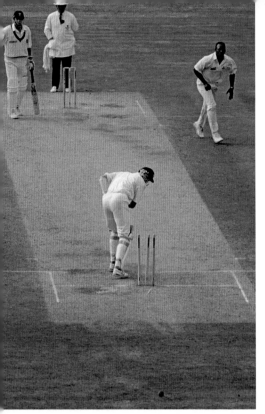

Devon Malcolm claims his ninth wicket in the South African second innings, setting up a series-saving victory at the Oval in August 1994.

The great Indian all-rounder, Kapil Dev, who scored 5,248 Test runs at an average of 31.05 and took 434 Test wickets at an average of 29.64.

Michael Atherton in a typical feisty duel with South African fast bowler, Allan Donald.

The great New Zealand all-rounder, Sir Richard Hadlee who scored 3,124 Test runs at an average of 27.16 and took 431 Test wickets at an average of 22.29.

The great Pakistani all-rounder Imran Khan who scored 3,807 Test runs at an average of 37.69 and took 362 Test wickets at an average of 22.81.

England's Graham Thorpe produced a typically defiant innings of 123 during the final Ashes Test match at Perth in February 1995 but could not avert a 329 run defeat.

England's 2005 Ashes winning cricket team with Queen Elizabeth and Prince Philip. Back row from left: Geraint Jones (Kent), Andrew Strauss (Middlesex), Simon Jones (Glamorgan), Kevin Pietersen (Hampshire), Matthew Hoggard (Yorkshire), Stephen Harmison (Durham), Paul Collingwood (Durham), Ian Bell (Warwickshire). Front row from left: Phil Neale (Manager), Marcus Trescothick (Somerset), Michael Vaughan (Yorkshire), Queen Elizabeth II, the Duke of Edinburgh, Duncan Fletcher (Coach), Andrew Flintoff (Lancashire) and Ashley Giles (Warwickshire). *All photographs are supplied by Getty Images.*

the ball struck his instep and ricocheted to Gower who took the catch and appealed immediately. Following a consultation between the two umpires, the aggrieved Phillips was given out, whereupon the remaining four Australian wickets collapsed like a house of cards. Australia were all out for 142 to lose by an innings and 118 runs. Ellison had match figures of 10-104. The tide had turned.

The first day of the final Test at the Oval featured a century of pugilistic power from Gooch (196) and a serene one from Gower (157) as the pair added 351 runs in 337 minutes for the second wicket. Although England's innings drained away quickly on day two, the Australians were bundled out for 241 and 129 to lose by an innings and 94 runs, allowing a delighted Gower to reclaim the Ashes. Once again, Ellison's swing bowling proved decisive as he achieved match figures of 7-81. Gower quipped that his triumphant presentation of the urn seemed like a scene from *The Life of Brian*. He said, 'The urn was so small that when I held it up to the Oval crowd, nobody could really see what I was holding.' 'Blessed are the cheesemakers.'

1986
Live to Tell

Once upon a time I had dismissed Madonna as a vapid vamp. Then I heard 'Live to Tell' and thought again. This is no celebrity affectation, no lachrymose indulgence. In 'Live to Tell' she veers from drained solemnity to beseeching anguish, wearied by the burden of incubating a long-held secret. The backing musicians on keyboard, synthesiser, guitar and drums are pitch-perfect in evoking a sombre, melancholy soundscape. There's no pop confection here. If this song is about child abuse, as many have surmised, it finds its mark more viscerally than, say, Suzanne Vega's sensitively imagined tale, 'Luka'.

After 'Live to Tell' I got the message. Madonna's extravagantly sexualised displays were not lascivious titillations. They were expressions of female power, just as 1980s shoulder pads and sprouting hairstyles were. Her workaholic dedication to her art and her hard-headed commercial acumen were indicative of her relentless pursuit of success. Her deconstruction of ostensibly salacious triggers mocked the notion that women are essentially men's playthings. Madonna supposed 'sexy feminism' was not an oxymoron. It represented her view of women on top.

This was certainly more diverting fare than what the England cricket team served up on the grim winter tour of the Caribbean in 1985/86. Once again the West Indies crushed England's feeble pretensions of competitiveness. All five Tests were lost by mighty margins. Upon his own admission, Gower allowed his players too much slack, leaving it largely to their discretion as and when and how they practised. There seemed to be no discernible game plan. The former Kent and Pakistan cricketer Asif Iqbal opined in a radio interview, 'Professionalism in a lawyer or an engineer is supposed to be an attribute, but when used in a cricketing context the term somehow insinuates indiscipline, boorishness – everything in fact that is traditionally not cricket.'

Gower was the only English batsman to average more than 30 during the five-match series, as his summer of love degenerated into a winter of discontent. Once again the press carped at the looseness of his shots outside the off stump. England's cause was hampered further when Gatting was ruled out of the Test series after a short ball from Malcolm Marshall shattered his nose in a one-day international. As for another summer hero, the mulleted Tim Robinson, he averaged only nine runs in his eight Test innings. It seemed as if most of the England batsmen were woefully unprepared for the extremity of pace and bounce produced by Garner, Holding, Marshall and Patterson. In seven out of their ten Test innings, England failed to reach 200 runs.

Meanwhile Botham continued to bowl in a faster style which had brought him 30 Ashes wickets at 27.58 during the summer series. But on the unforgiving, shining Caribbean surfaces his short-pitched deliveries stirred a feeding frenzy among the West Indian batsmen. Haynes, Richards and Richardson averaged over fifty runs with the bat while Botham conceded, on average, more than four runs per over with his 11 wickets costing 48.63 runs each. Gower seemed disinclined to counsel Botham on the folly of his ways as the cream of West Indian batting carved, cut, slashed, pulled and hooked with impunity. Glamorgan fast bowler Greg Thomas had supposedly suggested to a ducking Richards, 'The ball's red and round. Why not try hitting it?' Richards's response was to smash Thomas's next short ball out of the ground, reputedly retorting, 'You know what it looks like. Now go and fetch it.' At Antigua, Richards slammed a sensational century off just 56 balls in 83 minutes with seven sixes. Whether the exchange took place as described is open to question. Richards was equivocal when recently asked. However, there was no mistaking the West Indians' vindictive delight at this annihilation, particularly among those who had protested vociferously against the South African 'rebel' tourists – Gooch, Willey and Emburey – at Trinidad.

England then lost the first and second Tests of the summer to the rampant Indians, and might well have lost the third at Edgbaston had rain not intervened, although Gatting's gritty unbeaten hundred (183) proved crucial, too. The Indians had arrived with an awful Test record having won only one match in 42 attempts since defeating Keith Fletcher's side in Mumbai in December 1981, and yet they prospered here with disdainful ease.

India's five-wicket win in the first Test at Lord's was crowned with a graceful century from Dilip Vengsarkar (126 not out), who repeated the feat in India's 279-run win at Leeds. The occasion was less glorious for a demoralised David Gower as the England captaincy was passed to Mike Gatting. Once again the TCCB shuffled the pack, in searching for a credible opening partner for Gooch. During the six summer Tests, five different candidates were auditioned – Tim Robinson of Nottinghamshire, Wilf Slack of Middlesex, Mark Benson of Kent, Martin Moxon of Yorkshire and Bill Athey, then of Gloucestershire. Although Moxon made a promising debut against New Zealand, scoring 74 in his first innings, none of those chosen staked a solid claim.

Not that Gooch was performing well. After making a confident first innings ton at Lord's (114) he mustered only 61 over his next five knocks. In fact, Gatting was the only England batsman to average more than 29 in the Indian series. Maninder Singh took 12 wickets at 15.58 each with his orthodox left-arm spin while Chetan Sharma's brisk, slinging pace accounted for 16 dismissals at 18.75. Together they tore holes in the meek home batting, although it was Roger Binny's seamers which humbled England at Leeds.

Botham missed all but one of the six summer Tests having received a two-month suspension from the TCCB after admitting, in a press article, that he had smoked pot. In Botham's absence, the England pace attack was unproductively rotated with Graham Dilley, Richard Ellison, John Lever, Neil Foster, Greg Thomas, Derek Pringle and the two Test debutants – the Zambian-born Neal Radford and the Barbados-born Gladstone Small – coming and mostly going. Botham's talismanic return for the final Test at the Oval was eagerly anticipated. He did not disappoint, dismissing Kiwi Bruce Edgar with his first delivery, a tame half-volley. It was good enough, though, for him to equal Dennis Lillee's world record of 355 Test match dismissals. But his three first innings wickets and an explosive unbeaten innings of 59 runs, hit off only 36 balls, were in vain as an apocalyptic storm swept across the Oval, extinguishing England's last hope of salvaging the series. It was the first time that New Zealand had won a rubber in England and was richly deserved. While Gower and Gooch batted well, averaging over 50, so did Kiwi Martin Crowe, who averaged almost 70 in the series. Meanwhile a predatory Richard Hadlee took 19 wickets at little over 20 runs apiece.

England's shambolic summer was encapsulated by the 'four wicketkeepers' farrago at Lord's. With Bruce French knocked out by a Hadlee bouncer, Bill Athey donned the gloves but, as a non-specialist, Athey struggled to master the task. With Jeremy Coney's consent, veteran stumper Bob Taylor was then asked to take over for the rest of the second day. Taylor, who had retired two years previously, had been in a Lord's hospitality tent. However, Taylor was relieved on the third day when Hampshire's Bobby Parks (son of Jim) arrived.

Only Australia's insipid form in their twin home series with New Zealand, which they lost 1-2, and India, which they drew 0-0, gave Gatting's side any glimmer of hope Down Under. Martin Johnson, the *Independent* cricket correspondent, remained gloomy about England's prospects particularly after their underwhelming start to the tour. By the end of their first month in Australia, England's top four batsmen had single-figure averages. Chris Broad 'explained', 'We were acclimatising to the wine and socialising.' Johnson declared, 'There are only three things wrong with England – they can't bat, they can't bowl and they can't field.'

This dismissive assessment prompted vice-captain John Emburey to issue the team with T-shirts that bore the strapline, 'Can't bat, can't bowl, can't field'. It was a smart move. The self-deprecating message fired a competitive, siege-like spirit while mocking Australian conceit. However, England manager Micky Stewart had to step in quickly to foil a 'honey trap' when a tabloid newspaper mischievously despatched three women to fraternise with the England players, in the hope of extracting sensational revelations. While the media focused on England's limitations, the Australian shortcomings received little attention. And yet an Australian 'rebel' tour of South Africa had resulted in the banning of three of their most experienced seamers, Terry Alderman, Rodney Hogg and Carl Rackemann, while Geoff Lawson was expected to be sidelined having played very little first-class cricket in the previous ten months.

Emerging from beneath the radar, Gatting's team surpassed all expectations at Brisbane, winning the opening Test by seven wickets. It was England's first victory in 11 Tests, the last of which had been at the Oval in 1985. Border won the toss and put England in to bat. But his inexperienced pace trio – a giant, gangling Bruce Reid, a lively Chris Matthews and a combustible Merv Hughes – had a chastening reception. England compiled a first-innings total of 456 assisted ably by Athey (76), Gatting (61), Lamb (40), Gower (51) and debutant DeFreitas (40). However, it was left to Botham to pummel the Australians into abject submission. His incendiary century (138), hit off 174 balls, contained four sixes and 13 fours.

A savage drive off Hughes took Botham to 99, while a lofted smash off the same bowler earned him a hundred. Botham then blasted a six over the square leg boundary. When Hughes tried a bouncer, Botham hit the ball with such force that it crashed against the fence at midwicket, and rebounded almost as far as the square. Hughes tried a different tack, pitching the next one up but Botham contemptuously thrashed it over mid-on. Team mate, Steve Waugh thought that a mauling of this severity could scupper Hughes's Test career but he had no need to worry. The glowering pantomime villain brooded deeply upon his humiliation here before seizing his revenge two years later when he became a foul-mouthed scourge of the England batsmen.

I retain a brief audio extract of Botham's thunderous innings. Australian commentator Jim Maxwell had the misfortune to be at the microphone. Maxwell reported, '[Off-spinner Craig] Matthews bowls to Botham. He is down the wicket and swings at this. Look at this guys, it's straight over the sight screen, six, bang! It landed over the dog track, the third six of Botham's innings... The entertainment rolls on, 7/424. Botham and DeFreitas have added 73. There have been some crashing shots – a six behind point, one behind square, a pull... and Botham is down again, he is having a lash at it and it is going for six again... over the top near the dog track and into the Sir Gordon Chalk building. How do you bowl to a man in that mood? He is playing with complete disdain.'

Graham Dilley then produced one of his best England performances with the ball, taking 5-68 in helping dismiss Australia for 248. Gatting had no qualms about enforcing the follow-on. This time it was Emburey's off-spin which confounded the Australians. Although opener Geoff Marsh made a composed century (110), Emburey stifled the rest of the Australian batting, conceding less than two runs per over in taking 5-80.

One of Emburey's second-innings victims was Border whom he tucked up by bowling over the wicket at his leg stump, denying the left-hander the space to free his arms and play his favourite cut and sweep shots. Several times Border's bat jammed against his pads as he played too hard at the ball. It proved to be his undoing as Lamb eventually took a catch at silly mid-off.

Having won only three of the 22 Tests in which he had led Australia, Border was under fire. But Border was made of sterner stuff than his distraught predecessor Kim Hughes. While acknowledging that Botham's hundred was the defining moment in both the match and the series, he stood apart from his opponents, making snarling ripostes, and grumpily refusing to join Channel 9's post-match awards session, hosted by a garrulous Tony Greig. After his courteous concession of defeat at the Oval in 1985, it was 'no more Mr Nice Guy'.

At Perth, England seemed set to extend their advantage. On a belter of a wicket, Chris Broad (162) and Bill Athey (96) patiently made a 223-run opening stand. With Gooch remaining at home for personal reasons, Broad had seized his chance. He played in an upright, stately manner, driving strongly and straight, and scoring well off his legs. He largely eschewed hooking, pulling and, even, cutting, particularly against the spinners, unless the ball was invitingly short. As a measure of his success, Broad completed this series with an astounding average of 69.57 having made three very impressive centuries. Broad was well supported by his resolute opening partner Bill Athey.

Gower rediscovered his touch at Perth, making 136 glorious runs with the style that had graced the summer of 1985. In scoring 404 runs in the rubber at an average of 57.71, this was his most profitable series since then. Surrey wicketkeeper Jack Richards also demonstrated his prowess with the bat at Perth, posting a maiden Test ton (133) and his highest first-class score, as England racked up a massive total of 592/8 declared. Border's grim-faced, gritty hundred (125) enabled Australia to avoid the follow-on, which ultimately averted another defeat.

At Adelaide, the Australians chose to bat first on a flat track, reaching a first-innings total of 514/5 declared. All of their first seven batsmen made notable scores, particularly David Boon who reached 103. In reply, Broad (116) and Gatting (100) added 172 for the second wicket, in helping deny Australia a chance of victory.

At Melbourne, Gatting won the toss and put Australia in on a greenish surface. Finding much to encourage them, Small (5-48) and Botham (5-41) dismissed Australia for only 141. Botham was barely fit to play, having suffered a rib strain at Perth. Despite managing only a tentative amble to the crease and a gentle rotation of the arm, as might befit a father playing beach cricket with his young son, the Australians submitted wanly to his gentle swing.

Broad (112) and Athey (21) then strode off in pursuit, adding 58 for the first wicket. A second-wicket partnership of 105 between Broad and Gatting (40) took England into the lead with the loss of just Athey. Gatting had looked set for a bigger score for, like Macbeth, he 'murdered' Sleep, the Australian leg-spinner. However, he was eventually grateful for some lower-order clouting as England established a 208-run first-innings lead. Marsh (60), Border (34) and Steve Waugh (49) threatened to mount an Aussie fightback, but after Marsh was run out with his side on 153/4, Emburey and Edmonds ran through much of the remaining batting which added only 41 more runs. Against all expectations, England had retained the Ashes. Australia's late consolation lay in their 55-run victory in the final Test, thanks to Dean Jones's stupendous unbeaten first-innings hundred (184) and incisive spin bowling from Sleep and Taylor.

'Things Can Only Get Better'

1987 – 1999

England won 21 per cent of 131 Tests played
between June 1987 and August 1999

1987
Rent

While Mrs Thatcher's third consecutive victory at the polls was expected, the year's other headlining events were not. The cross-channel ferry, *Herald of Free Enterprise*, capsized in Zeebrugge harbour, killing 200 passengers. Michael Ryan went on a murderous shooting spree in the sleepy town of Hungerford. A hurricane-force storm left a £300m trail of devastation in south-east England. The bottom fell out of the Stock Market on 'Black Monday', and 30 people died in the King's Cross Tube station fire.

Sadly, England's post-Ashes euphoria proved as ephemeral as ever. Australia set aside their Ashes defeat by overcoming England in the ICC World Cup Final in Kolkata, winning by just seven runs. Pakistan then won the five-match summer Test series 1-0. As had been demonstrated in 1971, 1981/82 and 1985/86, an England Ashes victory was no longer a reliable indicator of their prowess in world cricket. The 1986/87 Ashes series had merely indicated that England had been the better of two languishing Test sides.

Bad weather played havoc with the summer's first two Tests at Old Trafford and Lord's, while Imran Khan's devastating bowling at Leeds – he took ten wickets for 77 runs in the match – earned Pakistan an overwhelming victory by an innings and 18 runs. England nearly achieved parity in an exciting finish at Edgbaston where they scored 109/7 in 17.4 overs chasing a victory target of 124. However, Pakistan's mammoth first-innings total of 708 at the

Oval ensured that they retained their narrow series lead. The Oval Test was a personal triumph for Javed Miandad who made a contemptuous double century (208). Imran Khan (118) and Salim Malik (102) made hefty scores, too. Had captain Mike Gatting not determinedly defied the bounding leg spin and googlies of Abdul Qadir with an unbeaten innings of 150, and had Botham (51) not supported him so ably in an unbroken fifth-wicket stand of 176, England might well have lost here, too. Defying the sleepy Oval surface, Qadir took ten wickets in the match for 211.

If the England Test cricket team was then under fire in the national press, the situation was worse for British social workers, having been severely censured for their failings in two headlining child abuse tragedies, both of which became the subject of judicial inquiries. It was the time when I undertook the unaccustomed role of office 'bouncer'. We had successfully applied to the High Court for leave to remove an infant considered to be at imminent risk of harm in a highly violent household. My task was to protect the office staff from the infant's young father who had a volcanic temper and a string of convictions for assault. He often stormed into the office demanding to be seen immediately by a senior member of staff. Whenever frustrated in his angry demands, he had a habit of pressing his shaved, heavily-tattooed head into a staff member's face, while berating them with shrieking obscenities. While he stopped short of physically assaulting anyone, neither our employing council nor the police seemed able to give us much protection.

The experience emphasised to me how disabling it can be for staff forced to work in such hostile circumstances. While in constant fear for their own safety it is difficult for social workers, particularly those working alone, to remain alert to the children's welfare. It was an issue upon which the 'Stockholm syndrome' shed important light. It was found that hostages trapped by violence often appeased, and even championed their abusers' causes. This happened in the Stockholm bank raid of 1973, and also during the hijacking of a Dutch train by South Moluccan terrorists in 1975. Patty Hearst – the abducted heiress turned terrorist – might well have been another example. While the judicial reviews emphasised that better practice could be secured by closer adherence to robust written procedures, without skilled supervision, specialist training and supportive provisions, such as paired working, those caught in such intimidating situations were less likely to operate effectively, irrespective of the calibre of documented professional guidance.

Broadly speaking, this is the deal with 'hostage syndrome'. You are given a bad, bad time. You lose all sense of worth and being. You have no one to turn to, except those who are giving you a bad, bad time. It's your only hope, your only identity. Perhaps this explains the blind loyalty of English cricket fans to their serially-failing national side.

I first heard 'Rent' in the autumn of 1987. The Pet Shop Boys mastered the knack of juxtaposing catchy, pulsating, electro-pop melodies with wry, snappy aphorisms. Here they cast a jaundiced eye upon the acquisitive, egotistical tendency, for which the eighties was castigated. In the guise of a kept woman or man, Neil Tennant expresses his cupboard love for his keeper, the payer of his rent. If the English Beat's 'Mirror in the Bathroom' evoked 1980s narcissism, 'Rent' seems to do the same for its venal values.

1988
Fast Car

If 'Rent' was also about louche affluence, 'Fast Car' was about wretched poverty. The song's writer, Tracy Chapman, is an African-American folk singer. Having been brought up by a single parent of modest means, she had direct experience of the circumstances she describes. The fast car is a fantasised symbol of escape for a young woman who has sacrificed her educational opportunities in order to care for her alcoholic father. Her steadfast optimism in the face of repeated knock-backs makes the song all the more affecting. At Nelson Mandela's 70th birthday tribute concert, at Wembley in June 1988, the song was given the global platform it deserved, harmonising with the African National Congress's demands for the end of apartheid and Nelson Mandela's immediate release.

In response to the rapidly changing South African political situation, the ICC, with the unanimous approval of its members, ruled on the issue of professional cricketers' visits to the country, and not before time. However, it did not prevent a further scandalous 'rebel tour' taking place in 1989/90, led, disappointingly, by the former England captain Mike Gatting.

If England's Ashes tour of 1986/87 was one of unalloyed triumph, the succeeding winter tour of Pakistan, Australia and New Zealand was tarnished with shame. The Test series in Pakistan, which was lost 1-0, was mired with bitter claims and counter-claims of cheating. Not pulling his punches, *Playfair Cricket Annual* editor Bill Frindall grumbled, 'When a Board so blatantly manipulates its grounds men, umpires and captain, it deserves to be expelled from the ICC.' Bill Frindall also berated the poor standards of etiquette shown by members of the England team, stating, 'When a batsman [Broad] refuses to leave the crease after being given out he should be rigorously punished. When a national captain allows himself to be provoked into a slanging match with an umpire [Shakoor Rana], however abrasive, he does the game of cricket and his country's honour a supreme disservice.' Interestingly, venerable English umpire Dickie Bird had been impressed with Shakoor Rana's umpiring when the two had stood together in a first-class match in England. Frindall might also have mentioned centurion Broad's petulant demolition of his stumps after his dismissal in the drawn Bicentenary Test at Sydney.

Depressingly, TCCB chairman Raman Subba Row, who had flown to Pakistan in an attempt to defuse the umpiring row, awarded every member of the English team a £1,000 hardship bonus! As tour manager in 1981/82, Subba

Row had previously defended captain Keith Fletcher after he had knocked off a bail in protest at his alleged wrongful dismissal.

Having escaped a TCCB reprimand, Gatting continued to lead the England side in Pakistan and Australia and in the three-match series in New Zealand, which resulted in a 0-0 draw, while Broad continued to open the England innings. Although the TCCB tolerated its players' gross improprieties on the field of play, they were unwilling to overlook Gatting's alleged impropriety in a hotel bedroom. For Gatting's time in charge was abruptly ended after a drawn opening Test against the West Indians at Trent Bridge in the summer of 1988. According to a tabloid report, Gatting had invited a female hotel employee to his room. He emphatically denied any wrong doing. The prurient press allegation was unproven, and yet the TCCB selectors, led by Peter May, considered Gatting's behaviour unbecoming, and sacked him, appointing his county colleague John Emburey in his place.

I was then setting up a joint child abuse investigation and assessment team with the local police. The catalyst was the NSPCC claim that child sexual abuse was hugely under-reported. While we recruited skilled and experienced social worker and police interviewers of children, they all had to undergo a demanding training programme which included instruction on the potential trauma brought about by disclosure. Our concern was that an investigation should not represent a further form of abuse. Given the almost hysterical, '*Crucible*'-like reactions to potential child sexual abuse, as occurred in Cleveland, where there were insufficient checks and balances, we tried hard to balance vigilance with a sense of proportion. Whether we did enough to help protect the children at risk, only those concerned can say.

Several of my police and social worker colleagues were also cricket fans. They, like me, reacted to Gatting's sacking with disbelief. One police colleague suggested that we invite Peter May to spend a day with us so that he might gain a better grasp of what *real* sexual impropriety meant. In fairness, the selectors accepted Gatting's account, but deemed him guilty of unbecoming behaviour as an England captain. It was unclear whether the earlier, and more important, Shakoor Rana incident had any bearing upon their decision.

The West Indian series was a disaster. Gower remarked that, with Gatting's dismissal, team morale fell immediately from 'something near good to rock bottom'. As a postscript to the Gatting 'affair', Peter May told the England players that they were not be seen in public after 10pm. Gower quipped that given the ultra-slow West Indian over-rate there was a fair chance that they might break their curfew while still playing.

John Emburey was unprepared for his sudden elevation. He was hideously short of form and confidence. While Dilley carried his excellent New Zealand form into the second Test at Lord's, England still lost by 134 runs. Only Lamb (113) and the tail-enders showed much resistance in their second innings. The third Test at Manchester was even worse. England managed scores of 135 and 93 as they rolled over feebly to Marshall, Ambrose and Walsh to lose by an innings and 156 runs. At Leeds, Worcestershire's opener Tim Curtis and Hampshire's South African-born middle-order batsman Robin Smith made their debuts.

Curtis was essentially a back-foot player. He seemed vulnerable to the West Indians' faster pitched-up deliveries. Some pundits thought he had a crooked backlift that caused him to play across the line. It was presumed that the extremity of the pace bowling exposed his technical limitations. The bare fact was that he had a Test average of 15.55 while his first-class average was 40.68.

Ebullient, hard-hitting Robin Smith also favoured the back foot, using his strong forearms to pummel fast bowling with muscular pulls, hooks and cuts. However, he was more vulnerable when thrusting forward at slow bowling with a heavy controlling hand. He also seemed rather two-eyed in his stance, not that this is necessarily a disadvantage as the late Ken Barrington demonstrated during his illustrious Test career. While Curtis made little impact at Old Trafford, Smith (38) supported Lamb (64) bravely in the first innings, helping raise 103 for the fifth wicket, before Lamb had to retire hurt with a torn calf muscle, whereupon England collapsed from 183/4 to 201 all out. Despite Gooch's second innings fifty, England capitulated once again to the West Indian pace quartet of Marshall, Ambrose, Walsh and Winston Benjamin. The tourists won by ten wickets.

Chris Cowdrey, son of Colin, was surprisingly selected to lead the England side at Leeds after May relieved Emburey of his ordeal. Given that Cowdrey was May's godson there were murmurs of nepotism, but in fairness to Cowdrey, he had been captaining County Championship leaders, Kent, at the time. Poor chap. First, the Headingley gateman failed to recognise him, turning him and his car away. Then he was dismissed for a duck and five before being set aside following a foot injury, which ruled him out of the Oval Test. He was replaced by Gooch, but Gooch, too, had to retire hurt after splitting his finger in the slips. Pringle, therefore, became England's fifth captain of the summer. It was an absolute mess. The West Indies duly won the final Test by eight wickets despite commendably punchy knocks from Smith (57) and Gooch (84).

England's first Test victory since their Ashes win Down Under came at Lord's against Sri Lanka. Curtis was dropped and replaced by Tim Robinson. Derbyshire's top order batsman Kim Barnett made his debut, as did Gloucestershire's genuinely fast bowler David 'Syd' Lawrence and Worcestershire all-rounder Phil Newport. Newport took seven wickets in the match with his fast-medium seamers, and Barnett made a first innings fifty (66), as England won by seven wickets. First-innings nightwatchman 'Jack' Russell played a leading role also, scoring 94 in helping Gooch (75) add 131 for the second wicket.

As promisingly as Barnett had batted in his first Test, Geoffrey Boycott remained sceptical about his technique, pointing out that Barnett's right foot slid outside his leg stump at the point of delivery. Boycott reasoned that Barnett then had to make a longer stride to play a ball pitched on or just outside his off stump, causing him to meet it at an angle. Although Barnett started the 1989 Ashes series well with a first-innings score of 80, he made only 61 in his next four Test innings. Barnett subsequently joined Mike Gatting's 'rebel' tour of South Africa in 1989/90.

The cancellation of England's planned tour of India in 1988/89 should not have come as a surprise to the TCCB. The Indian government had made its position clear on the Gleneagles Agreement. Once it refused to admit England captain Graham Gooch and seven members of his touring party, namely Phil Newport, Allan Lamb, Kim Barnett, John Emburey, Robert Bailey, Tim Robinson and Graham Dilley, all of whom had played in previous 'rebel tours', the TCCB realised that any further compromise was impossible. TCCB chief executive Alan Smith expressed his disappointment at the Indians' decision, but, as the Indian High Commissioner in Britain stated, the TCCB should have been cognisant of India's commitment to the Gleneagles Agreement. Given that the TCCB had selected a clutch of 'rebel tourists' for the winter tour, the Indian government were left to surmise that it was uncommitted to a Commonwealth policy agreed by the British government, and subsequently endorsed by the UN.

Conservative sports minister Colin Moynihan remarked, rather obviously, that India's stand had serious consequences for international cricket. This was underscored when New Zealand cancelled an alternative England tour, proposed by the TCCB, because of fear of disruption by Kiwi political activists. With a swathe of Australians and West Indian Test cricketers having also taken part in the 'rebel tours', the Gleneagles persona non grata list was growing exponentially. As *The Cricketer* editor Christopher Martin-Jenkins explained, though, there was a strong feeling among many county cricketers that something should be done to reward South African efforts in fostering multi-racial cricket. Perhaps it was sentiments such as these which blurred the issue, causing the TCCB to take their eye off the ball.

1989

I Am the Resurrection

In 1989 the world was in a state of flux. The fall of the Berlin Wall signified a sudden end of the Cold War, or so it seemed. Soviet leader Mikhail Gorbachev announced a radical policy of *perestroika* or reconstruction. A rapid, if fractious dissolution of Soviet and Iron Curtain states followed. He warned the Communist Party that it had no God-given right to rule. The Soviet Red Army's occupation of Afghanistan was also brought to an abrupt end, while US nuclear missiles were withdrawn at Greenham Common, a measure that was vociferously cheered by the women protesters encamped there. It seemed as if greater threats to Western security were posed by religious fundamentalist regimes or bandit states that condoned, incubated or sponsored terrorism. At the start of this year, Britain and the USA were still reeling at the December downing of a Pan Am jetliner over Lockerbie. Author Salman Rushdie was threatened, too, by an Iranian fatwa as Muslims at home and abroad reacted angrily to his new book, *The Satanic Verses*.

Repressive regimes became subject to greater challenge. In Beijing's Tiananmen Square, this had tragic consequences, while in Romania, the hated Ceausescu administration was brought to an end. Even the previously impregnable Thatcher government began to totter, thrown into turmoil by her sacking of foreign minister Geoffrey Howe over disputed European monetary policy. The angry resignation of Nigel Lawson, her Chancellor of the Exchequer, several months later, cast further doubt about the durability of her leadership. The impact of anti-Poll Tax demonstrations and the disaffection of her Cabinet members would eventually bring her down. British health and safety standards came under scrutiny, too, after a spate of fatal rail accidents and the horrific crush at Hillsborough, captured live on TV.

Cricket was not exempt from the political turmoil of the time. The increasing volatility of the South African situation saw to that. Anti-apartheid protests were growing there, both in number and intensity, exacerbated by angry black claims of police brutality. In the midst of this turbulence, plans were made for a further rebel cricket tour. In agreeing to lead the 1989/90 tour, Mike Gatting was either oblivious of or unconcerned about what he and his team might face in South Africa. Gatting had been upset by the TCCB's decision not to restore the English captaincy to him. A new chairman of the selectors, Ted Dexter, pressed for Gatting's reinstatement, but to no avail. TCCB cricket chairman 'Ossie' Wheatley vetoed the proposal. An angry and disillusioned Gatting therefore turned to the consolation of the South African rand. The pay-off was considerable – in the region of £80,000 to £100,000 per player. This was around twice what a top England cricketer might then earn in a year. It was also almost between eight and ten times better than the national average annual salary. Unsurprisingly, a strong team of recently-capped Test players was recruited including John Emburey, Graham Dilley, Chris Broad, Bruce French, Bill Athey, Kim Barnett, Neil Foster, Greg Thomas and Paul Jarvis. The possible threat of a five-year Test ban did not deter them. However, two black members of the party, Phil DeFreitas and Roland Butcher, had a change of heart once they realised how provocative their presence would be to black South African protesters. South African cricket administrator, Dr Ali Bacher was relieved having feared for their safety.

Arguably, the rebel tourists should have acquainted themselves better with the changing situation in South Africa before committing themselves. On the other hand, they were perhaps reassured by the knowledge that previous rebel tours had passed without incident. Warwickshire's Afrikaaner fast bowler Allan Donald said that he, too, had been unaware how dangerous the racial tensions were before undertaking armed patrols of the black townships, as a national service soldier, during the mid-1980s state of emergency. Donald wrote in his autobiography, *White Lightning*, that his eyes were not opened to the evil of the South African apartheid until he came to England in the late 80s, when he was confronted with the stark, unexpurgated evidence. He admitted that he had been insulated from the truth, having been brought up in the belief that the black South Africans were inherently violent and destructive while the supposedly fair-minded whites struggled to keep the peace.

South African political strife intensified in the six months before the 'rebel' tour began. Outgoing South African President P.W. Botha had already met the jailed African National Congress leader Nelson Mandela in Cape Town, in July 1989, sparking speculation about Mandela's imminent release. Acting president F.W. de Klerk then freed eight other black, nationalist prisoners in October while finally conceding that peaceful political demonstrations were legal.

Incidentally, these developments lent weight to Mrs Thatcher's lone stand in resisting Commonwealth calls for further sanctions. Having concluded that apartheid was almost at an end, she thought that additional sanctions would only increase the difficulties faced by black and mixed-race South Africans in finding work. Just as she predicted, on 2 February 1990, de Klerk lifted the 30-year ban on the ANC, the South African Communist Party and on 30 other anti-apartheid organisations. Nine days later Nelson Mandela was released from jail.

Gatting and his 16-man party were vilified by South African anti-apartheid protesters. The anger the 'rebels' had experienced from British demonstrators was pallid by comparison. The 'rebel' party were seen as part of a repressive regime then in full retreat. Had the protesters known that the tour was bankrolled by the South African government rather than by commercial interests, as had been falsely stated, their hostility would have been even more intense. As it was, Gatting and his men were exposed to the anger of thousands of black and mixed-race objectors. Upon their arrival at Johannesburg airport they were faced with hundreds of demonstrators waving placards and chanting, 'Gatting go home' and 'to hell with rebels, we want land'. The situation became a lot worse. Three thousand protesters halted their opening game at Kimberley. A bomb then destroyed a turnstile at Newlands before their following match, while at Bloemfontein, the police moved in to halt a furious demonstration, using tear gas and rubber bullets to disperse the crowd, severely injuring dozens. Some pitches were damaged and black waiters refused to serve the white South African cricketers in the hotels.

Nelson Mandela's release seemed to raise rather than reduce the heat of protest. Gatting then poured fuel on the flames with several ill-advised remarks, naively dismissing the protests as 'a few people singing and dancing', and stating that the evil of the apartheid regime was exaggerated. Gatting was frequently pelted with stones whenever he appeared in public. It was not only the South African protesters who were outraged by Gatting's presence, for on the streets of Kolkota, effigies of him were burned. But Gatting was not alone in the 'foot in mouth' stakes. When asked at a press conference what he thought about Nelson Mandela's release, Bill Athey flippantly replied, 'He can't bowl, can he?'

After enduring five weeks of vociferous opposition, Dr Ali Bacher courageously cancelled the tour. His development programme, that had done so much to foster cricket in the townships, was in danger of collapse as he received death threats, while many of his coaches were assaulted by angry black residents. The massive payment that Bacher had made to the 'rebel' tourists would have been better reserved for this programme.

There was no evidence that any of the English tourists were racist, just culpably blind to the impact of almost two centuries of brutal racial discrimination. For those claiming moral immunity on grounds that sport had nothing to do with politics, former BBC broadcaster John Arlott commented, 'To say that cricket has nothing to do with politics and you say that cricket has nothing to do with life.' According to human rights lawyer Theo Barclay, who completed a study of South African apartheid, the legacy of this 'rebel tour' was to leave black South Africans distrustful of the English cricket establishment.

Gower's Ashes side of 1989 had already been decimated by injuries to Lamb and Botham, and by Gooch's withdrawal on grounds of poor form and confidence. The 'rebels' unavailability compounded their dearth of resources. When Kent seamer Alan Igglesden was called up for the final Test, one newspaper jeeringly dubbed him as 'England's 17th best fast bowler'.

From an English point of view, the long, hot, summer series was a debacle. Gower's preparations were typically flimsy. According to Devon Malcolm's account, in his autobiography *You Guys are History*, he was shocked to find only lacklustre net and fielding practice, and no analyses of the Australians' strengths and weaknesses. Gower's team seemed left to make it up as they went along. Only Robin Smith with a series batting average of 61.44 and 'Jack' Russell with an average of 39.25 did themselves justice. The England bowling figures were just horrendous. Meanwhile, four Australian batsmen achieved averages in excess of 70 with Steve Waugh topping the pile having amassed over 500 runs at an average score of 126.50. He was followed by opener Mark Taylor who made 839 at an average of 83.90, and Border with 442 at an average of 73.66. Meanwhile, Alderman had a magnificent series with the ball, taking 41 wickets at 17.36, well supported by Lawson with 29 at 27.27 and Hughes with 19 at 32.36. Even 35-year-old Trevor Hohns's unremarkable leg breaks and googlies brought him 11 wickets at 27.27. A chopped and changed England side was fortunate to get away with only a 4-0 thrashing. The gulf between the two sides was colossal in terms of skill, technique, stability, combativeness, and tactical nous.

Border led from the front, adopting a ruthlessly aggressive manner throughout the six-match Test series. When batting on a hot afternoon, Robin Smith requested leave to call for a glass of water. Border replied, 'Can you have a drink? No, you f***ing can't. What do you think this is, a f***ing tea party?'

When England's debutant fast bowler Devon Malcolm joined the listing ship at Nottingham, he made the mistake of congratulating Terry Alderman on his fine bowling. Alderman threw Malcolm's praise back at him with a snarl. The Australians operated on a war footing. Border forbade any fraternisation between the teams until the Ashes were regained. Gower and his ever-changing team were either glared at or sledged mercilessly. But while Hughes would growl or holler choice vernacular at each of the England batsmen, once the battle was over, he could not have been nicer.

Border had been badly burned by the Ashes defeat Down Under in 1986/87. Prime Minister Bob Hawke had then compared Border's side unfavourably with new national hero, Pat Cash, who had just won the Davis Cup for Australia. Border was hell-bent upon an avenging mission. The princely Gower was no match for this grizzled, Sydney street fighter.

Just as 'Jack' Russell began his long, but ultimately vain resistance at Old Trafford, I was admitted to hospital with suspected testicular cancer. During the sleepless night that followed my operation, I played the Stone Roses' eponymous album quietly on my Walkman. Meanwhile, I kept an eye on an ailing double amputee in the next bed, summoning help when pain seemed to overwhelm him. I wondered whether either of us had much of a future.

One of the outstanding tracks on this memorable album is 'I am the Resurrection'. The song's portentous title mocked a message seen on a church noticeboard, although the thumping beat and melodious guitar work transcend the song's tetchy lyrics, as does the jangling, funk-fest epilogue. This was a rousing revival of 1960s rock for a 'rave'-bent dance culture. By the late 80s, British pop had become dominated by high-energy, electro-pop, dance beats. Quivering, pulsating, pounding, popping rhythms, and flickering, startlingly coloured strobe lighting were the new sound and vision, recreating the exuberance of the Ibiza clubs. Rapidly advancing electronic technology had enabled the pop archives to be raided, with the booty sliced and diced, put through a blender, and spattered on to a new canvas. The skill of the Stone Roses, and that of fellow Mancunians, the Happy Mondays, and Glasgow's Primal Scream, was to demonstrate that 'baggy' rock 'n' roll was as exciting and danceable as 'acid house'.

1990

Papa was a Rollin' Stone

The year began with another hurricane-force storm battering Britain, killing 46 people. It was followed by a political storm as the Poll Tax uproar swept through English towns and cities, with a full-scale riot in central London, mirroring the earlier unrest in Scotland. The Tories suffered heavily in the May local elections, but Mrs Thatcher remained resolute, rejecting the Delors plan for a single European currency and central bank. 'Up Yours Delors' crowed *The Sun* in puerile support. With the economy troubled by rising inflation and stumbling towards recession, the nation's manufacturing base shrunk further with British Steel's announcement of the closure of its Motherwell Ravenscraig steelworks. A loss of 11,000 jobs was forecasted. England's surprising World Cup football successes ended with what was to become a tradition – a semi-final, penalty shoot-out defeat at the feet of the Germans. This disappointment faded quickly, though, as Iraqi forces seized control of Kuwait triggering an international crisis that would result in the first Gulf War. There was a mounting crisis at home, too, as Tory divisions over Europe resulted in Mrs Thatcher being forced from office in November.

My operation was successful. But the reprieve prompted me to leave child care, realising that I needed more time to accommodate growing caring responsibilities for my parents and my aunt who had looked after me when I was young. My move to an adult social care planning and performance review post was timely as Liz and I also had to spend more time with her seriously ill mother. During one of these visits, in the winter of 1989/90, I managed to watch snatches of the first Test between the West Indies and England on Sky TV.

After the humiliating Ashes defeat, there was little hope that an England team, weakened by 'rebel' defectors, would have any chance of prevailing over the formidable West Indians. But a restored and revived Graham Gooch led a much more professional, determined, and tactically-aware team, despite its unproven middle order in which Nasser Hussain and Alec Stewart made their debuts. Much depended upon Gooch, Lamb and Robin Smith if England were to score enough runs to challenge the West Indians' supremacy. As for the bowlers, Small and DeFreitas were veterans of England's successful 1986/87 Ashes campaign, but Angus Fraser and Devon Malcolm were novices as was Northants' all-rounder David Capel. Viv Richards seemed to have little to fear from this attack.

The first Test took place at Sabina Park, Kingston, Jamaica, where England had not won since Len Hutton's time, 36 years before. The Sabina Park wicket was like a shattered mirror, its gleaming surface fissured like an irregular mosaic. A haughtily chewing Richards called correctly and decided to bat. Sturdy Devon Malcolm, back on his home turf, opened the England attack with Barbados-born Gladstone Small. It was black on black but it was home pair Greenidge and Haynes who prospered initially. Haynes leant easily into a stylish cover drive off Small, sending the ball zipping to the cover boundary, while Greenidge, having already flashed impetuously at Malcolm, slashed at another rising delivery, edging the ball just over the slip fielders' heads and down to the main stand wall at third man.

Although the wicket was hard, it was not especially fast, but excited by the occasion, Malcolm disconcerted both West Indian openers with his heavy 'perfume ball', while Small settled for frugal swing and seam, probing the 'corridor of uncertainty' just outside the right-handers' off stump. Malcolm had been instructed to focus upon producing high pace and lift. Despite the swooning heat and humidity he stuck to his task dutifully, bounding in eagerly, his muscular thighs exposed by his clinging whites. Being more of a shot putter in physique than a long- or middle-distance track athlete, Malcolm achieved his considerable speed from a rhythmic rocking run, and a high action that capitalised upon his massive shoulder strength. He seemed like our 'Diamond', our Wayne Daniel.

Malcolm's fielding was sometimes negligent and clumsy, though. After Greenidge and Haynes had taken the West Indians rapidly to 63/0, Greenidge flicked a ball straight to him at long leg. Malcolm fumbled, persuading Greenidge to convert a single into a couple. However, he reckoned without the strength of Malcolm's arm. Hurling in a fast, low, accurate return, 'Jack' Russell ran out Greenidge (32) with yards to spare. Small and Capel then frustrated Richardson and Haynes by bowling tightly on a line just outside their off stumps.

Irritated by this, Richardson unleashed a typically belligerent, back foot, square slash off Small, before spanking a good length ball on the rise for four. But when he tried to hoick a quicker, shorter ball from Capel over the on-side boundary fence, he miscued to Small at backward square leg. Richardson had departed for ten and the West Indians were 81/2. Incoming batsman Carlisle Best appeared to be in a hurry. Having clouted four runs, he fished at Capel's away-swinger which bounced more than he had anticipated and Russell grasped the edge – 92/3. Make that 92/4 as Haynes (36) mistimed a straight drive, presenting Small with a simple return catch.

Richards then appeared, to an excited roar from the home supporters. It was like the entrance of a matador, preening, pumped-up, and imperious. The West Indians had not dared speak with him as he had paced the dressing room in readiness for his emergence. He arrived at the crease helmetless, scornful of any threat. He took guard, dismissively regarding the field set for him before finally focusing upon Small. 'Do your damnedest,' his narrowed eyes seemed to say, 'it will not be nearly good enough.' As if to underline his contempt, he raced into the 20s with five boundaries, achieved mainly by laying back and flaying the ball through cover.

Malcolm was then restored to the attack. Former West Indian fast bowler Wes Hall had suggested that he might vary the degree of bounce by gripping the ball across the seam. This would have a 'grubbing' effect. Malcolm did as Hall suggested. Richards had been in his element, unleashing his speciality whipped drive through midwicket off deliveries speared into his pads. So when Malcolm produced a shorter delivery that, as a result of Hall's advice, he contrived to keep low, Richards was unprepared. Trapped on the back foot, Richards was given out lbw for 21. The West Indians were 124/5.

Fraser then joined the fun, belying his drooping, apparently exhausted demeanour. He whisked out the rest of the West Indian batting order. Fraser never swung the ball prodigiously, but allied to his probing line and length, he regularly produced just enough lateral movement to find the edge of the bat. Sky TV summariser Tony Greig greeted the departure of each forlorn West Indian batsman with a boorish, triumphalist whoop of 'goodnight Charlie!' So much for his impartiality as a pundit. Fraser took five wickets for 28 runs in 20 overs of stifling accuracy. His marginal, yet sufficient, seam movement, confounded the impetuous shot selection of the frustrated West Indians. The mighty West Indies were dismissed for 164.

Richards needed a quick and decisive response from his opening bowlers, but Ian Bishop and Patrick Patterson bowled profligately, notably the latter whose 18 overs went for 71 runs. Patterson, who had been a scourge of the English batsmen on the 1985/86 tour, claimed only one victim, Graham Gooch, who was unluckily caught down the leg side. The England heroes were Allan Lamb (132) and Robin Smith (57) who put on 172 for the fourth wicket, although Wayne Larkins (46) and 'Jack' Russell (26) made important contributions, too. As a result of their combined efforts, England gained an improbable 200-run first innings lead.

This was one of Lamb's finest innings for England. Defying the extremity of the Jamaican heat, he stood and delivered, rocking on to the back foot wherever possible and striking through the ball with nonchalant power and perfect timing. Meanwhile, Smith unleashed a series of slashes and hefty pulls, uninhibitedly fetching the ball from outside his off stump. It was a joy to behold, witnessing a daunting West Indian attack being demolished with the ferocity that their batsmen had so often inflicted upon the England bowlers. Only a belligerent Courtney Walsh did himself justice with impressive figures of 5-68 off 27.2 overs.

The West Indians began their second innings poorly with Malcolm flattening Haynes's leg stump (14) with a full-pitched delivery that the West Indian opener played across – 26/1. Greenidge and Richardson then took the West Indians uncomfortably to 69 before the latter fell into a trap set by a persevering Fraser. Noting the variability of bounce, Fraser encouraged Richardson to play his favourite pull shot, knowing that if and when one of his deliveries kept low, Richardson might be in trouble. The plan worked perfectly as Richardson (34) was dismissed, lbw. Best was almost out immediately afterwards. This time the 6ft 6in Fraser managed to extract surprising bounce, the ball clipping the shoulder of Best's bat and glove and flying past gully. But it was Greenidge (36) who was next to depart when a short flyer from Malcolm induced him to lay back and slash wildly at the rising ball, Hussain taking a sharp catch at backward point – 87/3. Hooper (8) did not stay long before he prodded unconvincingly at Small with Larkins, at first slip, rescuing Gooch's spill. But at 112/4 Richards returned to the crease with vengeance on his mind, beginning with two front-foot slashes for four. Undeterred by his first innings dismissal, he continued to plant his left foot down the pitch and whack the ball through midwicket. He and Best added 80 runs for the fifth wicket in very short time.

With the West Indian crowd savouring the fierce counter attack, Gooch recalled Malcolm. The Derbyshire fast bowler thundered in, unleashing a scorching yorker that Richards (37) played around. Instead of sending the ball whistling to the midwicket boundary, he was aghast to find his leg stump leant over in desolation – 192/5. The excited England players ran to a shyly smiling Malcolm, clambering all over him in jubilation.

Pining for his lost partner, Best (64) edged Small feebly to Gooch at second slip and the West Indians were almost sunk at 222/6, only two runs ahead. Malcolm's speed was too much for Geoffrey Dujon (15). Hanging back, Dujon jabbed at another quick delivery which he edged into his stumps, knocking out the middle and leg stumps. There was still just enough time for Small to dismiss Bishop (3) with Larkins taking the catch at first slip before the third day closed at 229/8. Although England fretted over a fourth day that was entirely lost to rain, the final day began brightly and so did Gooch's side in quickly wrapping up a nine-wicket victory. A tired but elated Gooch said, 'I've been waiting ten years for this moment,' while Viv Richards sarcastically replied, 'I don't want to take anything away from England. They won. Hip, hip, hooray but we'll be back.'

Unfortunately the second Test in Guyana was washed out without a ball being bowled. More frustratingly, England were poised to win the third Test at Port-of-Spain, despite Gooch having to retire hurt with a fractured left hand. Unfortunately, rain and poor light prevented England from reaching their victory target of 151, although they were only 30 runs short at the close with five wickets left. However, one of their remaining wickets was that of Gooch, who, unknown to the West Indians, was unable to bat again. Malcolm enjoyed another profitable match, taking ten wickets for 137. Had it not been for Gus Logie's sparkling first innings (98), the West Indians would certainly have lost here, too.

Gooch and Fraser's absence from the final two Tests proved crucial as big hundreds from Best, Haynes and Greenidge, and devastating fast bowling from Curtly Ambrose and Ian Bishop, turned the rubber on its head. An under-strength England side deserved a better result, but the value of disciplined play in support of carefully constructed game plans had been underscored as a recipe for future success.

Upon returning to England and restored to full fitness, Graham Gooch batted spectacularly against India at Lord's. He scored 333 and 123 in taking England to a 247-run victory that would decide the short series. Gooch had been lucky, though. Indian wicketkeeper Kiran More dropped him unaccountably when he had scored only 36 of his three hundred plus runs.

In Mohammed Azharuddin and Kapil Dev, India had their batting heroes too. Azharuddin made an immaculate hundred (121) while Kapil Dev plundered 77, averting the follow-on with four successive sixes struck off Eddie Hemmings' off-spinners.

After the wreckage left by the Ashes defeat, English cricket seemed to be on the rise once more, for New Zealand had already been beaten 1-0 in the summer's opening Test series. This was a personal triumph for 22-year-old Mike Atherton who scored 151 at Trent Bridge, and 82 and 70 at Edgbaston where England won by 114 runs. Atherton headed the England batting against the Kiwis, with an average score of 71.40. He then added a second Test century against the Indians on his home ground at Old Trafford (131).

Robin Smith, at the age of 26, also enjoyed a prodigious series against the Indians, making unbeaten centuries at Lord's (100) and Manchester (121), and averaging 180.5 in his six summer Test innings. Malcolm carried on his Caribbean form, too. He had the best bowling average of either side in the New Zealand series, taking 15 wickets at 17.93 – better even than Sir Richard Hadlee's 16 wickets at 24. This was a considerable feat, for Malcolm had his work cut out to extract any bounce from the docile wickets prepared for this series. But even his pounding pace made no impact on the featherbed surfaces sympathetically provided for the visiting Indians. Nevertheless, Fraser was rewarded handsomely for his dogged accuracy and seam movement, topping the England bowling averages with 16 Indian wickets at 28.75. The winter Ashes tour was anticipated in much better heart.

According to *Playfair* editor Bill Frindall, the summer of 1990 was a golden one for batsmen after the TCCB had insisted upon the preparation of better County Championship wickets, threatening to impose 25-point pitch penalties on those counties whose pitches did not come up to scratch. The high-seamed ball was outlawed also, forcing the pace bowlers to work harder and more cannily for their customary gains. Frindall delightedly exclaimed, '[With] few clouds around to encourage swing or swerve, batsmen were transported back to the Elysian fields of the 1930s.'

My lasting memory of the summer was cast in grey, though. This relates to the unusually overcast day on which Graham Gooch completed his triple Test ton, bristling with powerfully punched drives. While Gooch was completing his annihilation of the Indian attack, I was travelling to Norfolk. I had been asked to meet a young man who was formerly in our council's care, but then living in an east coast town. He was said to be in turmoil over whether to reveal more about the abuse he had suffered long before. He needed our reassurance about how any further disclosure might be handled, being fearful of its consequences. He was insistent upon speaking with a senior member of our staff. It was to be my final assignment as a child care specialist.

We sat together on a deserted, blustery clifftop overlooking the sombre North Sea. A continuous procession of grubby waves emerged from a heavy, wrinkled swell, collapsing lethargically with laboured sighs onto the shingle below us. He was hesitant, taciturn and flat. It was difficult to make a connection. Then I remembered the song that had caught my attention while travelling from London. It was a funky, hip-hop version of The Temptations' psychedelic soul hit, 'Papa was a Rollin' Stone'. This rendition, by Was (Not Was), contained a longer and harsher indictment of paternal neglect. The rapper's jabbing rage seemed to be magnified by the song's pitching, sole to heel, sprung rhythm. I passed my Walkman to the boy and invited him to listen while I stared at an opaque horizon. The boy eventually turned to me murmuring, 'That guy sounds *really* pissed off.' Anger is not necessarily bad. It can be an energy, a catalyst for change. Perhaps it was here, for we then began to talk.

1991
Unfinished Symphony

In 1991, there was a re-emergence of rioting in British towns and cities. The TV news bulletins carried footage of hooded adolescents 'burning rubber', if not torching their joy-ridden vehicles, on the mean streets of Oxford, Tyneside, Cardiff and Birmingham while the police and local authority officers looked on helplessly. As abhorrent as this misbehaviour was, it seemed like a seething riposte to a government seen to be fostering divisive social and economic policies. Here, were the snarling underdogs of an eighties underclass, stripped of purpose, ambition, hope, conscience or inhibition. Seen in this context, the construction of Canary Wharf appeared like a latter-day Babel tower, its occupants apparently oblivious to the disadvantaged communities scattered around them, as they paid blind homage to the voracious demands of high finance. How ironic it was that the London Docklands development, a paean to eighties affluence, should be built where working men and women once toiled, where commerce was once measured in tangible commodities. 1980s regeneration seemed to imply gentrification.

There was little winter cheer coming from Australia. Graham Gooch's side were decimated by injury, undermined by irresolute batting and compromised by a lack of athleticism and reliability in the field. Gower had been restored to the England team for the Indian series of 1990, justifying his recall with a majestic, unbeaten big hundred (157) at the Oval that denied India a series-saving victory. However, the tension between the intense, workaholic Gooch and a flamboyant, deceptively casual Gower grew as the team's adversities mounted, although Gower hardly short-changed his captain, top-scoring in the first three Tests, and making tons at Melbourne (100) and Sydney (123).

The preparatory disciplines that Gooch and Micky Stewart had introduced before the Caribbean Test series had paid dividends in improving the standard of team performances, until critical injuries and exhaustion overwhelmed them. But in Australia, Gooch possibly overplayed his hand, continuing to obsess about practice drills and insist upon arduous fitness routines when his party seemed in need of rest and recuperation – at least that was Devon Malcolm's view. Gooch's side had to contend with a punishing itinerary, and what with the intense heat and a succession of demoralising defeats, the players became drained and tetchy. Malcolm recalled that he reacted angrily when accused of laziness.

It did not help that Gooch had to miss the first Test with a poisoned hand. Had it not been for belated, yet decisive, medical action, his career might have been brought to a sudden end. With Allan Lamb deputising in the captain's absence, there was a relaxation in the intensity of performances demanded by Gooch, but then Lamb became sidelined, too, missing both the second and third Tests on account of a strained calf muscle. This was a legacy of Lamb's imprudent decision to jog back to the hotel, having exhausted himself in scoring a belligerent century in the extreme Ballarat heat. Fraser also missed the third and fifth Tests, after sustaining a potentially career-threatening hip injury. Frustratingly for England, this came after Fraser had taken 6-82 in the Australian first innings at Melbourne. Gooch's woes did not end there, though, as all-rounder Chris Lewis had to return home because of an injury. Lewis had bowled well at a steamy Brisbane where he helped Small, Fraser and Malcolm to dismiss Australia for 152 in their first innings. However, the 42-run lead England achieved here was instantly frittered away in a cataclysmic second innings collapse that gifted Australia a ten-wicket win.

At Melbourne, events took a similar course. Australia won by eight wickets with Marsh (79) and Boon (94) sharing a victorious unbroken third-wicket partnership of 187. However, greater resilience was shown at Sydney where Atherton scored his first Ashes hundred (105) and left-arm spin bowler Phil Tufnell bowled splendidly, taking 5-61 off 37 overs. Although Gooch and Gower boldly pursued a 255-run victory target, it was an unfeasible chase. A rapid loss of four wickets led Gooch to settle for a draw. It meant that Australia had retained the Ashes. At Adelaide, England were under the cosh for most of the game until Gooch (117) and Atherton (87) shared a 203-run partnership at the start of England's second innings, which ultimately denied Australia victory. However, another calamitous collapse at Perth resulted in a nine-wicket defeat, England's third loss of the rubber.

As if encouraged by the clamorous anti-monarchist sentiments of new Australian Prime Minister Paul Keeting, the Aussie players and supporters treated the England players with swaggering disdain. Phil Tufnell probably suffered the worst abuse. One Aussie barracker shouted at him, 'Lend me your brain, Tufnell, I'm building an idiot.' Tufnell found some of the Australian umpires equally frosty. When he asked one how many balls he had left to bowl, the umpire allegedly replied, 'Count them yourself, you pommie ****.'

An ill-judged prank by Gower and Morris did little to lift team morale. Gooch was understandably infuriated by their foolish indiscipline. The irony was that Gower had borrowed the money for the Tiger Moth stunt from his unsuspecting tour manager Peter Lush. At the end of the tour, a visibly strained Graham Gooch concluded with a downbeat assessment of his players' performances. It did little to improve a disgruntled mood. However, Gooch later expressed his regret at trying to strait-jacket Gower, recognising that he should have accepted Gower for what he was – a hugely talented big-match player, 'touched by genius' as he put it.

Mike Atherton's view was that the Australians were considerably stronger in all respects. He saw this as a product of substantial government investment in the pursuit of Australian sporting excellence. It was something that struck me, too, when I visited Australia in 2002, after my hosts told me of how much they contributed in taxes for this purpose.

Despite Mark Taylor and Steve Waugh losing form, David Boon, with a series average of 75.71, Greg Matthews, with an incredible one of 70.6, and Mark Waugh, with a maiden Test century on debut, ensured that Australia always had too many runs for England to chase. Only Gooch and Gower, with series averages of 53.25 and 45.22 respectively, came close to matching the best Australian batsmen. Meanwhile the Australian pace quartet of Bruce Reid (27 wickets at 16), Craig McDermott (18 at 20), Merv Hughes (15 at 24.33) and Terry Alderman (16 at 26.75) achieved better returns than any of the England bowlers, the best of whom was Fraser with 11 at 28.27.

The summer series against the West Indies began under the glowering clouds of Headingley. Gooch was magnificent. Standing tall in the Leeds gloom, he biffed and blunted the collective might of Ambrose, Patterson, Walsh and Marshall. In a low-scoring game, on a juicy wicket, Gooch's unbeaten big hundred (154) guided England to a 115-run victory. Dominican-born Phil DeFreitas was the pick of England's attack with match figures of 8-93 while debutant Glamorgan pace bowler Steve Watkin provided sterling support in taking 5-93. The eagerly awaited appearance of Zimbabwean Graeme Hick proved to be a damp squib, though, with the West Indian pace proving too hot for him to handle. He managed only six runs in his two innings at Leeds.

At Lord's, Robin Smith's abrasive batting (148) rescued England from disaster at 84/5, in replying to the West Indians' first-innings total of 419. 'Jack' Russell (46), Derek Pringle (35) and Phil DeFreitas (29) also gave sturdy assistance as England reached 354. Rain then intruded, regrettably curtailing an absorbing contest.

The West Indians drew level at Trent Bridge after taking a 97-run first-innings lead. A further second-innings collapse by England gave the visitors an easy victory target which they achieved for the loss of only one wicket. The fourth Test at Edgbaston followed a similar course. Viv Richards (73 not out) won the game with a straight driven six, ensuring that he remained unbeaten in the dozen series in which he had led the West Indian team. England all-rounder Chris Lewis had a fine game, taking 6-111 in the West Indies first innings, and in clubbing 65 in almost lone resistance. Unfortunately, the talented Lewis seemed to reserve his best Test displays for losing causes. Nevertheless, he contributed 47 late-order runs at the Oval, helping Robin Smith (109) and Graham Gooch (60) take England to 419, their highest innings total against the West Indies in 17 years.

Perhaps the most memorable feature of the victorious fifth Test came shortly before close of play on a sunny second day. It was when *Test Match Special* commentator Brian Johnston 'corpsed' over Jonathan Agnew's unwitting double entendre. In describing Botham's dismissal, hit wicket, Agnew solemnly announced that 'he just didn't get his leg over', whereupon Johnston dissolved into a helpless fit of giggles. Johnston's muffled snorts, sobbing chuckles and squealing protests seemed to go on forever, although it was probably no more than a minute. But it was enough to prompt BBC producer Peter Baxter to barge into the TMS box hissing 'Will someone please say something!' I heard the joyful farce somewhere between Sevenoaks and Ashford while driving to Canterbury. It remains as my, and many other BBC radio listeners', favourite broadcasting moment.

The game turned decisively on the Saturday as Phil Tufnell tied up the West Indian batsmen in knots, taking 6-25 off 14.3 overs. Only Haynes with an unbeaten 75 offered extended resistance as the West Indians were swept aside for 176. Gooch enforced the follow-on, and although Richardson (121) and Richards (60) fought valiantly, David Lawrence's raw, brawny pace accounted for five wickets at a cost of 106 runs. The Gloucestershire heavyweight fast bowler justified his selection in front of Malcolm who had been struggling with a shoulder injury sustained in Australia. England required only 143 to win and it was left to Botham to smite the winning boundary, giving him his first Test victory over the West Indians in 20 matches. It was also the first time that England had avoided a series defeat by the West Indies in six attempts, extending back 16 years to 1974.

However, only two English batsmen performed consistently well against the daunting West Indian pace quartet of Ambrose, Marshall, Patterson and Walsh: Robin Smith, with a brace of centuries, and a series average of 83.20; and Gooch with a series average of 62.50, boosted by his superb, match-winning ton at Leeds. The new boys, Mark Ramprakash, with a series average of 23.33, and Graeme Hick, with a very disappointing average of 10.71, failed to justify the hype that surrounded their selections. As for Mike Atherton, he endured a miserable summer, averaging only 8.77 in nine innings. It was not only the West Indians' testing pace that troubled him, for he was in considerable pain on account of a back problem which would require surgery.

Phil DeFreitas enjoyed a fine series, taking 22 wickets at 20.77 each, but he had little support of note except at Leeds, where Watkin and Pringle shared nine wickets, and at the Oval where Lawrence and Tufnell shared 14. DeFreitas's action was hardly a thing of beauty. After a hurried, slightly side-on run to the crease, in which his cock-eyed focus never left the batsman, at the point of delivery he flung both arms aloft as if flaying a swarm of insects. Although possessing wiry strength and nippy pace, his swing, cut and occasional off-breaks were most effective on home pitches. Although he made a promising debut as a 20-year-old in the Ashes-winning side of 1986/87, he found little success thereafter on overseas wickets where there was less lateral movement, and where his predominant back of a length bowling posed fewer concerns. Nevertheless, before Dominic Cork's spectacular debut in 1995, which brought DeFreitas's Test career to a close, he played in 44 Tests, taking 140 wickets at a respectable average of 33.57. It once seemed as if he, too, might succeed Ian Botham, but his destructive batting displays were rare, although at the Oval in 1994 and Adelaide in 1995 he produced game-changing cameos. Nevertheless, his athleticism, strong arm and dependable catching were always put to good use in the outfield.

The fact that the West Indians' pace quartet accounted for 76 dismissals at under 25 runs each suggested that England did very well to hold the tourists to a draw. Buoyed by their achievement, England proceeded to beat Sri Lanka in the summer's final Test at Lord's. The occasion was marked by Alec Stewart's maiden Test hundred (113 not out) which restored respectability to a stuttering first-innings effort. Gooch's second-innings century (174) then put England on the road to a 137-run victory, which Tufnell's 5-94 ultimately sealed.

Tufnell is now a jaunty, self-assured radio and TV personality, but in his playing days his obvious talent was too often compromised by self-doubt. Mike Atherton referred to this in his autobiography, *Opening Up*. He remarked that Tufnell repeatedly sought his and others' assurance that the ball was coming out alright and that he was spinning it enough. Tufnell was barracked unmercifully by the Aussies. His fielding was not as shambolic as they often scoffed, though. He took some outstanding catches as Devon Malcolm testified. However, his Aussie detractors seemed to sense his self-deprecation much like a shark spots a trace of blood in the water.

When Bristol's 'trip-hop' collective Massive Attack released their sublime single 'Unfinished Symphony' in February 1991, they agreed to temporarily drop 'Attack' from their name because the BBC deemed it 'unpatriotic' at a time when British armed forces were fighting in the first Gulf War. The BBC's reaction smacked of over-sensitivity. They had form in this respect, having banned 'J' t'aime... moi non plus' by Jane Birkin and Serge Gainsbourg in 1969, and 'Relax' by Frankie Goes to Hollywood in 1984, for quaintly prudish reasons. And yet its censors had been untroubled by The Who's 1967 single 'Pictures of Lily', a song about teenage masturbation, and Prince and The Revolution's 1985 hit, 'Little Red Corvette', the content of which was as sexually explicit as that of the banned 'Relax'. A Dutchman once told me that he thought Britain was absurdly over-sensitive on matters of trivial sexual impropriety, suggesting we would be less uptight had we endured 'the pornography of a Nazi occupation'.

There was no quarrel with the content or calibre of 'Unfinished Symphony', though. Its lush, swishing strings, multi-layered Hip-hop beats, scratches and samples, and jazzy piano chords, overlain by Shara Nelson's beseeching, husky soul voice, confirms this as a song of sumptuous quality, Play it to me and I am immediately whisked back to that dazzling August evening in 1991, when I was driving blithely through the verdant lanes of the 'Garden of England', entertained unforgettably by Brian Johnston's delightful gaffe.

1992
Crucify

Although my social work days were two years behind me, I often reflected upon the children and young people I had worked with. Tori Amos's harrowing song, 'Crucify', provided one such prod. Self-indictment does not come much more tortured than this, at least not in a pop song. Here, it is set to a tinkling, plunging piano score, with Tori Amos's quavering confessions hammered home with a thumping drum beat. When I first heard the song, I was immediately reminded of the anguish of a 15-year-old girl I had once known. She had craved our council's protective care while agonising about losing touch with her abusive family, suspecting that their depraved exploitation of her was the best that she merited, sensing, too, that she had invited their abuse, and fearing that she would be left with nothing if she jettisoned them. Guilt did once lead me to contemplate returning to child care, but the extent of my caring responsibilities held me back until the pangs of regret eventually faded.

Coincidentally, this was the year that our daughter Lydia developed a passion for football. As in my early years, it was distressing family circumstances that brought this about. It is strange that a game which generally confers more heartache than joy should serve as a sanctuary. It is perhaps all the more perplexing given that the team we chose to follow far and wide was modest Burnley. There again, living frugally on surprise is surely a better preparation for life than a rich diet of unabated success. Regrettably, she never really warmed to cricket although she joined in the raucous pub support of Devon Malcolm when he obliterated the South Africans in 1994, and was briefly intrigued by Saj Mahmood's hostility on the one occasion she accompanied me to a county game at Hove. Alas, it was an interest that flickered twice before spluttering out.

In 1992 we saw the restoration of South Africa to the Test-playing fraternity. As a result the Test bans imposed on 'rebel' tourists were lifted. The Commonwealth leaders had agreed to end sporting sanctions against South Africa in October 1991. South Africa began their rehabilitation by playing a one-off Test match at Bridgetown in April 1992 which the West Indians won narrowly after Ambrose and Walsh had dismissed the last eight South African batsmen for 25 runs. India then played four Test matches in South Africa during late 1992 and early 1993. This time the South Africans were the victors, thanks to Allan Donald's devastating pace bowling at Port Elizabeth where he had match figures of 12-139.

But it was Pakistan who probably presented the strongest challenge to Australian supremacy and West Indian might. On 25 March they defeated England in the World Cup Final in Melbourne by 22 runs – England's third World Cup final loss – and were victorious again in a five-match summer Test series played in England. The World Cup Final's man of the match was Wasim Akram, a devastating left-arm swing bowler who proved equally effective during the summer Test series.

The World Cup tournament was preceded by an England tour of New Zealand. The recently knighted Richard Hadlee had retired from Test cricket, which made England's task simpler. Lamb averaged 67.6 and Stewart 66 while Tufnell headed the Test bowling averages with 16 wickets at 22.93 each. Chris Lewis did well in his two appearances, averaging 42 with the bat and 24.9 with the ball. However, England's 2-0 series victory was overshadowed by the tragic injury suffered by David Lawrence whose left kneecap fractured horizontally while bowling at Wellington. Despite going through a 13-month recuperation period, 'Syd' was forced to call it a day after both of his attempted comebacks failed.

Lawrence's misfortune became Malcolm's renewed opportunity although he had to wait until the second Test at Lord's to make his mark. Another sluggish wicket at Edgbaston was largely responsible for a first Test bore draw. Feisty Pakistani captain Javed Miandad made a big hundred (153) as did Salim Malik (165) with Pakistan spending three and a half rain-interrupted days assembling 446 runs for the loss of only four wickets, while England took up the remaining time replying with 459 of their own, with Stewart (190) and Robin Smith (127) injecting iridescent entertainment into a dead contest. Sixty-two per cent of their runs came in boundaries. This helped dispel the ill feeling aroused by the TCCB's refusal to refund second-day admission fees when only two balls were bowled. The spectators' ensuing protests rightly prompted a rethink.

At Lord's, England struggled to impose themselves upon the Pakistani express pace pair Waqar Younis and Wasim Akram who provided a masterclass in reverse swing. Together they were responsible for 13 dismissals while the twirling leg-spinners and googlies of Mushtaq Ahmed accounted for a further five. England's middle and lower order fell apart in both innings. Had it not been for opener Stewart's unbeaten second-innings score of 69 – his second fifty of the match – England would not have been able to set Pakistan a three-figure victory target. The 138 runs Pakistan required to win proved to be a daunting task, though, with Lewis and debutant leg spinner Ian Salisbury sharing six wickets as the tourists slid to 81/7.

Neither Botham, in his final Test match, nor DeFreitas could bowl because of groin strains, so the load had to be shared between Malcolm, Lewis and Salisbury. At 95/7 Malcolm had Mushtaq caught at slip by Hick and suddenly England had a scent of victory. Gooch directed Malcolm to pepper the new batsman, Waqar, with bouncers, but allegedly refused his request for a short leg. If this is correct, it seemed to be a fatal loss of nerve as the discomforted Pakistani fast bowler immediately fended off a short ball in the direction of the absent short leg. Even then Gooch might have sealed victory had he brought Salisbury on to bowl at Waqar, before he was set, on a surface that was allowing sharp turn. By the time he was called upon, Waqar was more composed, helping Wasim take Pakistan to a two-wicket win.

Botham's farewell to Test cricket was an inauspicious occasion – two single-figure scores and a short wicketless spell. After the Ashes victory of 1986/87 he was rarely fit to play and when he did, it was with diminishing returns. Of course, his Test record – 5,200 runs at an average of 33.54 and 383 wickets at 28.4 – seemed impossible to replicate, so it was unsurprising perhaps that the selectors should repeatedly return to their former talisman as if he was El Cid.

It was not as if the selectors had a credible successor lined up. Derek Pringle had not really cut it at Test level. His containing medium pace was occasionally effective, as against the West Indians in the summer of 1991, but he never threatened to emulate Botham's feats. In 30 Test appearances, Pringle's batting average of 15.1 and his bowling average of 35.97 would have been commendable had they been reversed. The same could be said of David Capel who, in 15 Tests, had a similar batting average, but an inferior bowling one of 50.66.

Chris Lewis seemed a much better bet when he made his Test debut in 1990. He was a brisk seam bowler with a smooth, high action. Lewis was also a fluent batsman, capable of producing sizzling on-side drives and savage cuts. He was a sensationally athletic fieldsman, too. And yet his Test batting average was mediocre at 23.02 and his 93 wickets cost 37.52 runs each. Lewis seemed disengaged or absent-minded, at times, as on England's Caribbean tour of 1994 when he suffered sunstroke after failing to cover his recently shaved head. *The Sun* dubbed him 'the prat without a hat'. While his preening did not endear him to his team-mates, his unfounded allegations of English match fixing in 1999 brought about a more serious rift. Injury finally brought his disappointing career to an end, while his liberty was removed in 2008 after he was caught attempting to smuggle cocaine into Britain.

Darren Gough and Dominic Cork were also briefly considered as nominees for filling Botham's boots, although, like DeFreitas, they were primarily bowlers who could bat a bit as indicated by their respective Test batting averages of 12.57 and 18. Craig White and Dermot Reeve were other unsuccessful candidates, although White performed promisingly until injury curtailed his capacity to bowl. Ultimately, only Andrew Flintoff proved big enough to fit the bill, but his impact was not felt for a further decade. While Denis Compton accused Botham of setting an 'awful example' to young cricketers, Botham lifted the nation with his heroic feats, and not only on the field of play, for his charitable fund-raising efforts were also impressive. Whatever his shortcomings, he should be forever admired for his inspirational achievements with bat and ball.

The third Test at Manchester in 1992 featured another distasteful conflict which had marred too many contests between England and Pakistan. This spat began at Lord's after Devon Malcolm had peppered Waqar Younis and Aqib Javed with bouncers. At Old Trafford, Aqib retaliated but was frustrated when umpire Roy Palmer notified Aqib that he would receive an official warning if he persisted. Aqib and Pakistan captain Javed Miandad protested stridently. The contretemps escalated after Aqib accused Palmer of throwing his sweater at him. Actually, the sweater had sprung loose after becoming stuck in the loops of Palmer's jacket. With so much thin-skinned sensitivity about, though, it was almost inevitable that there would be explosive exchanges. As in 1982 and 1987/88, the impartiality of the umpires was questioned. This churlish Test ended in a high-scoring draw, rain having prevented any play on the second day. Aamir Sohail was the star of the truncated show with a double century (205) while Gower graced his return with a fine innings of 73. Chris Lewis delivered another impressive all-round performance with a fifty (55) and five wickets. It was a miserable return for Mike Atherton, though, having been caught at the wicket off Wasim Akram for a duck.

The heat of controversy was turned up further after Allan Lamb accused the Pakistanis of altering the shape of the ball in a one-day international at Lord's. Whereas some of the England batsmen doubted the legitimacy of the Pakistanis' bewildering reverse swing, the England seamers were more interested in how they could replicate their skill. Lamb's Test career ended at Lord's. It was sad that it should conclude in contentious circumstances since he had served England well during a lean period, scoring 4,656 Test runs, with 14 centuries, at an average of 36. While Warwickshire coach Bob Cottam thought Lamb was vulnerable to late away movement, having a tendency to move across his stumps at the point of delivery, Lamb continued to score heavily in county cricket, making 1,350 County Championship runs for Northants in 1992 at an average of 71.05.

Leeds then lived up to its reputation as a results pitch with Gooch (135) and Atherton (76) placing England on the road to a six-wicket victory with an opening first-innings stand of 168. Northants seamer Neil Mallender made a notable Test debut with match figures of 8-122. Despite Malcolm's impressive first-innings showing on a typically quick Oval wicket, where he took 5-94, even he was outgunned by Wasim Akram and Waqar Younis who shared 15 wickets as they dumbfounded the English batsmen with their pace and late reverse swing. Pakistan deservedly won the series 2-1.

1993
Animal Nitrate

The Queen declared 1992 to be an 'annus horribilis' for the British royal family. There was the Princess Royal's divorce. Then there was the Duke and Duchess of York separation and the humiliating topless photos of the Duchess. And, after much speculative muttering, news emerged of the Prince and Princess of Wales's marital difficulties. Finally, the Queen's misery was compounded when a fire engulfed her chapel and State Apartments at Windsor Castle. Fortunes were scarcely better for the Labour Party after John Major, lampooned by *Spitting Image* as the 'grey man' of British politics, triumphed over the supposedly more charismatic Neil Kinnock at the polls. And if 1992 was a bad year for English cricket, then 1993 was worse. A strangely selected, injury-hampered England side was thrashed in India, and beaten by Sri Lanka in Colombo in March.

To add to the despondency, the Indian leg of the tour was beset with civil unrest and inter-religious violence. Industrial action at the major Indian airlines led to the tourists undertaking some alarming internal flights, captained by grounded or retired pilots. Their only alternative was to take the train, only to increase their strain. Cross-country Indian train journeys were notoriously long, slow and uncomfortable with primitive sleeping and toilet facilities. It was small wonder that the photos taken of the dishevelled, exhausted and unshaven players, shortly after completing one such journey, aroused the concern of the chairman of selectors, Ted Dexter. But instead of focusing upon what could be done to remedy the inadequate travelling arrangements, he launched into a condemnation of the players' appearance, threatening to impose a ban on facial stubble. The screeching of Nero's fiddle pierced even the din and choking smog of Delhi and the hubbub and gagging pollution of Kolkata. In fairness, Dexter did take issue with the toxic conditions in which the England team were expected to play.

The only compensations to be drawn from this dismal tour were the maiden Test tons made by Graeme Hick at Mumbai (178) and Chris Lewis at Chennai (117). But these impressive knocks where pallid when compared with the huge weight of runs accumulated by the Indian batsmen. Azharuddin compiled a hefty hundred at Kolkata (182) in taking India to a winning score of 371. Sidhu (106) and Tendulkar (165) helped India make a demoralising score of 560/6 declared at Chennai. And Kambli's double century (224) took India to 591 at Mumbai, setting up a second successive innings victory.

While the Indians gorged themselves with easy runs, most of England's clamp-footed batsmen fell on their blades when facing Anil Kumble's leg-breaks. Kumble created havoc with the diffident English batsmen, taking 21 series wickets at an average cost of 19.80. Even Gatting, a highly accomplished player of spin, seemed distrustful of playing any shot other than the sweep. With Robin Smith and Alec Stewart less comfortable in combatting high class spin than outright pace, Gower's nimble footwork and 'soft hands' were sorely missed.

Mike Atherton had a poor tour. He was ruled out of the opening Test because of sickness, then passed over for the Chennai Test. Upon his own admission he became disgruntled and uncommunicative. When he was recalled for the Mumbai and Colombo Tests he did not do himself justice. In his autobiography, *Opening Up*, Atherton admitted that his attitude could have been better.

Hick achieved the distinction of heading both the England Test batting and bowling averages. Feeling more at home on the dusty, turning Indian tracks, without fear of his ribs being cracked by an endless assault of snarling bumpers, Hick averaged 52.5 with the bat. However, he was probably surprised to find his occasional off-spin being employed in a mainstay capacity. Given the ineffectiveness of Salisbury who took only three Test wickets at an average cost of 76.66, Emburey, who took two wickets at 72, and Tufnell who managed just four wickets at 68.50, Hick was required to bowl almost 77 overs during the series. The average cost of each of his eight wickets was a mere 25.25 runs. This was easily the best return achieved by any of the England bowlers, whether fast or slow. For the quicker bowlers, Malcolm, Jarvis and Lewis managed just ten wickets between them at an extravagant cost of 56 runs each. At no point during this series were India placed under any pressure.

Clearly, burn-out might have been a factor in the under-performance of the England bowlers. Emburey had bowled almost 850 first-class overs for Middlesex during the 1992 season while Salisbury had managed almost 750 for Sussex and England. Even 'shock' bowler Malcolm delivered 450 for his county and national side. This was before limited overs games were taken into consideration.

By sharp contrast, Graeme Swann delivered 290 first-class overs for his county and national side in 2013 while Stuart Broad completed 260 and James Anderson 277.

Malcolm's threat was largely nullified by the sluggish subcontinent surfaces, but he toiled uncomplainingly in the Indian heat and dust, whereas DeFreitas and Tufnell were unhappy with their lot. DeFreitas seemed unnerved by the surrounding violence and wanted to return home, while Tufnell was constantly exasperated at the Indian umpires' unwillingness to grant him an lbw decision. Tufnell might have had just cause. Malcolm thought that with greater encouragement from his captain Gooch, or coach Keith Fletcher, Tufnell might have ridden the knocks better. However, Gooch was not in a good place. His failing marriage had been exposed in the popular press, leaving him understandably distressed and distracted. He managed a Test average of only 11.75 in India before being allowed to return home early.

According to Malcolm, Keith Fletcher lacked Micky Stewart's instinctive grasp of how to re-motivate a struggling player. Despite his vast cricketing knowledge and tactical acumen, Fletcher appeared to be a man out of time. While his coaching relied heavily upon his own professional experience, the Australian and South African coaches were more forensic, assembling vast amounts of data in their analyses of technique, tactics and performance, which in turn fed into individual and team improvement plans, backed by specialist coaching and sports psychology. Such provisions might have helped right the listing ship on that disastrous winter tour, but adoption of these measures was several years away.

So England stumbled into another home Ashes series psychologically ill-prepared and technically and tactically inferior to their highly combative opponents. No preparations were made to combat the threat posed by new Australian leg-spinner, Shane Warne, despite accomplished New Zealand batsman Martin Crowe's warning that Warne was possibly the best of his type. This was no idle hype for in the opening Test, at Old Trafford, Warne produced 'the ball of the century' with his first delivery. Mike Gatting was the bemused batsman as Warne pitched the ball about a foot outside the leg stump before it ripped across Gatting's angled blade and hit the top of the off stick. Gatting was momentarily stunned, incredulous that a ball could turn so far, suspecting that wicketkeeper Healy had removed the bail with an attempted stumping. But then realisation struck. Peter Such, England's debutant off-spinner, had already prospered on this turning wicket, taking 6-67 in the Australian first innings, but Warne proved more deadly and no less so after the pitch had flattened. Only Gooch, who produced two gutsy innings of 65 and 133, could contend with Warne for long. With Warne achieving match figures of 8-137 and a growling, profane Merv Hughes keeping pace with 8-151, England lost by 179 runs.

At Lord's, the England players were humiliated. Batting first, Australia amassed 632/4 declared. Doughty Mark Taylor (111) ground out his second hundred of the series, while a fleet-footed Michael Slater exuberantly thumped his maiden Test ton (152). Not to be left out, David Boon (164 not out) recorded his first Test century in England. Only Mark Waugh's unaccountable aberration against Tufnell, when on 99, interrupted the succession of top order centuries. And by the time Border was bowled by Lewis for 77 the gnarled Aussie skipper had raised his Lord's Test average to three figures.

But here endeth the batting fun for in reply England closed day three on 191/9. This time it was Atherton's turn to play the lone stalwart (80). Following on, England batted with greater resolution. Nerves, poor judgement and a catastrophic slip led Atherton to be run out on 99. Nevertheless, half-centuries from Gatting (59), Hick (64) and Stewart (62) helped England to a better score of 365, although their last six wickets fell for only 61 runs. Australian off-spinner Tim May proved to be a much tougher adversary than initial intelligence suggested, maintaining constricting accuracy over long spells while displaying disconcerting variations of flight. He and Warne bowled almost 100 overs between them in England's second innings, sharing eight wickets for 183. England lost by an innings and 62 runs.

At Trent Bridge four English debutants were introduced – Somerset opener Mark Lathwell, Surrey's left-handed batsman Graham Thorpe, Essex left-arm bowler Mark Ilott and Larne-born but Australian-bred speedster Martin McCague. Seventeen players had represented England in the first three Tests. Thorpe distinguished himself with a stoical, unbeaten second-innings century (114) which alongside a more cavalier effort from Gooch (120), and sound support lent by Smith (50) and Hussain (47 not out), took England to the giddy heights of 422/6 declared. Set 371 to win in 77 overs, Australia crumbled under the unexpected pressure exerted by Caddick (3-32) and Such (2-58). At 115/6 they were in danger of defeat, but Steve Waugh (47 not out) and Brendon Julian (56 not out) added 87 runs to pull them out of the mire. Both Ilott and McCague made satisfactory debuts, the former taking four wickets with reasonable economy, and the latter displaying striking pace and aggression, notably in the first innings when he took four wickets for 121. The Australians were unimpressed by McCague's 'defection', though, deriding him as 'the only rat to join a sinking ship'.

At Leeds, Surrey seamer Martin Bicknell made his Test debut in place of Essex spinner Peter Such, but the four-pronged pace attack proved toothless as Australia racked up 653/4 declared with Border making an unbeaten double century (200), and Steve Waugh (157 not out) and Boon (107) also putting the England attack to the sword. Australian seamers Reiffel and Hughes then showed the flagging English pace quartet how it should be done as they shared 14 wickets for 278 runs. Australia won by an innings and 48 runs, and duly retained the Ashes, whereupon Gooch resigned as captain.

Twenty-five-year-old Atherton was invited to take his place, despite having had no experience of captaincy at county level. Although uncertain whether to accept Dexter's offer, Atherton was aware that he was unlikely to play beyond the age of 30 because of his troublesome back. He therefore felt compelled to accept the honour, as the chance might not come again.

There was no change in fortune at Edgbaston, Atherton's first Test in charge. This resulted in another heavy defeat, this time by eight wickets. Atherton did well, though. He batted resolutely in the first innings (72) and shuffled his bowlers intelligently, despite the adverse state of the game. He also dealt calmly with his players' exasperation as Mark Waugh (137), Steve Waugh (59), Healy (80) and Hughes (38) took the game away from England by compiling a 132-run first-innings lead. He dealt deftly with Stewart and Thorpe, too, when the Surrey pair were reported to the match referee Clive

Lloyd for dissent. Stewart had exuberantly congratulated Such on taking a wicket before umpire Shepherd had time to reject his appeal. Thorpe then threw down the ball in disgust after his appeal for a bat-pad catch was rejected. Atherton confirmed with Lloyd that Stewart and Thorpe had been out of order, but suggested that their actions were motivated by excessive enthusiasm rather than disrespect. Atherton proved nimble in scaling his steep learning curve.

Merv Hughes, who was the batsman at the centre of this row, thought highly of Atherton. When asked by Pilger and Wightman, authors of *Match of My Life – The Ashes,* why he sledged Atherton so vehemently, Hughes replied, 'If I didn't think Atherton could play, I wouldn't have wasted my breath upon him. He was one of the toughest competitors I have ever faced. His performances against Australia were sensational, he stood up to us and gave it a go. If you wanted someone to bat for your life, you would give him a call.'

Atherton knew that if his side was to prevail, he needed it to operate like a '19th county', with continuity of selection and an accent placed upon up-and-coming youthful talent. Twenty-nine players had represented England in the 1989 Ashes series and 24 in 1993. He knew there was no chance of recovering the Ashes with so much chopping and changing. However, his radical vision would not be enacted during his captaincy. It would require the appointment of a shrewd and far-sighted foreign coach, six years later, to bring about the necessary changes, including the introduction of central contracts.

For the final Test at the Oval, Robin Smith was dropped on account of his alleged difficulties in combating Warne. Smith disputed that he was too thrusting and firm-handed in playing Warne, leaving him vulnerable to bat-pad dismissals. He cited his success in dealing with both Aussie spinners at Nottingham, and also his mastery of Pakistan's Mushtaq Ahmed at Edgbaston and the Oval in 1992. Given that Smith was England's second strongest batsman during the 1990s, his omission was surprising, particularly when the fiery Oval wicket promised to suit his 'slash and burn' style of play.

Angus Fraser and Graeme Hick were recalled, and because the wicket was expected to be quick, so were Devon Malcolm and Steve Watkin. Fraser had taken two and a half years to recover fully from a misdiagnosed hip injury. Unfortunately, England's most successful batsman of the 1990s, Graham Thorpe, broke a finger while practising in the nets, so Mark Ramprakash was asked to cover. Even with the loss of Thorpe, Atherton believed he had a team capable of knocking over the Aussies, even if the Ashes were well gone.

Having won the toss, England batted aggressively and well, reaching 353/7 by the close of the first day. Gooch (56) and Atherton (50) began with a brisk 88-run opening partnership. Hick then strode to the crease, no longer the bowed, diffident figure who had allowed Hughes to intimidate him. As proof of his greater mental strength he began by creaming both Hughes and Reiffel through the covers before clipping them through midwicket. He also used his feet freely in attacking Warne and May. Alas, having regally lifted a delivery from May into the crowd he departed two balls later, caught by Warne at third man, from a reckless slash. Hick had made 80. Frustratingly, he had seemed capable of doubling that score. Although England's total of 380 was probably around 100 below par, the speed at which their batsmen scored had rattled the Australians. For the first time in the series the weary Australian fielders resorted to verbal assaults rather than focusing upon their game plans. As their attack tired, Alec Stewart took advantage, walloping 76 joyful runs.

At his best Stewart was a commanding batsman with a flamboyant array of drives, cuts and pulls with which he despatched the ball to the ropes at sizzling speed. Not even the most fearsome fast bowling could contain him then. As a specialist opening batsman he achieved a Test average of 46.9. Only Len Hutton, Geoff Boycott, Dennis Amiss and Alastair Cook have bettered that since the Second World War. His final career Test average of 39.54 would have been higher had he not loyally answered his country's need of a wicketkeeper/batsman, such was the fallibility of England's middle order for much of the 1990s.

Merv Hughes was just about spent. His damaged right knee was causing considerable pain. It had locked twice during this tour, forcing him to seek the advice of a British orthopaedic surgeon. He was told he would require surgery on his return home. However, Hughes was determined to carry on. He was desperate to claim his 200th Test wicket. Even the additional discomfort created by his sore back and ankles would not hold him back. A glaring, hooked-nosed, potty-mouthed Hughes was much more than a pantomime villain. He was a fearsome, courageous warrior. Off a stuttering, mincing run he completed 470 overs during the tour, 296 in the Test series alone, and 61 at the Oval. He typified rough, tough Aussie competitiveness, demonstrating the mental tenacity required to succeed at this level.

Former Australian captain Ian Chappell was highly critical of England's selection policy. He could not understand why Malcolm, whose pace and bounce troubled the Aussies, had not been chosen before. He was at a loss to understand Watkin's omission, too, given his county record. In 1993, Watkin took 92 first-class wickets at an average of under 22. Fraser's omission was equally inexplicable. He had taken 50 first-class wickets for eventual county champions Middlesex, at an average of 24.

There seemed to be a misperception at this time that Fraser had lost his 'nip' for he continued to bowl around 85mph. His county captain, Mike Gatting, griped about Fraser being over-bowled by England, yet he was a greater culprit. Eighty-two per cent of Fraser's first-class overs were completed in the service of Middlesex. Fraser remained philosophical, modestly ascribing his success to 'bowling the same ball 95 per cent of the time'. He explained in this BBC interview that he aimed to pitch the ball consistently on a length, on the line of the off stump, reasoning that if there was any movement even the best players in the world might struggle to deal with it. His Test career record of 177 wickets at 27.99 at a niggardly economy rate of 2.66 runs per over vindicates his assertion. At the Oval in 1993, Fraser was blessed with a quick top with impressive carry and duly revelled in the more auspicious conditions.

But he had to await his turn as Malcolm and Watkin were given the new ball. While Watkin focused on line and length, Malcolm was told to let rip. The faster Malcolm had both Taylor and Slater hopping around with a succession of sharply rising deliveries. The Aussie opening pair had thrashed England's slower pace bowlers in the previous five Tests, but facing Malcolm on a bouncy Oval wicket was a very different matter. Slater's back foot began to slide surreptitiously to leg. He wasn't quite so cocky here. This was the severest test yet of the Australians' technique and courage. For the first time in the series, the Aussie batsmen came to the crease clad in arm guards and chest protectors. Having softened up Taylor and Slater, Malcolm struck. A wickedly lifting ball had Slater poking the ball to Gooch at silly mid-on while another had Boon tucked up and fending a catch to Gooch who had been moved to short leg. Australia were 30/2, and after Fraser had replaced Malcolm, he had Mark Waugh caught at the wicket, with just enough seam movement to find the outside edge. The Australians were 53/3. Although Taylor (70) and Border (48) put on 79 for the fourth wicket, Malcolm returned to dismiss Taylor while Fraser had Border caught at the wicket. Fraser also bowled Steve Waugh for 20, and with Watkin chipping in with two wickets, Australia were languishing at 196/8. But then Healey (83) dug in, with Warne (16) and May (15), to drag his side back into contention at 303 all out. Fraser took 5-87.

England then built on their 77-run first-innings lead by patiently adding a further 313 runs with Gooch (79) and Ramprakash (64) top-scoring. Set 391 to win, Australia lurched to 30/3 with Watkin removing both openers and Boon. A 62-run fourth-wicket partnership between Mark Waugh (49) and Border (17) was ended by Malcolm who dismissed both batsmen, then snared Steve Waugh lbw for 26. At 106/6, the Australian batsmen were trapped on the ropes, with a fired-up Malcolm causing them to dodge and weave. Despite a spirited 75-run ninth-wicket stand between Reiffel (42) and Warne (37), Watkin and Fraser cleaned up the tail to give England victory by 161 runs. Malcolm (6-170), Fraser (8-131) and Watkin (6-152) shared all 20 Australian wickets. Until this trio had made their mark, the England bowling averages had looked very bleak. Only Such, with 16 wickets at 33.81, achieved respectability. By contrast, the Australians had two bowlers with over 30 wickets – Warne (34 at 25.79) and Hughes (31 at 27.25). Warne and May had bowled so tightly that they conceded barely more than two runs per over. Warne had demonstrated unprecedented control for a leg-spinner.

Five Australians achieved Ashes series averages in excess of 50: Steve Waugh (83.20); David Boon (69.37); Mark Waugh (61.11); Ian Healy (59.20);

and Allan Border (54.12). Their openers Mark Taylor (42.80) and Michael Slater (41.60) averaged over 40, too, whereas England's top-scorers Graham Gooch (56.08) and Mike Atherton (46.08) were the only home batsmen to exceed 40. Despite the euphoria aroused by England's Oval victory, the gulf in class was enormous.

Suede's 1993 song, 'Animal Nitrate', seemed to be a high-octane homage to glam-rock. With his strangled south London vowels, singer Brett Anderson morphed into David Bowie, while Bernard Butler's crashing power chords seemed in thrall of Bowie's lead guitarist, Mick Ronson. It was much later that I realised the song was about the twisted wreckage left by a sexually abusive relationship. Had the BBC realised this they might have banned it. But with ghastly reports of Balkan atrocities being broadcasted nightly on their radio and TV networks, perhaps they decided that there were more pressing moral concerns. With the Killing Fields still fresh in our memories and the Rwandan massacres just around the corner, it was clear that genocide had not been consigned to history as many of us had assumed. 'Ethnic cleansing' meant mass extermination.

1994
Hallelujah

Leonard Cohen is one of the greatest singer-songwriters of my lifetime. His mesmerising poetic imagery is matched by few other artists, although Bob Dylan is certainly one. But just as Jimi Hendrix provided the definitive version of Dylan's song 'All Along the Watchtower', Jeff Buckley gave the supreme rendition of 'Hallelujah'. The condensed, overblown version by X Factor winner Alexandra Burke is merely graceless.

The song is sprinkled with Old Testament references as the dissolution of a once passionate relationship is bitterly dissected. But whereas in Cohen's version, the words are wearily delivered as if the singer has been stripped bare by a raw separation, in Buckley's adaptation, his expressions of regret and reproach remain ardent and pointed. Buckley's tragic death in 1997 makes his rendition all the more poignant. 'Hallelujah' is one of the finest break-up songs of the 20th century.

1994 proved to be a valedictory year. We paid our respects to sadly departed broadcaster Brian Johnston, and we gratefully acknowledged the huge contributions made by Ian Botham, David Gower, Derek Randall, Viv Richards, and Malcolm Marshall as they bade farewell to first-class cricket.

Meanwhile Atherton looked to the future as he led his revamped, more youthful side on a Caribbean tour. England's jubilation at their Oval victory was lost quickly, though, as they were beaten badly in the opening three Tests. While the West Indian pace quartet of Ambrose, Kenny Benjamin, Walsh, and Winston Benjamin were ruthless with the ball, Adams, Chanderpaul, Arthurton and, above all, Lara dominated with the bat.

However, Atherton and Stewart established a robust opening partnership. Both completed a brace of Test centuries – Stewart compiling both of his in the unexpected victory in Bridgetown. Both batsmen completed the series with averages in excess of 50. Once Malcolm was ruled out with a knee injury, Fraser and Caddick formed an effective new-ball partnership, sharing 34 series wickets at an average of 29. Fraser took 8-75 in the first innings at Bridgetown while Caddick took 5-63 in the second, helping England to a 208-run win. This success was particularly gratifying after England had been blown away pathetically by Ambrose and Walsh for only 46 in their second innings in Trinidad, losing a game they were expected to win, by 147 runs.

The series ended with a Brian Lara gala performance at Antigua where he established a new world record for an individual Test innings by scoring 375. Thanks to centuries from Atherton (135) and Robin Smith (175), England matched the West Indian first innings score of 593, but once Lara had completed his phenomenal feat, Antiguan interest dwindled.

Atherton's physical and mental courage were exemplary. He was unflinching in grittily defying the intimidating, short-pitched West Indian bowling, riding the many blows to his ribcage while evading the clutches of the close catchers. His combativeness was inspirational, notably after the debacle at Port-of-Spain. For just eight days later, he and his opening partner Alec Stewart put on 171 for the first wicket at Barbados, establishing a winning platform. This was England's first victory in Bridgetown in almost 60 years.

In 1994, Raymond Illingworth succeeded Ted Dexter as chairman of the selectors. Following Fletcher's dismissal as England coach a year later, Illingworth also assumed the role of team manager. He thought that the England side needed greater discipline, direction and steel, believing it was his duty to knock the players into shape. Presuming he had overriding authority, Illingworth pronounced on coaching, tactical and selection matters. He also issued edicts on non-cricketing issues, too, banning the use of shades and mobile phones in the dressing room and on the pavilion balcony. Atherton found that his faith in youth and continuity of selection was not shared by Illingworth, who was swayed more by the proven records of 'old hands' such as Gooch and Gatting, seeing no problem in chopping and changing the England side on a 'horses for courses' basis.

One of Illingworth's first decisions was to recall Graham Gooch for the first Test series of the summer against New Zealand. This meant no place could be found for Mark Ramprakash, who had played in four of the winter Tests but had yet to find his feet at Test level. Although Ramprakash had not distinguished himself in the Caribbean, averaging a paltry 10.42 in seven Test innings, the less-demanding Kiwi bowling might have given him an opportunity to flourish. Although 40-year-old Gooch scored a double century (210) in England's innings victory over New Zealand at Trent Bridge, his Test-playing days were almost over, whereas 24-year-old Ramprakash's were just beginning.

Ramprakash was a batsman of extraordinary talent. Playing with a burning, combative intensity, he amassed 35,659 first-class runs in his career, averaging over 53 and scoring 114 centuries. And yet his Test record was mediocre. In 52 Tests he averaged only 27.32, half his first-class average. It was as if he put himself under too much pressure in his desperation to succeed. He proved vulnerable to expert 'sledgers', like Shane Warne, who could disturb his concentration, play on his nerves, and goad him into playing reckless shots. Had there been central contracts during the early 1990s, Ramprakash might have acquired the confidence to thrive. He, like 28-year-old Graeme Hick, was not helped by the divergence in outlook between Atherton and Illingworth. And while Atherton also rated both Fraser and Thorpe, Illingworth was less enthusiastic. Illingworth thought Fraser did not do enough with the ball.

Meanwhile, Andrew Caddick, another younger player of great potential was not selected for any of the summer Test matches. Admittedly, a shoulder injury caused him to miss six County Championship games. Nevertheless, he headed Somerset's County Championship bowling averages in 1994 with 49 wickets at 22.97. Even on the flat tracks of Taunton he was capable of devastating county sides. Despite suffering badly at the hands of the Australians in his debut Test series, he had recovered well in the Caribbean, becoming England's leading wicket-taker with eighteen at 30.27, producing a match-winning performance in Barbados. As with Ramprakash, Caddick had the qualities to succeed at Test level. Being 6ft 5in with a guardsman-like posture, Caddick could extract considerable bounce from the sleepiest of surfaces. He had a relaxed, rhythmic approach to the wicket, with a flowing, high action, that was modelled on fellow Kiwi Richard Hadlee. His impressive command of cut and swing was augmented by his lively pace of around 85mph.

Extraordinarily, Caddick had sought English qualification after finding progression difficult in his native New Zealand. The Kiwis would regret their unaccountable oversight. But also like Ramprakash, Caddick had a psychological frailty at Test level. Until he toughened up, his international performances were erratic, sometimes terrific but at other times frustratingly tepid. In his early Test career he often reserved his best displays for the second innings. Certainly, Caddick's bowling could disintegrate under sustained assault. It seemed as if his brash remarks and aloof manner thinly disguised a suspect self-belief. His time would come, though. Once he had established a potent opening partnership with Darren Gough, during the late 90s and early 2000s, his confidence and tenacity grew.

Illingworth also selected Yorkshire all-rounder Craig White and Worcestershire wicketkeeper/batsman Steve Rhodes for their Test debuts in 1994. Atherton said that he knew very little about the Australian-bred White when Illingworth announced his selection. Nevertheless, the 24-year-old started promisingly, scoring a fifty at Lord's and passing 40 at Old Trafford, where he also took four wickets. Bristling with typical Aussie combativeness, he had a penchant for slog-sweeping the spinners to, or over, the midwicket boundary or driving them above extra cover. He was not easily disconcerted by pace bowling, either. Originally an off-spinner, he reinvented himself as a fast bowler when doubts were expressed about his action. In his quicker style, he could reach a speed of 90mph. Using only a short run, he relied heavily upon his shoulder strength, which might have contributed to his later injury. He was also a dab hand at reverse swing. Until thwarted by fitness problems, he was a valuable member of both Test and one-day squads. Rhodes acquitted himself satisfactorily, too, in the twin summer series. As understandable as their selections were, it was difficult envisaging Illingworth, as England's captain, tolerating the subordinate role he expected Atherton to take in choosing the Test team.

Illingworth's other selections during the summer of 1994 were no less successful. Yorkshire fast bowler Darren Gough was blooded in the drawn third Test against New Zealand at Old Trafford where he took eight wickets, while recalled seamer Phillip DeFreitas had a fine series against the Kiwis, taking 21 wickets at an average of 21.47. England won the series 1-0 although only late-order resistance, led by Rhodes, saved them from defeat at Lord's. Here, classy Martin Crowe scored the first of two excellent centuries.

South Africa proved to be a tougher nut to crack. At Lord's they thrashed England by 356 runs on the back of a typically obdurate century by Kepler Wessels (105). Donald, De Villiers, Matthews and McMillan then cleaned up England twice in steamy conditions, dismissing them for 180 and 99. Atherton was censured, too, for drying the ball with dirt he kept in his pocket. While professing to match referee, Peter Burge, his innocence of ball-tampering, Atherton conceded later that the TV footage had looked incriminating.

Illingworth reacted quickly, imposing a £2,000 fine upon Atherton in order to avert a worse punishment by the match referee. He was convinced that he had saved Atherton from a ban. The South Africans were too elated by their victory to be bothered about pursuing this issue. They were more put out by Lord's refusal to allow them to display their new 'Rainbow Nation' South African flag on the balcony. Allan Donald was aghast given the importance of what the flag signified – a racially united South Africa collectively committed to its black President Nelson Mandela and a fairer constitution. South African frustration increased when Archbishop Desmond Tutu was refused entry into the Lord's pavilion because he was not wearing a jacket. He was in his ecclesiastical robes, having come to lead prayers with the South African team before the start of play. Fortunately, good sense prevailed and the Archbishop conducted prayers as planned. Atherton could have done without these slights for the South Africans' angry indignation was then heaped upon a reeling English team.

A high-scoring draw ensued at Leeds on an uncharacteristically docile surface. Thorpe was a notable beneficiary scoring 72 and 73 upon his return to the England side, vindicating Atherton's faith in him. With the Oval wicket expected to be once again fast and bouncy, the call went out to Devon Malcolm to help rescue the series. However, Illingworth refrained from announcing his team until 45 minutes before play was due to begin, leaving no time for preparation. Illingworth's inclusion of Malcolm meant that there was no place for left-arm spinner Phil Tufnell.

In his autobiography *Dazzler*, Darren Gough said that Malcolm did not make the impact Atherton had hoped for in South Africa's first innings. Gough claimed that Malcolm was reluctant to follow his captain's instruction to bowl fast and short, when South Africa were stumbling at 136/5. Atherton thought he had his opponents cornered and looked to Malcolm to finish them off. However, South African Jonty Rhodes was in hospital having ducked into a particularly fast ball from Malcolm. Malcolm was aware of Rhodes's epileptic condition and fearful of the possible consequences of the blow, although Rhodes was wearing a helmet. Perhaps this is why he was disinclined to follow his captain's instruction to pepper the South African tail-enders with short balls. He suggested to Atherton that it might be more profitable to pitch fuller given how much the ball was swinging. Angered by Malcolm's intransigence, Atherton replaced him with Gough. But perhaps Malcolm did know better as Gough's first four short-pitched deliveries were smacked to the fence. South Africa jumped jail with McMillan (93) and Richardson (58) adding 124 runs for the sixth wicket at indecent haste. Malcolm claimed that Atherton graciously conceded his tactical error at the close of play. This had not been a good day for Atherton. South Africa had recovered strongly, closing at 326/8, having made around 100 runs more than they should.

With Jonty Rhodes still unfit to continue at the start of day three, DeFreitas mopped up the final wicket for only six more runs. But Atherton was then given out, lbw to De Villiers, before he had scored. Atherton was clearly unhappy with the decision, convinced that he had nicked the ball. While umpire Ken Palmer was unmoved, referee Peter Burge was not, instantly fining Atherton £1,250 – half his match fee – for dissent. This was proving to be an expensive series for Atherton.

Gooch did not stay long, either, caught at the wicket for eight off Allan Donald, who still seemed incapacitated by the foot injury he had suffered at Leeds. Donald discovered after the game that he needed surgery to remove a cyst in his foot, caused by bowling largely on baked surfaces.

After these early setbacks, Hick (39), Thorpe (79) and Stewart (62) brought about a recovery, but at 222/7 England were in danger of conceding a substantial first-innings lead. DeFreitas and new batsman Darren Gough decided to launch an all-out attack, challenging one another as to who could hit the greater number of boundaries. In 30 minutes of carnage the pair added 59 runs in a frenzy of hooks, pulls, slashes and drives. England closed on 281/7. A first-innings lead was even possible. Illingworth was delighted, declaring the run-fest to be the most aggressive batting display he had ever seen. While the English dressing room was buzzing with excitement, the South Africans were very subdued. Captain Wessels was unhappy with Donald believing he should have done more to help his team despite his injury.

Upset by tabloid press criticism of his indiscretion at Lord's, and deflated by his run-ins with the match referee and his disagreements with Illingworth, Michael Atherton was said to be considering his position as captain. Illingworth was also doubtful whether Atherton would continue, indicating that Gatting would replace him should he decide to quit. When Atherton was out of the dressing room, Gooch gathered the team around him, urging them to back their captain wholeheartedly. Like a good ship captain, though, Atherton remained at the helm.

Although DeFreitas (37) was run out upon the resumption of play on the Saturday morning, Gough cuffed 17 more runs before running out of partners. England's deficit had been reduced to just 28. However, the game-changing moment came when De Villiers struck Malcolm on the helmet with a low bouncer. The normally slow-burning Malcolm was immediately moved to anger, hissing softly at the South African slip cordon, 'All you guys are f***ing history!'

Lydia and I watched history being made on a gigantic TV screen in a packed pub outside Turf Moor, Burnley. When Malcolm took the new ball he was in the zone, oblivious of everyone except the green-helmeted guy in his line of fire. Belying his heavy build, Malcolm seemed to glide to the wicket. His rhythm was perfect, his stride spot on. Every ounce of the momentum gained from his run went into his heaving shoulders. The first ball boomed off the pitch, flashing narrowly past Gary Kirsten's nose as he yanked his head aside, with Steve Rhodes taking it high to his right. Malcolm's gigantic follow-through ended with him head-to-head with Kirsten. This contest seemed like a cage fight. Each time Malcolm began his run to the wicket, the compressed pub watchers emitted a low growl, which was steadily stoked up until the point of delivery was reached, whereupon a shuddering, guttural war cry was released.

Gary Kirsten did not like the look of what was coming his way. Malcolm was dropping bombs. Half-turning his back at Malcolm's third delivery, his bat proffered awkwardly in feeble defence, the ball clattered against the top of the handle and looped upwards. Malcolm charged forward to gobble up the return catch pushing aside short leg, John Crawley, in his eagerness to snatch the falling ball. The pub rocked and rolled with delight. South Africa were 0/1. 'One-nil to the Engerrrland!' chanted the now crammed pub crowd. The next batsman was Cronje. His chequered final days were still several years ahead of him. He did not fancy facing Malcolm any more than his predecessor had as two balls scudded across his worried countenance. Cronje began bouncing around on his toes like a wired boxer waiting for the bell.

Peter Kirsten, Gary's half-brother, was next to go. Malcolm blasted a bouncer at him. Kirsten was not in position to play the hook. His feet were nailed to the spot. The ball was upon him too quickly. He swiped wildly at it anyway. As he pirouetted, the ball caught a top edge and spiralled skywards, slewing towards DeFreitas at long leg. There was a momentary hush before DeFreitas grasped the chance, his legs buckling beneath him. The Oval crowd went up as one and so did we. 'Two-one to the Engerrrland!'

Cronje was now facing but not for long. With the South African expecting a shorter delivery, Malcolm pitched up. Cronje was too tentative, too slow in pressing forward. The ball whistled through the gap between bat and pad, knocking back Cronje's middle stump. South Africa were 1/3. Hell, this was fun! Even Lydia was pitching in with the raucous cheers and chants.

With Atherton reluctant to crowd the new South African pair with close catchers, Cullinan and Wessels began a salvage operation. No further wickets fell before lunch, or immediately after. The 50-run mark was passed, so were 60 and 70. The South Africans found they could play shots, dominate even. Malcolm had been relieved. Neither Gough nor Benjamin were posing as much menace. Runs began to flow freely while Atherton resisted over-attacking, sticking with two slips and a gully. Finally, he turned again to Malcolm who was still high on adrenalin and refreshed by a lunchtime shower.

Wessels was described by Donald as a typical Afrikaaner – sturdy, durable, stubborn, undemonstrative but furiously driven. Wessels was determined that his native country should recover the pride and prestige it had lost while it was a political and sporting pariah. He glared at the returning Malcolm, looking to puncture his self-belief and draw his sting. Wessels knew that Malcolm was susceptible to self-doubt. His co-ordination sometimes let him down, particularly when he fell away in his delivery stride. Then, his radar became scrambled, offering the batsmen easy pickings, allowing them to thrash his wayward deliveries through point and cover or to flick and pull them through midwicket.

But on this day Malcolm retained a clarity of focus, a firmness of will. He decided to go around the wicket to the left-handed Wessels. Wessels had previously displayed vulnerability when his leg stump was targeted, but this was not the area that Malcolm probed. He retained a line outside the off stump, tempting Wessels with a series of fast, lifting balls which Wessels studiously ignored. Then Malcolm slipped in a fuller delivery on off stump. Wessels snapped at the bait and went for an expansive drive with little foot movement. The ball swung late and Steve Rhodes took the catch. It looked a shocking shot, but that was Malcolm's deserved reward for the pressure he had applied. The roar inside the pub was volcanic, fed as much with relief as elation. South Africa were 73/4, and Wessels out for 28.

With Jonty Rhodes still indisposed by his head injury, the all-rounder McMillan arrived in his place. He headed the South African batting and bowling averages in this series – a tough, dangerous opponent. Darren Gough got stuck into him, bruising his hands with a couple of sharp lifters. McMillan hung around, though, helping Cullinan add 64 but he then had a fatal lapse of concentration in dealing with a sharply lifting delivery from Malcolm that left him. Troubled by the damage inflicted by Gough, the leaden-footed McMillan played carelessly edging to Thorpe at slip. South Africa were 137/5. McMillan had made 25.

Thereafter, South African resistance crumbled. Richardson was trapped in front of his stumps, having decided to play French cricket. Malcolm's express delivery swung, beating Richardson's meek attempt at blocking it. Craig Matthews then received a brute of a ball from Malcolm, possibly his most lethal one of the day. The ball jagged back off the seam almost cutting Matthews in two, flicking his gloves as it bisected bat and body and forcing Rhodes to leap high to his left to take a fabulous catch down the leg side. South Africa had lost two wickets on 143 with only Jonty Rhodes, De Villiers and Donald to come.

Jonty Rhodes (10) bravely assisted Cullinan in adding 32 for the eighth wicket, but once Gough had induced Cullinan (94) to edge to slip, Malcolm's pace was too hot for the unnerved Rhodes. Rhodes could only manage a timid prod at a very quick ball pitched outside his off stump with his namesake snaffling a simple catch. Allan Donald made no pretence at defence against a Malcolm yorker and was bowled off his pads as he backed away. South Africa were all out for 175 in just 50.3 overs and Malcolm's figures were nine wickets for 57 runs off 16.3 overs.

England still needed 204 to win but with the evening shadows lengthening, Gooch and Atherton flayed the South African bowlers with such ferocity that their first 50 came off only 4.3 overs. Although Gooch departed shortly afterwards, having struck 33 in 20 balls, Hick moved seamlessly into his place as the savage assault continued. England eventually won by eight wickets at 12.41pm on the fourth day having reached their target in just 35.3 overs. Even the curmudgeonly Ray Illingworth was moved to applaud. But to Devon Malcolm, England's match-winner, with the best Test figures since Jim Laker, Illingworth could only manage to say, 'I suppose you're famous now.' Malcolm presumed it was meant as a joke. It certainly seemed to him to be grudging praise.

1995

Sorted for E's & Wizz

For much of the 1990s and 2000s, I co-ordinated the joint planning of local health, housing and adult social care services. Although much of my working life had been spent as a child care practitioner and manager, family caring responsibilities had helped bring me up to speed with adult care. For I had spent considerable time negotiating with health, housing and social care agencies on behalf of both parents and my aunt. The long car journeys I made as their carer were mitigated by the distractions provided by radio cricket and football commentaries. When there was no sport to listen to, I turned to the tape player. That is how the song 'Sorted for E's & Wizz' became associated with 1995. This song was written and performed by the whimsical Britpop band Pulp, whose leader, Jarvis Cocker, was like a 1990s version of Kinks' frontman Ray Davies. Both Cocker and Davies made jaundiced, if wry, examinations of contemporary obsessions and conceits. Pulp's song was considered to be controversial by some, notably by *Daily Mirror* journalist Kate Thornton. She alleged that the song glorified the consumption of illicit drugs, in this case, ecstasy and amphetamines. It seemed as if her attention halted at the title, though, for the song is clearly a sardonic take on a drug-fuelled 'rave' culture. What is emphasised here is the emptiness at its heart, where the escapism is brief and banal, and the social experience, vacuous and disengaging. Cocker's description of the sinking feeling experienced by revellers when 'coming down' during the morning after, is supplemented by a greater worry about their incapability of ever 'coming down'. Tragically, a number of revellers did not 'come down', losing their lives in a mistaken pursuit of chemically-enhanced joy. Gifted satirist Chris Morris ridiculed the press furore aroused by the song in an episode of *Brass Eye*, in which he gravely considered the pernicious qualities of a spoof drug, 'cake'.

The early 1990s had seen the growth of 'laddism' and its 'ladette' offshoot, carrying a 'boys will be boys' and 'girls can be boys' manifesto. It appeared to represent a backlash against what was glibly caricatured as po-faced, censorious political correctness. It was celebrated, if not promulgated, by magazines such as *Loaded,* while lampooned in the TV comedies *Men Behaving Badly* and *Fantasy Football League,* the latter being hosted by stand-up comedians David Baddiel and Frank Skinner. Laddism and ladettism thrived upon a staple diet of sex, drugs, booze, rock 'n' roll, cigarettes and football, but made relatively little impact upon cricket, at least initially, despite irritating episodes of vulgar, drunken chanting at some one-day games. The emergence of England's 'Barmy Army', during the 1994/95 Ashes series, was something of a game-changer, though.

For it was then that a football terraces, tribal culture invaded international Test cricket grounds in strength. The wild boors had arrived. While many of the Australian commentators were amused or bemused by the antics of the 'Barmy Army', the English cricket correspondents were horrified. This is what Martin Johnson had to say about them in February 1995, 'There was talk of the Barmy Army not being able to make it to Perth, but sadly they did… the radio stations are all clamouring to interview the English press. Not about England's prospects… but what we think about the loveable "Baaarmy Aaarmy"'… Well I suppose if loveable includes chanting obscenities, including a none too pleasant ditty alleging Shane Warne's sexual preferences, then they could scarcely have been cuter...' Sixteen years later, the massed ranks of the 'Barmy Army' helped bring Australia's 'Top Gun' fast bowler to his knees. While it was a humiliation that Mitchell Johnson avenged liberally, his demeaning treatment by the 'Barmies' underlined the fallacy of the 'sticks and stones' mantra.

From England's perspective, the 1994/95 series was a fiasco. The series was lost 3-1. There was a pile-up of injuries, and the relationship between Illingworth and Atherton remained fractious with disagreements over squad and team selection. Atherton wanted the party to include younger talent, namely Ramprakash and Hussain. Illingworth insisted upon choosing veterans Gooch and Gatting. Atherton wanted Angus Fraser, but Illingworth chose Joey Benjamin. Atherton felt largely powerless while fellow selectors Titmus and Bolus stood solidly behind Illingworth. When asked by the press about his relationship with England's manager, Atherton diplomatically described it as 'fine', but this was hardly convincing while their various disagreements were played out publicly.

Before Illingworth joined the England team just after the tour had begun, he complained to the press that Atherton had not rung him to discuss team matters. Illingworth appeared to be irked that Atherton had not acknowledged his debt to him over the 'dirt in pocket' affair. For Illingworth contended that, without his backing and pre-emptive sanctions, Atherton would have lost the England captaincy. Atherton's end-of-tour speech seemed equally critical of Illingworth, when he maintained that England needed selectors who were more cognisant of the needs of modern Test cricket. He suggested that the appointment of recently retired Test players might improve the prospects of better communication with the team. Illingworth was furious. His retort came in a later interview conducted by Geoff Boycott, which was published in *The Sun*. Illingworth claimed, 'Atherton is so stubborn, inflexible and narrow-minded.'

Of course, the pressure placed upon both men was considerable. England had lost four successive Ashes series heavily, and had not won a full Test series against anyone since 1987. The carping press was on their back. It was surprising, though, that Atherton should use the media to broadcast his discontent given his frosty relationship with the press after his 'dirt in the pocket' indiscretion. When Nasser Hussain became England's captain in 1999 he wisely strove to maintain a cordial relationship with the media, irrespective of any personal misgivings, reasoning that it was foolhardy to take journalists on in a war of words that could not be won.

However, Atherton must have been pleased that his faith in youth had been vindicated by the Ashes series batting averages. Thorpe had led the way with 444 runs at an average of 49.33 with a century (123), albeit in a losing cause at Perth. He was followed by Hick who averaged 41.60 in his three Tests including an unbeaten 98 at Sydney. Twenty-three-year-old John Crawley performed satisfactorily, too, with an average of 34.2, which was depressed by a pair in England's abject defeat in the fifth and final Test at Perth. It was his 71 at Adelaide, alongside Thorpe's 83 and DeFreitas's belligerent 88, which set up England's 106-run victory, a magnificent result, having been forced to field a threadbare team because of a rash of injuries. Had England been able to capitalise on the excellent batting of Atherton, Hick and Crawley, and the penetrative bowling of Gough and Fraser, in the preceding Test at Sydney, they might have won there, too, but their better display at the SCG gave them the belief that Australia could be beaten

Mark Ramprakash seized his one opportunity, too, created by injuries to Alec Stewart and Neil Fairbrother, making 72 and 42 at Perth, where only Thorpe scored more in the rout.

Atherton led well from the front, scoring 407 runs at an average of 40.7. Before Glenn McGrath found a chink in Atherton's armour, outside the off stump, his defence was almost Boycott-like. He played fast bowling assuredly and bravely, displaying good judgement about when to play. He continued to plunder an area square on the off side by turning the bat face at the point of impact. It was a habit he had acquired as a young adolescent when facing older and stronger opponents in club cricket.

He played short-pitched, rearing deliveries well, ducking and swerving where necessary, and when forced to play, rocking on to the back foot to cut, hook or pull, or to drop the ball dead at his feet. While his hooking was less circumspect, in that the ball was not always kept down, he gained many runs from this source. Besides, he realised the importance of hurting the opposition with bold stroke play. Atherton played Warne proficiently, judging flight, length, line and deviation astutely, employing neat footwork and a relaxed grip. Warne took his wicket only twice in the rubber. His concentration was unrivalled among his compatriots.

This was not a good series for 'older hands', Gooch and Gatting, though. Gooch averaged 24.5. He had been picked to bat in the middle order to combat the threat posed by Warne, but having failed in this position during the first two Tests, both of which were lost heavily, he reverted to opening. Apart from his watchful century at Adelaide (117), a vital factor in England's victory, Gatting's eight other Test innings realised only 65 runs. Moreover, with both Gatting and Gooch consigned to the outfield, because Atherton had better close catchers, the athleticism of England's fielding was severely compromised.

Atherton was criticised by some for not allowing Hick enough time to make his maiden Ashes ton at Sydney. With Hick appearing to dawdle in the 90s, Atherton lost patience with him and declared the innings closed, leaving Hick on 98 not out. Atherton reasoned that if England were to have any chance of keeping a series alive, in which they were 2-0 down, he had to declare imminently.

Hick refused to speak to Atherton for two weeks after. Gough said that Hick's disappointed response cast a shadow over the team's efforts to win the game. Atherton later reflected that he should have allowed Hick a little more time to complete what would have been a morale-boosting hundred, not only for Hick but also the England team. Unfortunately, the incident seemed to inhibit England's performance with the ball, despite Fraser's best efforts – he took 5-75. With Australia crumbling at 292/7 in pursuit of 449 for victory, Australian captain Mark Taylor was surprised that Atherton did not attack more, as it was clear that the Aussies had abandoned their run chase. Perhaps Atherton was still distracted by the Hick incident. Had England won here, the series would have been squared after their subsequent victory at Adelaide. Sadly, a slipped disc ruled Hick out of the remaining two Tests.

Darren Gough was the pick of the English bowlers, taking 20 wickets at 21.25 in just three Tests before suffering a stress fracture in his left foot. Gough's blistering half-century (51) at Sydney had helped England raise a first-innings score of 309, while his subsequent six wickets for 49 led the way in blasting out the Australians for 116 in their first innings. Gough's efforts had dispelled the gloom in the England camp, after successive defeats.

Because of McCague's injury, and Benjamin's and Malcolm's unavailability due to chickenpox, Atherton called upon Fraser who was playing grade cricket in Sydney. While the absent Illingworth was unimpressed with Atherton's choice, Fraser bowled exceptionally well at Sydney, remaining in the side for the rest of the series, and taking 14 wickets for 389 runs at an average of 27.78.

While Malcolm had limited impact (13 wickets at 45.23), not helped by his early sickness, he played an essential role in the Adelaide triumph in taking seven wickets in the match for 117, displaying the hostility that had routed the South Africans at the Oval. He was no slouch at Perth, either, as a YouTube clip confirms. Here he is shown peppering a jumpy Michael Slater with a succession of 92mph 'throat balls' that the sprightly Aussie opener had difficulty in evading.

A curious feature of Malcolm's bowling was the juxtaposition of his vicious pace with his blithely benign demeanour. While glowering expressions and histrionic oaths are part and parcel of fast bowling, Malcolm's manner was akin to a man of the cloth, blessed with beatific calm. Perhaps that was why he was nicknamed 'Dude'. He remains as the most improbable 'head hunter' I have ever seen. Darren Gough claimed not to have heard Devon Malcolm's famous oath when batting with him at the Oval. Conceivably, Malcom's words were whispered so inoffensively that they did not carry the 22 yards to Gough.

Once again, the Australian batting figures were superior. Five of their batsmen averaged over 40: debutant Greg Blewett (83); Michael Slater (62.3); Steve Waugh (49.28); Mark Taylor (47.1); and Mark Waugh (43.5). Their bowlers had better figures, too. Craig McDermott bowled menacingly, taking 32 series wickets at an average cost of 21.09. His six wickets for 38 runs at Perth consigned England to a 329-run defeat. Gooch and Gatting had mastered McDermott ten years before, but found their reflexes no longer sharp enough to combat his pace and movement. Warne also had a fine series, taking 27 wickets at an average cost of 20.33. The hat-trick he took at Melbourne, reduced England to 91/9, and an imminent 295-run loss.

The Ashes defeat signalled the demise of coach Keith Fletcher. Although hugely experienced and well-liked he was inclined to shift the blame onto the players when confronted by critical members of the press. Nevertheless, as Gough testifies, he encouraged his players to play their natural game. Before the series began, Fletcher gained little credit from his ill-judged boast that the England team had a better pace attack than that of Lillee and Thomson. With Malcolm and Benjamin incapacitated by chickenpox and McCague injured during the first Test, Fletcher's bragging was made to look very silly. At Fletcher's departure, Illingworth added the role of head coach to his bulging portfolio. The temptation to micro-manage seemed overwhelming, leaving Atherton uncertain about the security of his position and whether he would be leading a side that accorded with his choice.

The West Indian party arrived in England in the summer of 1995 to contest a six-match Test series. They were smarting, having lost a spring home rubber to Australia, in which Steve Waugh had averaged over one hundred runs, after scoring a decisive double century in Jamaica. The West Indians seemed determined to make England pay for their humiliation.

After putting Atherton's side in to bat in the opening Test at Leeds, Bishop and Benjamin revelled in the seamer-friendly conditions, sharing nine wickets for 92 runs in dismissing England for 199. Only Atherton, England's belatedly reprieved skipper, exhibited any staying power. Despite restarting his innings seven times on account of the many rain interruptions, Atherton remained steadfastly at his post for over three and a half hours, making a defiant 81. Although Devon Malcolm summarily dismissed Carl Hooper for a duck when the tourists began their reply, Brian Lara launched a venomous counter-attack. Malcolm's opening two overs went for 24 runs. The West Indians gained an 83-run first-innings lead, and with Gough breaking down with a back injury, the visitors won by nine wickets on the fourth day.

The tables were turned at Lord's, though. Batting first, England were indebted to Thorpe (52) and Robin Smith (61) whose 111-run fourth-wicket partnership cemented an innings that was faltering at 74/3. Both batsmen pulled, cut and drove with relish. Their almost simultaneous demise was followed by Ramprakash's soft dismissal for a duck. With England back in trouble, debutant Dominic Cork (30) came to their aid helped by fellow pace bowler Peter Martin (29). Thanks to their efforts respectability was achieved with a 283-run total.

Gough and Fraser then respectively removed Campbell and Lara with only 23 runs on the board. But the flamboyant, flashing blades of Richie Richardson (54) and Keith Arthurton (75), and the more restrained stroke-play of Jimmy Adams (54), put the tourists 41 runs ahead at the halfway stage. Fraser was the pick of the England seam bowlers with 5-66 runs in 33 typically tight overs.

When England batted again, Hick (67) not only stood his ground against the barrage of short-pitched bowling, he delivered some powerful rebukes, although his champagne moment arrived when he struck an elegant six off the gentle off-spin of Carl Hooper. Once again Smith (90) bludgeoned the West Indian attack, being particularly harsh on the inexperienced Gibson. Having recovered from a blow on the helmet, inflicted by a Walsh beamer, Thorpe kept him company, punching and nudging 42 runs, helping England achieve a position of prosperity at 290/5, only for a late collapse to swing the game back in the tourists' favour. The upshot was that the West Indians needed 296 runs to win. Although Gough removed Hooper with only 15 on the board, Lara and Campbell set off in belligerent pursuit of their victory target, with Lara striking 38 off only 44 balls before the close of play on the fourth day. There was an unwelcome similarity to the Lord's Test of 1984.

Perhaps Lara found inspiration in this precedent for there was no letting up on the next morning. His rasping cover drives off a footsore Gough were as dazzling as the morning sun, with the echoing 'pocks' produced by his mighty blade momentarily silencing the hubbub of passing traffic. But Gough was not fazed, continuing to invite Lara to drive expansively at his fully pitched out-swingers. With the West Indian score at 99/1, and Lara on 54, Gough managed to find a little more swing than the great batsman had expected. Lara prodded forward tentatively with minimal movement of his feet, the face of his bat turned slightly towards cover. The ball nicked the outside edge but was destined to fall short of first slip before Alex Stewart intervened, hurling himself to his left to clutch it in his outstretched left glove. It was an extraordinary catch, justifying Illingworth's decision to recall him in place of Steve Rhodes who had endured a dismal Ashes tour.

However, the game was decided after Dominic Cork's introduction into the attack. His first innings bowling performance had been unremarkable – one wicket for 72 runs with tail-ender Ian Bishop his sole victim. However, his second innings display proved spectacular. Cork seemed to be a man in a hurry. He bristled with irritability and impatience as he bustled to the wicket from a curved approach, his head turned curiously to the right, while continuing to observe the batsman obliquely. But his action was pleasingly high with a sharp rotation of his trunk in the delivery stride to achieve a classical sideways posture. Continually bearing a scowling expression, and forever sniping at the facing batsman, he hurried through his overs as if making up for lost time, as well he might. His performance here confirmed that his selection had been long overdue.

Being not much quicker than medium-fast, his irksome bark seemed greater than his bite, but his hooping in- and away-swing spelt trouble for the remaining West Indian batsmen. Carrying on where Gough had left off, his out-swinger was a too good for left-hander Jimmy Adams. Adams launched a lacerating cover drive only to find that the ball had swung late, nicking the outside edge and flying fast and high to Hick at second slip who, in a jolting reflex action, took the catch in both hands at full stretch, staggering backwards with the force of the take. Hick was a terrific slipper. Adams was gone for 13 and the tourists were 124/3. Richardson followed shortly afterwards. Cork fooled the West Indian captain into expecting a booming out-swinger. Richardson moved across his stumps to counter the ball's expected movement only to find that there was none. The ball was gun-barrel straight and Richardson was out lbw for a duck. The West Indians were 130/4.

Cork cleverly controlled his use of swing much like a slow bowler does with an 'arm ball'. Another left-hander, Arthurton, was next to fall into his trap with the score at 138. He, too, played for absent swing, presenting a soft bat-pad catch to substitute short leg Paul Weekes. Gibson hung around long enough to help Campbell raise the score to 177/5 but he, too, became trapped in front of his stumps for 14. Then, crucially, Cork induced an increasingly desperate Campbell to play a wild drive outside his off stump. Cork's in-dipper found the inside edge and Stewart took a regulation catch. With Campbell's dismissal for 93, England were almost home and dry. Cork made short work of the West Indies' tail. Ambrose gave Richard Illingworth gentle catching practice at cover while Walsh obligingly deflected a shorter delivery into Stewart's waiting gloves. England had won by 72 runs and Cork had taken 7-43 in 19.3 overs, surpassing John Lever's 7-46 as the best analysis for an England player on Test debut.

Disappointingly, England reverted to capitulation mode on a fast track at Edgbaston where the West Indian pace quartet dismissed Atherton's men for 147 and 89 to win by an innings and 64 runs. Smith's batting and Cork's first-innings figures of 4-69 were the only bright spots for Atherton.

Raymond's Illingworth's response was to relieve Stewart of the gloves at Manchester and bring back Russell while strengthening the batting order with two all-rounders, Craig White and Lancashire captain Mike Watkinson, who could bowl both seam-up and off-spin. Veteran off-spinner John Emburey was restored to bat at ten meaning that Angus Fraser was the only 'rabbit' in the side. England became harder to beat.

At Old Trafford England did rather better than that, winning by six wickets. Importantly, they started well. Fraser and Cork shared eight first innings wickets as the West Indians were dismissed for 216. England's reinforced tail wagged so boisterously that, after Atherton (47), Thorpe (94) and Smith (44) had taken England to 264/5, Russell (35), Watkinson (37) and (Cork 56 not out) added a further 173 which realised a 221-run first innings lead.

On the fourth morning I drove mum to Brighton for a period of recuperation after an exploratory back operation in a London hospital.

Relieved by the outcome and by the prospect of a fortnight's reprieve in caring for dad, she listened with interest to the radio commentary, sharing my excitement at Cork's hat-trick which decimated the West Indian second innings. Although Lara played extravagantly (145) in averting an innings defeat, Crawley and Russell duly took England to victory. This was one of those rare occasions when mum and I happily shared a sporting event just as we had done many times during the 1960s. In the years that followed there were so many urgent health issues to attend to that my frequent visits home were more often calls of duty rather than times of relaxed pleasure.

The fifth Test featured centuries from Atherton (113) and Hick (118) and a big hundred from Lara (152). However, an unbroken tenth-wicket partnership of 80 between Watkinson (82) and Richard Illingworth (14), who was nursing a fractured finger, saved the day for England. The sixth Test resulted in a high-scoring draw in which Hick (96 and 51 not out), Atherton (36 and 95), Thorpe (74 and 38) and Russell (91) excelled with the bat for England, while Lara (179), Campbell (89), Richardson (93), Hooper (127) and Chanderpaul (80) played notable innings for the West Indies. Malcolm was recalled for the Oval only to find a dead surface, ill-suited to his pounding pace. But he still gave it his best shot, bowling 39 overs, and taking three wickets, including those of Lara and Hooper, as the West Indians amassed 692/8 declared in their first and only innings.

The exasperatingly inconsistent Hick had stepped up during this rubber, averaging 50.38, demonstrating emphatically what a class player he was. Opinions had varied on whether his fallibility in Test cricket had been a matter of technique or temperament. Umpire Dickie Bird believed it was a matter of technique, claiming that Hick's feet were poorly positioned, leaving his head and eyes off-line. Steve Waugh thought that Hick had been pampered, having played mostly on benign surfaces against inferior opposition. Kiwi John Bracewell agreed, dubbing him a 'flat track bully'. Cricket correspondent Christopher Martin-Jenkins considered Hick to be suspect against the short ball. Allan Lamb elaborated upon Martin-Jenkins' observation, suggesting that the one bouncer per over restriction, then applying in county cricket, gave Hick little opportunity to hone his technique against short-pitched fast bowling. And yet when he was at his confident best, Hick was capable of hammering world class fast bowling as he demonstrated amply at the Oval in 1993 and 1994 and in Sharjah in 1999, where he thrashed the bowling of the world's fastest paceman, Shoaib Akhtar, in a one-day international. So perhaps temperament did play a part in his under-performance in Test cricket. When facing aggressive opponents such as Curtly Ambrose, Courtney Walsh or Merv Hughes, he was inclined to avert his gaze if they snarled at him, as if incapable of staring them out. His apparent diffidence seemed to encourage their belief that they could get inside his head, and wreak havoc with his confidence. When he recalled Hick to the Test side at Nottingham

Illingworth accused him of being 'mollycoddled'. Illingworth challenged Hick to produce the major innings that would confound his detractors. Creditably, Hick did exactly that, making a sweet, unbeaten ton (118), which comprised 17 boundaries, representing almost 60 per cent of his runs.

After his heroics of the year before, Malcolm endured a frustrating summer in 1995. His knee injury threatened to scupper his eagerly-anticipated tour of South Africa, and yet, according to his autobiography, *You Guys Are History*, a magazine article, published during that summer, bothered him more. It allegedly claimed that England Test cricketers born abroad of a non-white ethnicity, were not as strongly committed to their team's success as their white counterparts. The claim had no validity. Take the case of the mixed-race Nasser Hussain, for example. He had been born in India, spending his first seven years there. It was clearly absurd to question his commitment to the national team for his patriotism was as fierce as anyone chosen to represent England.

According to Malcolm, nothing was said in the article about the commitment of white England cricketers born and/or bred overseas, of which there had been several since the start of the 1980s, including: South African-born batsmen Chris and Robin Smith and Allan Lamb; Zimbabwe-born batsman Graeme Hick; New Zealand-born fast-medium bowler Andrew Caddick; Australian-born batsman Jason Gallian and Zambian-born fast-medium bowler Neal Radford. Each of these players had qualified for selection on the basis of their parents' nationality. In addition, UK-born players Martin McCague, Craig White and Alan Mullally were picked for the England Test team, despite spending much, if not all, of their youth in Australia. Mullally had even represented an Australian under-19 side.

These white recruits from abroad had sought qualification for England because of frustrated ambitions in their home countries. There is no evidence to suggest that their loyalty to the England team was compromised by their upbringing, although some English journalists, such as 'Jim' Swanton, and players, such as Chris Cowdrey, seemed uncomfortable about anyone playing for England who had not been born and educated in the UK.

The Jamaican-born Devon Malcolm and Dominican Republic-born Phillip DeFreitas took exception to the article, jointly suing the publisher for libel, contending that the article constituted a 'racist slur'. Damages were awarded to the plaintiffs in an out-of-court settlement. Malcolm donated his award to two charitable causes: a local children's hospital and a Sheffield cricket centre that bore his name, where underprivileged children of all races were encouraged to play the game.

The offending article seemed to reflect an unease felt by some British people at the growth of multiculturism and its impact upon national identity. In 1990, Conservative politician, Baron Norman Tebbit spoke of his concern in this regard, when he referred to what he perceived to be a lack of loyalty among South Asian and Caribbean immigrants and their children towards the England cricket team. He did not suggest that those of a non-white ethnicity were necessarily disposed to behave unpatriotically towards their 'adoptive' country, but concluded that those who supported their country of ethnic origin, rather than England, in a Test match between the two, were not integrated successfully within British society.

Heaven knows what Baron Tebbit would have made of the events I witnessed at a one-day international, in Cardiff in 2014, where thousands of British Asians sung and chanted in support of India with discernible Welsh accents, interspersing their adapted football repertoires with frequent renditions of 'Bread of Heaven'. A well-lubricated Indian supporter cordially, if indelicately, inquired of our party whether we were 'sheep sh*****s', too. When a friend confirmed that he was, this jolly supporter urged us all to stand and join him in a raucous celebration of what he presumed to be our shared geographical identity. While these Indian fans rooted for their country of ethnic origin, and not their place of birth and / or residence, their loyalty was not singular, being laced with Welsh pride and British 'laddism'. It is doubtful whether Baron Tebbit's rather facile test was designed to contend with such complexities of identity. Besides, why should such a test apply solely to foreign-born immigrants of a non-white ethnicity?

1996
Firestarter

In 1996 there was the horrific Dunblane shooting. It was also the year in which the IRA exploded two massive bombs in Manchester's city centre and at South Quays, in the London Docklands district. Their purpose was to derail a Northern Ireland peace process which was gathering momentum after almost 30 years of bloody strife. It was the year in which former 'rave' band The Prodigy re-invented themselves as techno-punks, and unleashed their aural assault, 'Firestarter'. This was not so much a song as an explosion of feral energy. It was small wonder that the BBC attempted to hide the accompanying video from younger audiences. The footage shows Keith Flint, a studded, heavily mascaraed vocalist, with a double Mohican crop, twitching and gesticulating threateningly in a dark, abandoned Tube station to a wild soundtrack of brutal beats, samples and jagged guitar licks. His manically hissed message seemed to announce *Apocalypse Now*!

A few months after the song's release, England lost a European Championship semi-final at Wembley to Germany, almost inevitably after another penalty shoot-out. Meanwhile Ian Botham and Allan Lamb lost an expensive High Court case after suing Imran Khan for libel with regard to his supposed allegations of ball tampering.

Having held the West Indians to a creditable 2-2 draw England embarked upon what became a dispiriting tour of South Africa. In his autobiography,

Allan Donald was highly critical of the preparations made by Illingworth for the winter Test series, drawing unfavourable comparisons with the scientific approach instigated by the South African cricket manager, and ex-England Test player, Bob Woolmer. Donald referred to the advanced health and fitness regimes devised by Woolmer's appointee, Professor Tim Noakes, and to the welter of video and statistical performance analysis maintained by Woolmer. Each of the South African players were shown films of themselves in action, dissecting their batting, bowling and fielding techniques as a basis for formulating individual and collective improvement plans. Detailed examinations were undertaken of the England batsmen, to determine how they had been dismissed, and where they sought to score, so that bowling and field placement plans could be put in place to capitalise upon this intelligence. Donald maintained that his side, ensconced in a training camp, were well ahead of England in terms of planning and attention to detail.

Donald was unimpressed with the standard of England's coaching. In South Africa this was provided by ex-Test players Peter Lever and John Edrich. Donald believed they were yesterday's men, over-reliant upon their playing experience of over 20 years before, when the game was very different. Both served with distinction under Illingworth, during the late 1960s and early 70s, which had presumably commended their selection. Darren Gough and Devon Malcolm found that they were hampered more than helped by Peter Lever's attempts at improving their actions, and yet Illingworth insisted that they should comply with his coach's instructions. It was only after Atherton lost patience with Gough's lack of zip in a net session, demanding that he 'bowl properly', that Gough reverted to his original style. Gough also thought that Illingworth and Lever were wrong to meddle with Malcolm's action. Their misguided efforts left him distressed and demoralised, undermining the strike bowler whom the South Africans feared most.

In fairness, Gough and Malcolm had technical faults that impaired their effectiveness. In Gough's case his left foot twisted in his delivery stride which was thought responsible for the stress fracture he sustained during the 1994/95 Ashes tour, while Malcolm had a tendency to fall away at the point of release resulting in him spraying the ball down the leg side. But the well-intentioned cures seemed to cause more problems than they solved.

At first, the disparity in strength between the two sides was not immediately obvious. A series of cataclysmic thunderstorms severely curtailed play at Centurion Park, although there was sufficient time for Graeme Hick to score a sublime century (148) as England compiled 381 runs in the only innings to be completed. While Illingworth and Atherton felt that they had been denied a realistic winning opportunity, Donald disputed this because of the flatness of the pitch.

In the second Test at Johannesburg, only Atherton's heroic steadfastness and 'Jack' Russell's attritional defence saved England from defeat as they batted together throughout the final day while the South Africans strove desperately to separate them. Digging in like a Western Front combatant, Atherton scored 185 unbeaten runs, displaying amazing clenched-jaw concentration, focusing fiercely on each ball, oblivious to the jibes and chatter around him or the baying crowd. He severely curtailed his attacking strokes, choosing only to play those which might rotate the strike or disturb the bowler's rhythm. He left anything which could be ignored. Only a momentary shiver of nerves, when on 99, disturbed his obduracy. It was then when he poked a short, lifting ball into the hands of Gary Kirsten at short leg, who inexplicably dropped it. This was a match-defining moment. But without the incredible resolution of Russell, his scrapping partner, Atherton's marathon effort would have been in vain. Russell continually shuffled into line proffering a dead bat to just about everything hurled at him, whether pitched up or short. One-day pyrotechnics are fine, but stubborn rearguard actions of this ilk are more compelling. I remain in awe of those adhesive battlers whose backs bear an imprint of the wall against which they are pressed.

Rain also wrecked the game at Durban while a painfully slow wicket at Port Elizabeth denied any prospect of victory with both sides consumed with caution. The series hinged upon the outcome of the final Test played on a result wicket at Cape Town. Upon winning the toss, England batted first and badly, making only 153. But they hauled themselves back into the game, first by stifling the South African batsmen and then by steadily picking them off as Cronje's men succumbed to impatience. With South Africa hardly better placed at 171/9, Atherton threw the new ball to Malcolm expecting that the man Nelson Mandela dubbed as 'the destroyer' would blast out the final South African batsman. But Malcolm had not played for a month. He had been shunned and carped at by Illingworth. His confidence was at a very low ebb. Unsurprisingly, he bowled like a drain. Wicketkeeper David Richardson and the unconventional 'frog in a blender' spinner Paul Adams smashed South Africa 91 in front. England folded once again, managing only 157, and lost by ten wickets. Illingworth was incandescent with rage berating the whole team, but reserving his sternest criticism for Malcolm. Poking Malcolm in the chest he yelled, 'And you, you've lost us the f***ing Test match.'

Malcolm stifled his anger at Illingworth's outburst but subsequently told the South African press of his resentment, whereupon the story went viral, compounding his team's low spirits. England had played badly at Cape Town, but arguably Illingworth should have picked a stronger batting line-up. Russell had been steadfast at Johannesburg, but his position at six in the order was at least one place too high.

At the end of the South African tour, Illingworth made the astonishing announcement that Robin Smith, Mark Ramprakash, Alec Stewart, Angus Fraser, Mike Watkinson and Richard Illingworth had almost certainly played their final Test matches when three of these players were representing England in the impending World Cup competition. As a confidence-building exercise, it left a lot to be desired.

It was no surprise that England lost the succeeding one-day series 6-1. Their form in the World Cup was dire, too. They were eliminated after being thrashed by Sri Lanka, who came of age by unexpectedly seizing the world title, maintaining an Asian monopoly of the trophy. Their triumph was not without controversy, though, as Australia and New Zealand forfeited their group games, designated for Sri Lankan venues, on account of Tamil Tiger terrorist scares.

While Smith, Illingworth and Watkinson were not picked again for the England Test side, Stewart, Fraser, Ramprakash and Malcolm were recalled, although Malcolm was rightly reprimanded by the TCCB for washing the dirty linen in public, making a resolution of the problem more difficult to achieve. Illingworth did not escape censure, though, and was persuaded by the TCCB to release a statement that it had never been the intention of the England management to 'cause offence or distress' to Malcolm. It was accepted that Malcolm remained totally committed to playing for England.

While the courageous scrapper Robin Smith was arguably dropped too soon, given his Test batting average of a shade under 44, his colourful reputation as a 'party animal' did not impress Illingworth. While Illingworth was heading the selection panel, there was no chance that Smith would be recalled. When David Graveney replaced Illingworth as chairman of the selectors in 1997, Smith was almost 34 years old, and by then England were looking at younger players.

When the Indians arrived in England in the spring of 1996, Atherton was unsure whether he would be asked to lead his side in the three-match series. He insisted that he was eager to continue in the role, and once re-confirmed as skipper he adroitly guided his side to victory in the opening Test. At Edgbaston he rotated his new pace trio of Cork, Lewis and debutant Alan Mullally with a sureness of touch, supporting them well with shrewd field placements. The Indians seemed to be ring rusty, having played only three Test matches in the previous 18 months because of precedence given to the more lucrative one-day game. Consequently, they were hustled out in their first innings for only 214 with Dominic Cork (4-61), Alan Mullally (3-60) and Chris Lewis (2-44) inflicting the main damage. Nasser Hussain then compiled a memorable maiden Test ton (128) after spending the previous two years in the cold. Although fortunate to be reprieved on 14 when he appeared to glove a leg-side catch to wicketkeeper Mongia off Srinath, Hussain took England to a 99-run first-innings lead.

India's new ball pair Srinath and Prasad bowled intelligently with testing variations in pace, disconcerting lift and movement. They deservedly shared eight first-innings wickets, but they had little support from their colleagues. Vaunted leg-spinner Anil Kumble was particularly disappointing, being erratic in both line and length, and leaking too many runs, particularly on the leg side. Even England tail-ender Min Patel gave him some stick. Tendulkar stood firm, providing further evidence of his genius. His innings of 122 contained 19 fours and a six, but it was the only reprisal India could manage as they crumbled once again for 219, with Lewis taking 5-72. England won by eight wickets.

At Lord's, Azharuddin won the toss and invited England to bat on a seamer's wicket, in gloomy conditions. Srinath and Prasad were particularly menacing, zipping a succession of deliveries past the outside edge. They found unlikely support from medium-paced Sourav Ganguly who chipped in with two wickets, dismissing Hick for one run with only his sixth ball in Test cricket. It was a poor shot by Hick who flat-batted an apparently innocuous delivery to mid-off. When Thorpe (89) and Russell (124) came together, England's first innings was falling apart at 107/5. Their 136-run sixth-wicket partnership played a major part in mounting a respectable first-innings score of 344. Ganguly (131) and the technically impeccable Dravid (95) responded bullishly, enabling India to establish an 85-run first-innings lead. However, with England deliberating over their second-innings score of 278 runs, there was insufficient time left to force a result.

In the final Test at Nottingham, India completed their re-acclimatisation to Test cricket, achieving an imposing first-innings total of 521 with elegant hundreds from Tendulkar (177) and Ganguly (136), and a more workmanlike fifty from Dravid (84). On a flat track, England batted with equal resolution. Atherton (160) and Stewart (50) put on 130 in their opening partnership, while Hussain (107) and Atherton added 192 for the second wicket. Unfortunately Hussain had to retire hurt with a cracked index finger, a vulnerability that dogged his Test career. Although Atherton was rarely fluent, and occasionally blessed with good fortune, his concentration never wavered as England racked up 564 in reply. Mark Ealham, the latest English all-rounder to be auditioned at Test level, performed well after replacing Ronnie Irani. He scored a half-century on debut (51) and took six wickets in the match for 111 with his medium-paced seamers. Hampered by an injury to their opener Rathour, the Indians ended the short series as they began, in a state of disarray. On a blameless wicket, they were dismissed second time around for just 211. However there was not enough time for England to make 169 for victory. While England deservedly won the rubber, in Tendulkar, Ganguly and Dravid India had three young batsmen of the highest calibre.

Pakistan's tour of England took place against the backcloth of a High Court hearing after Botham and Lamb had sued Imran Khan for libel. The former England players had alleged that, in an *India Today* magazine article, Imran had accused them of racism and 'ball tampering'. They also claimed that Imran had defamed them by suggesting that they were not properly educated and of an inferior social standing. Imran denied each of these allegations. He said that his words had been taken out of context and that he had only been defending himself against allegations, made in a previous newspaper article, that he was a 'ball-tampering' cheat. Much to Botham's and Lamb's dismay, Imran was vindicated, leaving them £400,000 out of pocket, prompting a revival of the 'Beefy and Lamby' raconteur roadshow. Not that this controversy fazed the tourists as they beat England comprehensively 2-0.

Five of the Pakistan batsmen achieved series averages in excess of 60 – Moin Khan (79), Ijaz Ahmed (68.8), Salim Malik (65), Inzamam-ul-Haq (64) and Saeed Anwar (60.33). Only Stewart, with an average of 79.20, boosted by an exhilarating innings of 170 at Leeds, and Crawley, with 59.33, thanks to a resolute 106 at the Oval, came close to matching Pakistan's batting standards.

Having selected and rejected Kent's Mumbai-born slow left-arm spinner Min Patel, England failed to identify a replacement capable of troubling the Pakistan batsmen. The four wickets that leg-spinner Ian Salisbury and off-spinner Robert Croft shared in this rubber cost 87 runs each, whereas Pakistan's mesmerising leg-spinner Mushtaq Ahmed took 17 wickets at 26.29. His cunningly concealed googly proved particularly menacing.

I rarely had time to watch much televised Test cricket during the 1990s, but I spent an hour watching Mushtaq bowl on the final day of the Oval Test, failing abysmally to spot which way his twirling deliveries would turn. In his autobiography, *The Gloves Are Off*, Matt Prior admitted that he had been nonplussed, too, when he first kept wicket to Mushtaq after the Pakistani magician's arrival at Sussex during the early 2000s.

Despite the resolution shown by Atherton (43), Stewart (54) and Hussain (51), the remaining English batsmen seemed bemused. Mushtaq took six second-innings wickets for 78 off 37 exuberant overs, setting up a nine-wicket Oval victory. Little did I realise that he would help propel my languishing county side, Sussex, then at the bottom of the Second Division, to three County Championship titles. The second of these I would witness at a dank Trent Bridge, while running the gauntlet of a persistent Sky reporter who inadvertently threatened to expose my inexcusable absence from a council managers' conference.

As if Mushtaq did not present sufficient threat on his own, there was Wasim Akram and Waqar Younis to slice through the English batting with pace and reverse swing. This opening pair shared 33 wickets at a combined average of 27. With Gough incapacitated by injury, the England attack had neither the venom nor the wiles to trouble the Pakistani batsmen. With the Australians due to return in the following year, England were no nearer to producing an Ashes-winning side than they had been in 1989. The only consolation was that after their winter World Cup humiliation, Atherton's men beat both India and Pakistan in the summer's one-day series. They also had a new head coach following the appointment of David 'Bumble' Lloyd. His arrival signalled the end of Illingworth's reign as team supremo. The whacky-humoured Lloyd ushered in a more vibrant and positive mood in the England dressing room. Certainly, Lloyd had no intention of forcing Johnny Mathis upon his players as Illingworth had done during the South African tour.

1997
Heroes

'Things Can Only Get Better', D:Ream's politically-abducted club anthem, 'Blaired' out again as the 'New Labour, New Britain' message appealed to a majority of the British electorate. For 43-year-old Tony Blair, the youngest British Prime Minister for 185 years, won a landslide victory at the polls, giving his Labour Party the largest Parliamentary majority since the Second World War. New Labour's success was attributed to its willingness to embrace most aspects of the Thatcher 'revolution', such as the privatisation of nationalised industries, low direct taxation, tight limits on union power and a culture of enterprise, having courted the support of media mogul Rupert Murdoch and that of prominent businessmen including Richard Branson. Of the 119 women MPs elected to Parliament, 100 were members of the Labour Party, prompting coinage of the yucky sobriquet, 'Blair's Babes'.

This was the year in which all-party peace talks began in earnest in Northern Ireland after a resumption of the IRA ceasefire and an edgy compromise over the re-routing of an Orange parade. But the devastating Omagh bombing of 1998 was to prove that the Irish 'Troubles' were not yet at an end.

Despite Labour's overwhelming victory not everyone was sold on their supposedly 'new' politics. Take the 'eco warriors' for example. No new motorway, bypass or airport extension could be planned or built without prolonged battles between these well-organised, dedicated environmentalists and the public authorities. The 'eco warriors' literally dug themselves in at contested sites, creating a complex of tunnels beneath land identified for development, and erecting protest camps high in the trees, with precarious inter-connecting walkways. Characters bearing nicknames such as 'Swampy', 'Muppet Dave' and 'Animal' infiltrated the ranks of modern celebrities with 'Swampy' invited to appear on the TV news quiz programme, *Have I Got News for You*.

This was the year that Diana, Princess of Wales died tragically in a car crash in Paris while her car was being pursued by the paparazzi. In days of yore, that is to say when I was still a child, celebrities were remote, unobtainable, glitzy, Hollywood-style icons. Yet during the 1990s a new accessible, fallible, endlessly-confessing model emerged, one that had greater identification with ordinary lives. Canonised Princess Diana seemed to embrace the old and the new – in one sense a pure Hollywood-like fabrication, with her glossy glamour and immaculate costumes, but in another sense a TV reality celebrity with her personal confessions and intimate disclosures. Put together with her admirable sensitivity and accessibility to those suffering severe disability and illness, it was small wonder that her death should prompt such a massive outpouring of collective grief in what became the 'necrothon' of the 20th century.

A further restructuring of the administration of British cricket took place on 1 January 1997 with the England and Wales Cricket Board (ECB) replacing both the Test and County Cricket Board (TCCB) and the Cricket Council. The new, all-purpose organisation was led by Lord MacLaurin, a former chairman and moderniser of Tesco. He immediately set to work in attempting to radically revitalise an English game that was failing to develop sufficient players of international quality.

Looking at the example set in Australia, he wanted to establish a ladder of opportunity that encouraged talented school and club cricketers to progress upwards through a series of feeder competitions, enabling the best of them to play at the highest level. Lord MacLaurin began to realise, though, that most county chairmen did not prioritise the success of the England side, as he did. He found them preoccupied with ambitions for their own sides. Unabashed, Lord MacLaurin exalted the principle of 'Team England'. Somewhat grudgingly, the counties fell into line, acceding to the creation of two divisions of the County Championship, with only Glamorgan dissenting. Given the uncompetitive nature of much of county cricket, the proposal was generally supported by the press, and by the wider public, at least by those prioritising the success of the national side. The regular followers of the domestic game were divided, though, some fearing that this change might result in inferior entertainment for followers of lower-division sides. Nevertheless, the change took place in 2000.

By this time county cricket clubs were deriving very little income from gate money, which amounted to around three per cent of their total yearly revenue. Member subscriptions did not deliver a lot more with these comprising, on average, 11 per cent of the county clubs' annual income. It seemed as if county clubs were standing or falling by their ability to attract substantial commercial funding, with those counties boasting greater star quality and international venues, such as Lancashire, Warwickshire and Surrey, prospering considerably more than their rivals.

For those, like me, who were brought up on, and inspired by, extensive terrestrial TV coverage, it became clear that its days were numbered. And just as Joni Mitchell suggested in her song 'Big Yellow Taxi', many of us would not appreciate what we had lost until it was gone. A foot had been wedged in the door by a deal struck in 1995 involving both terrestrial and satellite TV companies, making the game richer by £60m over four seasons. With this extra investment an average county player's salary increased to £30,000 per year, although Sussex went further in offering a three-year contract worth £200,000 to Derbyshire's Chris Adams to turn around their ailing fortunes.

A few years later, Sky Sports and Channel 4 trumped a BBC bid in agreeing an exclusive £100m deal with the ECB to cover international and domestic cricket, promising to improve the game's alleged 'stuffy image'. If English cricket was to continue to profit from such deals then its international sides had to be considerably more successful. While England's international cricket sides remained in the doldrums, domestic cricket was threatened with dwindling revenues. And yet without a thriving domestic game, international success could not be assured.

England's winter engagements included a brief yuletide tour of Zimbabwe. It began badly when ECB chief executive Tim Lamb refused to allow the players' wives permission to visit their husbands in Harare at Christmas. This did not go down at all well. The players complained that this was the third Christmas in succession spent far away from home. To rub salt into their wounds, as Darren Gough put it, Lamb exempted himself from his embargo by inviting his wife to join him in Harare over the festive period. New ECB chairman Lord MacLaurin was concerned by the gulf existing between the ECB administrators and the England players. He was horrified by the standard of accommodation provided for the England players in Zimbabwe, insisting that the time-honoured tradition of room-sharing should cease forthwith. He made it clear that the team should receive the same benefits previously reserved for the management, such as first-class accommodation and travel. Whether or not the row with Lamb played any part in this, England performed dismally in Zimbabwe.

England struggled to subdue their combative opponents in both Test matches, although Nick Knight's (96) and Alec Stewart's (73) bold batting almost secured victory in the uniquely drawn first Test at Bulawayo. At the end of the final over, the scores were level with England having four wickets in reserve. Exasperated at failing, so narrowly, to win the game, England's head coach David Lloyd crowed intemperately, 'We flippin' murdered them,' earning himself an ECB reprimand.

However, Zimbabwe merited their reprieve. Andy Flower made a gutsy first-innings hundred (112) on day two, well supported by his captain Alistair Campbell (84), as the hosts posted a challenging score of 376. Although Hussain (113) and Crawley (112) helped England to a 30-run lead, Zimbabwe continued to battle stubbornly in overcoming a poor start to set England a tough 205-run victory target in 37 overs.

The second Test at Harare gave Lloyd no cause for joy either as England were dismissed for 156 having been put into bat by Campbell. England trailed by 59 at the halfway stage, and although an unbeaten second innings century by Stewart (101) gave his team some hope of forcing victory, rain washed away that prospect.

As for the one-day contest, England were utterly humiliated, losing the first game by two wickets and the second by a massive margin of 131 runs, having been bowled out for only 118. The press had a field day, deriding England's demise at the hands of chicken farmer Eddo Brandes, who completed a hat-trick. England had badly underestimated their opponents, overlooking, perhaps, how tough the Zimbabweans needed to be, living and working under an oppressive regime. Alistair Campbell rightly accused England of 'having a superiority complex'. The subtext, of course, was that the England cricket team had no right to consider itself superior to any other international side.

In New Zealand, the arrival of Dominic Cork improved England's bowling options while strengthening their tail. However, Atherton's men started disappointingly. At Auckland, Atherton put New Zealand in to bat in conditions ideal for seam bowling. Cork, Mullally and Gough wasted their advantage. Thanks largely to Stephen Fleming's fine maiden Test ton (129), New Zealand reached a first-innings total of 390. Atherton (83), Stewart (173) and Thorpe (119) batted marvellously in reply, though, enabling England to gain a 131-run lead.

Piqued by their poor showing on the first day, Cork, Mullally, Gough and Tufnell caused havoc the second time around. New Zealand stumbled to 105/8. Although Simon Doull (26) helped Nathan Astle avoid an innings defeat, New Zealand's prospects did not look good as last man Danny Morrison strode to the wicket. New Zealand were only 11 runs in front and Morrison's Test batting record was poor, featuring a world record 24 ducks. Unabashed, Astle proceeded to smack the ball around while his humble partner defended solidly. Together, they added 106 runs in an unbroken last-wicket partnership that lasted almost two sessions. A British tabloid paper depicted the England bowlers staring dolefully out of a cartoon rocket that had been blasted into outer space. It seemed as if the England team was still in the dog house, albeit one that belong to Laika.

A reinvigorated Andy Caddick was restored to the attack at Wellington. He took four wickets for 45 and Gough 5-40 as New Zealand were dismissed for only 124 in 48.3 overs. England then batted patiently, reaching a first-innings total of 383 with Thorpe making an outstanding ton (108), with Stewart (52), Hussain (64) and Crawley (56) contributing well. Caddick, Gough, Croft and Tufnell then ripped New Zealand apart again as England won by an innings and 68 runs.

At Christchurch, Atherton was able to field an unchanged England side for the first time in 33 Tests. He celebrated with an unbeaten first-innings score of 94, and although England trailed New Zealand by 118 runs at the halfway stage, Atherton's second-innings hundred (118) proved vital as his side made 307/6 to win by four wickets. It was only the second time in their Test history that England had chased down a 300-plus winning target. After Atherton's steadfast, five-and-three-quarter-hour vigil, Crawley (40) and Cork (39) took England across the line with an unbroken 76-run seventh-wicket partnership. The match was a personal triumph for Robert Croft too. He took 5-95 in the New Zealand first innings and 2-48 in the second, chipping in with 31 important runs when England were stumbling at 145/6 in their first innings.

The summer home Ashes series was approached in good heart. The preliminary Texaco one-day series was won handsomely by England with 19-year-old Ben Hollioake producing a wonderfully fluent fifty on a glorious day at Lord's. Not to be outdone, his older brother Adam hit the winning runs in all three Texaco games. Nobody seemed at all concerned that both Hollioakes had been born in Melbourne, Australia. What seemed more important was that the Aussies were spluttering. It was difficult to comprehend the degree of punishment that Glenn McGrath took at Lord's where England surged to victory, smiting 270 runs in front of a raucously patriotic crowd.

The Edgbaston Test arrived and still the midnight chimes remained silent. What could be heard, though, was the Barmy Army's boisterous reinvention of the Euro 96 anthem 'Football's Coming Home' with 'Ashes' substituted for 'football'. Judging by the TV highlights, which I caught late on the first day, their chanting was incessant as England blasted out the Australians for only 118. Mark Taylor had chosen to bat on a strip that had been flooded only ten days before. The wicket oozed with moisture. It might have been much worse for the Aussies, for at one stage they were 54/8. Only Warne's frenzied swatting and Kasprowicz's hardy resistance rescued them from utter desolation.

To Geoffrey Boycott's delight, Devon Malcolm was recalled. Malcolm wasted little time in making an impact, tempting a horribly out-of-form Taylor to drive, only for him to edge a searing delivery into Mark Butcher's safe hands at slip. With Gough having already shattered Elliott's stumps, Australia were 15/2. Gough also castled Mark Waugh for five, and induced Blewett to nick a swinging delivery to Hussain at slip (7), having bowled him with a no-ball immediately before. The Australians were sinking fast at 28/4.

Incoming batsman Michael Bevan did not fancy Malcolm at all, having been strafed with a succession of sharply lifting deliveries. One snorting, short-pitched ball, aimed at Bevan's throat, hurried him into playing an ugly, protective shot that had Boycott whooping with pleasure. 'That's it Devon. Make them hop around on the back foot. They don't like it!' Bevan did not stay much longer, involuntarily deflecting a skidding bouncer to Mark Ealham at gully, having managed only eight nervously-acquired runs. His departure with 48 on the board signalled a further mini-collapse with Caddick snaffling both Steve Waugh and Ian Healy with no addition to the score. Although Warne threw the bat, particularly against Caddick, the Somerset pace bowler was not to be denied, cleaning up the tail and earning the impressive figures of 5-50 off 11.5 overs.

Although England stuttered in reply, quickly losing Atherton (2) and Butcher (8), with Stewart (18) also departing with the score on 50, Hussain (207) and Thorpe (138) took the game away from Australia with a superlative record-breaking fourth-wicket stand of 288 runs.

Hussain had progressed considerably since his Test debut in 1990 when Boycott was critical of his impetuosity, and particularly his tendency to play open-blade slashes against the pacemen, which risked being caught at gully. Hussain's technique had become tighter. The ball no longer slid off the face of his bat as before. While he was prepared to cut fiercely, he was proficient in keeping the ball down. At Edgbaston, he batted resplendently helped by a drying, albeit stodgy wicket that sapped the sting of McGrath and Warne. McGrath's two wickets cost 107 runs while Warne's solitary success was at the expense of 110 runs, with his effectiveness diminished further by a sore shoulder.

Whenever Warne bowled a little short, Hussain was quickly on to the back foot, cutting him savagely but precisely. And when McGrath, Kasprowicz or Gillespie over-pitched he drove them with relish. Hussain's double century, off 337 balls, contained 38 boundaries, while Thorpe's fluent innings was completed off 245 balls with 19 fours. Thorpe's confident execution of cut and sweep shots against Warne were key features in England grasping the initiative. Both batsmen achieved their highest Test scores.

The Australians had mistakenly believed that Hussain's volatility could be exploited. Twelfth man Justin Langer tried to capitalise on this only for Hussain to deride him as 'the bus driver'. England eventually declared at 478/9, which was 360 runs ahead of the Australians.

It was crunch time for Australian captain and opening batsman Mark Taylor. He had not scored a Test fifty in the previous 18 months. His wretched form had compelled the selection of an additional batsman as cover, meaning that his team's bowling options were squeezed. He had left himself out of the final one-day international and was contemplating dropping himself for the second Test at Lord's should he fail here.

With his back pushed up against the wall, Taylor produced one of the bravest innings seen in Test cricket. It was not a pretty knock but it was certainly effective. He and Matthew Elliott began with an opening stand of 133 before Elliott (66) was bowled by Robert Croft. Undeterred, Taylor ground on, supported weightily by Greg Blewett (125) as a further 194 runs were put on the board, taking Australia to 327 before their second wicket fell.

Taylor had realised that, in his anxiety to regain his 'mojo', he had neglected the mundane essentials of batting, opting instead for expansive cover drives and explosive hooks to reassure himself that the force was still with him. Here, he settled for nudges off his hip and squirting deflections to third man, restraining the temptation to play aggressively. Unconcerned by the odd false shot and by balls that narrowly missed the edge, he patiently accumulated vital runs for his side. When Croft induced Taylor to provide a return catch with his score on 129, Australia were still in a perilous position, but Taylor had rediscovered his touch and confidence.

Croft bowled well on a wicket that gave him little help, dismissing the first three Australian batsmen before the deficit was erased. Gough then made a triple breakthrough, leaving the tourists effectively 71/6. With the hobbling

Gillespie run out for a duck, Ealham mopped up the tail, leaving England to make 118 to win. Atherton (57) and Stewart (40) knocked off the runs with aplomb at a rate of almost six per over, taking their side to a nine-wicket victory.

It was too good to be true. Sure enough, normal service was resumed at Lord's. Had it not been for a profusion of heavy showers, and a stubborn opening partnership of 162 between Mark Butcher (87) and Michael Atherton (77) on the final day, England would have probably lost. Glenn McGrath had proved almost unplayable in England's first innings finding darting, late movement off a good length. His control was so immaculate that his 20.3 overs yielded just 38 runs. Having been put into bat by Taylor, only three England batsmen made double figures as Atherton's side was dismissed for just 77. Of the eight wickets that McGrath took in the England first innings, five of his victims were caught behind the wicket. Fortunately for Atherton's men the conditions were less in McGrath's favour when England batted again.

Atherton had hoped for a flat track at Old Trafford that would once again stifle both McGrath and Warne. He was to be disappointed. It was a moist, green surface with bare patches at either end, tailor-made for McGrath and Warne. However, he was amazed that the Australian captain chose to bat first. Taylor thought that, despite its obvious perils, the wicket would probably be at its best in the early stages of the game. If that meant sacrificing his own run-scoring opportunities, then so be it. It was this attitude which defined Taylor as a terrific captain.

Kent's fast-medium bowler Dean Headley made his debut here. He had an impressive pedigree, being the son of the former West Indian and Worcestershire opening batsman Ron Headley and the grandson of the great West Indian batsman George Headley. Headley wasted little time in making his presence felt, dismissing Taylor for two with a fiery ball that squared up the Australian captain, and found the outside edge of his bat, presenting Thorpe, at first slip, with a sharp catch.

Headley threw himself, heart and soul, into the fray. Sprinting to the wicket off a long run, he completed his delivery stride with a wrenching sideways twist of his torso, an outward thrust of his guiding arm, and a cocking of the right wrist at the hip, before hurling the ball at the batsmen with wiry power. Being almost 6ft 6in tall he achieved disconcerting bounce, too, as Taylor found to his cost after ducking into one of his skidding bumpers. Although less quick than Malcolm, Headley was decidedly swift while having a better command of length, line and movement. He could swing the ball prodigiously, conventionally and in reverse mode, cutting it back into the left-handers at pace, which made him a dangerous proposition. His jolting action seemed to demand a lot of him, though, particularly when striving for extra pace. Perhaps the back injuries, which enforced his premature retirement, were attributable to the stress his action imposed. His departure from Test cricket in 1999 was a sad loss, since during his short England career he was consistently menacing, even on unsympathetic tracks.

At Old Trafford, Headley took eight wickets in the match for 176 runs off 56.3 hostile overs. It was a very impressive Test debut. He and Gough formed a formidable new-ball partnership. And it was Gough who capitalised upon Headley's initial success by demolishing Elliott's stumps, leaving the Australians tottering at 22/2. Although first-change bowler Mark Ealham had Mark Waugh caught at the wicket for 12, even at 42/3, Australia were still in the game while Steve Waugh was batting.

Waugh needed a rub of the green, though. He was very fortunate to survive his first ball from Caddick which hit him on the pads in front of his stumps. Nevertheless, the umpire was unmoved by Caddick's impassioned appeal. Although Waugh received little help from his specialist batsmen after Elliott (40) departed at 85, caught at the wicket off Headley, the Australian tail provided gritty backing. Paul Reiffel (31) helped Waugh add 70 essential runs having joined the fight with his side in a mess at 160/7. Reiffel's resolution allowed Waugh to progress to a typically tenacious ton (108). It might have been very different had Stewart held on to a chance given by Reiffel, off Headley, when he had scored only 13.

Waugh was never fazed by narrow misses. Throughout his innings he rode his luck, playing and missing, and edging high and wide of the slips, but he was never perturbed by such narrow escapes. On the contrary, he revelled in such close calls, convinced that these confirmed his supremacy.

Australia's first-innings score of 235 might have appeared modest but Taylor's decision to bat first in such challenging conditions was fully vindicated as the dents the English pacemen left on the moist surface deepened as the pitch dried. Only Mark Butcher (51) did himself justice as Warne ripped the England innings apart with 6-48 off 30 fizzing overs. Australia gained a 73-run lead, and although Headley struck twice in the opening overs of the Australian second innings, the Waugh brothers took the game away from England with a 92-run fourth-wicket partnership. If Mark (55) was princely, older brother Steve was a teak-tough hero as he ground out a second century (116) while grimacing with pain from his badly-bruised right hand. With the help of Healy's aggression (47) and Warne's swinging from the hip (53), the Waugh brothers indemnified Australia against defeat. Crawley was the sole member of the England side to display any resistance, with a determined innings of 83, while his colleagues were skittled for very little. Australia won by 268 runs.

At Leeds, where England fielded abysmally, Matthew Elliott (199), Ricky Ponting (127) and Jason Gillespie (7-37) enabled Australia to grasp an overwhelming first-innings lead of 329 runs, which was converted rapidly into an innings victory. Only Hussain (105) and Crawley (72) acquitted themselves well with the bat. Gough wryly asked why the selectors had meddled with the bowling attack when it had been the batting that had let England down at Old

Trafford. For in defiance of Atherton's wishes, the ECB selectors, Graveney, Gooch and Gatting, had decided to blood the Gloucestershire left-arm seamer Mike Smith at Leeds, instead of re-selecting Caddick who had bowled so well at Edgbaston and Lord's, but less effectively at Manchester. Atherton was unimpressed with their decision, believing that it had been made in ignorance of the conditions at Leeds where he expected the tall Caddick to have posed a greater threat on a strip of uneven bounce.

Poor Smith had a miserable debut. He was denied the new ball, and his solitary chance of a wicket was spilled by Thorpe. Smith was left firing blanks while leaking almost four runs per over. A two-man pantomime cow provided some consolatory amusement to the dejected crowd by cavorting around the boundary, in the company of a man dressed as a giant carrot. Alas, the ground stewards played the party-poopers. Having been clumsily crash-tackled by the over-zealous officials, the unconsciously uncoupled cow's rear end had to be despatched to hospital for restoration. If only England's fate could have been remedied so easily.

At Nottingham, Australia duly retained the Ashes. With Gough ruled out because of injury, Malcolm and Caddick were recalled. Together with Headley, they bowled with fire and purpose on a flawless track, the first of the series. But Australia still ran up a hefty first-innings total of 427 with all of their top batsmen, except Ponting, recording half-centuries. England managed 313 in reply with Stewart, restored as opener, playing his finest innings of the series, displaying his full range of attacking shots (87). Thorpe added a further half-century (53) and the debutant Hollioake brothers chipped in with some useful runs. However, once Australia had built a 450-run lead with devastating efficiency, Atherton's side was left with only dignity to fight for. Unfortunately, that objective was beyond them, too, as McGrath, Warne and Gillespie dismissed them for 186, seizing a 264-run victory and the rubber.

The final Test at the Oval threatened to be a repeat of the three preceding matches as McGrath slit open the England batting order on the opening day, taking 7-76 as England made only 180. But on the second day, the dry Oval surface began to crumble. Tufnell seized his opportunity, bowling with great guile and accuracy, turning the ball sharply without any assistance from the rough patches. Until Warne's late thrash, the Australian batsman were unable to master him. Tufnell took 7-66 in 34.3 overs. It was an impeccable display of high-class spin bowling. Nevertheless, thanks to Warne's bold bash, England faced a deficit of 40 runs. Warne had strained a groin muscle, though. He was clearly hampered as he stepped gingerly to crease, unable to apply his customary degree of spin. Undeterred, Kasprowicz made light of Warne's indisposition, taking 7-36 as England subsided to 163 all out, with only Thorpe (62) and Ramprakash (48) tarrying, in a fourth-wicket partnership of 79. This left Australia with just 124 to make for victory, and over two days still to go.

Atherton was left with the conundrum of how best to balance attack with defence. He was unsure whether he should use Malcolm at all, fearing that a few poor overs from him could accelerate defeat before Tufnell had an opportunity to work his magic. Malcolm later said that he had to persuade Atherton to let him open the bowling. Atherton was not won over at first, but eventually threw the ball to his fastest bowler and told him he had two overs in which to make an impact. It was a wise decision. In his opening over a pumped-up Malcolm proved too quick for Elliott, straightening a ball that trapped the Australian opener in front of his stumps for four, detonating a bellowing roar from the Oval crowd (5/1). But Atherton wasted little time in turning to his most dangerous bowlers, Tufnell and Caddick. Tufnell bowled from over the wicket subduing the Australian batsmen with his tight control and vicious turn. Lifted by Tufnell's containment of the Australian stroke-makers, Caddick swept in with rare confidence. He bowled beautifully, constantly probing their 'corridor of uncertainty', finding movement both in the air and off the wicket.

Blewett (19) was Caddick's first victim. The ball jagged back sharply off the seam requiring Stewart to throw himself to his left to take a low catch (36/2). Although West Indian umpire Barker upheld Caddick's appeal, the TV replay indicated that the ball had brushed Blewett's pad not bat. Six runs later, Taylor failed to counter Caddick's seam movement and was out lbw on the back foot for 18 (42/3). Almost unbelievably the Waugh brothers departed quickly, too. Tufnell removed Mark for just a single (49/4), and then Steve edged a swinging, lifting ball from Caddick to Thorpe at first slip for six (54/5).

On the first day of the Premier League season, the Oval crowd morphed into a football crowd, hectoring and hollering England towards victory. Ponting (20) and the big-hitting Healy (14) began to right the listing ship, putting on 34 as the England fans' nerves began to fray faster than their finger-nails could be chewed. But Caddick then hung on to a return catch from Healy, after agonisingly juggling with the ball, first with his right hand, and then with both, finally trapping it against his chest as he spun around (88/6). Tufnell followed up by dismissing Ponting lbw (92/7).

Batting with a runner, Warne decided upon an all-out attack and whacked a ball from Tufnell high into the outfield where Martin positioned himself in readiness for the catch. Hearts were in mouths as the *TMS* commentator informed us that Martin was one of England's less reliable fielders, having spilt a 'sitter' off Warne during the first innings. The cataclysmic explosion that ensued told anyone relying upon radio coverage all they needed to know (95/8).

Kasprowicz was in Caddick's sights now. It was no contest. Caddick produced a brute of a delivery that stopped and stood up. Kasprowicz could only fend off the ball to Adam Hollioake at silly mid-off (99/9). Glenn McGrath had a burning desire to hit the winning runs for his country, but sadly for him he was unable to rise to the occasion, striking the first ball of Tufnell's 14th over into Thorpe's safe hands at mid-off. Once again England had shown they had the steeliest nerves in tight, low-scoring finishes. They might even have won a penalty shoot-out against the Germans.

Tufnell was rightly chosen as man of the match having taken 11 wickets for 93 runs off 46.4 overs, but the estimable efforts of Caddick, Thorpe and Ramprakash had also made victory possible, while Atherton's cool demeanour, and tactical precision during this 32.1 over run-chase, was exemplary. England's euphoria was understandable but the final series score of 3-2 certainly flattered England, for it was neither a true reflection of Australian dominance nor of England's shortcomings.

In 1997, the British Mercury Prize for a popular music album was awarded to *New Forms*, by Roni Size's Reprazent. The album was praised for its inventive drum 'n' bass improvisations, a musical style with roots in Jamaican reggae and the British 'jungle' genre, which was once hilariously lampooned by a sociopathic priest character in the TV sitcom *Father Ted*. In its darker manifestations, 'jungle' was the music of choice for many disaffected black and some white British youths, living in deprived urban areas. However, 'Heroes' offers neither an angry confrontation nor a call to arms. Instead, a husky, female vocalist, named Onallee, trails her sultry voice, with its jazzy and soulful inflections, skilfully across breakbeats of shifting timbre and tempo, evoking the style and flourish of Billie Holiday.

1998
Praise You
England's Caribbean tour lived down to expectations. Atherton had wanted to end his captaincy at the Oval but was persuaded against his better judgement to do one last tour of duty. He suffered awful luck with the toss when it mattered most. England lost in Guyana largely because they had to bat second on a rapidly deteriorating wicket. In Antigua, too, England were put into bat on a damp pitch which allowed Walsh, Ambrose and Ramnarine to bundle them out for 127. Once it had dried, the West Indian batsmen capitalised, racking up 500/7 declared with almost nonchalant ease. England struggled and ultimately failed to avert an innings defeat, despite Hussain (106), Thorpe (84 not out) and Stewart (79) putting up a spirited fight.

However, England could only blame themselves for squandering a position of strength on an under-prepared wicket in Trinidad. Here, Fraser, Headley and Tufnell had the West Indians wobbling at 124/5, when in pursuit of 282 for victory. However, a sixth-wicket partnership of 129 runs between Carl Hooper (94 not out) and wicketkeeper David Williams (65) set up a three-wicket win.

Trinidad had to host two consecutive Tests following the abandonment of the opening match in Jamaica because of a dangerous pitch. In the second of the Trinidadian Tests, England briefly restored parity to the rubber, having also won by three wickets. Atherton (49) and Stewart (83) provided the spade work with a second-innings opening partnership of 129 runs.

Former Hampshire captain Mark Nicholas attributed England's 3-1 series defeat – their fourth in succession in the Caribbean – to a lack of individual and collective toughness. He considered this to be a by-product of a domestic game which fostered complacency, nepotism and parochialism, despite Lord MacLaurin's attempts at changing this mindset. Nicholas pointed out that since 1963, when the amateur/professional distinction was ostensibly abolished in English first-class cricket, the England team had managed to win only 26 per cent of the 352 Test matches it had played. The case for radical reform seemed irrefutable.

Although this was a Test series too far for England's weary captain, it was a largely happy trip for his players, and particularly for Mark Ramprakash, whose series Test average of 66.50 was a much better reflection of his talent. His splendid big hundred at Barbados (154) lit up a game that was ruined by unseasonal rain.

Having been recalled to the colours after two years in the Test wilderness, Angus Fraser performed heroically, returning the best figures of his first-class career in the second Test in Trinidad. Alas, his first-innings figures of 8-53 and match figures of 11-110 were in a losing cause. However, he followed this feat up by taking 5-40 and 4-40 in England's subsequent win on the same ground a few days later. Caddick had a fine match here, too, taking 5-67 in the first innings and 2-64 in the second, while Headley took 4-77 in the second innings.

Alec Stewart batted well throughout the series, recording an average of 40.79. Both Hussain and Thorpe made centuries, too. But the West Indians had the stronger batting line-up, with Lara and Hooper excelling. They also had the stronger bowling attack – Curtly Ambrose took 30 wickets at an average of 14.26 while Walsh took 25 at 25.63. Even West Indian spinners Ramnarine and Hooper took 24 between them at a cost of just under 21 whereas the 13 wickets that Croft and Tufnell shared cost over twice that figure at 44.46.

As Atherton was about to relinquish the England captaincy to a fiercely competitive Alec Stewart, he reflected upon how England's cause had been hampered during his time in charge by the excessive workloads placed upon his key bowlers, particularly Fraser, Gough and Caddick. Not once did he have this trio at his disposal at the same time. In fact, in only half of the 54 Test matches he captained, did even two of them play together. Strange selections had some bearing upon this, but injury played a greater part, a legacy of their debilitating county workloads. The top Australian pacemen were then bowling over half of their first-class overs in the service of their country, whereas Fraser, for example, bowled less than a fifth of his for England.

During the early 1990s, I devoted as much time to the care of my aunt as I did to my parents. She had Parkinson's disease, requiring considerable assistance from me, and paid and unpaid helpers, with her personal, practical and health care. She was very frightened, and not only because her degenerative condition progressively robbed her of her strength and independence. The powerful medication that she was prescribed to slow her decline had alarming side effects. She began calling me at work and home, in distressed states, saying that long departed friends and relatives were haunting her house. Because these people appeared so vividly to her, she found it hard to believe that they were no more than medication-induced hallucinations. The only way I could dispel her fear was by standing or sitting in the places they were said to inhabit, whereupon they disappeared from her sight. In her dingy house, these 'exorcisms', particularly those conducted at night, were eerie experiences for me, but for her they were an endless torture. Poor aunt, her final years were consumed with torment.

By the time she died in the mid-90s, I had to step up my support for dad as he succumbed to dementia. Because mum was experiencing difficulty in looking after him, I often had to step into the breach, sometimes at short notice when she was exhausted or re-admitted to psychiatric hospital. I looked after him in his home in Hastings and in mine in London, arranging home care, day care, and short breaks in specialist homes. Sometimes, kind relatives and friends helped out, but most of these people were ageing, too. What these years taught me was that, as a carer, the buck stops with you no matter how good the support services might be. Someone has also to co-ordinate whatever help is on offer – paid or unpaid – and deal with the queries and concerns that follow. And if the care arrangements fail, for whatever reason, the carer has to be prepared to stand in, irrespective of pressing work, family and other commitments.

There was nothing at all unusual about my situation, though. As the 2001 Census revealed there were 4.8 million unpaid carers in England. By 2011, this figure had grown to 5.4 million – almost certainly a significant underestimate. This means that at least 10.2 per cent of the population were looking after around 6.5 million disabled or ill spouses, partners, parents, children, other relatives or friends. These unpaid carers provided on average around 22 hours of care per week, although almost a quarter of carers provide 50 hours or more weekly care. Generally speaking, 80 per cent of the nation's social care needs are met by unpaid carers. Their duties encompass help with bathing, dressing, preparing food and drink, feeding, toileting, mobility, administering medication, laundry, shopping, housework, handling housing and financial affairs, attending health and other appointments, emotional support and much more.

Although two-thirds of those cared for are people of pensionable age, there are a significant number of younger people who need their carers' regular assistance. These include people with mental health needs, learning or physical disabilities, visual and hearing impairments. And with the population rising, and people living longer, those requiring their carer's help is increasing. In the ten years between the 2001 and 2011 Censuses, there was an 11 per cent increase in the number of carers and eight per cent increase in their average weekly hours of care. Meanwhile, there was a 27 per cent drop in the number of older people receiving council help at home, such as home care. Since 2010 there has been an estimated £4.6bn or 31% reduction in government funding of council adult social care, halving services at home for older people in some areas.

With unpaid carers having to absorb an ever-increasing share of social care there is less scope for pleasurable activities for themselves and for those they care for. Nevertheless, when dad stayed with me in his declining years, I often took him to watch Brentford play, as this was the football team he supported as a young man. I am not sure whether the football made much impact upon him. Perhaps that was a blessing for Brentford was not a very good team during this period, but he seemed to find an elusive sense of calm at Griffin Park despite the baying voices around him. For as his faculties deserted him, he was often agitated at the perceived unpredictability of his narrowing world.

And in summer, we would visit leafy Sussex village greens where he had played cricket during the 1950s. Some he recognised, most he did not. On one afternoon of tall, slumbering heat we stopped at the village cricket field where he had often played. The heroic image I have of him smiting the ball around is located here. He had no recollection of having played there, though, despite being a regular team member for five or six years during the 50s, and having visited the nearby village pub many times since. Dementia not only snatched away much of his past, but also cast doubt about some of mine, as our shared memories fluttered away like loose pages of a disintegrating book. Although I used photos as well as visits in trying to shore up his rapidly receding memory, I had to take care not to agitate him. He tended to panic when asked questions he could not answer. None of us like being reminded of our waning powers.

We watched a lot of village cricket during the summer of 1998. During the 70s, when mum had several extended stays in psychiatric hospital, he took great comfort if we could spend an hour or so watching a local game together after visiting hours. He loved the willowy echo of a sweetly struck shot, the honeyed scent of blossoming spring, the cleansing freshness of newly-cut grass, and the gentle rustling of a warm, caressing breeze. Above all, he loved the pub lunches. His appreciation of food was one of the last senses to desert him.

We also watched some Test cricket on TV, although it was entirely by chance that we watched a series-defining interlude of play at Trent Bridge. England were 1-0 down in the rubber. They had drawn at Edgbaston but had been thrashed at Lord's. Only Nasser Hussain's reproving century (105) had lifted patriotic pride. At Old Trafford, England had simply jumped jail, thanks to a doughty rearguard action begun by Atherton (89) and Stewart

(164), and completed by Robert Croft (37 not out) and Angus Fraser. But at Trent Bridge, England had fought so well with bat and ball that they were left with 247 to win with around four sessions left in which to complete their task. England had not made as many runs as this to win a Test match at home since 1902. According to one tabloid newspaper this was the series England *dare* not lose. So no pressure then.

Dad and I sat together watching Atherton and Butcher cautiously acquire 40 runs. Their key objective, though, was to bat out the evening session unscathed. While I helped dad to understand what he was watching, it was important not to overload him with information he could not digest. Just as I felt that the opening pair were entering calmer waters, Shaun Pollock, the son of the former South African Test fast bowler Peter, found the edge of Butcher's bat, and wicketkeeper Mark Boucher took the catch. Pollock was a mean bowler, rarely giving much away with his vexing line and length. Bowling close to the stumps Pollock made the most of the lateral movement he summoned. A third of the wickets Pollock took in this series resulted from catches at the wicket.

Hussain joined Atherton and initially played with greater freedom than his partner. Atherton remained circumspect, studiously pushing a run or two here or nudging a single there. Only a brutal cut or flamboyant drive from Hussain gave any real momentum to the scoring. But Atherton's principal objective was to remain at his post until play ended. The light was passable but it was a sullen evening.

Disturbed by England's steady progress, at 82/1 Cronje recalled his ace fast bowler Allan Donald. Donald customarily slashed white sun block horizontally across his nose and cheeks as if he was leading a Sioux war party. But in these overcast conditions he settled for smearing his bottom lip. Actually, this looked more sinister, as if he had been rabidly foaming at the mouth. Not that Donald ever needed brutalising cosmetics. At his fastest he was terrifying. Tall and wiry he arrived at the wicket with a pronounced leap, the ball held high in his right hand as if exhibiting an item of torture to his victim, while his left forearm, crossed his chest, mimicking a crash bar. His speed was generated in a single rotation of the arm. The momentum acquired from his swift and direct approach to the wicket was enhanced by the elasticity of his shoulder power, and the gravitational force of his landing.

Hussain had suffered on account of a 'poppadum' index finger. A hefty blow on this finger might put him out of the game as it had before. Hussain knew that Donald's fast, rearing deliveries posed a significant threat but he was not inclined to duck or dodge unless there was no option. His overriding instinct was to take the fight to the aggressor. Not that he had too much opportunity to do so here, for it was Atherton who initially took much of the flak.

The 40-minute period which followed featured one of the most vicious, absorbing duels I have ever witnessed on a cricket field. Donald was so pumped up with hissing adrenalin, knowing that the outcome of the match probably depended upon what he could achieve in this spell. He urged wicketkeeper Boucher to keep the sparks flying, exhorting him to gee up the slip cordon into blitzing Atherton and Hussain with disdainful invective. Donald wanted to be in the batsmen's faces and inside their heads. The phlegmatic Atherton had other ideas, though.

Donald went round the wicket to Atherton. His first ball was short and lifted alarmingly. Atherton had not adjusted to the new line and instinctively half-turned away from a ball he had not picked up. While throwing his bottom right hand clear, he failed to get his left hand out of the ball's path soon enough. The ball seemed to brush his left glove before being caught by a diving Boucher, low and at full stretch in front of first slip. Donald sprinted gleefully towards Boucher and the slip cordon, his left arm raised in triumph. But their crestfallen expressions stopped him dead in his tracks. Swivelling around he saw that umpire Steve Dunn was unmoved. Cronje smiled contemptuously at Atherton. Donald was not so restrained, though. In the full gaze of the TV camera he snarled at Atherton, 'You better be f***ing ready for what's coming... There'll be nothing in your half.' At least that's Donald's version of what he said. My lip-reading skills are not that great although I did pick up his expletive. Atherton did not flinch or avert his eyes. Unmoved and unrepentant, he returned Donald's menacing stare with cussed bravado, his lips pressed firmly together.

The next ball was lethally quick. Atherton was marginally late on his back-foot shot, inside-edging the ball to fine leg for four. Donald gave him another long malevolent stare before uttering with smouldering malice, 'You f***ing cheat.' Atherton was determined not to be bullied into a war of words. He composed himself once more, took guard and patiently awaited the next delivery, his eyes never leaving Donald as the bowler returned to his mark.

Donald was true to his word for the following ball was a skidding bouncer. Atherton ducked, the ball thwacking into Boucher's gloves at a speed somewhere in the 90s. More profanities from Donald followed.

Next up was a fizzing delivery aimed at Atherton's chest. Atherton let the ball find its mark, breasting it into the gully region off his chest protector. Although recoiling fractionally with the force of the blow, Atherton wasted no time in recovering his position. An involuntary hint of a smile hovered upon his lips before his inscrutable mask was quickly re-applied. The sentinel stance was resumed. Donald yelled at him, 'Come on! I've got you in my pocket!'

The ball after was the quickest of the lot. It reared wickedly from just short of a length. Atherton leapt, but realising in the nick of time that it was about to decapitate him, jerked his head aside while still in mid-air. Commentating on BBC TV, David Gower gasped, 'Vicious! Really, really vicious! That was straight and aimed at the target. The target in this case being the head.'

But as if tiring of playing the punchbag, Atherton went for what seemed to be a premeditated hook shot off the ensuing short ball. Perhaps this battering had slowed his feet, because his positioning appeared awry. Atherton had to fetch the shot while nailed to the spot. Atherton made imperfect contact, and as he spun around the ball looped up off the splice but fell safely to earth in a vacant deep square leg area. Atherton took two runs from this imprudent hoick. Donald fumed. He had thought of putting a fielder there for a mistimed hook, but Atherton's obduracy had dissuaded him. Now his chance had gone. Atherton would not repeat this error.

Donald resumed his short-of-a-length assault, the ball fired across Atherton but the former England captain merely dropped his wrists and allowed it to hiss through to Boucher. Gower remarked, 'These two could write a book about what's going on out there except the transcripts would not be publishable.'

Finally Atherton moved off strike. Pollock bowled him a fuller pitched delivery outside his off stump. Reaching for it with minimal foot movement, Atherton square drove the ball to the point boundary. The Trent Bridge crowd roared their approval.

Donald was so fixated on removing Atherton that he paid less attention to Hussain. But at 100/1, it was Hussain who gave him his best chance of a breakthrough. First Donald beat Hussain's stroke, the ball flicking the Essex man's hip and carrying to Boucher who elatedly threw the ball aloft. Donald joined in the appeal before realising that Hussain had not made contact. Donald beamed at Hussain. Hussain returned a wry smile. But the next ball should have dismissed him. A leg-cutter found the outside edge of Hussain's bat as he prodded forward uncertainly. The degree of movement had deceived Hussain. Unfortunately for South Africa, it had deceived the reliable Boucher also. He fumbled the chance, the ball popping out of his gloves. Had Kallis not left his post in a dash to embrace Donald he might have redeemed the error.

Donald flew down the pitch eyes bulging, veins protruding, roaring 'Nooooo!!' A prostrate Boucher banged his forehead against his gloves in woeful contrition. Hell hath no fury like a fast man spurned. Except Donald was bigger than that. After stomping off to long leg at the end of the over, with impressive magnanimity he ran back to Boucher before play could resume, patting him affectionately on the back. But Boucher remained desolate. With their cheerleader nobbled, the combative energy seemed to seep out of the South Africans. They remained in morose silence until the close, when England were strongly placed at 108/1 with Atherton on 43 and Hussain on 25.

Belatedly, dad caught on. Without being prompted he remarked, 'That's quite a fight going on there.' It was as if his fading faculties could only compute erratically and slowly what he saw. I enthusiastically agreed. We even managed a brief conversation about cricket being a game for the brave. Foolishly, I grasped at the notion that all was not yet lost. Sometimes, lingering, odds-defying hope is the hardest to live with.

Next day, while I was at work Atherton (98 not out) steered England to an eight-wicket victory, helped by Hussain (58) and Stewart (45 not out) who was in spanking form. Donald had been right. That 40-minute duel did determine the outcome of the game. England were back on terms. Later that evening dad and I spoke on the telephone. We had often phoned one another in past years to natter about cricket or football. I told him the result. He seemed pleased but I was not sure he really understood what I was telling him.

Donald and Atherton put aside their feud over a drink. Regarding the glove incident, Atherton asked Donald what he would have done if their situations had been reversed. With commendable honesty, Donald replied that he would not have walked either. Donald admired Atherton for the guts he showed in standing up to his fierce assault, and for brazening out his guilt. Atherton agreed that the offending glove should be auctioned to swell Donald's benefit fund. Atherton even signed it for him – on the culpable spot.

Ten days later the rubber was decided at Leeds. England had the better of several poor umpiring decisions, notably at the start of the fourth innings when South Africa slipped to 27/5. However, Cronje's men rallied strongly on a flattening wicket. Driving back from Hastings, I listened nervously as Rhodes and McMillan clubbed 117 for the sixth wicket, putting England's second-string bowlers Salisbury and Flintoff to the sword. At this point in his career, Flintoff seemed no more than an amiable medium-pacer. Stewart had a problem. Gough was suffering stomach cramps while Fraser's back was sore. Cork was his only go-to bowler.

Cork was often at his best when the chips were down. Turning on his 'Mr Nasty' act, that got up the noses of so many opponents, he goaded McMillan into taking him on, knowing that the strapping South African had a short fuse. Jibes were as much a part of Cork's armoury as swing, and on this hot, cloudless afternoon, with only a pappy ball at his disposal, he was getting little of the latter. Eventually McMillan snapped, flailing at a short ball from Cork that he intended to smack out of the ground. His anger had got the better of his technique, though, as he merely cuffed the ball to Alec Stewart behind the stumps. It was not the first time or indeed the last that Cork would sucker an opponent into giving away his wicket. Here, it was priceless. What's more, it revived Darren Gough. Steaming in from the main stand end Gough speared a pitched-up delivery into Rhodes's pads. The South African's eyes lit up at the prospect of finding the midwicket boundary only to locate Flintoff's waiting palms at short midwicket.

At 167/7, South Africa were back in the soup, and when Gough trapped Boucher lbw for only four the tourists faced the prospect of imminent defeat at 175/8. But Stewart's three pace bowlers were shattered. Stewart knew he could ill afford to bring back Salisbury or Flintoff with so few runs to play with. Cronje also realised this and wanted to claim the extra half hour of play, believing that his all-rounder Pollock and Donald would deliver victory against an exhausted attack. Cronje failed to get his message to the batsmen in time, though. The umpires were unaware that either captain could call for extra time, so when Stewart made it clear that he wanted to go off at the close, they concurred. On the following morning, in front of a large, boisterously patriotic crowd, Fraser had Donald caught at the wicket before Gough took England to victory by trapping fast bowler Ntini, lbw for a duck.

It had been a special match for the ebullient Gough who took 6-42 in the second innings and 9-100 in the match. It was a special occasion for Fraser, too. Fraser had emphasised what Raymond Illingworth had missed by returning series-winning figures of 10-122 at Nottingham, and 8-92 at Leeds.

However, England's euphoria dissipated far too quickly as a weary team then lost a stormy one-off Test against Sri Lanka. The brilliant if controversial Sri Lankan spinner Muttiah Muralitharan was given a tailor-made strip on which to practise his arts. Seizing the opportunity with glee, he took 16 wickets in the match for 220 runs.

Reflecting the modernising process that Lord MacLaurin championed, England's 1998/99 Ashes party included a fitness coach, a sports psychologist, an analyst and a media-relations manager. But some of the selection decisions remained as baffling as ever. It seemed inconceivable that Andy Caddick should be passed over, for he had been the only England-qualified bowler to take 100 first-class wickets in 1998. Phil Tufnell missed out also despite his startling success against the Australians at the Oval in 1997.

Nevertheless, the selection of Alex Tudor, Surrey's highly promising fast bowler, was an exciting one despite the capricious use of his talents on tour. With Gooch as tour manager and Alec Stewart as captain it was inevitable that a high premium would be placed on exacting fitness drills. But it seemed counterproductive to drive the players so remorselessly in heat of suffocating intensity.

At Brisbane, England's new wine gushed out of their old skins as seven catches were shelled off Gough's bowling alone. Mullally also botched a straightforward run-out opportunity when Steve Waugh was on 29. Waugh made 83 more. With Healy clobbering 134, Australia made 485. Although England summoned a spirited reply, led by Mark Butcher's fine ton (116), and augmented by half-centuries from Hussain (59), Thorpe (77) and Ramprakash (67 not out), Australia were about to complete a rout when a tropical storm thwarted them.

At Perth there was no reprieve. England lost a low-scoring game by seven wickets inside two days and two sessions. The only bright spots in England's performance were Graeme Hick's 68, the highest individual score made in the game, and Tudor's first-innings figures of 4-89 on his Test debut.

The third Test at a baking Adelaide was equally one-sided. Christmas was still ten days away when Australia summarily retained the Ashes. With a Republican government in power, Australians were voting on whether their president should replace the Queen as head of state. Reflecting the prevalent iconoclastic mood, some Australian journalists suggested that it was time to downgrade future Ashes contests, reducing these to three match mini-series. This was the size of Australian triumphalism.

Then came the amazing Melbourne Test. England had made 270 in their first innings, having been put in to bat by Taylor. A revitalised Alec Stewart led the way with a hard-hit century (107) supported once again by Ramprakash (67). The match seemed evenly poised as Australia teetered at 252/8, only for Stuart MacGill (43), deputising for the injured Warne, and Steve Waugh (122) to put together an 88-run ninth-wicket partnership. It seemed as if the game had been yanked out of England's grasp. And yet England batted staunchly in their second innings with Stewart (52), Hussain (50) and Hick (60) recording half-centuries. However, the game was to hinge on the modest 23-run final-wicket partnership between 'Audi' Mullally – a sobriquet earned on account of his four consecutive ducks – and Gough.

Australia required only 175 runs to win, and at 103/2 they seemed home and hosed. Then Mark Ramprakash made an astonishing catch to dismiss Langer (30) from a full-blooded pull off Mullally. Flinging himself to his right at square leg, Ramprakash managed to grasp the ball with his outstretched right hand. His phenomenal athleticism and subsequent roar of defiance lifted England's flagging spirits. Headley was recalled to the attack. Delivering reverse swing at a hostile pace he induced a dumfounded Mark Waugh (43) to nick a lifting ball to Hick at slip. Australia were 130/4, but still hot favourites to win their third consecutive victory. After all, Steve Waugh was still at the crease.

Headley continued to steam in with the intensity of Headingley hero Bob Willis. First he had Darren Lehman caught at the wicket by Hegg for four, then the dangerous Ian Healy was dismissed for a duck, Hick taking another fine slip catch, before Damien Fleming was trapped in front of his stumps for a duck. Suddenly Australia were 140/7. Only Steve Waugh (30) seemed to stand in England's way. Nicholson (9) stood his ground while a further 21 runs were added. However, Headley was not finished. Nicholson edged to be caught by a cavorting Warren Hegg. Having seen how competently MacGill had defied the England attack in the first innings, Waugh took a single off the first ball of Gough's next over. Gough sneered at him, 'After a not-outer?' before immediately yorking MacGill for nought, and then trapping McGrath lbw also without scoring.

The 'Barmy Army', who had rowdily cheered England to this 12-run victory, were beside themselves with joy, as were the foot-sore England players. A pumped-up Gough seized a stump, gesticulated angrily at the cocky Australian crowd and bawled at a TV camera that he mistakenly took to be Australian, 'Shove that up your arse, you Australian w*****s.' The arrogance of the Australian press had stung the whole England team, but Gough in particular. I took in these astounding events while driving to a meeting on the other side of the county. Leaving the profanities to Gough, I mused how intoxicating the sour smell of crushed invincibility was from those who deodorise with hubris.

England might have even squared the Test series at Sydney had Slater (123) not been unaccountably reprieved early in his innings. The TV evidence suggested he was well short of his ground. In another low-scoring game dominated by spin, that let-off probably made the difference as Australia eventually won by 95 runs with MacGill returning match figures of 12-107. While MacGill was probably Warne's equal in terms of delivering wicket-taking deliveries – his googly was particularly devilish – his inferior control meant that Warne remained ahead.

As I returned home late from work I heard Norman Cook's (aka Fatboy Slim) 'Praise You' for the first time. How vigorous and stirring it sounded, like a supercharged gospel track with various samples thrown into the mix, a crackling keyboard score, a funky guitar, muttered asides, and a thumping beat driving home a simple, repetitive message of love. That message represented a tiny extract of Camille Yarbrough's 1975 song, 'Take Yo Praise'. Yarbrough is an African-American musician, poet, and activist. She rather liked Fatboy Slim's 'big beat' adaptation when it was played for her. And so she should.

1999
Rise

The sixties were framed by two obscenity trials, the first of which took place in 1960. This concerned Penguin Books's publication of an unexpurgated version of *Lady Chatterley's Lover*. The second happened in 1971, after the publication of a 'School Kids' edition of *OZ*, an underground magazine. The offending issue, published in 1970, featured an unusually libidinous Rupert Bear. Both trials bear testament to the moral conservatism prevalent within this period notwithstanding the 1960s' licentious reputation. As for the 1990s, this decade seemed book-ended by two demolitions. For in 1989, the Berlin Wall was breached while in 2001 a horrific terrorist assault made upon Manhattan's World Trade Center brought about its complete destruction.

While acknowledging the inherent problem with 'decaditis' – the fallacious practice of splitting time into ten-year segments as a basis for legitimate historical enquiry – these twin 'demolitions' are signifiers of the times in which they occurred. The fall of the Berlin Wall denoted the demise of the Iron Curtain, with Glasnost, Perestroika and the anticipated end of the Cold War raising hope of greater freedoms and political independence. Whereas the horrific attack in Manhattan marked a return to the politics of fear. Fundamentalist insurgency then became the new global threat, stalking areas of political instability, particularly where collapsing oppressive regimes released previously suppressed racial and religious animosities.

In keeping with the demolition motif, England's 2-1 defeat in a four-match Test series with New Zealand confirmed its cataclysmic fall from grace. In the space of 40 years England's Test side had dropped from the top, at least unofficially, to rock bottom of the official world rankings, below Zimbabwe.

In 1999, Britain's economy was sustained by a thriving global financial sector but its manufacturing base, which had formerly upheld its status as a world power had withered. England's bottom place in the world's cricket hierarchy seemed to be a symbolic reflection of what had been lost since the end of the Second World War: industrial might, military strength and imperial power.

The summer of 1999 was a disastrous one for English cricket. As hosts of the World Cup, England's hapless one-day team were eliminated by India before England's tournament song could be released. Afterwards, captain Alec Stewart and head coach David Lloyd were relieved of their responsibilities. But the buck did not stop with them. The opening ceremony at Lord's was an abject spectacle. It was as if it had been organised by the spoof 2012 Olympics 'Deliverance' team. The firework display was miserly, apparently consisting of little more than the contents of a budget selection box with a few mortars thrown in to wake up dozing MCC members. And then the PA system crackled and spluttered before falling silent, leaving Prime Minister Tony Blair quite literally speechless. Not all bad then.

So when Alan Mullally skied a ball from Chris Cairns to mid-off confirming the Kiwis' Test victory at the Oval by 83 runs, England's newly appointed captain Nasser Hussain had only a poisoned chalice to hold aloft. As he appeared on the pavilion balcony he was roundly booed by the grumpy English crowd, some of whom remained loyal to Stewart.

England's new head coach was to be the former Zimbabwe player Duncan Fletcher, who had done such a fine job in reviving Glamorgan's fortunes. However, as with the appointment of Hussain as captain, there was some equivocation within the ECB. Lord MacLaurin was thought to have preferred ex-England batsman Bob Woolmer as head coach, who had performed well in a similar role with the South African side. However, the sometimes gruff but always constructive Fletcher became their chosen candidate. As with the ambivalent selection of Alf Ramsey as England's football manager in 1962, the rest was, indeed, history.

My song of the year was 'Rise', not out of any sarcasm, I must add. Gabrielle's husky R 'n' B number is a sad contemplation of a broken relationship, backed by a sample of Bob Dylan's song, 'Knockin' on Heaven's Door'. And no trite allusion to the state of English cricket is intended here, either. Dylan allowed free usage of the sample because he liked the song so much. I guess, if the song is good enough for Bob then it is good enough for me.

'Race For The Prize'

2000 – 2005

England won 47 per cent of 78 Tests played between November 1999 and August 2005

2000–2005

Lose Yourself

The new millennium arrived with pomp and angst. Although the Dome did not pull or the river catch fire, or the Eye go around, at least the Bug did not bite. Airliners did not crash to earth and we could still use the ATM. On the morning of 1 January 2000, the world seemed to be much the same as it was at the end of the 20th century.

After the millennium I ceased recording my past in annual instalments. It seemed like bad accountancy as I sped towards later life with one year blending obscurely into another. The period that followed is probably the most disturbing that many of us, Baby Boomers, have ever experienced. Far from defeating insurgency, the 'War on Terror' seems to have multiplied the threat of international terrorism while associated refugee problems have mounted catastrophically. In the meantime, global environmental sustainability has repeatedly been called into question as has internet safety and security. With the world becoming an ever more dangerous place, concerns have risen about intensifying surveillance and the suspension of human rights and freedom, supposedly in the interests of civic safety.

International cricket has not escaped the fall-out of increasing instability. For example, Pakistan is currently prevented from hosting international games on account of a residual risk of terrorist atrocities, although the Afghanistan cricket team now competes in the one-day World Cup competition. And yet in the first five years of the new century, in the midst of so much international strife, English cricket made a dramatic recovery, at least at Test level.

This improvement began erratically. The 1999/2000 winter tour to South Africa did not go well. It was Duncan Fletcher's first series as England's head coach and Hussain's first full Test series as captain. South Africa won the first and fourth Test matches by an innings, and although England won a rain-drenched fifth Test by two wickets, it later transpired, after Cronje's transgressions became known, that this contrived, yet successful, finish might have been incentivised by shady gambling interests.

The summer Test series against the West Indians featured an astonishing reversal of fortune, though. After England had been thrashed in the opening Test at Edgbaston, it appeared as if the Lord's Test was following a similar pattern as England trailed the West Indians by 133 runs at the completion of their first innings. But the English lions recovered their roar. Caddick (5-16), well supported by Gough and Cork, then rolled over the tourists for just 54 in their second innings, with Lara making only five. Nevertheless, a victory target of 188 seemed to be a daunting task with Ambrose and Walsh in full cry. But the English batsmen rose to the occasion, remarkably. Atherton (45) and Vaughan (41) added 92 to take England to 95/2, but it needed Cork's chutzpah (33 not out) to see England home, with two wickets to spare, in a nail-biting finale.

Then at Leeds, Caddick (5-14) and Gough (4-30) shot out the West Indians for 64 in their second innings, delivering victory by an innings and 39 runs inside two days. Caddick completed the win by dismissing four West Indian batsmen in a single over. I could hardly believe my ears as the West Indians' last six wickets fell for 12 runs in less time than it took me to drive the five miles between meetings in Godalming and Guildford.

The genial, wholehearted Gough and the reclusive, sometimes contrary Caddick emerged as a world-class act with the new ball. Gough's bustling style and skidding pace neatly complemented the loping Caddick's booming swing and bounce. Nevertheless, it took Fletcher's wise counsel to cement their pairing after Caddick had irked Gough by boasting of his place on the Lord's honour board, a commendation that Gough had coveted.

Dad died in a nursing home in October 2000. A series of strokes had reduced him to catatonic silence. Although visited regularly by family and friends, he became oblivious of our presence. I felt badly about this for years after, for I had arranged his nursing home admission when it was clear that, even with considerable help, mum could no longer look after him. To my lasting regret, neither could I. With mum needing so much assistance on account of a rapid deterioration in her physical health, and with dad no longer around, only the car radio and late night TV highlights sustained my interest in cricket.

However, I did register news of England's momentous victory in the Karachi twilight. Thorpe (64 not out) and Hick (40 not out) had braved the gathering gloom to take England to a six-wicket victory, while Atherton had prepared the ground with a first-innings hundred (125). By slowing the game to a crawl, Pakistani wicketkeeper and captain Moin Khan had attempted to exhaust the light before the winning runs could be made. Much to his disgust the umpires thwarted his blatant gamesmanship. Despite repeated complaints that his fielders could not see the ball, the umpires allowed play to continue. This was England's first series victory in Pakistan since the days of Dexter, almost 40 years before.

England then surpassed themselves by winning in Sri Lanka having recovered from a drubbing in the first Test. Here, Hussain led the fightback at Kandy with a scruffy but invaluable century (109), bringing to an end a dismal run of form that caused him to question his position as captain. His exultant celebrations said it all.

Although Darren Gough was voted the man of the series, Thorpe's mastery of Muralitharan was essential to England's success. Left-arm spinner Ashley Giles was another key performer, both in Sri Lanka and Pakistan, benefitting from an over-the-wicket plan devised with Fletcher and Hussain. In Karachi, he took 7-132, while in Colombo, he returned figures of 6-70, where his leg stump line of attack offered more than containment, comprising subtle variations in spin, pace and flight. Fletcher also believed that Giles was capable of raising his game as a batsman and fielder. He was right on both counts, as Giles completed Ashes-winning innings at Trent Bridge and the Oval, in 2005, and held important catches, notably in the gully.

England therefore prepared for the arrival of the 2001 Australian team in good heart. The first warm-up Test against Pakistan, at Lord's, was won by an innings, with Gough and Caddick sharing 16 wickets for 207 runs. But the second was lost by 108 runs, due mainly to Inzamam-ul-Haq's superb batting (114 and 85). Although Michael Vaughan (120) and Graham Thorpe (138) batted well for England, this was an untimely setback. Steve Waugh's side proved to be the most powerful Australian team to visit this country since Bradman's 'Invincibles'. They annihilated England, requiring only 11 days of Test cricket to take the series. Steve Waugh led the way with a series batting average of 107, followed by his brother Mark with 86, Damien Martin with 76.4 and Adam Gilchrist with 68. Meanwhile McGrath (32 wickets at 16.93) and Warne (31 at 18.7) shattered the English batting almost at will. Only at Leeds, where Mark Butcher (173) batted with a style and power reminiscent of Adam Gilchrist, were the Australians rattled. However, England's six-wicket victory here owed much to the complacency, if not arrogance, of substitute Australian captain Adam Gilchrist. In closing the Australian second innings at 176/4, he left England a full day to chase 314 for victory. England were expected to roll over in time-honoured fashion.

As testament to his belligerent approach, almost 100 of Butcher's 173 runs came in boundaries – 23 fours and one spectacular six behind point. Butcher achieved a series average score of 56.36, but, with the exception of Ramprakash, who averaged a shade under 40, and Hussain who averaged

35.4, no other England batsman threatened to get on top of the Australian attack for long. And although Caddick and Gough shared 32 series wickets, these cost, on average, 44 runs each. Australia deservedly won the rubber 4-1.

This was Michael Atherton's final Test series. His Test average of 37.69 was a fine reflection of his value but would surely have been better had his taxing back problems not periodically inhibited his movement and shot-making. It was almost inevitable that his final dismissal should be at the hand of his nemesis Glenn McGrath, who had taken his wicket on 18 previous occasions in Test cricket. Atherton left the Oval field to a standing ovation, generously joined by each of the Australians. He had been a stalwart in a twilight period of English cricket.

Whether overawed by Tendulkar's batting brilliance or mesmerised by Harbhajan's and Kumble's magical bowling, England lost a subsequent three-match series in India 1-0. Marcus Trescothick's performances with the bat and Flintoff's with the ball were promising, though. Hussain was encouraged, too, that his bowlers had restrained the Indian shot-makers so well. Giles had the distinction of dismissing Tendulkar with a stumping. It was the only time he was dismissed in this way.

On the New Zealand leg of the 2001/02 tour, England had to settle for a 1-1 draw after comfortably winning the first Test in Christchurch. Hussain (106), Thorpe (200 not out) and Flintoff (137) had excelled with the bat, just as Caddick and Hoggard had with the ball. But the principal star was Kiwi Nathan Astle, who blasted 222 from only 153 balls in a last-wicket thrash. His second hundred required just 39 balls.

In 2002, 12-month central playing contracts were introduced. The first ones, of six months' duration, were brought in during 1999. Central contracts represented a quantum leap for the England team. Not only did these result in higher annual incomes for the contracted players – up to £1m each if appearance and sponsorship deals were taken into account – they also helped enhance the calibre of their performances.

Before central contracts were awarded, England won 29.9 per cent of the 521 Test matches played since 1946, but of the 78 Tests played between autumn 1999 and August 2005, 47.4 per cent were won. Vindication of the value of central contracts could hardly have been more emphatic. There is little doubt that the protection central contracts afforded enabled both Caddick and Gough to stay fit throughout the summer of 2000, an unprecedented achievement for this injury-prone pair. It was a crucial factor in England's victory over the West Indians. With both bowlers in their early 30s, it was all the more important to shield them from overwork in domestic cricket, while supporting them with the ECB physiotherapist and fitness coaches.

The summer of 2002 began well for England. The Sri Lankans were dispatched 2-0, admittedly in conditions favourable for seam bowling.

And when India were subsequently beaten by 170 runs at Lord's, Hussain having scored 155, England's confidence was high. However, neither Michael Vaughan's glorious 197, nor the stinging pace and leaping bounce of debutant Steve Harmison, could drive home England's advantage at Nottingham. The Indians capitalised upon this reprieve by squaring the series at Leeds. Although Hussain's rich vein of form continued (110), Tendulkar (193), Dravid (148) and Ganguly (128) set about the England bowlers as India won by an innings and 46 runs. With the winter Ashes series next up, there was concern for Andrew Flintoff's fitness after he suffered a double hernia, a legacy of the strain imposed by his long run-up. A bore draw ensued on a featherbed at the Oval where Vaughan's mighty score of 195 was trumped by an even bigger one by Dravid (217).

The winter Ashes series was disastrous. Thorpe had to withdraw because of personal reasons. Neither Gough nor Flintoff were fit to play. Gough's knee problem had not been cured and Flintoff could not run. Simon Jones had already sustained a rib injury before a horrific cruciate injury at Brisbane brought his tour to an end. Trescothick could not throw because of a shoulder problem.

A bruised hip ruled Crawley out of the second and third Tests. Stewart's bruised hand forced him to miss the fourth. After missing the opening Test through injury, Harmison broke Giles's left wrist in the nets, sidelining the spinner for the rest of the series. Caddick's sore back kept him out of the third. Substituting for Jones, Chris Silverwood managed only four overs in the third Test at Perth before breaking down with an ankle injury. Alex Tudor was struck on the head by a Brett Lee thunderbolt in the same match. Craig White missed the final Test with a muscle injury while Jeremy Snape – a one-day specialist – broke his thumb facing Lee. England employed no fewer than 31 players on this star-crossed tour.

At Brisbane, Hussain made the mistake of putting Australia in to bat, although Fletcher admitted he had agreed with the decision. Matthew Hayden made 197, having been dropped four times, while Ponting made 123 as Australia thundered to a total of 492. Lacking a full complement of bowlers, Jones having been stretchered off, Caddick (3-108) and Giles (4-101) did well to contain the Australian assault. But after a spirited first-innings reply of 325 with Trescothick (72), Butcher (54), Hussain (51) and Crawley (69 not out) recording half-centuries, England collapsed pathetically in their second innings, being dismissed for 79 and losing by 384 runs.

In each of the first four Tests, Australia never made less than 456 in their first innings. However England had the consolation of unveiling a new world-class batsman in Michael Vaughan. He made three huge hundreds in this series, the third of which (183), at Sydney, helped take England to an astonishing 225-run victory. Butcher made a vital first-innings ton (124), while Caddick's valedictory seven-wicket haul polished off the remaining Australian resistance.

Had McGrath and Warne been fit to play, though, it is doubtful whether England would have won.

With England losing the Ashes series 4-1, Fletcher and Hussain decided in was time for radical surgery. They sought a new team to be built around Vaughan, Trescothick and Harmison. As doughtily as Stewart and Butcher had played for England, Fletcher wondered whether they had become too 'punch drunk' with defeat to serve in an Ashes-winning side. Even the fiercely combative Hussain seemed to be having doubts about his ability to rise above the wreckage.

Another wretched 2003 World Cup campaign ensued. The England players had not wanted to play in a group game in Zimbabwe. The political situation was worsening with democracy under increasing threat. Some were uncomfortable about morality of playing there. But the British government would not issue a directive on whether England should play. With the ICC unprepared to intervene, this left the ECB with an awkward decision, knowing that British firms still traded with Zimbabwe and British Airways flights continued to operate in and out of Harare. The ECB also feared the adverse financial consequences of forfeiting the game. There was the possibility that South Africa might cancel their summer tour of England as a gesture of solidarity with Zimbabwe. But once a Zimbabwe rebel group began issuing death threats to any England player arriving in the country, the ECB felt it had no option other than to withdraw the team on grounds of personal security. Understandably, England did not perform very well in the competition, being eliminated in the first round.

After England had scraped a draw in the first Test against the visiting South Africans, Hussain decided to relinquish the captaincy. Vaughan was appointed in his place. Although he lost his first Test match in charge, at Lord's, Vaughan steered England to a highly creditable 2-2 series draw. The South Africans proved to be tough opponents. Their abrasive young skipper Graeme Smith led from the front, scoring double centuries at Edgbaston and Lord's. Although England lost by an innings and 92 runs at Lord's, Flintoff gave further notice of his pounding power with the bat (142).

County champions-elect Sussex then provided England with their match-winner at Nottingham. Test debutant James Kirtley proved unstoppable on a wearing surface with his swingers and shooters. His second-innings figures of 6-34 enabled England to win by 70 runs. This was after Butcher (106), Hussain (116), Stewart (72) and fellow new-boy Ed Smith (64) had taken advantage of the easier batting conditions on the first two days. But at Leeds, the momentum was lost once more as South Africa recovered from a poor start to win by 191 runs with Gary Kirsten (130) and Kallis (9-92) their principal match-winners.

And so to the Oval for the final Test. South Africa flew out of the traps, putting 362 runs on the board on day one for the loss of four wickets. Herschelle

Gibbs made 183 and South Africa eventually totalled 484, apparently safe from defeat. It was here that England began to play like the Australians, scoring at almost four runs per over. Trescothick set the tone with a crunching innings of 219. Thorpe then biffed 124, leaving Flintoff to bring up the rear with an explosive 95. England made 604/9 declared, giving their bowlers around five sessions to win the game. They did not need as much time as this, though. Harmison rattled the South Africans with his speed and lift while Martin Bicknell probed them with lateral movement. The South Africans were in a pickle at close of play on the fourth day, having made 185/6, only 65 ahead. Little did we know that this 'all guns blazing' fightback would provide the springboard for an Ashes victory two years later.

Hussain's part in that transformation was pivotal. He consistently led from the front. Patriotic to the core, he was zealous in all that he did, with the possible exception of fitness routines like long-distance running, which he did not enthuse over, making him less a pupil of Gooch and Stewart than Vaughan proved to be. He was uncompromising in his demands for performance improvement, though, assiduous in practice sessions, paying close attention to technical and tactical detail. He was also massively courageous, as he demonstrated in the extreme heat of Colombo in 2001. Hussain had sustained a hip strain early in the match, but insisted on remaining at his post until England had won. By this time he could hardly walk.

Although renowned for his incandescent outbursts, particularly after an avoidable dismissal, Hussain could control his temper quickly when the situation demanded, such as at a press conference. He generally handled the media in a helpful, open-handed manner, realising that there was little mileage in defensiveness and negativity. He was tough-minded but understanding and supportive of team-mates experiencing rough patches. There was a period, during his captaincy, when in the course of 18 Test innings he averaged less than 13 runs. He never forgot the generous support his team gave him during that bleak period.

He and Fletcher seemed to complement one another well although they did not agree on everything. Hussain was intensely proud to lead his country. His tearful reaction when relinquishing the captaincy said as much. Notwithstanding the heavy Ashes defeats suffered, under his watch England improved considerably.

It was on the October 2003 tour of Bangladesh that Vaughan laid down his marker. He wanted England to be fitter and stronger than ever before. They spent rainy days pounding away in the gym while bonding closely as a unit. Fletcher's bowling coach, Troy Cooley, helped the pace bowlers become more proficient in reverse swing and in cutting the ball, essential skills when bowling on the slow, dusty surfaces of the Indian subcontinent. Fletcher also recommended that Simon Jones place his fingers wider either side of the seam to enable him to swing the ball more. Although England lost a three-match

Test series in Sri Lanka, they showed impressive resilience in averting defeat at Galle, and also at Kandy where Vaughan led the rearguard action with a century (105). Fletcher was pleased that lower-order batsmen were helping England to bat longer.

The trail of glory began in Jamaica in March 2004. Harmison had spent the winter training with Newcastle United. He responded well to the rigorous demands made of him at St James' Park, arriving in the Caribbean in the best shape of his life – and how it told! He was unplayable at Sabina Park, returning figures of 7-12 in the West Indian second innings. At one stage, Vaughan had eight catchers in the slip and gully regions. The West Indies made only 47 and lost by ten wickets.

I caught sight of Harmison's devastating spell on TV while waiting for a London train. There was a spring in his step that I had not seen before. Jogging to the crease with relaxed conviction, his black hair plastered with glistening sweat, with his exuberant leap, both arms flung aloft, he gave the impression of someone joyfully joining a beach rave, except the product was anything but fun-packed, as he delivered an incessant salvo of vicious thunderbolts that reared menacingly at the batsmen's throats. It is hard to reconcile his aggressive intensity here with the anguished waywardness that haunted his later Test career.

In Trinidad, Simon Jones swung England around with five second-innings wickets for 57. The West Indians lost by seven wickets. Then, in Barbados, Flintoff probed the West Indians' vulnerability against shorter-pitched balls outside their off stump, earning him first-innings figures of 5-58. It was his first Test 'five-for'. Not to be outdone, Matthew Hoggard broke the back of the West Indies second innings with a hat-trick, hastening their collapse to 94 all out.

But it was Graham Thorpe's outstanding unbeaten hundred (119) that enabled his bowling colleagues to seal a series victory in Barbados, England's first in the Caribbean since 1968. On a tricky wicket which threatened to derail his side's efforts, Thorpe resolutely defied the skidding, slinging speed of Fidel Edwards, the pounding pace of the whirling Tino Best and the canny leg-cutters of Corey Collymore, withstanding six hours of intense heat and humidity. Always resolute in defence, he cut and pulled rapaciously whenever safe to do so. His innings exuded bristling bravado. And yet his fierce combativeness contrasted oddly with an expression of vulnerability. His lips were pressed together as if suppressing sorrow, while his dark eyes seemed touched by loss. The sunblock he thinly applied to his face accentuated his state of exhaustion, which was apparent whenever he wearily emptied his helmet of accumulated perspiration. But nothing distracted him as he steadily chipped away at the West Indian lead, finally overhauling their first innings total of 224 by two runs. As a result of their eight-wicket victory in Bridgetown, England's ICC ranking went up to third. England's ambition of a 4-0 series win was denied, however, by Brian Lara's gala in Antigua as he compiled an unbeaten score of 400, snatching back the world record for the highest individual Test innings from Matthew Hayden.

The summer of 2004 featured the 'Magnificent Seven', comprising England's complete domination of New Zealand who were beaten 3-0, and the West Indians who were defeated 4-0. Middlesex opener Andrew Strauss made a century (112) against the Kiwis on his Test debut at Lord's while wicketkeeper Geraint Jones made his maiden Test ton (100) against the same opponents at Leeds in only his second Test appearance.

The West Indian series was also a personal triumph for Kent batsman Robert Key who scored 221 runs in the first innings at Lord's and an unbeaten match-winning 93 at Old Trafford. It was a prosperous summer for Ashley Giles who took 24 West Indian wickets during the four-match series, while Steve Harmison's 21 wickets against New Zealand and 17 against the West Indians pushed him into top place in the ICC's world bowler rankings. Not to be outdone, Flintoff became the world's leading all-rounder. England seemed to be on an unstoppable roll, with their summer successes moving them up to second on the ICC ladder, 20 points behind Australia.

The summer of 2004 represented an important change in my life which led me back to county cricket after a 40-year absence. I had been pushing myself far too hard at work: co-ordinating a major departmental reconstruction; setting up a new county-wide housing support scheme with 11 constituent district or borough councils; and leading preparations for a comprehensive review of adult social care services by the national inspectorate. Meanwhile my caring commitments had to be accommodated.

The epileptic seizures that brought me to a halt were probably a blessing. Being no longer able to race around in my car, as I had been doing for years, I had to reorganise my life, both at work and outside. This included negotiating extra support for my mum so she was no longer so reliant upon my direct help. In reducing my hours of work to manageable proportions, I also agreed a flexible nine-day fortnight work pattern, allowing me to resume watching Sussex County Cricket Club.

Reliance upon public transport was actually a boon, offering more preparatory time for the many meetings I attended, helping me become more efficient and productive. I also loved the days I spent at various Home Counties cricket grounds, notably Arundel, Horsham and Hove. My visits to mum became less like a frenzied duty call and more like a companionable day out. With more of mum's care needs being met by health and social care staff, it was possible to find time to wheel her along Hastings promenade on warm, sunny days or to watch tennis, cricket or a video together. It enabled us to rediscover the pleasure of being together which had become lost under an accumulation of urgent care tasks.

England's tour of South Africa in the winter of 2004/05 was the first series that I was able to follow closely in around 15 years. Having neglected myself I got back into shape at a local gym while watching the coverage on Sky TV. Andrew Strauss was outstanding, topping the England batting averages with 77.28, having made three crucial Test centuries. He batted with complete conviction, peppering the cover boundary with beautifully timed drives. Having remedied a former technical weakness outside his off stump, Marcus Trescothick scored prolifically, too, particularly when his side needed this most. At Durban, Strauss (132) and Trescothick (136) put on a 273-run first-wicket stand, turning a game that England were losing into one they were winning, before poor light on the final afternoon intruded. When the umpires ended play, South Africa were placed perilously at 290/8, 88 runs short of their victory target, with 15 overs remaining. In the fourth Test at Johannesburg, Trescothick hammered 180 in the style of Matthew Hayden, giving England a winning opportunity which Hoggard seized with the ball.

Among the bowlers, Flintoff, with 23 wickets at 24.95 each, and Hoggard, with 26 at 25.50, took the honours. Hoggard's 12-205 at Johannesburg proved to be a series-winning performance. His in-swingers troubled the South African left-handers, particularly Graeme Smith, whose tendency to shuffle across his crease left him vulnerable to lbw dismissals. Hoggard took his wicket in this way on three occasions in the series.

South African-born batsman Kevin Pietersen made his debut for England in the subsequent one-day series, having qualified on the basis of his mother's British nationality. Pietersen seemed oblivious to the hostile reception he received from the South African crowds. In fact he relished it. As Duncan Fletcher had stressed, England had to bat aggressively against the Australians, scoring at around four runs per over, if there was to be sufficient time to dismiss their strong batting line-up twice. On the basis of his one-day performances, Pietersen seemed to fit this bill perfectly. Regrettably, his selection for the Ashes team would result in Graham Thorpe's exclusion, which appeared rough justice given Thorpe's battling qualities that he displayed once again, scoring 118 not out at Durban and 86 at Pretoria.

As the Ashes hype soared into overdrive, fired by England's emphatic Twenty20 victory over Ponting's men at the Rose Bowl, I first became acquainted with Eminem's 'Lose Yourself'.

It was a new millennium but the beat went on. And it still stirred my pulse. There was feisty Polly Harvey with her scalding lyrics, squally guitar and growling bass. There was the petulant drawl of the insouciant Strokes, reminiscent of The Velvet Underground and Iggy Pop. There was the raw blues of The White Stripes, and the haunting, warbling lament of transgender Antony Hegarty of Antony and the Johnsons. And there was 'Rock el Casbah', a superb Arabic makeover of the Clash song, sung by French-Algerian singer and activist Rachid Taha. But my song of the early 2000s is 'Lose Yourself'.

Hip-hop may not be to everyone's taste. It wasn't to mine until I heard 'Lose Yourself'.

It is a stonking, adrenaline-pumping track. No wonder it is such a favourite among sports competitors psyching themselves up for a big, winning performance. It begins with a synth-pop wash, topped by a plaintive piano phrase. Then a throbbing guitar cuts in, steadily growing in intensity as Eminem cranks up the urgency of his message. He demands to know, if we had just one chance to seize our prized ambition, would we take it. Jabbing us in the chest with the force of the song's sprung rhythm and his punchy rap, Eminem insists that success is the only option, failure is not. The tinkling piano drifts in and out of the chorus, but there is no letting up. It is a simply a case of do or die. Finally, an exhausted Eminem signs off, wearily reminding us that we can do anything we set our mind to. As Fletcher's England cricket team girded themselves for their biggest challenge yet, 'Lose Yourself' had stirring resonance.

As everyone knows, England prevailed. The Ashes were recovered after a 16-year absence. In such a hard-won, close victory, the margins of performance between the two sides might have been slender, but they were crucial. For the first time in almost twenty years, England's planning was informed by better intelligence than the Australians'. Captain Michael Vaughan, head coach Duncan Fletcher and batting and bowling coaches Matthew Maynard and Troy Cooley spent much time with analyst Tim Boon in studying video footage of the opposition. They rigorously examined technique, the shots played by their batsmen, their favoured scoring zones, their means of dismissal and potential vulnerabilities. The areas targeted by the Australian bowlers were studied carefully, too, taking in varieties of pitch, flight, spin, cut and swing, and their preferred field placements and so on. It was only after Fletcher's appointment that England's preparations became so systematic and forensic. The insights gathered here provided a basis for focused practice sessions and detailed game plans which Vaughan, as captain, had the freedom to adjust during a game as he saw fit.

Out of such analyses came the successful plan to put two men on the drive for the aggressive Matthew Hayden and probe his defence outside the off stump with conventional and reverse swing. At Manchester, Hayden became so concerned about countering the reverse swing, he had difficulty in reading that he shuffled too far over to the off side, exposing the leg stump which Flintoff targeted and hit. Hayden completed his Test career with an average score of 50.73. In this series, however, he managed 35.33 with this average belatedly inflated by his century at the Oval (138). Another prolific dasher, Adam Gilchrist, was shackled by Flintoff bowling from around the wicket on or just outside the line of off stump at high pace, confusing Gilchrist with an awkward angle of attack, persistent pace and darting movement both in and out. On four occasions Gilchrist was dismissed by a catch at the wicket or in the slip or gully region. He completed his Test career with an average of 47.6 but in this series he mustered only 22.62.

The Merlyn bowling machine proved very successful also in helping the England batsmen hone their technique against Warne as it was capable of replicating his variety of deliveries, his spin and dipping flight. But Warne still took 40 English wickets at 19.92 each. Importantly, though, Strauss played him with increasing confidence as the series progressed, helped by his intense practice with 'Merlyn'.

Secondly, the key targets set by Fletcher's 'think tank' were achieved. In order to create the necessary momentum for pressuring the Australians, it was agreed that England should aim to make at least three first-innings scores of 400 plus in no more than 130 overs. While England achieved this on three occasions – at Edgbaston and Trent Bridge, where they won, and at Manchester, where they almost won – not once did Australia make so many. Moreover England reversed the pattern of previous Ashes contests by scoring their runs at a slightly faster rate (3.9 per over) than the Australians (3.7), and although the margins were fine, Ponting's men were disconcerted by the forcefulness and confidence of the English batsmen. Fletcher was keen to see lower-order resistance, too, and at Trent Bridge and the Oval this was evident as Hoggard and Giles took England to a tight victory in the former, while Giles helped protect England's 2-1 lead in the latter. Prompted by Troy Cooley the fast bowlers operated as a tight unit, capable of delivering two out of three balls in the right area and on the right line. Previous England pace attacks had lacked this degree of consistency.

Thirdly, England had the better captain in Vaughan. Whereas Ponting was easily rattled, exhibiting indecision, defensiveness, and slowness in reacting to mounting pressure, Vaughan was cool, alert, flexible, steely, tactically imaginative, and prepared to take risks. At lunch on the final day at the Oval, Vaughan was worried that the England batsmen might sell themselves short in their attempt to defend their narrow series lead. He was concerned that an over-defensive approach might allow the Australians to take control and square the series. He therefore instructed Pietersen to 'stop messing about and go out and express yourself'. Pietersen did as he was bid and smashed 35 runs off Brett Lee's first three overs after lunch. Pietersen went on to record a dismissively aggressive, match-saving hundred (158), off only 187 balls, and containing 15 fours and seven sixes, thereby trumping Botham's big hitting record at Old Trafford in 1981. As for Vaughan's coolness under pressure, his captaincy during the anguished final stages of the Edgbaston Test bears testimony to that. And his handling of his team's disappointment at not winning the Manchester Test was exemplary, pointing out how ecstatic the Australians were about drawing the game. Vaughan rightly interpreted this as an expression of inferiority. Vaughan was rarely wrong-footed by his opponents. On one occasion when Ponting was foolish enough to 'sledge' him, he made the cutting retort, 'You're no Steve Waugh. Get back to second slip.'

Fourthly, England were able to bat first in four Tests, helped by Ponting's mysterious decision to put England in to bat at Edgbaston. This meant that England had the better batting conditions in four Tests. It also meant that their batsmen were not exposed to Warne on a wearing final-day surface in three out of the five Tests, although they did have to bat out the final day at the Oval. The hairy fourth-day run chase at Trent Bridge indicated how much of a challenge this might have been had they also needed to do this at Edgbaston and Manchester.

Fifthly, the Australians seemed to be perplexed by reverse swing. At least this was the impression given by their media which described the phenomenon as if it was some startling anthropological discovery. It almost defies belief that the Australians were unaware of the Pakistani tricks of the trade, having faced Sarfaz Nawaz, Wasim Akram and Waqar Younis. However knowledge of the weapon is one thing, thwarting it is another.

Sixthly, the Australians were guilty of complacency. Both Hayden and McGrath boldly predicted a 5-0 drubbing of England after the hosts' disappointing performance at Lord's. Ricky Ponting's decision to put England in at Edgbaston was surely borne out of arrogance. It seemed incredible that he should have done so after losing his premier fast bowler, Glenn McGrath, to a ligament injury during a warm-up session. In fact, McGrath's absence from the two Tests that England won was clearly important. And as the Australians faced the prospect of defeat, they began to gripe increasingly about England's use of substitute fielders. A moaning team is often a losing one.

'Feels Like We Only Go Backwards'

2006 – 2012

England won 40 per cent of 85 Tests played between November 2005 and August 2012

2006–2012
Harder Than You Think

When I resumed watching county cricket in 2004, it became immediately clear of how much had changed in the 40 years I had been away. The fielding was considerably more athletic and agile. With reflexes sharper, spectacular catches were taken almost as a matter of course. I discovered that my original home county side, Sussex, had employed a baseball coach to help raise their standards in the field. It was exhilarating to see them in action. The standards that Colin Bland introduced in the mid-1960s had become commonplace. Of course, I had seen the baseball slides and the doubling up on ball chases on TV, but watching the action live made me realise just how swiftly the ball was pursued, and how powerful, rapid and accurate most of the returns were from the deep. The TV cameras had minimised this because of its narrower perspective.

As for the batting, the County Championship scoring rates seemed markedly faster than I remembered from my youth. In a game between Sussex and Glamorgan in 2005, a rate of four or five runs per over was maintained throughout a day of scintillating entertainment. During the same fixture in 1966, although Glamorgan achieved their victory target by scoring at an average rate of four runs per over, the overall run rate during the preceding two days of play averaged no more than 2.3. Even the supposedly brighter one-day game produced some sluggish rates of

256

scoring during the 1960s. This was illustrated in the first Gillette Cup Final of 1963, in which both Sussex and Worcestershire scored at an average 2.6 runs per over.

There seemed to be a greater intensity in the bowling I saw, too, with the close fielders chirping away continuously, either at one another or the batsmen, while the swapping-over process, at the end of an over, was commonly conducted at a canter. The modern game seemed more enjoyable to watch with the predatory fielding often proving as exciting as the batting and bowling. I liked this game. It was vibrant, highly competitive and briskly-paced. With the live county action seeming more attractive than the radio or TV Test coverage, my interest in the national side began to wane after 'The Greatest Series' of 2005, but this loss of appetite was also attributable to England's disappointing progress after that glorious summer.

In November 2005, England played a three-match Test series in Pakistan which they were expected to win. They failed lamentably, only avoiding a 3-0 clean sweep because of the merciful intervention of bad light in Faisalabad, with England on the rack at 164/6 while ostensibly chasing 285. Crucially, Vaughan's arthritic right knee had ruled him out of the first Test at Multan. England had been well on top for much of the game. Deputy captain Trescothick made a superb 193 in the first innings. His bowlers also stuck to their task admirably on a bland surface, dismissing Pakistan twice for below-par totals of 274 and 341, with Flintoff taking eight wickets in the match for 156. Despite having only 198 runs to find to win the game, England collapsed calamitously as a result of undisciplined batting, veering from a position of strength at 64/1 to 175 all out, allowing Pakistan to snatch victory by only 22 runs.

Thereafter, Pakistan grasped total control. Inzamam-ul-Haq scored centuries in each innings in the drawn game at Faisalabad while Mohammad Yousuf made a double century at Lahore where Pakistan won by a demoralising margin of an innings and 100 runs. The 'Rawalpindi Express', Shoaib Akhtar, and leg-spinner Danish Kaneria shared nine second-innings wickets as England subsided from 205/2, with Bell (92) and Collingwood (80) apparently in command, to 248 all out. The news was passed to me in my 'Transylvanian' bunker situated beneath County Hall, while my colleagues and I grappled to find necessary budget cuts without imperilling essential adult social care services.

The three-match series in India had a more positive outcome, although I was still not seeing much daylight actually or figuratively. At one point it seemed uncertain whether England could raise a full team at Nagpur. But the Ashes spirit was revived as the team scrapped together to achieve a worthy draw. They were helped considerably by young Essex opener Alastair Cook, who, on debut, scored a composed 60 and an unbeaten hundred (104). He had been drafted into the side just hours after his arrival from the West Indies where he had been touring with the England A team.

Cook had been summoned as an emergency replacement for Marcus Trescothick who had left the tour because of a stress-related illness, although this was not then known to be the reason. Monty Panesar, a Northamptonshire slow left-arm bowler with impressive command of flight, line and length, with the ability to produce biting turn, also enjoyed a memorable debut, excitedly trapping the great Sachin Tendulkar lbw for only 16.

Although England lost by nine wickets at Chandigarh, replacement captain Flintoff led from the front to achieve a 212-run victory at Mumbai. Here, he contributed a brace of boldly biffed half-centuries, and produced a match-winning burst of 3-14 in the Indian second innings which fell apart for just 100 runs. He was indebted also to the determined batting of Andrew Strauss (128) and debutant Owais Shah (88) in the first-innings. After previous false starts, James Anderson confirmed his pedigree as a top Test performer, taking six wickets in the match for 79 runs. However, the most surprising hero was Hampshire's off-spinner Shaun Udal, who celebrated his 37th birthday and his final Test cap with match figures of 5-67. According to Hoggard and Flintoff, the inspiration for England's demolition of the Indian second innings had come in the dressing room as they played Johnny Cash's 'Ring of Fire' at incinerating volume before taking the field. As the hard-rocking Australian band AC / DC claimed, 'Rock 'n' Roll Ain't Noise Pollution'.

But as well as England had fought in India, the team which had taken them to Ashes glory was breaking up as injuries took their toll. Vaughan had not played at all in India, neither had Giles who was struggling with a hip injury. Simon Jones's career seemed in doubt, too, because of a persistent ankle problem that had emerged at Trent Bridge in 2005. Although Trescothick returned to the Test side during the summer of 2006, his stay would be brief as his stress-related illness returned, bringing his illustrious Test career to a premature close. At this time little was known about the impact of depression upon sportsmen and women. The wild media speculation concerning the absence of players such as Trescothick only intensified their torment as they struggled with an illness which is debilitating both mentally and physically.

As for Vaughan, he had sought specialist treatment for his knee during the winter of 2005/06 which encouraged his ambitions of a comeback during the following summer. Meanwhile, he remained upbeat about resuming his international career. However, as Sussex took control of the County Championship game with Yorkshire at Arundel in 2006, with former Zimbabwe Test batsman Murray Goodwin (235) flaying the Yorkshire attack, Vaughan was conspicuous by his absence in the field. No explanation was given, but those watching feared the worst. Vaughan's absence was so protracted that he had to bat at seven. As he shuffled tentatively to the wicket with Yorkshire in dire straits, he rightly received an enthusiastic reception from all present. Alas, his stay was all too brief. Having played a sumptuous, trademark cover drive for four, with elegance and power perfectly aligned, he succumbed to

Yasir Arafat's next delivery, a fully-pitched ball that cut back and trapped him in front of his stumps. The osteoarthritis in his right knee clearly impeded his movement, at the wicket and in the field. I wondered then whether I had seen him play for the last time. Actually, I did see him play once more. It was not an auspicious occasion for him or for Yorkshire, though. Vaughan's stumps were wrecked by Rana Naved-ul-Hasan's hooping swing, after he had made only five runs. Following his dismissal Yorkshire subsided for a paltry 89 runs, to lose by an innings and 261 runs.

With Jones unavailable through injury and Harmison continuing to blow hot and cold, the heavily-built Flintoff undertook a ruinous burden of responsibility with the ball. The jarring impact of bowling long spells on unforgiving surfaces finally told on his ankles. England's previously potent pace attack was in disarray. Anderson had bowled well at Mumbai but Hampshire's Chris Tremlett was as yet untried, while Durham's Liam Plunkett was a mere novice at Test level, despite some encouraging performances against the Sri Lankans.

Duncan Fletcher's answer was to blood the promising 6ft 4in Lancashire quick bowler Sajid Mahmood in the opening summer Test at Lord's. He proved decidedly slippery in his first spell, dismissing three Sri Lankan batsmen, including Kumar Sangakkara, as the visitors tumbled to 192 all out. But despite gaining a 359-run first innings lead, thanks mainly to the efforts of Pietersen (158) and Trescothick (106), England were unable to force victory. The three-match series ultimately ended in a disappointing 1-1 draw. Pietersen seemed to be the only England batsman capable of mastering Muralitharan. His century (142) at Edgbaston proved decisive as England won by six wickets. But even he had difficulty contending with Muralitharan at Trent Bridge where the Sri Lankan spin bowler took 8-70 in England's second innings to bring about a 134-run victory.

Like Vaughan, Flintoff was ruled out of the four-match Test series against Pakistan. After a high-scoring draw at Lord's, England crushed Pakistan by an innings and 120 runs on a fiery surface at Old Trafford. Both Cook (127) and Bell (106 not out) made successive Test centuries, allowing England to declare at 461/9, the visitors having been blasted out for only 119 in their first innings with Harmison taking 6-19. The Pakistanis did little better in their second innings as Harmison and the rapidly improving Panesar shared ten wickets equally. At Leeds, a game that appeared destined for another high-scoring draw suddenly lurched England's way on the final day. Defying cries of 'traitor' from the watching British Pakistani contingent, Mahmood ran through the visitors' middle and late order, taking 4-22. Baron Tebbit might have been as interested by Sajid's reception as with his achievement.

Mahmood had the physique, athleticism and aggression to have been a top pace bowler. His approach to the wicket was relaxed and rhythmic while his action was high, flowing, and economical, capable of producing genuinely fast, swinging deliveries. I watched him at action at Hove during the summer of 2007. He seemed miffed that he had been ignored until Sussex openers Chris Nash and Richard Montgomerie had put on 78 runs in apparent comfort. His indignation was understandable because Anderson and Smith had bowled like drains before him. Mahmood reacted with a steaming spell, as hostile as I had ever seen on Hove's then dry, slow, low track. Immediately he achieved sharp lift, raising puffs of dust whenever he banged the ball hard into the slumbering surface. It was as if the wicket was wincing at his rough treatment. In next to no time he had dismissed both openers: Montgomerie caught at the wicket and Nash snaffled in the slips. Having had both of them hopping about, ducking and even diving, beneath his salvo of deadly, skidding bouncers, Mahmood astutely slipped in the fuller, swinging deliveries, which brought about their downfall.

Lydia, our daughter, had accompanied me on this occasion, intending to enjoy a long read in the Sussex sun, but she was briefly distracted by Mahmood's 'head-hunting', causing her to remark, 'I hadn't realised cricket was such a dangerous game. Couldn't someone become seriously hurt?' As we now know, someone was, when Phillip Hughes tragically lost his life in 2014. As for Mahmood, he rarely exhibited such sustained hostility thereafter. Frustratingly inconsistent, the nascent talent that had once attracted Duncan Fletcher's attention slipped away. It was a great shame, not only for Mahmood, but for other British Asians who are significantly under-represented in English first class cricket.

The fourth Test against the Pakistanis erupted with controversy after Darrell Hair, the senior umpire, declared that the ball, which was to be replaced, had been doctored. Furious at his implication of cheating, the Pakistan players refused to return to the field after tea, ultimately forfeiting the match. It was the first incident of its kind in 129 years of Test cricket.

From an English perspective, the winter Ashes series was a fiasco. An injury-ravaged England team was ill-prepared to face their boot camp-hardened opponents, hell bent on revenge for their 2005 defeat. The Australians were unbeaten since their Ashes loss, winning 11 out of 12 Tests. Australia's 2005 stars remained in fine fettle, while their new additions – Mike Hussey, Andrew Symonds and Stuart Clark – made a much greater impact than England's Ashes debutants – Cook, Anderson and Mahmood. Mike Hussey averaged 91.60 with the bat, while Andrew Symonds averaged 58, whereas Cook managed just 27. Australian seamer Stuart Clark with 26 Ashes wickets at 17.03 was also more penetrative than either Mahmood (five wickets at 52.8) or Anderson (five wickets at 82.6).

Harmison's first ball at Brisbane was taken at second slip. That wayward delivery seemed to epitomise the ragged, brow-beaten performance of the England squad. Despite excellent batting performances from Collingwood (206) and Pietersen (158) at Adelaide, their sterling efforts were shamefully squandered in a hapless second-innings collapse. As was the case with Ian Botham, the burden of captaincy inhibited Flintoff's all-round talents. And with Flintoff's troublesome ankle preventing him from bowling at full pace, the Australians took advantage. Flintoff's batting did improve as the series progressed, but only Pietersen and Collingwood batted with authority and success in this one-sided affair.

Fletcher seemed unduly swayed by the 2005 success, investing excessive faith in yesterday's men, notably Ashley Giles and Geraint Jones both of whom had poor series. Giles took just three wickets in the first two Tests for 262 runs whereas Panesar took eight on his recall at Perth. As for Jones, the Australians ruthlessly exposed his batting limitations. In six completed Test innings, Jones realised 63 runs at an average of 10.5. His replacement, Chris Read, proved no better with the bat despite being a superior stumper. Although Cook had an indifferent series, he made 116 at Perth sharing a 170-run second-wicket partnership with Bell (87), but this was insufficient to avert a 206-run defeat.

The England bowling was awful. In 2005, the England pace attack stifled and shook the Australian batting. Here, it could have been filed under 'buffet fare'. Flintoff bowled well at Brisbane in a losing cause, but spluttered thereafter. Hoggard took 7-109 at Adelaide as Australia amassed 513 in reply to England's 551, but was otherwise innocuous. Anderson was no better, and despite taking four wickets at Melbourne, Mahmood had to withstand heavy punishment from Hayden (153) and Symonds (156). On average, Mahmood went for over five runs an over. Australia were vastly superior in all aspects of the game, including mental strength, and deservedly won the series 5-0.

In a suitably buoyant mood they set off for the Caribbean, where they won the World Cup for the third time running, whereas England faltered in the second group stage, amid unwelcome publicity concerning Andrew Flintoff and the alleged 'Fredalo' incident. It seemed as if the 2005 Ashes victory was an over-celebrated dream.

England's head coach Duncan Fletcher was left to face the angry British pundits and cricket correspondents. He promptly resigned to be replaced by ECB Academy supremo Peter Moores. Some doubted Moores's ability to turn around England's fortunes, as he had with Sussex, not having played the game at international level. However, he responded quickly to the wicketkeeping problem by bringing in Matt Prior for his England Test debut against the West Indians, at Lord's.

Early in Prior's career with Sussex, Moores had suggested that he should don the gloves. Moores had been impressed with Prior's athleticism and quick reactions. The Johannesburg-born and Brighton-schooled young man had already proved his worth as an attractive and often brutal batsman. I can vouch for that having seen him obliterate strong county bowling attacks on several occasions, but I was aware that his wicketkeeping was inconsistent. His positioning was said to be occasionally faulty, leaving him to make hurried leaps and awkward takes. In his book, *The Gloves Are Off*, he said that his catching technique was insufficiently grooved. He proved to be a quick and determined learner, though. The concentrated remedial sessions he arranged with former Nottinghamshire and England stumper Bruce French were very successful in smoothing out the rough edges, enabling him to become a highly proficient, agile international 'gloveman'. Meanwhile, the sessions he spent with county pal Mushtaq Ahmed sharpened his reading of 'mystery' spin.

Prior enjoyed a remarkable Test debut at Lord's in 2007, scoring a rapid hundred (126). He was one of four centurions in England's first innings – the others being Cook (105), Collingwood (111) and Bell (109 not out). The West Indians creditably refused to cave in. Chanderpaul (74) led a fightback, joined by Dwayne Bravo (56) and wicketkeeper Ramdin (60), as the tourists made 437, 116 runs behind England's score. Despite Panesar's excellent figures of 6-129 the West Indians held out for a draw.

Having recovered from his broken finger, Michael Vaughan resumed the England captaincy at Leeds. His arthritic knee had enforced an 18-month absence from Test cricket. In celebration of his return, he made a ton (103) only to be upstaged by Pietersen's 226 as England reached a first-innings total of 570. England won by an innings and 283 runs with Ryan Sidebottom achieving match figures of 8-86.

At Manchester, the West Indian medium-paced bowler Darren Sammy took seven second-innings wickets for 66 on debut, but despite Chanderpaul's game resistance (116 not out), Panesar took 6-137 and England won by 60 runs. Panesar was also an architect of victory at Chester-le-Street with another 'five-for'.

The other summer visitors, India, were stronger opponents, though, winning the three-match series 1-0 after gaining a seven-wicket victory at Trent Bridge. The Indians had previously denied England victory at Lord's in the first Test with their last remaining batsmen Dhoni (76) and Sreesanth (4) at the crease. In the final Test at the Oval India ensured their 1-0 series lead remained intact after making a mammoth first innings total of 664, featuring a maiden Test ton from 36-year-old spinner Anil Kumble. India's left-arm seamer Zaheer Khan was the outstanding bowler of the series, displaying expert command of conventional and reverse swing.

A three-match series in Sri Lanka before Christmas also resulted in a 1-0 defeat, with Sri Lanka having slightly the better of the drawn game in Colombo and much the better of the one in Galle. Once again Muralitharan was the leading bowler on either side. In the second Test in Colombo, he took the 62nd five-wicket haul of his career. However, Cook had a good series. In making a back-to-the-wall century (118) in Galle, he became only the fourth player to make seven Test centuries before reaching his 23rd birthday. The Galle Test was a highly emotional occasion for it was the first Test match played there since the tsunami on Boxing Day 2004.

England's 2008 tour of New Zealand was very short – all three Tests were squeezed into March – but ultimately successful after a shambolic collapse in Hamilton had resulted in a 189-run defeat. Having replaced Prior, his former Sussex colleague, Tim Ambrose made a debut Test hundred at Wellington (102) setting up England's equalising 126-run victory. Then centuries from Pietersen (129), Strauss (177) and Bell (110), at Napier won both the game and the rubber. The man of the series award went deservedly to the curly haired left-arm fast-medium bowler Ryan Sidebottom, who picked up 24 wickets at an average cost of 17. Anderson also played a significant part in England's equalising victory at Wellington with match figures of 7-130, including a first innings 'five-for'.

Anderson's future England new-ball partner, Stuart Broad, performed well with the bat and ball in the final Test at Napier, although it was Panesar's left-arm spin which saw England home by 121 runs. His second-innings figures of 6-126 included the dismissals of four of New Zealand's top five batsmen. Nevertheless, New Zealand put up a spirited fight, particularly the 19-year-old tail-ender Tim Southee who smashed 77 runs from 40 balls, including nine sixes, in recording New Zealand's fastest Test fifty. It was a remarkable debut for Southee who, in returning first-innings figures of 5-55, produced the best bowling statistics of any New Zealander playing in their first Test match.

The first of the summer series was also against New Zealand. The rain-interrupted first Test ended in a draw although the tourists were thankful for Jacob Oram's century (101) on the final day for steering them away from the rocks. England were equally grateful to Monty Panesar at Old Trafford for turning a game which New Zealand were winning into one that they ultimately lost. Panesar's second innings figures of 6-37 skittled the Kiwis for 114 after they had established a 179-run first-innings lead. Thanks to Strauss's 12th Test ton (106) and solid support from Vaughan (48) and Pietersen (42), England reached their victory target of 294 for the loss of only four wickets. At Trent Bridge, Pietersen (115), Ambrose (67) and Broad (64) rescued England from a poor start to post a first-innings total of 364. Anderson then cut a swathe through the New Zealand first innings batting, taking 7-47, while Sidebottom did much the same in their second knock (6-67). England won by an innings and nine runs.

The South Africans provided a sterner test, though. They recovered well from a first-innings drubbing at Lord's, where Pietersen (152) and Bell (199) put on 286 for the fourth wicket and England totalled 593/8 declared. After the South Africans had replied with only 247, their leading batsmen Smith (107), McKenzie (138) and Amla (104 not out) dug in the second time around, ensuring their side held out for a well-merited draw. Then at Leeds, South Africa turned the tables. Having gained a 319-run first innings lead, they drove home their advantage, winning by ten wickets. Although Collingwood (135) and Pietersen (94) gave England a realistic prospect of victory at Edgbaston, helping to set the tourists a 281-run winning target,

Graeme Smith's unbeaten big hundred (154) took his side to victory with five wickets to spare. On a wicket that gave equal encouragement to pace and spin bowling, England should have done better. At 93/4 the South African chase appeared to be faltering, but an attack comprising Sidebottom, Anderson, Flintoff and Panesar failed to perform as well as expected.

Michael Vaughan bade farewell to Test cricket at Edgbaston. He had batted poorly in this series. Taking the mounting media criticism to heart, he decided to fall upon his sword. He remained in first-class cricket for only one more year before deciding that his knee was no longer strong enough to withstand the rigours of professional cricket.

Pietersen stepped into Vaughan's shoes at the Oval, scoring a century (100) which helped England gain a consolatory six-wicket victory. He was therefore chosen to lead England in a two-match series in India in December. There was considerable doubt whether the matches would take place, though, after a horrific terrorist attack in Mumbai resulted in the deaths of 166 people. But as was the case before, it was decided that the show must go on.

England lost the first Test in Chennai despite being in control of the game for three and a half days. Strauss scored a century in each innings. But having been set 387 runs to win, India stormed home to win by six wickets, with Tendulkar (103) and Yuvraj Singh (85) leading the final assault with an unbroken fifth-wicket partnership of 163 runs.

The second Test had been originally designated to take place at Mumbai, but in light of the terrorist attack, it was moved to Chandigarh. The chilly, foggy conditions were hardy conducive to Test cricket. Pietersen led from the front, top-scoring for England with 144, but with England collapsing from 280/4 to 302 all out, he was left with a 151-run deficit at the halfway stage. Not that Indian captain Dhoni seemed interested in pursuing victory, allowing the game to peter out into a dull draw. Nevertheless, off-spinner Graeme Swann emerged from this short, stressful tour with his reputation enhanced, having spun the ball considerably while maintaining tight control. Swann's jesting persona belied a fierce determination to succeed at Test level. He had the necessary attributes, having mastery of disconcerting flight and drift with a well-disguised 'arm ball'. Above all, the degree of spin he imparted meant that he was capable of producing viciously turning off-breaks, as Ponting would discover when facing him at Edgbaston in 2009. He was also an agile and reliable slip fielder and an effective, bludgeoning, lower-order batsman.

After the England team had returned home it became apparent that a damaging rift existed between captain Pietersen and head coach Moores. Before the February tour of the Caribbean, the ECB responded by replacing Pietersen with Strauss, and Moores with the former Zimbabwe wicketkeeper/batsman Andy Flower. Flower had a brilliant Test record. He had a Test batting average of 51.54 and had been rated as one of the best wicketkeeper/batsmen in the world alongside Adam Gilchrist. Unlike Moores, Flower commanded respect not only because of his coaching ability but because of his prowess as a top Test player.

The Caribbean tour began very badly for England. West Indian pace bowler Jerome Taylor took 5-11 as he and his team-mates dismissed England for only 51 in their second innings to win the first Test by an innings and 23 runs. It was England's third-lowest innings total in their Test history, and a curious reversal of what happened during their previous visit to Jamaica, when Harmison inflicted a similar humiliation upon the 'Windies'. Although Strauss led a strong English recovery in the three remaining Tests, scoring a century in each, the West Indians clung on tenaciously to deny England victory at Antigua and Trinidad, therefore winning the series 1-0.

England had to wait until the West Indian visit in May to gain their revenge. This they did with ease, winning by ten wickets at Lord's, where debutant Durham seamer Graham Onions took 7-102 with his wobbling swing, and by an innings and 83 runs at Chester-Le-Street, where Anderson returned match figures of 9-125. Bopara scored a ton in each game while Cook notched one of his 'daddy' hundreds (160) at the Riverside. Although Taylor, the West Indian destroyer in Jamaica, was largely innocuous in both games, his new-ball partner Fidel Edwards was more challenging, notably at Lord's where he took 6-92 in the England first innings. It seemed as if the Australian trainers had done their work well in toughening up and sharpening the West Indian pace attack, raising their previously suspect fitness levels.

However, the main event of the summer of 2009 was a resumption of the Ashes contest. Although this was a tight, absorbing series of fluctuating fortunes, illuminated by memorable individual performances, both sides lacked the depth of quality that had made the 2005 rubber one of the greatest in the history of Test cricket. Determined not to lose the mind games, the generally diplomatic Andrew Strauss taunted Ricky Pointing with the observation that the Australians had 'lost their aura'. It stung Ponting all the more because it happened to be true. He had lost five world-class performers in Justin Langer, Matthew Hayden, Adam Gilchrist, Shane Warne and Glenn McGrath.

In the first Test at Cardiff Australia failed to nail an overwhelming advantage, allowing Anderson (21) and Panesar (7), the last Englishmen standing, to secure a draw by batting for over an hour together on the final afternoon. It was an incredible escape. Australia had accumulated 674 in their first innings for the loss of just six wickets – Ponting, who made 150, was one of four Aussie centurions. Facing a first-innings deficit of 239, England seemed lost at 70/5. Although Collingwood (74) held the fort for five and three quarter hours, even he could not have imagined that England's last pair would survive 69 balls to save the game.

The second Test at Lord's was a very different affair. Strauss (161) and Cook (95) put on 196 for the first wicket, feasting on the waywardness of the out-of-sorts left-armer Mitchell Johnson, who went for over six runs per over. England made 425 at a canter but Australia faced a considerably more challenging task as they began their reply. The floodlights were on while the misty, overcast conditions proved most sympathetic to the England swing bowlers. Anderson took 4-55 while Onions took 3-44. The Australians were toppled for 215. Batting again, England added a further 311 at over four per over, setting Australia 522 to win. Undeterred by his painful right knee, Flintoff gave it his all, bowling at the lightning pace that had formerly made him such a dangerous adversary. The five wickets he took for 92 eventually consigned Australia to a 115-run defeat, despite brave and aggressive knocks by Michael Clarke (136), Brad Haddin (80) and Mitchell Johnson (63). This was a fitting swansong from Flintoff who announced he would be retiring from Test cricket at the end of the series on account of his recurrent injuries.

Even without the injured Pietersen, England bossed the third Test at Edgbaston, too, only for Clarke (103) and North (96) to steer the Australians to a comfortable draw after rain had washed out the third day's play. So it came as a nasty shock when the Australians roared back at Leeds. Here they dismissed England on a seaming strip for only 102 with Siddle proving almost unplayable. After seizing a 343-run first-innings lead Australia won by an innings and 80 runs within three days.

But it was England who had the final say at the Oval. Having made 332 in their first innings, England took a stranglehold on the match when Stuart Broad (5-37) and Graeme Swann (4-38) dismissed Australia for 160. South South African-born Jonathan Trott patiently accumulated a magnificent, maiden Test century (119), while some lower order merriment left Australia needing 546 to win. At 217/2, and Ponting and Hussey batting serenely, the Australians were on course for an improbable victory. Then Flintoff made his final decisive intervention, brilliantly running out Ponting (66) with a direct hit. Hussey (121) successfully marshalled the lower order for a while, but eventually the England bowlers wore him down. Harmison's recall to the attack resulted in a late clatter of wickets, leaving the Australians 197 runs short and stripped of the Ashes.

The series was notable for the timely emergence of Anderson and Broad as world class fast bowlers. Throughout the rubber, Anderson swung the ball prodigiously and late, using conventional and reverse movement. No longer allowing his head to fall away in his delivery stride, he maintained tighter control, although he remained prepared to gamble with fuller-pitched balls in order to induce an imprudent drive.

Despite swinging the ball less than Anderson, Broad proved adept at achieving sharp movement off the seam, and, when in the groove, he had a knack of destroying sides with relentless spells of high intensity fast bowling. His 'five-for' at the Oval was one such example. Belying his choirboy appearance, Broad was a feisty competitor, seemingly more at ease with his hostility than Anderson whose snarling asides seem more petulant than threatening, as if pushed reluctantly into a confrontation by a macho older brother. And as stubbornly as Anderson has batted for England, Broad seemed to be the more talented player, at least before 2014 when he was struck on the head by a bouncer. Before then, Broad demonstrated a penchant for sizzling back-foot drives that at their best were reminiscent of the stroke play of the great Garry Sobers.

After recovering the Ashes, England drew creditably 1-1 with South Africa in the winter series. Late-order resistance held off their hosts in Pretoria while centuries from Cook (118) and Bell (140) put England on a winning course at Durban where Swann (9-164) and Broad (6-87) led their side to an innings victory. Onions and Swann denied South Africa at Cape Town with a heart-stopping last-wicket partnership, before Smith, with a second successive Test ton, set up an innings win for the hosts in Johannesburg.

It had been a good year for Matt Prior. After being restored to the England team in India he made one Test hundred and seven fifties, averaging 39.71 over the 15 Tests he played in 2009. His pugnacious batting and wicketkeeping made him a key member of an increasingly combative England side. Strauss (47.73), Collingwood (47.47), Bopara (46) and Cook (44) also enjoyed a successful year, as did Swann with 61 Test wickets at 29.54 and a batting average of 39.53. It was a more subdued one for Kevin Pietersen (39.25), though, a legacy no doubt of his feud with Moores and his Achilles injury. A mercurial personality who seemed to attract admiration more than affection, Pietersen, like David Gower before him, continued to be criticised for losing his wicket to injudicious shots. Meanwhile he maintained a Test batting average that placed him among the top ten England batsmen since the Second World War. Employing both classical and improvised shots, he was capable of taking a game away from strong opponents with glorious attacking stroke-play that few could emulate. His series-saving ton at the Oval in 2005 clearly illustrated this. And yet Duncan Fletcher insisted that Pietersen's cavalier flourishes were not the product of whim but of intense net practice during which he would rehearse the same shot repeatedly until satisfied that he had mastered it.

The 2010 cricket season began triumphantly for England as they won the ICC World Twenty / Twenty Championship in Barbados, its first ICC one-day international title. England also beat Bangladesh 2-0 and Pakistan 3-1 in the ensuing summer Test series. The latter series ended in high controversy, though, when it was discovered that some of the Pakistanis had been embroiled in a spot betting scandal. Three of the team – captain Salman Butt and fast bowlers Mohammad Asif and Mohammad Amir – were subsequently jailed for their crimes in November 2011. Their convictions questioned the legitimacy of the entire series.

Nevertheless, England travelled to Australia in good heart. After an initial wobble at the start of the Brisbane Test, England recovered strongly to crush the Australians in three of the four remaining Tests, running up huge totals and overpowering the Australian batsmen with high class seam bowling and off spin. The England batting averages were Steve Waugh-like. Leading the way was Alastair Cook who amassed 766 runs, averaging 127.66. Jonathan Trott (89), Ian Bell (65.80), Kevin Pietersen (60), Matt Prior (50.40) and Andrew Strauss (43.85) followed.

Only Ryan Harris and the persevering Peter Siddle made much impact with the ball for Australia, although Mitchell Johnson managed to disrupt England at Perth with match-winning figures of 9-82. Otherwise, his erratic, low-slung pace was treated disrespectfully. His 136.3 series overs conceded on average four runs apiece. The Barmy Army's targeting of Johnson's fragile self-belief was as effective as it was puerile. To the tune of the Beach Boys' song, 'Sloop John B', they repeatedly sang, 'He bowls to the left, he bowls to the right, Mitchell Johnson's bowling sh**e.' The singing was almost incessant when Johnson was in action with either ball or bat. His psychological destruction seemed to be a crucial factor in England's 3-1 victory. As for the Australian batting, only Mike Hussey (63.33), Shane Watson (48.33) and Brad Haddin (45) seemed capable of holding England back. Both Ponting (16.14) and Clarke (21.44) had particularly poor series, with Anderson (24 wickets at 26.04), Chris Tremlett (17 at 23.35) and Tim Bresnan (11 at 19.54) so dominant.

The glorious summit was finally reached in the summer of 2011 when the Sri Lankans were beaten 1-0 and the Indians thrashed 4-0. These twin victories took England to the top of the ICC World Test Championship, a position that they had last held, albeit unofficially, in January 1959. It had been a long, sharply undulating climb taking up most of my lifetime. Strangely, perhaps, I found England's long-awaited triumph anti-climactic, possibly because the Indians had capitulated so wanly. Cook, Bell and Pietersen racked up a succession of gigantic individual scores while an out-of-sorts Tendulkar could not manage a single Test ton.

The question was whether England could retain this crown having grafted so long and hard to grasp it. The answer was a resounding 'no'. The Pakistanis proceeded to wreck their party, just as they had done in 2005, steamrolling England 3-0 in a short series in January and February 2012. The series was hosted in Dubai and Abu Dhabi because of continuing political instability and terrorist activity in Pakistan. Curiously echoing events 53 years before, the England players thought they had been cheated, claiming that the Pakistani off-spinner, Saeed Ajmal 'threw'. As was the case in 1959, this was not the principal reason why England lost. Put simply, they did not play as well as their opponents. In the summer of 2012, South Africa ended the debate by snatching away the world title with an emphatic 2-0 series win. With Kevin Pietersen's alleged text message to the South Africans arousing ill-feeling among his colleagues, it was a dispiriting end to England's brief period of glory.

In choosing the song with which to close this diary, there were several worthy artists to consider, ranging from classy, yet sadly wasted, Amy Winehouse to percussive LCD Soundsystem, but I eventually plumped for Public Enemy and their confrontational hip-hop number, 'Harder Than You Think'. It was adopted by Channel 4 as its theme for the TV coverage of the 2012 Paralympics. Like Eminem's 'Lose Yourself', it is an uncompromising rallying call, set to a stirring horn sample taken from an obscure Shirley Bassey track. Public Enemy's message here is that, with the government seen as their principal adversary, rap is deemed to be an authentic voice of protest, aiming to arouse unity in a pursuit of black liberation. Considering themselves to be the true torch bearers of rap, Public Enemy take issue with rappers emerging in their wake, whom they berate for desecrating the purity of their political aims through self-aggrandisement and exploitation of other blacks. Irrespective of whether Public Enemy's presumption of moral superiority is justified, the propulsive force with which they deliver their message is as compelling as its content is challenging. Such visceral demands for political integrity have featured more often in popular music than its detractors might presume. As the selection of songs for this book suggests, popular music has embraced many harsh and edgy subjects. It's not just about hearts and flowers.

Final Thoughts

During the 60 years I have followed the England Test cricket team, its supporters have expected it to prosper, at least most of the time. It is a perspective which the media fosters. Their damning and sometimes virulent criticisms of England's defeats imply this, as if failure is perfidious. The England football team is punished by a vindictive media, too, when it loses important games, hence tabloid headlines such as 'Swedes 2 Turnips 1' and 'The Wally with the Brolly'.

If this represents a misalignment between expectation and reality, how has this arisen? Is it a vain vestige of imperialist privilege, or is it merely misplaced patriotic valour? For long gone are the days when Britain's superior strength could dictate victory on the battlefield or the sports field. And yet, contrary to Bill Bryson's opinion, Britain is not such a small island, at least in terms of its population size. At 63.2 million, Britain is the third largest nation in the European Union. More to the point, its population is 165 per cent greater than that of Australia and 22 per cent higher than that of South Africa, both of whom have significantly better Test match win percentages since the Second World War (see Appendix). On this basis it seems reasonable to question why the England Test cricket team has not performed better over the last 60 years. Whereas Australia has won almost half of the Test matches they have played in this period, England has won only a third.

After a 'Golden Age' during the 1950s, when the England team, under Hutton's and May's captaincy, won just over a half of the Test matches it played, it took the national side almost half a century before it came close to emulating that degree of success, with the English game taking an inordinate amount of time to catch up with the best examples overseas, and then only achieving this after the appointment of two foreign coaches, Duncan Fletcher and Andy Flower. And having caught up in 2005, the England team fell backwards, almost immediately, although injuries to its key players played an important part here. Even a subsequent recovery, between 2009 and 2011, resulted in only a brief restoration of glory. England's wretched performance in the 2015 World Cup confirmed just how far it had slipped behind the best and the rest in the one-day game, having been the World Twenty / Twenty champions as recently as 2010.

Thanks to the insights shared by Nasser Hussain, Michael Vaughan, Duncan Fletcher and Steve James, it is apparent that the shake-up in English cricket that took place after the millennium had a startling effect in raising the performance of its Test side. For the introduction of central contracts, better coaching, forensic intelligence and sharper fitness regimes, culminated in the recovery of the Ashes in 2005 and the capture of the world crown in 2011. Possibly Fletcher's and Flower's most notable achievements were to draw the very best performances from their most experienced players. Their unresolved problem, it seemed, was in succession planning, although that was not an issue they were able to address without wider ECB involvement.

The England Test team's pathetic capitulation in Australia during the 2006/7 and 2013/14 Ashes series underlined the degree of difficulty England has faced in replacing its declining or ailing stars quickly enough, despite the creation of a national academy and the greater competitiveness of the county game after its divisional reorganisation. The emergence of fine young Test players, such as Joe Root, Gary Ballance and Moen Ali, gives some cause for optimism. But what happens at the top of the pyramid is not the sole defining factor of success. Without a solid base in grass roots cricket, the top cannot sustain itself.

When I was at a state senior school, during the early 1960s, cricket was played and coached with a similar level of dedication and intensity as was expected in the classroom. Our inter-school games were highly competitive, often watched by many of our class-mates. This no longer appears to be the case, at least in the state sector. Interested youngsters can, of course, join local clubs or coaching schemes but only in an extracurricular capacity. Does this provide sufficient incentive in developing the leading English players of tomorrow, taking account of those from all ethnic backgrounds? Of course, the selling-off of state school playing fields and the constraints applied by the National Curriculum have hardly helped the game to flourish in the state-funded schools.

While I celebrate cricketing success and continue to be disappointed by failure, I remain largely philosophical about the achievements of my national and club sides. I suppose dad's message to me was not to expect too much from life. It is a lesson that has generally served me well without necessarily impeding my determination to succeed. Great expectations rest uneasily on my shoulders, and while my support of modest cricket and football teams has often left me disappointed and defeated, their unexpected triumphs have been so much sweeter. Take the glorious Ashes series of 1981 and 2005 or Burnley's improbable promotions to the Premier League in 1999 and 2014.

But dad belonged to a generation decimated by war, accustomed to privation and loss. He considered himself fortunate to have survived when some of his friends did not. For the most part, he accepted his lot with good grace. And when in later life he was stripped of his strength, personality and dignity, he resigned himself to that awful fate, too. It was left to me to expect more on his behalf, as befits someone born and bred in an age of greater entitlement.

Since my love of cricket became so entwined with caring responsibilities over the past 25 years, it seems appropriate to conclude with a brief observation about the current state of adult social care.

While the *Help for Heroes* initiative has campaigned well on behalf of all who have served in the British armed forces, particularly those who have suffered physically or mentally, its focus has been primarily on those involved in recent conflicts and their families. Arguably, the needs yesteryear's heroes have received less attention. Here, I refer not only those who fought in the Second World War, like dad, but also to those who sustained the war effort at home, like mum. So many of these heroes now struggle to receive adequate social care. Do they not deserve more than frequently delayed and rushed home visits by overstretched and minimally-trained care assistants, on little more than the minimum wage? That is, supposing they can obtain such a service. Do they not merit more than underfunded, hectic, and often cursory residential and nursing home care? And what about the millions that are compelled to fill the yawning gaps in the quality and quantity of these services?

Should the 5.2 million people in England, who provide such essential care, on an unpaid basis, ever develop a stronger voice with the 6.5 million people they care for, then politicians will find they have to answer to around one fifth of their electorates on this vexed subject. That, of course, might help re-align the inequitable resource allocations that currently impair the lives of cared-for people and those who look after them.

Appendix

LEADING ENGLAND BATTING AVERAGES

Minimum qualification: 1,000 runs and an average above 29.99 (Test records up to 1 March 2015)

Name	Runs	HS	Ave	Main playing period
Sir Len Hutton	6,971	364	56.67	1950s
Denis Compton	5,807	278	50.06	1950s
Peter May	4,537	285*	46.77	1950s
Tom Graveney	4,882	258	44.38	1950s
Rev. David Sheppard	1,172	119	37.80	1950s
Peter Richardson	2,061	126	37.47	1950s
Reginald Simpson	1,401	156*	33.35	1950s
Ken Barrington	6,806	256	58.67	1960s
Ted Dexter	4,502	205	47.89	1960s
Geoffrey Boycott	8,114	246*	47.72	1960s
Colin Cowdrey	7,624	182	44.06	1960s
Geoff Pullar	1,974	175	43.86	1960s
John Edrich	5,138	310*	43.54	1960s
Peter Parfitt	1,882	131*	40.91	1960s
Basil D'Oliveira	2,484	158	40.06	1960s
Bob Barber	1,495	185	35.59	1960s
Jim Parks junior	1,962	108*	32.16	1960s
M.J.K. Smith	2,278	121	31.63	1960s
Dennis Amiss	3,612	262*	46.30	1970s
Tony Greig	3,599	148	40.43	1970s
Keith Fletcher	3,272	216	39.90	1970s

Name	Runs	HS	Ave	Main playing period
Mike Denness	1,667	188	39.69	1970s
Brian Luckhurst	1,298	131	36.05	1970s
Derek Randall	2,470	174	33.37	1970s
Bob Woolmer	1,059	149	33.09	1970s
Alan Knott	4,389	135	32.75	1970s
David Gower	8,231	215	44.25	1980s
Graham Gooch	8,900	333	42.58	1980s
Chris Broad	1,661	162	39.54	1980s
Tim Robinson	1,601	175	36.38	1980s
Allan Lamb	4,656	142	36.09	1980s
Mike Gatting	4,409	207	35.55	1980s
Sir Ian Botham	5,200	208	33.54	1980s
Chris Tavaré	1,755	149	32.50	1980s
Graeme Fowler	1,307	201	35.32	1980s
Graham Thorpe	6,744	200*	44.66	1990s
Robin Smith	4,236	175	43.67	1990s
Alec Stewart	8,463	190	39.54	1990s
Michael Atherton	7,728	185*	37.69	1990s
Nasser Hussain	5,764	207	37.18	1990s
John Crawley	1,800	156*	34.61	1990s
Graeme Hick	3,383	178	31.32	1990s
Joe Root	1,732	200*	50.94	2000s
Kevin Pietersen	8,181	227	47.28	2000s
Jonathan Trott	3,763	226	46.95	2000s
Alastair Cook	8,423	294	46.02	2000s
Ian Bell	7,156	235	45.00	2000s
Marcus Trescothick	5,825	219	43.79	2000s
Michael Vaughan	5,719	197	41.44	2000s
Andrew Strauss	7,037	177	40.91	2000s
Matt Prior	3,920	131*	40.83	2000s
Paul Collingwood	4,259	206	40.56	2000s
Mark Butcher	4,288	173*	34.58	2000s
Andrew Flintoff	3,795	167	31.89	2000s

LEADING ENGLAND BOWLING AVERAGES
Minimum qualification: 50 wickets (Test records up to 1 March 2015)

Name	Wkts	Ave	Main playing period
Frank Tyson	76	18.56	1950s
Johnny Wardle	102	20.39	1950s
Jim Laker	193	21.24	1950s
Brian Statham	252	24.84	1950s
Alec Bedser	236	24.89	1950s
Tony Lock	174	25.58	1950s
Roy Tattersall	58	26.08	1950s
Trevor Bailey	132	29.21	1950s
Ken Higgs	71	20.74	1960s
Fred Trueman	307	21.57	1960s
John Snow	202	26.66	1960s
David Brown	79	28.31	1960s
David Allen	122	30.97	1960s
Ray Illingworth	122	31.20	1960s
Barry Knight	70	31.75	1960s
Fred Titmus	153	32.22	1960s
Ted Dexter	66	34.93	1960s
Bob Willis	325	25.20	1970s
Derek Underwood	297	25.83	1970s
Mike Hendrick	87	25.83	1970s
John Lever	73	26.72	1970s
Chris Old	143	28.11	1970s
Geoff Arnold	115	28.29	1970s
Geoff Miller	60	30.98	1970s
Tony Greig	141	32.20	1970s
Pat Pocock	67	44.41	1970s
Sir Ian Botham	383	28.40	1980s
Graham Dilley	138	29.76	1980s
Nick Cook	52	32.48	1980s
Neil Foster	88	32.85	1980s
Gladstone Small	55	34.01	1980s

Name	Wkts	Ave	Main playing period
Phil Edmonds	125	34.18	1980s
Derek Pringle	70	35.97	1980s
John Emburey	147	38.40	1980s
Norman Cowans	51	39.27	1980s
Eddie Hemmings	43	42.44	1980s
Angus Fraser	177	27.32	1990s
Dean Headley	60	27.85	1990s
Darren Gough	229	28.39	1990s
Dominic Cork	131	29.81	1990s
Andrew Caddick	234	29.91	1990s
Alan Mullally	58	31.24	1990s
Phillip DeFreitas	140	33.57	1990s
Devon Malcolm	128	37.09	1990s
Chris Lewis	93	37.52	1990s
Phil Tufnell	121	37.68	1990s
Chris Tremlett	53	27.00	2000s
Simon Jones	59	28.23	2000s
Ryan Sidebottom	79	28.24	2000s
Steven Finn	90	29.40	2000s
James Anderson	380	29.72	2000s
Stuart Broad	264	29.90	2000s
Graeme Swann	255	29.96	2000s
Matthew Hoggard	248	30.50	2000s
Steve Harmison	226	31.82	2000s
Tim Bresnan	72	32.73	2000s
Andrew Flintoff	219	33.34	2000s
Monty Panesar	167	34.71	2000s
Craig White	59	37.62	2000s
Ashley Giles	143	40.60	2000s

PROBABLY THE BEST ENGLAND TEAM OF MY LIFETIME:
Sir Len Hutton (captain)
Geoff Boycott or Alastair Cook
Ted Dexter
Kevin Pietersen
Ken Barrington
Andrew Flintoff
Sir Ian Botham
Alan Knott or Alec Stewart
Jim Laker
Johnny Wardle or Derek Underwood
Fred Trueman or Jimmy Anderson

Other reserves: Denis Compton, Peter May, Graeme Swann, Bob Willis.

Note: Had Denis Compton not been troubled so much by his knee during this period he would have been chosen in my first 11. There are many others I would have liked to find room for including: Alec Bedser, Colin Cowdrey, Tom Graveney, Brian Statham, John Edrich, David Gower, Graham Gooch, Ray Illingworth, Michael Atherton, John Snow, Darren Gough, Matthew Hoggard and Graham Thorpe.

INTERNATIONAL TEST RECORDS UP TO AND INCLUDING AUGUST 2005

1946-2005	P	W	D	L	T	Win%
Australia	504	230	151	121	2	45.6%
South Africa	215	84	71	60	0	39.1%
West Indies	404	145	137	121	1	35.9%
England	599	193	235	171	0	32.2%
Pakistan	315	98	135	82	0	31.1%
Sri Lanka	156	41	55	60	0	26.3%
India	383	86	174	122	1	22.5%
New Zealand	310	59	128	123	0	19.0%
Zimbabwe	83	8	26	49	0	9.6%
Bangladesh	40	1	4	35	0	2.5%

ENGLAND'S AND AUSTRALIA'S TEST RECORDS AFTER THE 2005 ASHES SERIES

2005-2012	P	W	D	L	T	Win%
Australia	75	44	14	17	0	58.7%
England	85	34	25	26	0	40.0%

Includes England's and Australia's respective home series against South Africa in 2012.

ENGLAND'S AND AUSTRALIA'S TEST RECORDS SINCE SECOND WORLD WAR

1946-2012	P	W	D	L	T	Win%
Australia	579	274	165	138	2	47.3%
England	684	227	260	197	0	33.2%

ENGLAND'S TEST RECORD SINCE SECOND WORLD WAR

	P	W	D	L	T	Win%
1946-1999 #	521	156	215	150	0	29.9%
1999-2005 $	78	37	20	21	0	47.4%
2005-2012 *	85	34	25	26	0	40.0%

\# Up to and including 1999 summer home series against New Zealand
$ Up to and including 2005 home Ashes series
* Test record after 2005 Ashes series

References

A Century of Great Cricket Quotes; David Hopps; Robson Books ©; 1998.

Chronicle of the 20th Century; Derrik Mercer (Editor); Longman ©; 1988.

A Corner of a Foreign Field: The Indian History of a British Sport; Ramachandra Guha; Picador ©; 2002.

A Social History of English Cricket; Derek Birley; Aurum Press ©; 1999.

A Spell at the Top; Brian Statham; Souvenir Press Ltd ©; 1969.

A Typhoon Called Tyson; Frank Tyson; William Heinemann (reprinted by permission of Random House Group Ltd ©); 1962.

*Anatomy of Brita*in; Anthony Sampson; Hodder and Stoughton ©; 1962.

As It Was; Fred Trueman; Pan Books (an imprint of Pan Macmillan, London ©); 2005.

Ashes Regained; The Coach's Story; Duncan Fletcher; Pocket books, an imprint of Simon & Schuster UK Ltd. Duncan Fletcher ©; 2005

Australia 55; Alan Ross; Constable & Co Ltd ©; 1985.

Basingstoke Boy: The Autobiography; John Arlott; Fontana (reprinted by permission of HarperCollins Publishers Ltd ©); 1992

Betrayal; The Struggle for Cricket's Soul; Graeme Wright; H.F. & G Witherby (Cassell imprint) ©; 1993.

Beyond a Boundary; CLR James; Yellow Jersey Press (reprinted by permission of Random House Group Ltd ©); 2005.

Bill Edrich: A Biography; Alan Hill; Andre Deutsch (reprinted by permission of Carlton Books ©); 1994.

Boycott on Cricket; Geoffrey Boycott; Partridge Press / Transworld Publishers Ltd; ©; Partcount Limited 1990.

Calling the Shots; My Story as England Captain; Michael Vaughan; Hodder & Stoughton ©; 2005.

Chucked Around; Charlie Griffith; Pelham Books ©; 1970.

Cricket Cauldron: With Hutton in the Caribbean; Alex Bannister; Pavilion Books ©; 1990.

Cricket Conflicts and Controversies; Kersi Meher-Homji; New Holland publishers.com ©; 2012.

Cricket at Hastings; Gerald Brodribb; Spellmount Ltd. ©; 1989.

Cricket at the Crossroads; Class, Colour and Controversy from 1967 to 1977; Guy Fraser-Sampson; Elliott and Thompson Limited Guy Fraser Sampson ©; 2011.

Cricket for South Africa; Jackie McGlew; Hodder and Stoughton ©; 1961.

Cricket from the Grandstand; Keith Miller; The Sportsmans Book Club ©; 1960.

Cricket Musketeer; Freddie Brown; Stanley Paul & Co Ltd ©; 1954.

Cricket Rebel; John Snow; Hamlyn Publishing Group Ltd ©; 1976.

Crisis? What Crisis? Britain in the 1970s; Alwyn Turner; Aurum Press Ltd; Alwyn Turner ©; 2009.

Dazzler; The autobiography; Darren Gough; Michael Joseph; Penguin Books©; 2001.

Denis Compton: The Untold Stories of the Greatest Sporting Hero of the Century; Norman Giller; Andre Deutsch (reprinted by permission of Carlton Books ©); 1997.

D'Oliveira; An Autobiography; Basil D'Oliveira; Collins ©; 1968.

End of an Innings; Denis Compton; Pavilion Books ©; 1958.

England Down Under: MCC in Australia 1958-59; John Kay; Sporting Handbooks ©; 1959.

England v South Africa 1955; Bruce Harris; Hutchinson ©; 1955.

Family Britain 1951-57; David Kynaston; Bloomsbury; David Kynaston ©; 2009.

Fifteen Paces; Alan Davidson; Souvenir Press Ltd ©; 1965.

Fifty Years in Cricket; Sir Leonard Hutton; Stanley Paul & Co Ltd (reprinted by permission of Random House Group Ltd ©); 1984.

Flying Stumps; Ray Lindwall; Arrow Books (reprinted by permission of Random House Group Ltd ©); 1957.

Flying Stumps and Metal Bats; Cricket's Greatest Moments – by the People Who Were There; The Wisden Cricketer; Aurum Press.co.uk ©; 2008.

Frank Worrell: A Biography; Ivo Tennant; Lutterworth Press; 1987.

Fred Trueman: The Authorised Biography; Chris Waters; Aurum Press Ltd ©; 2011.

Frith on Cricket; Half a Century of Writings by David Frith; Great Northern Books David Frith ©; 2010.

Grovel; the story and legacy of the summer of 1976; England v West Indies; David Tossell; Pitch Publishing Ltd ©; 2012.

Innings of a Lifetime; Ralph Barker; Collins ©; 1982.

Jimmy; My Story; James Anderson; Simon & Schuster UK Ltd. James Anderson ©; 2012.

Just My Story; Len Hutton; Hutchinson ©; 1956.

Keith Miller: A Cricketing Biography; Mihir Bose; George Allen & Unwin (an imprint of Harper Collins ©); 1980.

Lasting the Pace; Bob Willis; Willow Books ©; 1985.

Match of My Life: The Ashes: Sam Pilger & Rob Wightman; Pitch Publishing Ltd. ©; 2013.

MCC: The Autobiography of a Cricketer; Colin Cowdrey; Hodder and Stoughton (reproduced by permission of the publisher Hodder & Stoughton Ltd ©); 1976.

Naught for Your Comfort; Trevor Huddleston; Collins ©; 1956.

Never Had It So Good: A History of Britain from Suez to the Beatles; Dominic Sandbrook Little; Brown ©; 2005.

Opening Up; Michael Atherton; Hodder & Stoughton ©; 2002.

Operation Ashes; Arthur Morris & Pat Landsberg; Robert Hale Ltd ©; 1956.

Over to Me; Jim Laker; Frederick Muller Ltd (reprinted by permission of Random House Group Ltd ©); 1960.

Peter May: A Biography; Alan Hill; Andre Deutsch (reprinted by permission of Carlton Books ©); 1996.

Peter May's Book of Cricket; Peter May; Cassell & Co ©; 1956.

Phoenix from the Ashes: The story of the England-Australia Series 1981; Mike Brearley; Unwin Paperbooks ©; 1982.

Pitch and Toss; Roy McLean; Hodder & Stoughton ©; 1957.

Playfair Cricket Annual 1949; Peter West (Editor); Playfair Books Ltd ©; 1949.

Playfair Cricket Annual 1951; Peter West (Editor); Playfair Books Ltd ©; 1951.

Playfair Cricket Annual 1953; Peter West (Editor); Playfair Books Ltd ©; 1953.

Playfair Cricket Annual 1954-62; Gordon Ross (Editor); Playfair Books Ltd ©;

Playfair Cricket Annual 1964; Gordon Ross (Editor); The Dickens Press ©; 1964.

Playfair Cricket Annual 1977-85; Gordon Ross (Editor); Queen Anne Press ©;

Playfair Cricket Annual 1986-92; Bill Frindall (Editor); Queen Anne Press ©; *Playfair Cricket Annual 1993-2009*; Bill Frindall (Editor); Headline Pub. PLC ©;

Playfair Cricket Annual 2010-13; Ian Marshall (Editor); Headline Pub. PLC ©;

Richie Benaud: Cricketer, Captain, Guru; Mark Browning; Kangaroo Press ©; 1996.

Rough Guide to Cult Fiction; Paul Simpson, Helen Rodiss, Michaela Bushell (Editors); Rough Guides ©; 2005.

Rough Guide to Cult Movies; Paul Simpson, Helen Rodiss, Michaela Bushell (Editors); Rough Guides ©; 2004.

Rough Guide to Cult Pop; Paul Simpson (Editor); Rough Guides ©; 2003.

Shadows Across the Playing Field: 60 Years of India-Pakistan Cricket; Shashi Tharoor, Shaharyar Khan; Roli Books ©; 2009.

Stiff Upper Lips and Baggy Green Caps: A Sledger's History of the Ashes; Simon Briggs; Quercus ©; 2006.

60 Years on the Back Foot; Sir Clyde Walcott; Orion Books; 2000.

Sweet Summers: The Classic Cricket Writing of JM Kilburn; Duncan Hamilton (Editor); Great Northern Books ©; 2008.

Summer Spectacular; The West Indies v England, 1963; JS Barker Sportsmans Book Club ©; 1965.

Ted Dexter Declares: An Autobiography; Ted Dexter; Stanley Paul ©; 1966.

Ten Great Innings; Ralph Barker; Chatto & Windus ©; 1965.

Test Match Diary 1953; John Arlott; James Barrie (an imprint of Random House Group Ltd ©); 1953.

Test Diary 1964; Denis Compton; Sportsmans Book Club ©; 1965.

Thatcher's Britain: The Politics and Social Upheaval of the 1980s; Richard Vinen; Pocket Books (an imprint of Simon & Schuster UK Ltd) Richard Vinen ©; 2009.

The Art of Captaincy; Mike Brearley; Hodder & Stoughton Ltd. ©; 1985.

The Ashes; Ray Illingworth & Kenneth Gregory; Collins ©; 1982.

The Ashes: Highlights Since 1948; Peter Baxter, Peter Hayter; BBC Books ©; 1989.

The Ashes Captains; Gerry Cotter; The Crowood Press ©; 1989.

The Australian Challenge; John Arlott; Sportsmans Book Club ©; 1963.

The Bedsers: Twinning Triumphs; Alan Hill; Mainstream Sport ©; 2001.

The Captain's Tales; Battle for the Ashes; David Fulton; Mainstream Publishing Company ©; 2009.

The Complete Who's Who of Test Cricketers; Christopher Martin-Jenkins; Macdonald Queen Anne Press ©; 1987.

The D'Oliveira Affair: Forty Years On*; Rob Steen; Bodacious.com ©; 2008.

The Faber Book of Pop; Hanif Kureishi, Jon Savage (Editors); Faber ©; 1995.

The Fast Men; David Frith; Van Nostrand Reinhold ©; 1975.

The Fight for the Ashes 1956; Peter West; George G Harrap ©; 1956.

The Gloves Are Off; My Life in Cricket; Matt Prior; Simon & Schuster UK Ltd. Matt Prior ©; 2013.

The Plan; How Fletcher and Flower Transformed English Cricket; Steve James; Bantam Press; Transworld Publishers © Steve James; 2012.

The Nineties: When Surface was Depth; Michael Bracewell; Flamingo (an imprint of Harper Collins) Michael Bracewell ©; 2003.

The Noughties: a Decade that Changed the World 2000-2009; Tim Footman; Crimson Publishing; Tim Footman ©; 2009.

The Seventies: Portrait of a Decade; Christopher Booker Allen Lane; Christopher Booker ©; 1980.

The Toughest Tour: The Ashes Away Series Since the War; Huw Turbervill; Aurum Press Ltd ©; 2010.

The Wisden Book of Test Cricket 1876-77 to 1977-78; Bill Frindall; Macdonald & Jane's ©; 1979.

The Wisden Book of Test Cricket 1977-2000; Bill Frindall; A&C Black Publishers Ltd. ©; 2010.

The Wisden Book of Test Cricket 1876-77 to 1977-78; John Wisden & Co; A&C Black Publishers Ltd. ©; 2009.

The Ultimate Hit Singles Book; Dave McAleer (Editor); Carlton Books ©; 1988.

Thrown Out; Ian Meckiff, Ian McDonald; Stanley Paul & Co Ltd (reprinted by permission of Random House Group Ltd ©); 1961.

Tony Lock: Aggressive Master of Spin; Alan Hill; The History Press Ltd ©; 2008.

When the Lights Went Out: What Really Happened to Britain in the Seventies; Andy Beckett; Faber & Faber Ltd; Andy Beckett ©; 2009.

White Heat: A History of Britain in the Swinging Sixties: Dominic Sandbrook; Little, Brown; Dominic Sandbrook ©; 2006.

White Lightning; The Autobiography; Allan Donald; CollinsWillow ©; 1999.

Wickets, Catches and the Odd Run; Trevor Bailey; Willow Books (reprinted by permission of HarperCollins Publishers Ltd ©); 1986.

Wisden Cricketers' Almanac 1967-78; Norman Preston; Sporting Handbooks ©;

Wisden Cricketers' Almanac 2004-07; Matthew Engel; John Wisden & Co. Ltd ©;

Wisden Cricketers' Almanac 2008; Scyld Berry; John Wisden & Co. Ltd ©; 2008

Wisden on the Ashes; The Authoritative Story of Cricket's Greatest Rivalry; Steve Lynch (editor); John Wisden & Co. Ltd ©; 2011.

You Guys Are History!; An Autobiography; Devon Malcolm; CollinsWillow ©; 1998.

REFERENCES

Young Jim; The Jim Parks Story; Derek Watts; Tempus Publishing Limited ©; 2005.

1001 Albums You must Hear Before You Die; Robert Dimery, Octopus Books ©; 2008.

1001 Songs You must Hear Before You Die; Robert Dimery, Cassell Illustrated ©; 2013.